AF348877

Guide to the Unified Process featuring UML, Java and Design Patterns

Springer
London
Berlin
Heidelberg
New York
Hong Kong
Milan
Paris
Tokyo

John Hunt

Guide to the Unified Process featuring UML, Java and Design Patterns

Springer

John Hunt
JayDee Technology, Corsham, Wilts, UK

British Library Cataloguing in Publication Data
Hunt, John, 1964-
    Guide to the unified process featuring UML, Java and design
    patterns. - (Springer professional computing)
    1. Object-oriented methods (Computer science) 2. UML
    (Computer science) 3. Java (Computer program language)
    I. Title.
    005.1'17

    ISBN 1852337214

Library of Congress Cataloging-in-Publication Data
Hunt, John, 1964-
    Guide to the unified process featuring UML, Java and design patterns / John Hunt.
        p. cm. -- (Springer professional computing)
    ISBN 1-85233-721-4 (alk. paper)
      1. Object-oriented methods (Computer science) 2. UML (Computer science) 3. Java
    (Computer program language) I. Title. II. Series.

QA76.9.O35H84 2003
005.1'17--dc21   2003042773

ISBN 1-85233-721-4 Springer-Verlag London Berlin Heidelberg
A member of BertelsmannSpringer Science+Business Media GmbH
http://www.springer.co.uk

First published 2003

Typeset by Ian Kingston Editorial Services, Nottingham, UK
Printed and bound in the United States of America
34/3830-543210 Printed on acid-free paper SPIN 10905425

This book is dedicated to Beverley and Rebecca, without whom none of my books would have been written

Contents

Part 2 Design Patterns

Part 3 The Unified Process in the Real World

Part 1

The Unified Process

1

Introduction

1.1 Introduction

This book introduces and guides the you through the use of the Unified Modeling Language (UML) and the Unified Process (both originally devised by Grady Booch, James Rumbaugh and Ivar Jacobson) and their application to Java systems. This means that the book will present you, the reader, with the notation used in the UML and the steps described by the Unified Process with particular reference to the Java environment (including the classes and the syntax).

The book itself is structured in three parts. Part 1 introduces object-oriented analysis and design and the Unified Process. The UML is introduced, as necessary, to support the Unified Process steps. Part 2 discusses the topic of design patterns, while Part 3 looks at the Unified Process and UML in the real world.

The first part of the book is structured in the following manner:

Chapter 2: Object -Oriented Analysis and Design
This chapter surveys the most significant object-oriented design and analysis methods to emerge since the late 1980s.

Chapter 3: An Introduction to the UML and the Unified Process
This chapter provides the background to the UML and the Unified Process. It also presents a summary of both.

Chapter 4: Software Architecture and Object-Oriented Design
This chapter explains and justifies why an architecture is essential to the successful design and implementation of a large object-oriented system.

Chapter 5: Requirements Discipline: Use Case Analysis
This chapter introduces the requirements discipline (which may also be known as Use Case Analysis). This discipline attempts to identify what the functionality of the system will be. These use cases will be essential as the backbone to the whole design process.

3

Chapter 6: The Analysis Discipline
This chapter considers the analysis of the requirements as described by the use cases. This process helps to identify the primary system requirements necessary to support the use cases.

Chapter 7: The Design Discipline: System and Class Design
The design discipline chapter moves the results of the analysis discipline forward to the actual design of the system.

Chapter 8: Implementation Phase
Having produced a design it is then necessary to move the design into an implementation in Java.

Chapter 9: The Test Discipline: How it Relates to Use Cases
Testing is a huge subject in its own right. This chapter therefore focuses on the use of use cases as the driving force behind the identification of test cases.

Chapter 10: The Four Phases
The Unified Process is made up of four phases that a project may cycle through during its lifetime. These phases apply the disciplines described above. This chapter considers and describes the four phases and highlights the focus of each phase.

Chapter 11: The JDSync Case Study
This chapter presents a detailed worked case study.

The second part of the book relates to the use of design patterns:

Chapter 12: Software Patterns
This chapter presents a detailed look at the design pattern concept.

Chapter 13: Patterns Catalogs
This chapter describes a number of the best established patterns.

Chapter 14: Applying the Model–View–Controller Pattern
This chapter describes the Model–View–Controller (MVC) pattern in detail.

Chapter 15: The Hierarchical MVC
This chapter looks at how the MVC pattern can be extended to become hierarchical.

Chapter 16: The Visitor Framework
This chapter describes the design of the visitor framework.

Chapter 17: The EventManager
This chapter presents the event manager.

Chapter 18: J2EE Patterns
This chapter discusses the J2EE patterns

Chapter 19: The Fault Tracker J2EE Case Study
This chapter presents a case study of a J2EE-based design.

The third part of the book relates to the real-world Unified Process and UML and has the following format:

Chapter 20: Are UML Designs Language Independent?
This chapter considers UML and Java and how UML can be mapped into Java.

Chapter 21: Customizing the Unified Process for Short Time-Scale Projects
This chapter discusses the issue of customizing the Unified Process for short-term projects (rather than the long-lived projects assumed by default in the Unified Process).

Chapter 22: Augmenting the Unified Process With Additional Techniques
A description of how the Unified Process can be augmented with additional techniques.

Chapter 23: Inheritance Considered Harmful!
This chapter describes why you should be careful of over using inheritance in your designs.

Chapter 24: Incremental Software
This chapter discusses how an incremental software project can be managed.

Chapter 25: Agile Modeling
This chapter describes how Agile Modeling can be used to control the model generation processes within the Unified Process.

1.2 Why UML and the Unified Process?

A question which should be answered straight away is "why use the UML and the Unified Process?". The simple answer to the first part of this is that the UML, or Unified Modeling Language, has become the *de facto* standard. This is not necessarily a cast-iron reason for adopting a particular approach or notation. However, in this case the *de facto* standard has been adopted by the Object Management Group (the OMG) and by (almost) all vendors of object modelling tools. This allows a common language to be used whether you are working with Rational's Rose, Select's Enterprise Modeller or indeed Visio Enterprise. As the UML is not tied to a particular modelling approach you can also apply it via whichever design method you wish.

This is actually a very important point – the UML is a notation, not a method. I personally have heard numerous people talk about adopting or applying the UML method. This is a warning flag that these people probably don't know very much about object-oriented design. As the UML is a notation you cannot say you are going to apply the UML method – it is just plain nonsense.

The final reason for adopting the UML is that it has been a long time in gestation and has been open to public review for a number of years now. This has ensured that many people worldwide have been able to have input into the UML, rather than just a few behind the closed doors of some university or company. The result is not necessary the final word on notations, but it is certainly better than anything else around at present.

This should have justified the presentation of the UML in this book, but what about the Unified Process? Like the UML, the Unified Process was developed by the "three amigos", Booch, Rumbaugh and Jacobson, with support from Rational, their employer. It is explicitly designed to work with the UML and indeed was developed in tandem with the UML, but has taken longer to come out into the public domain. This is partly due to the fact that it is easier to produce a notation than it is to produce a whole design method which covers the majority of the life cycle of a software product. However, the ambitious goal of the Unified Process is to do just that!

So, other than the fact that the same people who developed the UML developed the Unified Process, is there any other reason for choosing the Unified Process? Actually, yes. I have been recommending for some time that projects should adopt a hybrid approach to their object-oriented analysis and design, primarily based around the Object Modeling Technique (OMT), some elements of Objectory and a bit of Booch and Fusion. However, this was a rather informal hybrid, directed more by personal judgement than by an explicit process. Nevertheless, this is essentially what the Unified Process does, but it does it far more formally than I ever did and goes much further than I ever went. It addresses many of the areas with which I was not comfortable in my own efforts and introduces techniques to deal with issues which I had not even considered. I therefore decided to adopt this design method.

1.3 Why This Book?

We have now covered what this book is about and justified the choice of the UML and Unified Process as the notation and method respectively that we have adopted. What we have yet to cover is why I felt that it was necessary to write this book in the first place. Essentially I was moved to write it, as, having waded through the weighty tomes on the Unified Process and read many books on the UML, I felt that I had not been presented with a clear guide on how to apply the notation and the method for the project work I am involved in, which concentrates on Java. This book therefore focuses on applying the notation and the method to Java. This does not mean that it is without value to someone who is not interested in Java. A major problem that I have had with the Rational books on the Unified Process is that I do not find them very accessible. They are written (to my mind at least) more as academic texts than as a practitioner's workbook. This book therefore attempts to focus on actual practitioners and on providing an easily accessible step by step guide to applying UML and the Unified Process.

1.4 Where to Get More Information

The following books are useful additional references on the Unified Process and the Unified Modeling Langauge.

Booch, G., Rumbaugh, J. and Jacobson, I. (1999). *The UML User Guide*, Addison-Wesley, Reading, MA.

Eeles, P., Houston, K. and Kozaczynski, W. (2002). *Building J2EE Applications with the Rational Unified Process*. Addison-Wesley: Reading, MA.

Eriksson, H. and Penker, M. (1998). *UML Toolkit*. Wiley, Chichester.

Fowler, M. and Scott, K. (1997). *UML Distilled*. Addison-Wesley, Reading, MA.

Hunt, J. (1999). *Java for Practitioners*. Springer-Verlag, London.

Jacobson, I., Booch, G. and Rumbaugh, J. (1999). *The Unified Software Development Process*. Addison-Wesley: Reading, MA.

Kruchten, P. (2000). *The Rational Unified Process: An Introduction*, 2nd edn. Addison-Wesley: Reading, MA.

1.5 Where to Go Online

One important point about both the UML and the Unified Process is that both have Web sites dedicated to them. The places you should start with include the OMG (Object Management Group) and Rational Corp.

OMG for UML: http://www.omg.org/
Rational for UML and Unified Process: http://www.rational.com/
UML User Group: http://www.valtech.com/about/umlug.htm
Unified Modeling Language Revision Task Force: http://uml.systemhouse.mci.com/
Object References: http://www.jaydeetechnology.co.uk/

Object-Oriented Analysis and Design

2.1 Introduction

This chapter surveys the most significant object-oriented design and analysis methods to emerge since the late 1980s. It concentrates primarily on OOA (Coad and Yourdon, 1991), Booch (Booch, 1991, 1994), Object Modeling Technique (Rumbaugh *et al.*, 1991), Objectory (Jacobson, 1992) and Fusion (Coleman *et al.*, 1994). It also introduces the Unified Modeling Language (Booch *et al.*, 1996; Booch and Rumbaugh, 1995).

This chapter does not aim to deal comprehensively with either the range of methods available or the fine details of each approach. Rather, it provides an overview of the design process and the strengths and weaknesses of some important and reasonably representative methods.

2.2 Object-Oriented Design Methods

The object-oriented design methods that we consider are all architecture-driven, incremental and iterative. They do not adopt the more traditional waterfall software development model; instead they adopt an approach which is more akin to the spiral model of Boehm (1988). This reflects developers' experiences when creating object-oriented systems – the object-oriented development process is more incremental than that for procedural systems, with less distinct barriers between analysis, design and implementation. Some organizations take this process to the extreme and adopt an evolutionary development approach. This approach delivers system functions to users in very small steps and revises project plans in the light of experience and user feedback. This philosophy has proved very successful for organizations that have fully embraced it and has led to earlier business benefits and successful end-products from large development projects.

2.3 Object-Oriented Analysis

We first consider the Object-Oriented Analysis approach (OOA) of Coad and Yourdon (1991). The identification of objects and classes is a crucial task in object-oriented analysis and design, but many techniques ignore this issue. For example, neither the Booch method nor OMT deal with it at all. They indicate that it is a highly creative process that can be based on the identification of nouns and verbs in an informal verbal description of the problem domain. A different approach is to use a method such as OOA as the first part of the design process and then to use another object-oriented design method for the later parts of the process.

OOA helps designers identify the detailed requirements of their software, rather than how the software should be structured or implemented. It aims to describe the existing system and how it operates, and how the software system should interact with it. One of the claims of OOA is that it helps the designer to package the requirements of the system in an appropriate manner (for object-oriented systems) and to reduce the risk of the software failing to meet the customer's requirements. In effect, OOA helps to build the Object Model that we look at in more detail when we look at OMT.

There are five activities within OOA which direct the analyst during the analysis process:

- Finding classes and objects in the domain.
- Identifying structures (amongst those classes and objects). Structures are relationships such as *is-a* and *part-of.*
- Identifying subjects (related objects).
- Defining attributes (the data elements of the objects).
- Defining services (the active parts of objects that indicate what the object does).

These are not sequential steps. As information becomes available, the analyst performs the appropriate activity. The intention is that analysts can work in whatever way the domain experts find it easiest to express their knowledge. Thus, analysts may go deeper into one activity than the others as the domain experts provide greater information in that area. Equally, analysts may jump around between activities, identifying classes one minute and services the next.

2.3.1 Class Responsibility Collaborator (CRC)

CRC (Class Responsibility Collaborator) is an exploratory technique rather than a complete method. It was originally devised as a way of teaching basic concepts in object-oriented design. The CRC technique can be exploited in other methods (for example, Booch; it is explicitly used as an early step in Fusion). It is also the foundation of the responsibility-driven design method (Wirfs-Brock *et al.*, 1990), where it constitutes the first phase.

CRC deals primarily with the design phase of development. The process is anthropomorphic and drives development by having project teams enact scenarios and play the parts of objects. Classes are recorded on index cards. The steps in the process can be summarized in Figure 2.1.

Identification of Classes and Responsibilities
In this stage, the classes are identified. Guidelines include looking for nouns in the requirements document and modelling physical objects and conceptual entities. Object categories are candi-

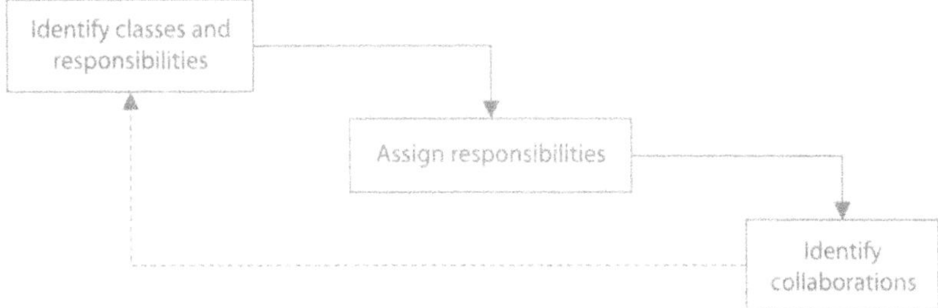

Figure 2.1 Steps in CRC.

date classes. Grouping classes by common attributes gives candidates for abstract superclasses. The classes are written on cards. The classes form the vocabulary for discussion. Subclasses and superclasses are also identified and recorded on the class card. The requirements are then examined for actions and information associated with each class to find the responsibilities of the classes. *Responsibilities* are the essential duties that have to be performed. They identify problems to be solved and are a handle for discussing solutions. An example of a CRC class card is presented in Figure 2.2.

Assignment of Responsibilities

The responsibilities identified in the previous stage are allocated to classes. The goal is to distribute the "intelligence" of the system evenly around the classes, with behaviour kept with related information. Information about one thing should appear in just one place. If necessary, responsibilities can be shared among related classes. Responsibilities should be made as general as possible and placed as high as possible in the inheritance hierarchy.

Identification of Collaborations

This stage identifies how classes interact. Each class/responsibility pair is examined to see which other classes would need to be consulted to fulfil the responsibility and which classes make use of which responsibilities. The cards for classes that closely collaborate are grouped together physically. This informal grouping helps in the understanding of the emerging design.

Class Name	
Superclasses	
Subclasses	
Responsibilities	Collaborations
...	...

Figure 2.2 A CRC class card.

Refinement

The design process is driven toward completion by considering execution scenarios. Each member of the design team takes the part of a class enacting the scenario. This process uncovers missing responsibilities and collaborators. The restricted size of the index cards helps stop classes becoming too complex. If a card becomes too cluttered, then it is reviewed. The outcome can be simplified statements of responsibilities, new subclasses or superclasses, or even new classes.

The output of the design is a set of classes that are related through inheritance. The hierarchy is refined with common responsibilities placed as high as possible in the graph. Abstract classes cannot inherit from concrete ones and classes that add no functionality can be discarded.

Strengths and Weaknesses

In assessing CRC it should be noted that CRC is a technique and does not claim to be a method (even though there are practitioners around who use it as a method). CRC is primarily an exploratory technique can be very useful in this role. However, it does not produce a design which can be directly implemented – it is at too high a level. As the index cards produced during the design process are the only form of documentation associated with the design (i.e. the only record of the design decisions taken as well as the end result) they are clearly inadequate. It can be a very powerful technique for identifying initial classes and class relationships (both inheritance and uses relations); however, it does not deal with object creation, object partitioning, object interactions (only collaborations) or any issues related to the implementation of the system. In summary CRC is a powerful technique which has its place within other design methods during the very early stages of class and object identification.

2.4 The Booch Method

The Booch method (also known as Booch and Object-oriented Development, or OOD) is one of the earliest recognizable object-oriented design methods. It was first described in a paper published in 1986 and has become widely adopted since the publication of a book describing the method (Booch, 1991, 1994).

The Booch method provides a step-by-step guide to the design of an object-oriented system. Although Booch's books discuss the analysis phase, they do so in too little detail compared with the design phase.

2.4.1 The Steps in the Booch Method

- *Identification of classes and objects* involves analyzing the problem domain and the system requirements to identify the set of classes required. This is not trivial and relies on a suitable requirements analysis.
- *Identification of the semantics of classes and objects* involves identifying the services offered by an object and required by an object. A service is a function performed by an object, and during this step the overall system functionality is devolved among the objects. This is

another non-trivial step, and it may result in modifications to the classes and objects identified in the last step.

- *Identification of the relationships between classes and objects* involves identifying links between objects as well and inheritance between classes. This step may identify new services required of objects.
- *Implementation of classes and objects* attempts to consider how to implement the classes and objects and how to define the attributes and provide services. This involves considering algorithms. This process may lead to modifications in the deliverables of all of the above steps and may force the designer to return to some or all of the above steps.

During these steps, the designer produces

- Class diagrams, which illustrate the classes in the system and their relationships.
- Object diagrams, which illustrate the actual objects in the system and their relationships.
- Module diagrams, which package the classes and objects into modules. These modules illustrate the influence that Ada had on the development of the Booch method (Booch, 1987).
- Process diagrams, which package processes and processors.
- State transition diagrams and timing diagrams, which describe the dynamic behaviour of the system (the other diagrams describe the static structure of the system).

Booch recommends an incremental and iterative development of a system through the refinement of different yet consistent logical and physical views of that system.

2.4.2 Strengths and Weaknesses

The biggest problem for a designer approaching the Booch method for the first time is that the plethora of different notations is supported by a poorly defined and loose process (although the revision to the method described in Booch (1994) addresses this to some extent). It does not give step-by-step guidance and possesses very few mechanisms for determining the system's requirements. Its main strengths are its (mainly graphical) notations, which cover most aspects of the design of an object-oriented system, and its greatest weakness is the lack of sufficient guidance in the generation of these diagrams.

2.5 The Object Modeling Technique

The Object Modeling Technique (OMT) is an object-oriented design method which aims to construct a series of models which refine the system design until the final model is suitable for implementation. The design process is divided into three phases:

- The Analysis Phase attempts to model the problem domain.
- The Design Phase structures the results of the analysis phase in an appropriate manner.
- The Implementation Phase takes into account target language constructs.

2.5.1 The Analysis Phase

Three types of model are produced by the analysis phase:

- *The object model* represents the static structure of the domain. It describes the objects, their classes and the relationships between the objects. For example, the object model might represent the fact that a department object possesses a single manager (object) but many employees (objects). The notation is based on an extension of the basic entity–relationship notation.
- *The dynamic model* represents the behaviour of the system. It expresses what happens in the domain, when it occurs and what effect it has. It does not represent how the behaviour is achieved. The formalism used to express the dynamic model is based on a variation of finite state machines called statecharts. These were developed by Harel and others (Harel *et al.*, 1987; Harel, 1988) to represent dynamic behaviour in real-time avionic control systems. Statecharts indicate the states of the system, the transitions between states, their sequence and the events which cause the state change.
- *The functional model* describes how system functions are performed. It uses data flow diagrams which illustrate the sources and sinks of data as well as the data being exchanged. They contain no sequencing information or control structures.

The relationship between these three models is important, as each model adds to the designer's understanding of the domain:

- The object model defines the objects which hold the state variables referenced in the dynamic model and are the sources and sinks referenced in the functional model.
- The dynamic model indicates when the behaviour in the functional model occurs and what triggers it.
- The functional model explains why an event transition leads from one state to another in the dynamic model.

You do not build these models sequentially; changes to any one of the models may have a knock-on effect in the other models. Typically, the designer starts with the object model, then considers the dynamic model and finally the functional model, but the process is iterative.

The analysis process is described in considerable detail and provides step-by-step guidance. This ensures that the developer knows what to do at any time to advance the three models.

2.5.2 The Design Phase

The design phase of OMT builds upon the models produced during the analysis phase:

- *The system design step* breaks the system down into subsystems and determines the overall architecture to be used.
- *The object design step* decides on the algorithms to be used for the methods. The methods are identified by examining the three analysis models for each class, etc.

Each of the steps gives some guidelines for their respective tasks; however, far less support is provided for the designer than in the analysis phase. For example, there is no systematic guidance for the identification of subsystems, although the issues involved are discussed (resource management, batch versus interactive modes etc.). This means that it can be difficult to identify where to start, how to proceed and what to do next.

2.5.3 The Implementation Phase

The implementation phase codifies the system and object designs into the target language. This phase provides some very useful information on how to implement features used in the model-based design process used, but it lacks the step-by-step guidance which would be useful for those new to object orientation.

2.5.4 Strengths and Weaknesses

OMT's greatest strength is the level of step-by-step support that it provides during the analysis phase. However, it is much weaker in its guidance during the design and implementation phases, where it provides general guidelines (and some heuristics).

2.6 The Objectory Method

The driving force behind the Objectory method (Jacobson *et al.*, 1992) is the concept of a *use case*. A use case is a particular interaction between the system and a user of that system (an actor) for a particular purpose (or function). The users of the system may be human or machine. A complete set of use cases therefore describes a system's functionality based around what actors should be able to do with the system. The Objectory method has three phases, which produce a set of models.

2.6.1 The Requirements Phase

The requirements phase uses a natural language description of what the system should do to build three models.

- *The use case model* describes the interactions between actors and the system. Each use case specifies the actions that are performed and their sequence. Any alternatives are also documented. This can be done in natural language or using state transition diagrams.
- *The domain model* describes the objects, classes and associations between objects in the domain. It uses a modified entity–relationship model.
- *The user interface descriptions* contain mock-ups of the various interfaces between actors and the system. User interfaces are represented as pictures of windows, while other interfaces are described by protocols.

2.6.2 The Analysis Phase

The analysis phase produces the analysis model and a set of subsystem descriptions. The analysis model is a refinement of the domain object model produced in the requirements phase. It contains behavioural information as well as control objects which are linked to use cases. The analysis model also possesses entity objects (which exist beyond a single use case) and interface objects (which handle system–actor interaction). The subsystem descriptions partition the system around objects which are involved in similar activities and which are closely coupled. This organization structures the rest of the design process.

2.6.3 The Construction Phase

The construction phase refines the models produced in the analysis phase. For example, inter-object communication is refined and the facilities provided by the target language are considered. This phase produces three models:

- Block models represent the functional modules of the system.
- Block interfaces specify the public operations performed by blocks.
- Block specifications are optional descriptions of block behaviour in the form of finite state machines.

The final stage is to implement the blocks in the target language.

2.6.4 Strengths and Weaknesses

The most significant aspect of Objectory is its use of use cases, which join the building blocks of the method. Objectory is unique among the methods considered here, as it provides a unifying framework for the design process. However, it still lacks the step-by-step support which would simplify the whole design process.

2.7 The Fusion Method

The majority of object-oriented design methods currently available, including those described in this chapter, take a systematic approach to the design process. However, in almost all cases this process is rather weak, providing insufficient direction or support to the developer. In addition, methods such as OMT rely on a "bottom up" approach. This means that developers must focus on the identification of appropriate classes and their interfaces without necessarily having the information to enable them to do this in an appropriate manner for the overall system. Little reference is made to the system's overall functionality when determining class functionality etc. Indeed, some methods provide little more than some vague guidelines and anecdotal heuristics.

In contrast, Fusion explicitly attempts to provide a systematic approach to object-oriented software development. In many ways, the Fusion method is a mixture of a range of other approaches (indeed, the authors of the method acknowledge that there is little new in

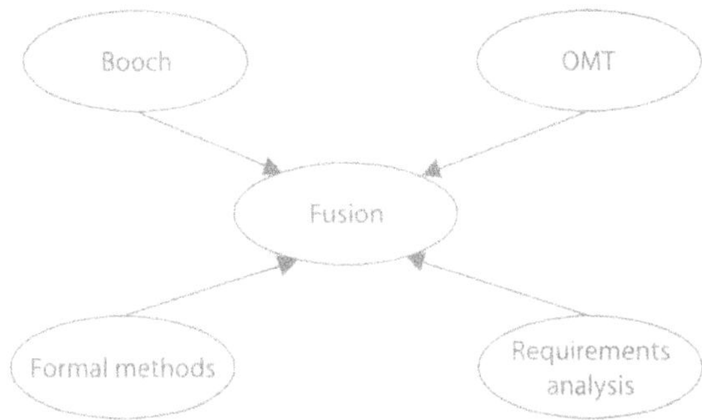

Figure 2.3 Some of the influences on Fusion.

the approach, other than that they have put it all together in a single method; see Figure 2.3).

As with other object-oriented design methods, Fusion is based around the construction of appropriate models that capture different elements of the system and different knowledge. These models are built up during three distinct phases:

- *The analysis phase* produces models that describe the high-level constraints from which the design models are developed.
- *The design phase* produces a set of models that describe how the system behaves in terms of a collection of interacting objects.
- *The implementation phase* describes how to map the design models onto implementation language constructs.

Within each phase a set of detailed steps attempts to guide the developer through the Fusion process. These steps include checks to ensure the consistency and completeness of the emerging design. In addition, the output of one step acts as the input for the next.

Fusion's greatest weakness is its complexity – it really requires a sophisticated CASE tool. Without such a tool, it is almost impossible to produce a consistent and complete design.

2.8 The Unified Modeling Language

The Unified Modeling Language (UML) is an attempt by Grady Booch, Ivar Jacobson and James Rumbaugh to build on the experiences of the Booch, Object Modeling Technique (OMT) and Objectory methods. Their aim is to produce a single, common, and widely useable modelling language for these methods and, working with other methodologists, for other methods. This means that UML focuses on a standard language and not a standard process, which reflects what happens in reality; a particular notation is adopted as the means of communication on a specific project and between projects. However, between projects (and sometimes within projects), different design methods are adopted as appropriate. For example, a design method intended for the domain of real-time avionics systems may not be suitable for designing a small payroll system. The UML is an attempt to develop a common meta-model which unifies semantics and from which a common notation can be built.

2.9 Summary

In this chapter, we have reviewed a number of object-oriented analysis and design methods and the Unified Modeling Language. We have briefly considered the features, strengths and weaknesses of each method.

In all these systems, during the design process it is often difficult to identify commonalities between classes at the implementation level. This means that, during the implementation phase, experienced object-oriented technicians should look for situations in which they can move implementation-level components up the class hierarchy. This can greatly increase the amount of reuse within a software system and may lead to the introduction of abstract classes that contain the common code.

The problem with this is that the implemented class hierarchy no longer reflects the design class hierarchy. It is therefore necessary to have a free flow of information between the implementation and design phases in an object-oriented project.

2.10 References

Boehm, B.W. (1988). A spiral model of software development and enhancement. *IEEE Computer*, May, pp. 61–72.

Booch, G. (1987). *Software Components with Ada*. Benjamin Cummings, Menlo Park, CA.

Booch, G. (1991). *Object-Oriented Design with Applications*. Benjamin Cummings, Redwood City, CA.

Booch, G. (1994). *Object-Oriented Analysis and Design with Applications*, 2nd edn. Benjamin Cummings, Redwood City, CA.

Booch, G. and Rumbaugh, J. (1995). *The Unified Method Documentation Set*, Version 0.8. Rational Software Corporation (available at http://www.rational.com/ot/uml.html/).

Booch, G., Jacobson, I. and Rumbaugh, J. (1996). *The Unified Modeling Language for Object-oriented Development, Documentation Set*, Version 0.91 Addendum, UML Update. Rational Software Corporation (available at http://www.rational.com/ot/uml.html/).

Coad, P. and Yourdon, E. (1991). *Object-Oriented Analysis*. Yourdon Press, Englewood Cliffs, NJ.

Coleman, D., Arnold, P., Bodoff, S., Dollin, C., Gilchrist, H., Hayes, F. and Jeremes, P. (1994). *Object-oriented Development: The Fusion Method*. Prentice Hall, Englewood Cliffs, NJ.

Harel, D. (1988). On visual formalisms. *Communications of the ACM*, 31(5), 514–30.

Harel, D. et al. (1987). On the formal semantics of Statecharts. *Proceedings of the 2nd IEEE Symposium on Logic in Computer Science*, pp. 54–64.

Jacobson, I. et al. (1992). *Object-Oriented Software Engineering: A Use Case Driven Approach*. Addison-Wesley, Reading, MA.

Rumbaugh, J. *et al.* (1991). *Object-Oriented Modeling and Design.* Prentice Hall, Englewood Cliffs, NJ.

Wirfs-Brock, R., Wilkerson, B. and Wiener, W. (1990). *Designing Object-Oriented Software.* Prentice Hall, Englewood Cliffs, NJ.

An Introduction to the UML and the Unified Process

3.1 Introduction

This chapter introduces the Unified Modeling Language (UML) notation, its motivation and history. It then presents the Unified Process as a design method, supported by the UML notation, for designing object-oriented systems.

3.2 Unified Modeling Language

The Unified Modeling Language (or UML) was an attempt to bring together the best of the notations currently in use in the early 1990s. It was developed by Rational Corp., originally by Grady Booch and James Rumbaugh. In the early days of UML (and in particular when I first came across it) it was part of the Unified Method, and indeed the first document I read about the UML was actually entitled "Unified Method 0.8". The intention was to produce not just a notation but a best practice method as well. However, producing a notation is one thing; producing a design method is quite another. Therefore the Unified Method developed into the Unified Modeling Language (UML), which focuses on the notation and is not a design method. Ivar Jacobson later joined Rational and became the third member of the triad that developed the UML.

The UML attempts to be a unifying notation that incorporates the best of a number of other notations as well as current best practice in one generally applicable notation. That is, you should equally be able to apply the UML to a real-time system, a payroll system or a Web browser. Each project might make more or less use of different parts of the UML (and indeed some parts may be ignored by different projects). However, the UML should act as a common vocabulary for all object-oriented design projects. Possibly surprisingly, this is what has begun to happen. Almost all (if not all) object-oriented design tools now support the UML (often in addition to their own notation), and many books have been written on how to apply the UML in different situations (in some cases with additions being made).

One of the most significant aspects of the UML is that it possesses a meta-model. This is a model which explicitly describes the UML (in fact this meta-model is written in UML!) thus allowing different tool vendors to implement the UML with the same meaning. It also allows different tool vendors to exchange models if they wish. It also provides a concrete basis upon which others can assess, review and respond to the UML. This was a very significant development when the UML was first released, and provided a very firm foundation for the UML as the notation of choice.

3.2.1 History of the UML

The UML was not developed overnight (see Figure 3.1). It has gone through an extensive development process which started in the mid-1990s. As stated earlier, my first encounter with what was to become the UML was when it was first documented as part of the Unified Method (release 0.8) in October 1995. At this point in time its heaviest influences were OMT (where I was coming from) and the Booch method. This was primarily because the two key architects at this time were Rumbaugh and Booch. However, OMT has had many influences and has taken many elements from other design methods (see Figure 3.2).

At this time the Unified Method was an impressive exercise, as it had only been under development for the best part of a year. However, things did not stand still, and by the middle of the next year (1996) version 0.9 was released (and version 0.91 three months later). The name had at this point changed and the release was now called the Unified

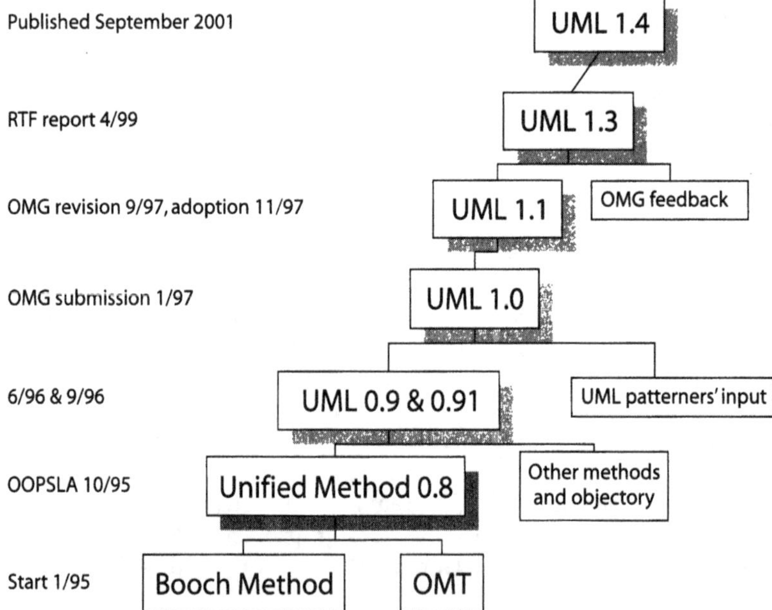

Figure 3.1 A potted history of the UML.

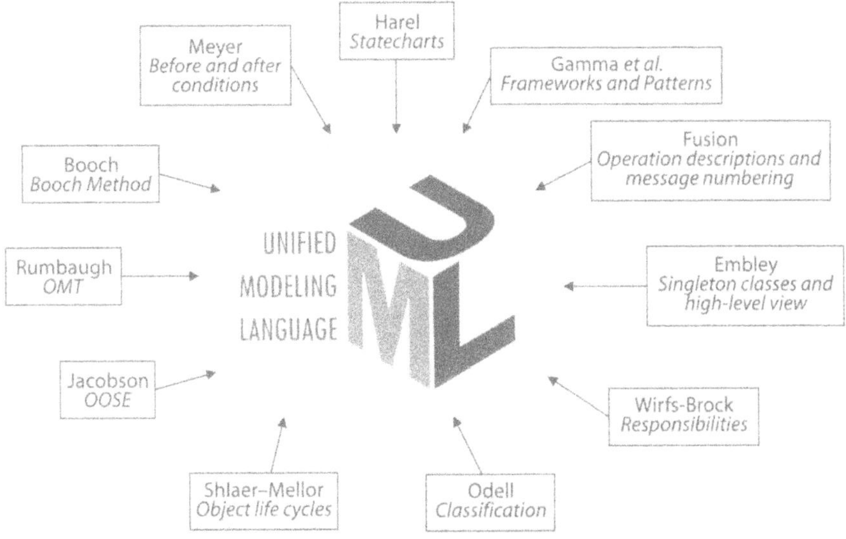

Figure 3.2 Influences on the UML.

Modeling Language. This release focused on the notation and mostly ignored the process. However, much had happened during this time. Not only had many people worldwide commented on the 0.8 release (as it was freely available for download from Rational's Web site – http://www.rational.com/), but the influence of Ivar Jacobson was now being felt. Jacobson had been one of the key architects of the Objectory method, which was most notable for its use of use cases. He had joined Booch and Rumbaugh at Rational at just about the same time as the 0.8 version was released. In UML 0.9 use cases were seen for the first time.

Other partners were now becoming involved in the UML development process, ensuring that a wide variety of backgrounds, expertise and experience was brought to bear. Companies such as IBM, Hewlett-Packard and Microsoft all contributed. Then, at the beginning of 1997, the UML 1.0 standard was presented to the OMG for acceptance as an OMG standard. Version 1.1 of the UML was promulgated as a standard by the OMG towards the end of 1997.

Development of the UML has not stood still, however, although it is now under the control of the OMG. Rather it has continued to develop, and we are now at version 1.4 of the UML (September 2001). At the time of writing there were at least three initiatives looking at developments to the UML, including UML 1.4 with Action Semantics, which adds to UML the syntax and semantics of executable actions and procedures, including their run-time semantics. These semantics are contained within one package, labelled Actions, which defines the various kinds of actions that may compose a procedure. In addition the RTF has been published for UML 1.4.1.

UML is now almost universal as the language used to describe object-oriented models. Indeed, incorporating UML as an OMG standard has ensured that many organizations have adopted it as a non-proprietary standard and that the standard has maintained pace with current developments in computer science – the Internet and Java in particular.

3.2.2 Introduction to the UML

The UML is made of a number of models that together describe the system being designed. Each model comprises one or more diagrams with supporting documentation and descriptions (note that the diagrams alone are not enough). Each model is intended as a complete description of the system being designed from a particular perspective (for example, the static structure of the classes or the dynamic behaviour of the operating system). Each diagram can be part of more than one model, or different parts of the same diagram can be part of different models.

The primary diagrams that comprise the UML are listed below and presented in Figure 3.3.

- *Use case diagrams.* Essentially, these present the interactions between users (human or otherwise) and the system. They therefore also highlight the primary functionality of the system.
- *Class diagrams.* These diagrams present the static (class) structure of the system. They are the core of the UML notation and of an object-oriented design.
- *Object diagrams.* These diagrams use notation which is almost identical to class diagrams, but they present the objects and their relationships at a particular point in time. Object diagrams are not as important as class diagrams, but can be very useful.
- *Activity diagrams.* These describe the flow of activities or tasks, typically within an operation. They are a bit like a graphical pseudocode.
- *Sequence diagrams.* These diagrams show the sequence of messages sent between collaborating objects for a particular task. They highlight the flow of control between the objects.
- *Collaboration diagrams.* These diagrams show the sequence of messages sent between collaborating objects for a particular task. The diagrams highlight the relationships between the collaborating objects. Tools such as Rational Rose allow you to generate collaboration diagrams from sequence diagrams (and vice versa).

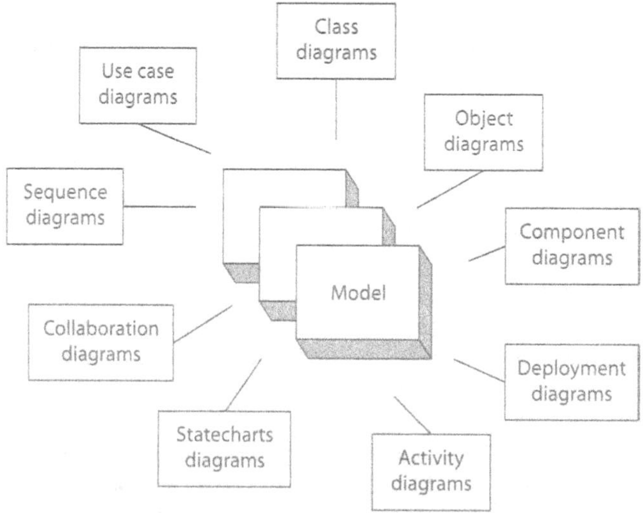

Figure 3.3 Relationship between diagrams and models.

- *Statecharts.* A statechart, or state diagram, illustrates the states an object can be in and the transitions which move the object between states.
- *Component diagrams.* These diagrams are used to illustrate the physical structure of the code in terms of the source code. In Java this means the class files and Java Archive Files (JAR), as well as items such as Web Archive Files (WAR) and Enterprise Archive Files (EAR) in the Java 2 Enterprise Edition architecture.
- *Deployment diagrams.* Deployment diagrams illustrate the physical architecture of the system in terms of processes, networks and the location of components.

3.2.3 Models and Diagrams

UML diagrams are comprised of model elements (a complete listing of which is provided in Appendix A). A diagram represents a particular view into the model. This is because modelling a software system is a complex process in its own right. Ideally the whole system could be described in a single, easily comprehensible diagram. However, only the simplest systems might achieve such an aim. Instead, a model of a software system will only ever be that: a model of the real thing. Models abstract or hide some of the details of the real thing. In the same way, a UML model presents a particular view of a system, abstracting or hiding particular details. Even so, a single model is a complex entity in its own right and is likely to be difficult to present meaningfully within a single diagram. Instead, a particular model can be viewed in different ways. Each UML diagram is just such a view.

One of the key aspects of the UML is that each diagram should be consistent with any other diagrams representing the same information. That is, if one operation is mentioned in two diagrams it should have the same name, with the same return type and the same parameters in each.

When a design is documented using the UML, multiple models are created. Each model captures a different aspect of the emerging design. These aspects are documented in terms of the diagrams, additional notes and documentation. The key element of each model is the visual aspect of the design; however, this visual aspect is augmented by additional textual descriptions and specifications. Indeed, within many diagrams detailed specifications as well as adornments and notes may be included.

The UML is thus a language for:

- visualizing,
- specifying,
- describing, and
- documenting a software system.

However, the UML is not a design method, it is purely a notation for documenting a design (note that the above all relate to describing the design). A notation on its own is not enough: a method indicating how to apply that design is required. Conceptually the UML can be used with any appropriate object-oriented design method. In this book we use it with the Unified Process, the design method developed by Jacobson, Booch and Rumbaugh as a complement to the UML. This design method is introduced in the remainder of this chapter.

3.3 Analysis of the UML

First, it is worth trying to dispel one of the major myths surrounding the UML – it is *not* a methodology or a process! The UML is a notation that can be used to describe object-oriented systems. This notation tells you nothing about how you should go about carry out a design, producing the elements of a UML diagram or identifying how you should structure your models. Indeed, it is for this very reason that Rational produced the Unified Process as one methodology that can use the UML. Note that I have just said "one methodology", as the UML can be used with any appropriate methodology and is not directly tied to the Unified Process.

It is important to address the question of why so many people seem to think that UML must be a method or that it is inherently tied to the Unified Process. I believe that there are a number of reasons, including:

1. Originally, notations and methods were very tightly coupled (for example the OMT, OOD, BOOCH etc. all had their own notations, as well as methods). Indeed this was a motivation behind the UML: to try to get away from the "my notation is best" attitude and to overcome the notation wars!
2. Confusion between the UML and the Unified Process. An understandable confusion exists between the UML notation and the method that has been developed (with a similar name) that uses the UML. Of course, this is made worse because both originate from the Unified Method work of the late 1990s.
3. The bandwagon effect. By this I mean that people tend to jump on the UML bandwagon without necessary understanding what UML is, and make assumptions that fit their own knowledge and experience. Hence the number of job adverts that include "must have knowledge and experience of the UML method".

Another myth to deal with is that the UML is complete. It is not! You will almost always find things that cannot easily be described in UML or that appear to be missing (for example, there is nothing in UML to support describing the data model that your object-oriented application (be it Java , C#, C++ etc). might be working with. In such situations you must resort to using another notation in conjunction with UML. If you are using a UML diagramming tool, this may mean that you must also switch to a different diagramming system.

Finally, UML is actually quite large, and it can take time to get familiar with each type of diagram in UML and how you use them. However, in the main you do not need all of UML for a particular project. For example, there are very many classes in Java. In the last Java software system you built, how many of those packages (let alone classes) did you use? I would be surprised if it was not a core subset that, in general, you use on most projects. It is the same with UML. You should therefore get familiar and comfortable with the appropriate subset that you will need to use for the types of projects you are likely to undertake.

3.4 The Unified Process

The Unified Process is a design framework which guides the tasks, people and products of the design process. It is a framework because it provides the inputs and outputs of each activity, but

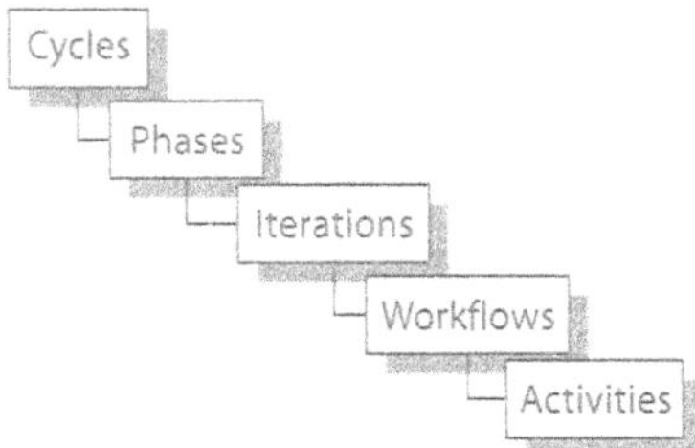

Figure 3.4 Key building blocks of the Unified Process.

does not restrict how each activity must be performed. Different activities can be used in different situations, some being left out, others being replaced or augmented (this is discussed in more detail later in this book). Why then is the Unified Process call a process and not the Unified Framework? It is called a process because its primary aim is to define:

- Who is doing what.
- When they do it.
- How to reach a certain goal (i.e. each activity).
- The inputs and outputs of each activity.

It is thus an engineered process. In fact, it is comprised of a number of different hierarchical elements (see Figure 3.4).

The Unified Process actually comprises low-level activities (such as finding classes), which are combined together into disciplines (formerly known as workflows) which describe how one activity feeds into another). These disciplines are organized into iterations. Each iteration identifies some aspect of the system to be considered. How this is done is considered in more detail later. Iterations themselves are organized into phases. Phases focus on different aspects of the design process, for example requirements, analysis, design and implementation. In turn phases can be grouped into cycles. Cycles focus on the generation of successive releases of a system (for example, version 1.0, version 1.1 etc.).

3.4.1 Overview of the Unified Process

There are four key elements to the philosophy behind the Unified Process. These four elements:

- are iterative and incremental
- are use case-driven
- are architecture-centric
- acknowledge risk

Iterative and Incremental

The Unified Process is iterative and incremental, as it does not try to complete the whole design task in one go. One of the features of the waterfall model of software engineering used by many design methods (see Figure 3.5) is that it primarily assumes that you will complete the require-

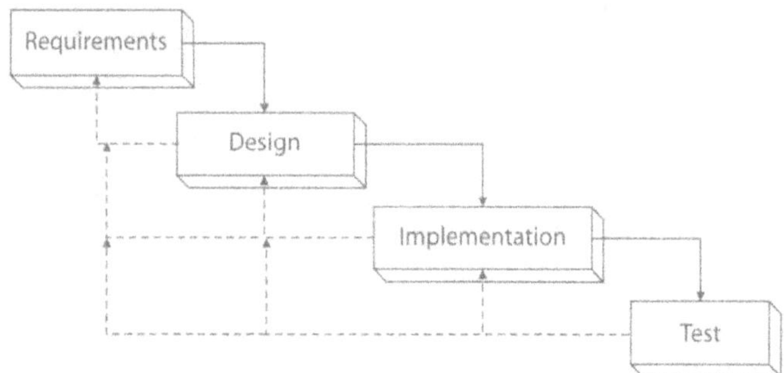

Figure 3.5 The waterfall model.

ments analysis before you start the design phase. In turn, you will complete the design phase before you start the implementation phase and so on. It does accept that there may be some feedback of information from one phase to any preceding phases and that this feedback may have an impact on the products of the preceding phases. However, this is a secondary issue and the assumption is that you will be able to complete the vast majority of one phase before ever considering the next phase. This may be true if this is the fifth or sixth system you have built in the same domain for the same type of application. It is unlikely to be the case with your first application in a new domain (such as your first e-commerce project!).

In contrast to the waterfall model, the Unified Process has an iterative and incremental model. That is, the design process is based on iterations which either address different aspects of the design process or move the design forward in some way (this is the incremental aspect of the model). This does not mean that the Unified Process is a process based on rapid prototyping. Any prototypes that are developed in the Unified Process are used to explore some aspect of the design. This could be to verify some architectural issue for which the design options are similar. Indeed, the use of an iterative and incremental approach in the Unified Process requires more planning (rather than less planning) compared with approaches such as those based on the waterfall model.

Essentially the following holds with the iterative approach in the Unified Process:

- You plan a little.
- You specify, design and implement a little.
- You integrate, test and run.
- You obtain feedback before next iteration.

The end result is that you incrementally produce the system being designed. While you do this you explicitly identify the risks to your design/system up front and deal with them early on (see later). Notice that this does not mean that you are hacking the system together; nor are you carrying out some form of rapid prototyping. However, it does mean that a great deal of planning is required, both initially and as the design develops.

Use Case-driven

The Unified Process is also use case-driven. Remember from earlier that use cases help to identify who uses the system and what they need to do with the system (i.e. the top-level functionality).

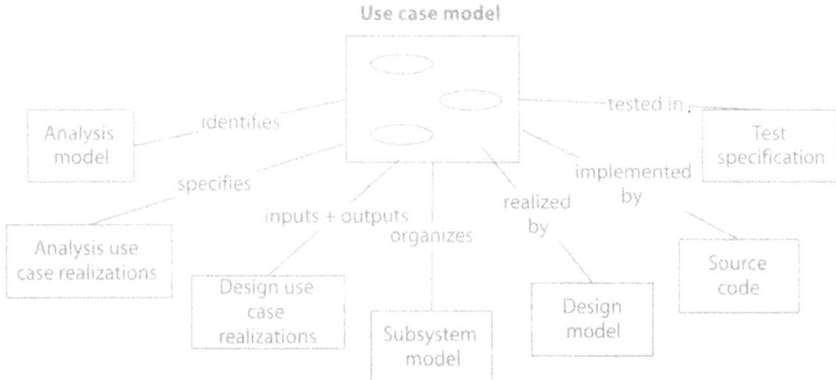

Figure 3.6 The role of use cases.

Thus use cases help identify the primary requirements of the system. One problem with many traditional approaches is that once the requirements have been identified there is no traceability of those requirements through the design to the implementation. Instead, designers (and possibly implementers) must refer back implicitly to the requirements specification and make sure that they have done what is required of them. This is then verified by testing (by which time it is often too late to make any major modifications if the functionality is either wrong or missing).

In the Unified Process use cases are used to ensure that the evolving design is always relevant to what the user required. Indeed, the use cases act as the one consistent thread throughout the whole of the development process, as illustrated in Figure 3.6. For example, at the beginning of the design phase one of the two primary inputs to this phase is the use case model. Then, explicitly within the design model, there are use case realizations which illustrate how each use case is supported by the design. Any use case which does not have a use case realization is not currently supported by the design (in turn, any design elements which do not in some way partake in a use case realization do not support the required functionality of the system!).

To summarize the role of use cases they:

- identify the users of the system and their requirements
- aid in the creation and validation of the system's architecture
- help produce the definition of test cases and procedures
- direct the planning of iterations
- drive the creation of user documentation
- direct the deployment of the system
- synchronize the content of different models
- drive traceability throughout models

Architecture-Centric

One problem with having an iterative and incremental approach is that while one group may be working on part of the implementation another group may be working on part of the design. To ensure that all the various parts fit together there needs to be something. That something is an

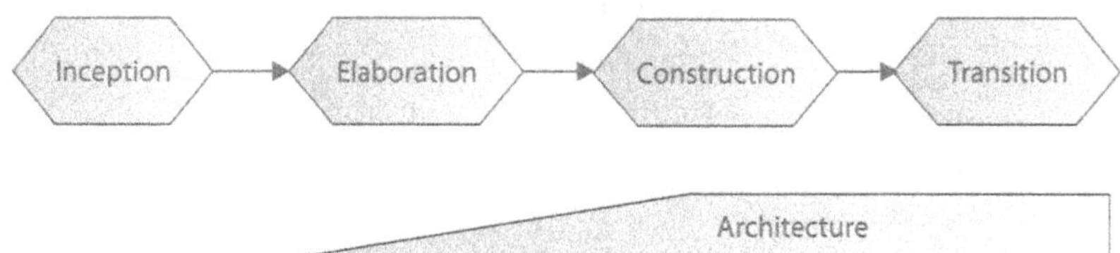

Figure 3.7 The development of the architecture.

architecture. An architecture is the skeleton on which the muscles (functionality) and skin (the user interface) of the system will be hung. A good architecture will be resilient to change and to the evolving design. The Unified Process explicitly acknowledges the need for this architecture by being architecture-centric. It describes how you identify what should be part of the architecture and how you go about designing and implementing the architecture (Figure 3.7). The remainder of the Unified Process then refers back to that architecture.

Obviously, the generation of this architecture is both critical and very hard. Therefore the Unified Process prescribes the successive refinement of the executable architecture, thereby attempting to ensure that the architecture remains relevant.

Acknowledges Risk

Finally, the Unified Process explicitly acknowledges the risk inherent in software design and development. It does this by highlighting unknown aspects in the system being designed and other areas of concern. These areas are then targeted as either being critical to the system and therefore part of the architecture, or areas of risk which need to be addressed early on in the design process (when there is more time) rather than later on (when time tends to be short). Thus it tries to force the riskiest aspects of the system to be designed and implemented early on, hence ensuring that the risk in the system is addressed and managed in a professional manner. Note that it is typically the areas of a design which we do not really understand which end up having the biggest impact on an architecture or the final system. This is often because we do not realize the impact that such areas will have and therefore do not take into account how to deal with their requirements. This is why late on in projects, when such areas are addressed, the system either needs to leave out that functionality or requires major modifications to incorporate the functionality.

Additional Features of the Unified Process

There are two additional features of the Unified Process which are worth making explicit at this stage. The first is that it really requires tool support. That is, it requires a tool that not only supports an appropriate notation (such as the UML; indeed we will assume the UML is the notation used with the Unified Process from now on), but actually supports the Unified Process itself: i.e. a tool which guides you through the various phases, disciplines and activities of the Unified Process. Such a tool can greatly simplify the design process and provide essentially cross-checks and additional support.

The second aspect to note about the Unified Process is that it actually covers the whole of the software development life cycle. That is, it starts by considering the development of the business case for a software system. It then ends with the long-term ongoing maintenance of a large long-lived software system (the sort of system which is still running after 20 or 30 years, as has been the case with a significant number of COBOL systems which were affected by the millennium bug!).

In this book we do not cover the whole of the software development life cycle from initial concept onwards. Instead, we focus on the stages between the start of the use case analysis (requirements capture) through to the end of the implementation of the software with a brief discussion of the testing phase. We also focus on the four phases which comprise the Unified Process and leave a discussion of the role of cycles until near the end of the book.

3.4.2 Life Cycle Phases

The Unified Process is composed of four distinct phases. These four phases (presented in Figure 3.8) focus on different aspects of the design process. The four phases are Inception, Elaboration, Construction and Transition.

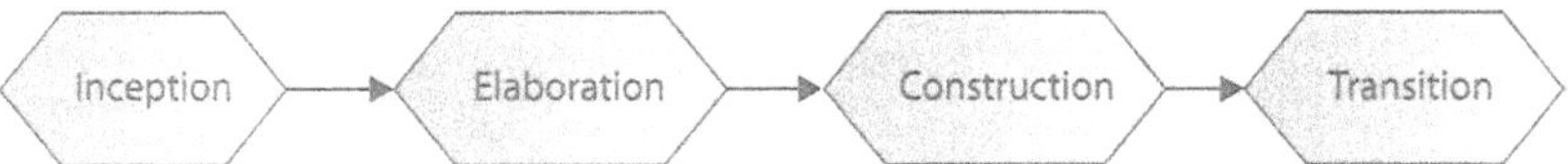

Figure 3.8 The four phases of the Unified Process.

The four phases and their roles are outlined below:

- *Inception.* This phase defines the scope of the project and develops the business case for the system. It also establishes the feasibility of the system to be built. Various prototypes may be developed during this phase to ensure the feasibility of the proposal. Note that we do not focus on the development of the business case in this book: it is assumed that the system to be designed is required and that a business case has already been made.
- *Elaboration.* This phase captures the functional requirements of the system. It should also specify any non-functional requirements to ensure that they are taken into account. The other primary task for this phase is the creation of the architecture to be used throughout the remainder of the Unified Process.
- *Construction.* This phase concentrates on completing the analysis of the system, performing the majority of the design and the implementation of the system. That is, it essentially builds the product.
- *Transition.* The transition phase moves the system into the user's environment. This involves activities such as deploying the system and maintaining it.

Each phase has a set of major milestones that are used to judge the progress of the overall Unified Process (of course, with each phase there are numerous minor milestones to be achieved). The primary milestones (or products) of the four phases are illustrated in Figure 3.9.

A milestone is the culmination of a phase and comprises a set of artefacts (such as specific models) which are the product of the disciplines (and thus activities) in that phase. The primary milestones for each phase are:

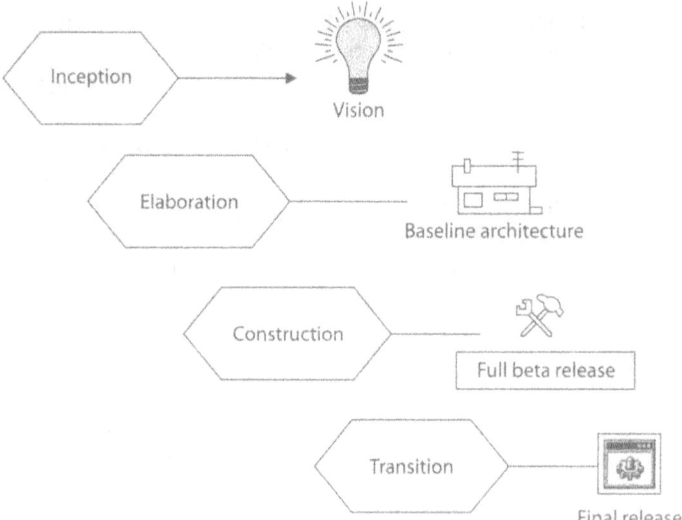

Figure 3.9 The major deliverables of each phase.

- *Inception.* The output of this phase is the vision for the system. This includes a very simplified use case model (to identify what the primary functionality of the system is) and a very tentative architecture, and the most important or significant risks are identified and the elaboration phase is planned.
- *Elaboration.* The primary output of this phase is the architecture, along with a detailed use case model and a set of plans for the construction phase.
- *Construction.* The end result of this phase is the implemented product which includes the software as well as the design and associated models. The product may not be without defects, as some further work has yet to be completed in the transition phase.
- *Transition.* The transition phase is the last phase of a cycle. The major milestone met by this phase is the final production-quality release of the system.

3.4.3 Phases, Iterations and Disciplines

There can be confusion over the relationship between phases and workflows, not least because a single discipline can cross (or be involved in) more than one phase (see Figure 3.10). One way to view the relationships is that the disciplines are the steps you actually follow. However, at different times we can identify different major milestones that should be met. The various phases highlight the satisfaction of these milestones. For example, during the elaboration phase, part of the requirements, analysis, design and even implementation disciplines may be active. However, the emphasis at this time, within these disciplines, will be on elaborating what the system should do and how it should be structured, rather than on the more detailed analysis, design and implementation which occurs during the construction phase.

For the majority of this book we will focus on the various disciplines (not least because this is the emphasis which the designer typically sees). We shall come back to the four phases in Chapter 10.

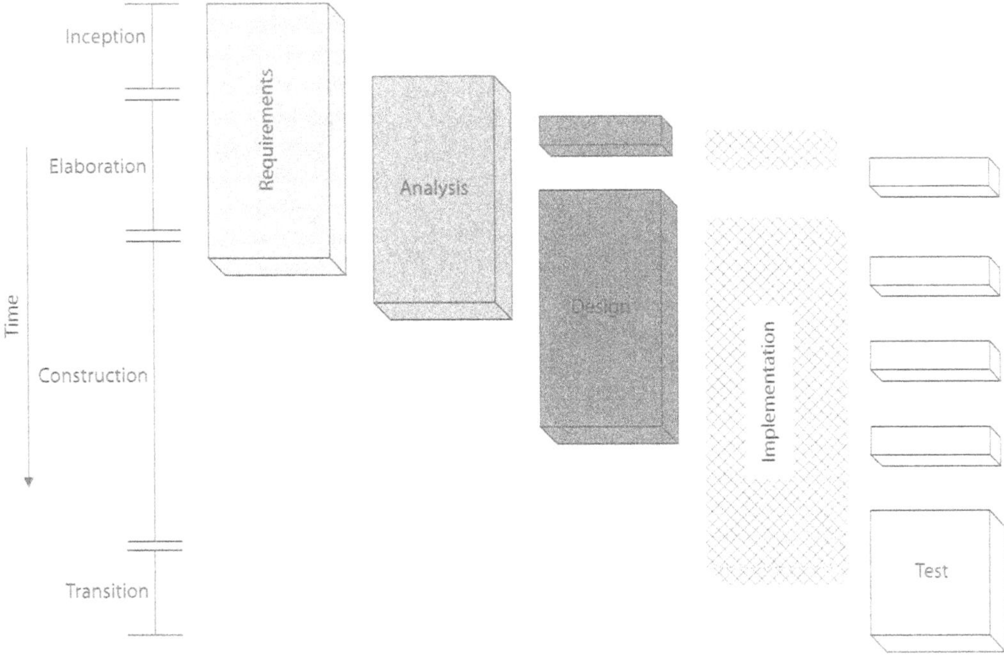

Figure 3.10 Disciplines versus phases.

The five disciplines in the Unified Process are Requirements, Analysis, Design, Implementation and Test (as indicated in Figure 3.10). Note that the Design, Implementation and Test disciplines are broken up. This is to indicate that elements of each disciplines may take place earlier than the core parts of the discipline. In particular, the design, implementation and testing of the architecture will happen early on (in the elaboration phase). Thus part of each of the Design, Implementation and Test disciplines must occur at this time.

The focus of each disciplines is described below (their primary products are illustrated in Figure 3.11):

- *Requirements*. This discipline focuses on the activities which allow the functional and non-functional requirements of the system to be identified. The primary product of this discipline is the use case model.
- *Analysis*. The aim of this discipline is to restructure the requirements identified in the requirements discipline in terms of the software to be built rather than in the user's less precise terms. It can be seen as a first cut at a design; however, that is to miss the point of what this discipline aims to achieve.
- *Design*. The design discipline produces the detailed design which will be implemented in the next discipline.
- *Implementation*. This discipline represents the coding of the design in an appropriate programming language (for this book that is Java), and the compilation, packaging, deployment and documenting of the software.

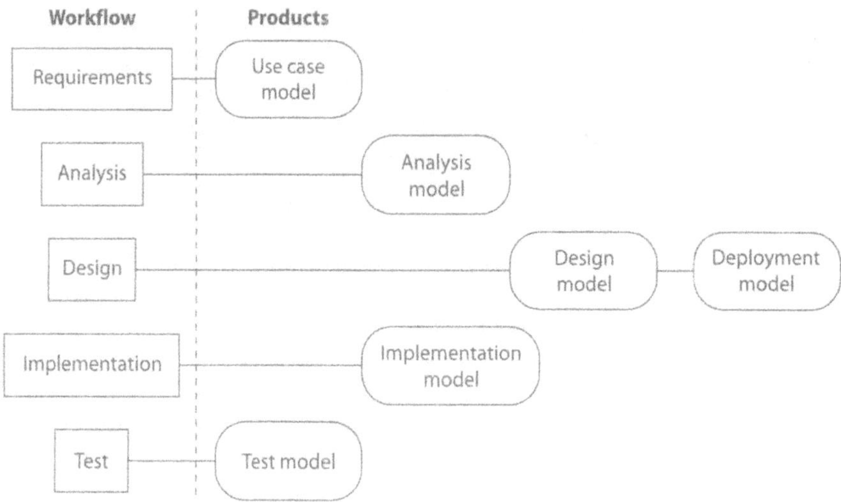

Figure 3.11 Discipline products.

- *Test*. The test discipline describes the activities to be carried out to test the software to ensure that it meets the user's requirements, that it is reliable etc.

Notice that the disciplines all have a period when they are running concurrently. This does not mean that one person is necessarily working on all the disciplines at the same time. Instead, it acknowledges that, in order to clarify some requirement, it may be necessary to design how that requirement might be implemented and even to implement it to confirm that it is feasible.

In fact, this acknowledges that the Unified Process is a spiral (as indicated by its iterative and incremental nature). This is illustrated in Figure 3.12 (note that as a phase moves around the spiral multiple iterations may occur; we have assumed only one iteration in this figure for simplicity's sake). As can be seen from this diagram the five disciplines are

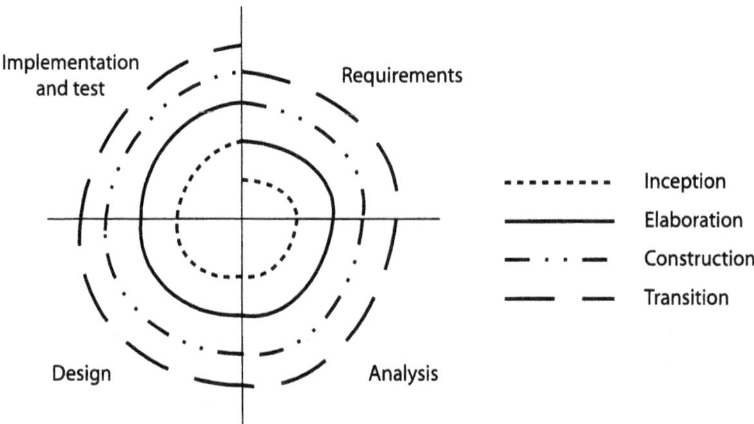

Figure 3.12 The Unified Process is a spiral.

involved in each of the four phases. Each phase moves around the various disciplines producing outputs which feed into the next phase. Each phase examines the requirements (to a greater or lesser extent). Each phase involves the analysis discipline, the design discipline and so on. This is in fact one of the Unified Process's greatest strengths: it represents a practical iterative design method, which is held together by an architecture and which acknowledges risk up front and makes it one of the driving elements of the whole design process. It then ensures that what is being produced will be relevant to users of the system by holding everything together via use cases. Indeed, it is the use cases which help a designer to identify what should be performed in any particular iteration.

3.4.4 Disciplines and Activities

Having discussed disciplines we should mention what disciplines do and what they are comprised of. A discipline describes how a set of activities are related. Activities are the things that actually tell designers what they should be doing. An activity takes inputs and produces outputs. These inputs and outputs are referred to as artefacts. An artefact that acts as an input to a particular activity could be a use case, while the output from that activity could be a class diagram, etc. The actual activities that comprise each of the disciplines will be discussed in more detail in appropriate chapters later in the book; however, Figure 3.13 lists the primary activities for each of the disciplines.

3.4.5 Applying the Unified Process

When it comes to applying the Unified Process to a real-world project, you should notice that it is a framework (see Figure 3.14). This means that there is no universal process which will always be applicable in its entirety. Instead, the Unified Process is designed for flexibility and extensibility. It allows a variety of life cycle strategies and also allows the selection of what artefacts should be produced. It defines what activities should be performed when and which workers should

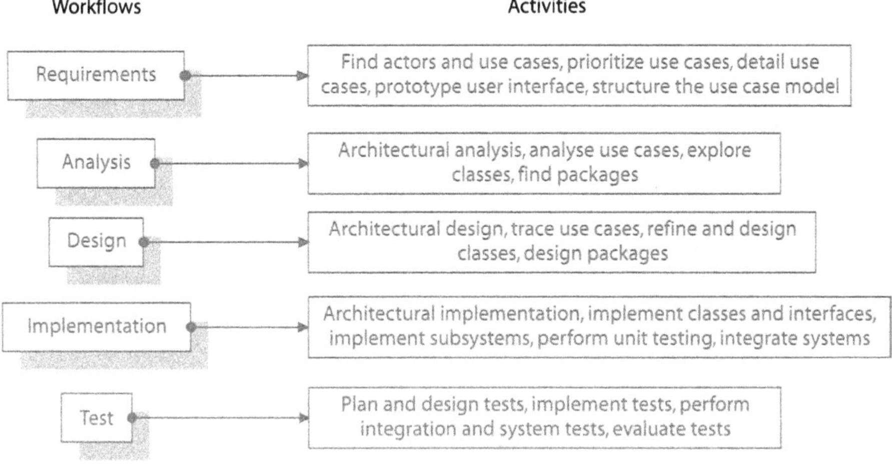

Figure 3.13 Disciplines are comprised of activities.

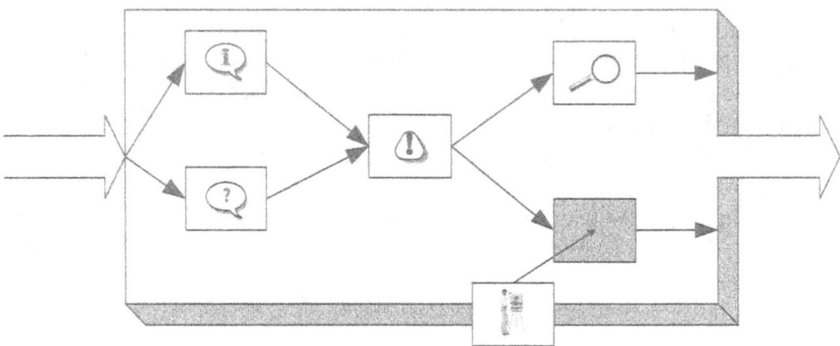

Figure 3.14 The Unified Process is a framework.

perform those activities. Thus it is possible to leave out those elements that don't fit the current project. For example, you might leave out deployment diagrams if you are only deploying on one processor, or if you are working with a batch processing oriented system you may decide to ignore some of the dynamic elements produced, such as statechart diagrams.

In turn, you can add in additional elements if they are required. For example, you may decide to incorporate some real-time extensions into the UML, and some activities to support them. You might decide to incorporate a security view of your system. You might also feel the need to incorporate additional processes. For example, you might incorporate additional activities to help identify an initial set of classes, attributes and relationships. In fact, you may even decide to leave out whole phases, iterations and disciplines as appropriate: for example, a simple system may not need an explicit analysis model!

3.5 The Rational Unified Process

You may have read about the Rational Unified Process (or RUP) elsewhere, so you might think that this is just the Unified Process under another banner (after all, Rational did create the Unified Process in the first place). Well, not exactly. The Rational Unified Process (Kruchten, 2000) is an instantiation of the Unified Process (as is the Enterprise Unified Process or EUP (Ambler, 2001)). Remember that the Unified Process itself is a framework that can be adapted to different situations, types of projects, and detailed techniques. The RUP is a configuration of the Unified Process that is directly supported by the RUP product from Rational. This product specifies many processes and describes how to apply other Rational tools on software projects. It also provides the framework for various documents and artefacts that need to be produced and generally controls the flow of work through a project. This is great if you want to follow this particular instantiation of the Unified Process (but of course it comes at a price). The end result can be that the tool and the process take over! However, it should be noted that the RUP product now has a tool, RUP Builder, for selecting and deploying specialized RUP configurations.

3.6 Summary

To conclude, the Unified Process is a design process framework that is hierarchical, as it is made up of cycles, comprising phases which are themselves made up of workflows that describe how activities are linked. It is engineered because it specifies these activities, who should carry them out (although we don't explicitly identify particular roles for those carrying out activities in this book) and the artefacts produced by the activities. Finally, the key elements of the Unified Process are that it is:

- iterative and incremental
- risk-driven
- architecture-centric
- use case-driven.

3.7 References

Kruchten, P. (2000). *The Rational Unified Process: an Introduction*, 2nd edn. Addison Wesley Longman, Reading, MA.

3.8 Online References

Ambler, S. W. (2001). Enterprise Unified Process White Paper: `http://www.ronin-intl.com/publications/unifiedProcess.htm`
Rational Unified Process: `http://www.rational.com/products/rup/`
OMG Unified Modeling Language: `http://www.omg.org/technology/documents/formal/uml.htm`

4

Software Architecture and Object-Oriented Design

4.1 Software Architecture – the Very Idea

4.1.1 Why Have an Architecture?

Why have an architecture? This is a very valid and important question, not least because the Unified Process, on which this book is based, is said (among other things) to be architecture-centric. Let us consider what role requirements (and in this case use cases) have. They help to identify what the system should do; that is, its functionality. They do not state anything about how that functionality should be provided. In some cases non-functional requirements may also be identified which may impose restrictions on the realization of the system, but even these say very little about how the system should be structured or designed.

However, many people have taken the *requirements* of a system (i.e. its required functionality) and used them as their *sole starting point* in producing a design and implementation of a software system. In some cases this has been successful, and in many others it has not been so successful. Indeed, in software engineering this is exactly the series of steps that are advocated in many development methods. That is, find out what the system should do and then implement it. This may well be acceptable if this is the nth time that you have produced such a system; however, if this is the first time you have produced a system to these requirements (and the system is large) it is likely to be fraught with danger.

Consider the equivalent case within the domain of the built environment (i.e. buildings). If you were to construct a simple *garden shed* you might well start by thinking about what you need to do with it: for example, "store the grass mower", "store shovels and forks" or "keep dangerous liquids away from children". You might then produce a design which exactly matches these requirements. This end result could be a simple 5' × 6' × 7' shed or it could be a smaller 5' × 4' × 6' construction. It could be made out of wood, for example. You might also add other functional requirements, such as "must be high enough to walk into" and "must have light for germinating plants". This might direct you towards a higher shed

39

and one with a window in it. You might well produce a design in your head with minimal paperwork and go along to your local wood merchant and purchase the required amount of materials. You could then fabricate the shed at your convenience. Such an approach is satisfactory because most of us have witnessed a garden shed at some time or another and have a reasonable idea of what it should look like. In addition, the requirements are fairly basic and can easily be realized.

However, let us now consider constructing a house from just its functions, having never seen a house (merely hearing from someone else what they want it to do). The list of functions might be:

- Park car securely inside.
- Have a place to cook food and do the clothes washing.
- Be able to sleep inside.
- Have amenities to allow relaxation including music and television etc.

What might the end result of providing these functions be? This list of functions says nothing about the relationships between them. Indeed some bright aspiring young designer might note that the car will be inside the house. The car might reasonably have a stereo. If the car could be upgraded to include a television, well then this would be the ideal place to provide relaxation. Thus the "car secure inside" function and the "relaxation with music and television" could be achieved together by placing the car in the middle of the house and requiring the users to sit inside the car!

If you think this example seems a little absurd, have a think about some of the software systems you or others have "endured" and see if you can make a connection – I certainly can!

What is required is something which expresses the overall relationship between the elements which will satisfy the required functions. In the case of a house these are the architectural blueprints. These describe where everything should go, presenting different views for different contractors (i.e. those for the heating system, those for the wiring, those for the physical structure of the walls, floors and ceilings, etc.). In the case of automobiles there are equivalent diagrams (e.g. the wiring harness, the suspension). In fact, in almost every example of large-scale engineering endeavour there are architectural blueprints. Software engineering really is no exception, and thus the software architecture represents the blueprints for the software system.

You might at this point argue that you have built a number of systems without the need to resort to an architecture. However, ask yourself the question "did I have an implicit architecture in mind?". Often with simple systems people have an architecture which they have adopted subconsciously. They often argue that it's the obvious way to structure the system. That may well be so, but it is obvious either because the system is straightforward or because they have seen similar systems before. This is really why the shed example worked – we had a mental model/architecture of the shed. With the house, as we had never seen a house before, we had no mental model or architecture to follow.

It should also be fairly clear to you by now that if your system is straightforward (in that you already know how to approach the problem or it is relatively simple) you may not need to produce an explicit architecture – but that doesn't mean you don't have one, just that it is not being made explicit!

4.1.2 Why We Need an Architecture

Let us review the argument being made about why an architecture is a critical element of the object-oriented design process. We need an architecture to:

- *Understand the system.* Software systems can be large and complex, and must meet conflicting requirements. An architecture provides a convenient blueprint or model of the system to be produced. It abstracts out much of the implementation detail, but "positions" the elements which must meet the various functional requirements.
- *Organize development.* That is, it helps organize "plumbers" and "electricians". In other words, it helps firstly to separate out different concerns so that those involved in the "plumbing" of the system only need to worry about plumbing issues. It also identifies how the different concerns are related, so that the points at which they intersect are well documented and clearly specified (for example in the central heating boiler).
- *Promote reuse.* The problem with writing reusable code is that you need to identify that what you are producing is reusable. I have personally been in situations where two people on one project were reproducing the same solution but from different aspects. In at least one case they were sitting opposite each other. It is certainly easier to produce reusable code the second, third or even fourth time you are designing and implementing a system than the first. However, if this is the first time it is a great deal more difficult. Indeed, in many systems, the only form of reuse that occurs is at the class level (i.e. at a very detailed level), and is identified by the coder during implementation. However, an architecture can help at a much higher level by identifying critical systems and subsystems early on. Common subsystems can then be made reusable.
- *Promote continued development.* Few systems of any size or consequence are produced and never altered. Instead, it is much more common for a system to evolve over time, with new requirements being identified and new functionality added or existing functionality modified. The original architecture can be essential in helping to control the evolution of the system over time (both within a single release and between releases of a system). Indeed, a good architecture need change little over the life cycle of a system, but can be instrumental to the success of future releases. This is because it provides the overall structure into which the new additions or modifications must be fitted. Often the actual design of the system is too detailed to allow an overview to be gained, and thus future designers and implementers may misinterpret part of a design or (worse) ignore it. The architecture can help to minimize such problems.

4.1.3 Architecture Myths

At this point let us stop, stand back and consider some of the myths that surround the concept of an architecture. For a start it is important to realize that the architecture and the design are not the same thing (indeed, we hinted at that in the last paragraph) but it is important to reiterate this. The architecture highlights the most significant elements of the design. These include the major systems and subsystems, their interfaces, how the system will be deployed, etc. It does not include many details of the systems and subsystems and how they are implemented – that is the job of the design. It is useful to picture the level of detail in the architecture and the level of detail in the final

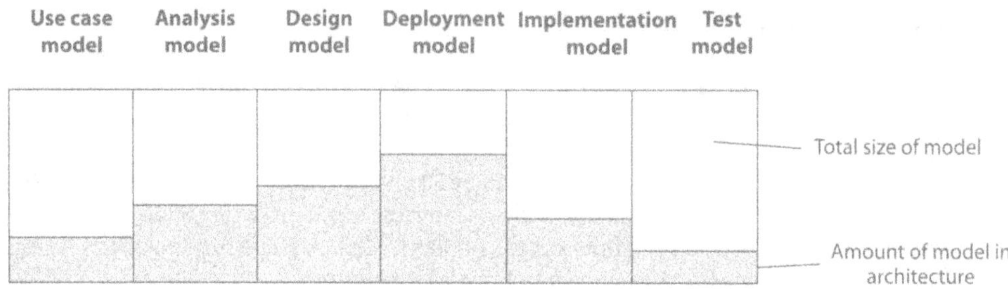

Figure 4.1 The relationship between design and architecture.

design as bar charts, as is done in Figure 4.1. As can be seen from this diagram, the architecture leaves much out, while the design must address many more aspects in detail.

Another myth to be debunked is that the architecture and the infrastructure are the same thing. This is an easy mistake to make (not least given what we have said about the role of the architecture). However, it is important to remember that the architecture only captures those elements of the design which are necessary to provide an understanding of the overall design of the system. In fact Jacobson, Booch and Rumbaugh state that only about 10% of all the classes in a design are architecturally significant. The remaining 90% may well be functionally significant, but are not important in understanding the overall structure of the system. However, for the infrastructure of the system, i.e. the essential functionality of the system, it is likely that many more classes will be needed (indeed it is likely that at least 50% of the classes in the design will make up the infrastructure).

Another myth is that "my favourite technology" is the architecture. The architecture does not relate to any particular technology, and should be implementable in whatever manner is appropriate, whether this is straight Java, JavaBeans, Enterprise JavaBeans or whatever. Such technologies do not dictate the architecture, although they may well make it easier or harder to implement!

If we are talking about any system of significant size it will be impossible for a single architect to get right. Thus the concept that a good architecture will be the work of a single architect is unlikely to be true. Rather, it is likely that a good architecture will be the product of a group of people (the architecture team), all of whom have brought their own particular skills and experience to the production of the architecture. It may well be that there is a lead architect whose vision has been realized in the architecture, but he or she will have benefited from the input and collaboration of others. This peer review and multi-skill input is often essential (consider a house: will one architect produce the full set of plans required, including all electrical, plumbing and heating designs?).

Another issue is what form the architecture should take. An architecture should not, and indeed is not, flat. An architect, when producing the plans for a house, will not merely produce a single diagram with one elevation presented. Instead different views will be presented, some of different elevations (front, side and three-dimensional), some of different aspects, and some of the interior spaces, wiring, plumbing etc. Each view will pick up on a particular aspect of the design, and none is likely to include all aspects of the design. Imagine being presented with a diagram including all piping, all wiring, all heating ducts, windows, doors, walls, coving, lighting, walls and exterior fitments. It would be a confusing jumble that would not be of use to anyone!

A common mistake (which I encountered numerous times when I was a lecturer within a software engineering department, where undergraduate students were attempting to produce their first object-oriented designs) is to think that a set of diagrams are sufficient to document a design (or an architecture). The architecture is much more than just its basic structure. In producing an architecture the architect has made multiple assumptions and trade-offs, and these should be included in the documentation supporting the architecture. In the world of the designer it is common to produce scale models (in some cases large ones) to study the effects of various stresses and strains on the design. For example, bridge builders often produce scale models of bridges, and car designers produce clay models of their designs. These may then be tested against real-world scenarios (for example, cars are often tested in wind tunnels). Thus a good architecture should be implemented to test out its validity. The architecture may then resemble a mini-system in which all the building blocks for the full system have been identified and put into place.

The end result of the architecture should be a complete set of documents covering the functions supported by the architecture, the design of the architecture, the implementation of the architecture, the testing of the architecture etc. In some cases the architecture implementation may form the basis of the actual system, or it may be used purely as a reference. Either way the architecture is much more than just a set of diagrams representing the overall structure of the system.

One very useful analogy for the architecture (which was actually suggested by a couple of designers from a software development company in Cardiff) is that the architecture is like a space station. Within the core element of the space station all the conduits and connections have been put in place for future modules to be plugged into. Then, as new modules for the space station are designed and developed, they can be plugged into this core and will work safely with the rest of the system. In addition, Java facilities such as interfaces can be used to provide "airlocks". These act as fire doors between different parts of the space station, so that if one part of the architecture (space station) fails or needs to be redesigned, an airlock protects the remainder of the architecture from being affected. This is illustrated in Figure 4.2. Note that the information exchanged between various parts of the architecture will be vital in ensuring that the architecture is resilient to change. The analysis discipline (considered later in the book) helps to identify the key entities in a system. In terms of the architecture, these indicate the key concepts in the system and may well highlight the types of information to be exchanged between parts of the architecture.

Finally, let us address the myth that "architecture is an art". Although this may currently be true, there is no reason why it should be. Producing an architecture is no more and no less of an art than producing a software system. It should be subject to, and controlled by, the same guidelines as used to produce the overall design. However, a different set of criteria need to be applied to identify the appropriate classes, interfaces, objects, subsystems and systems than are used for the overall design. In the case of the architecture what we are looking for are the architecturally significant features: that is, those aspects of the system which, if modified, will have a significant impact on other elements, or which are so fundamental to the system as to defines its core behaviour.

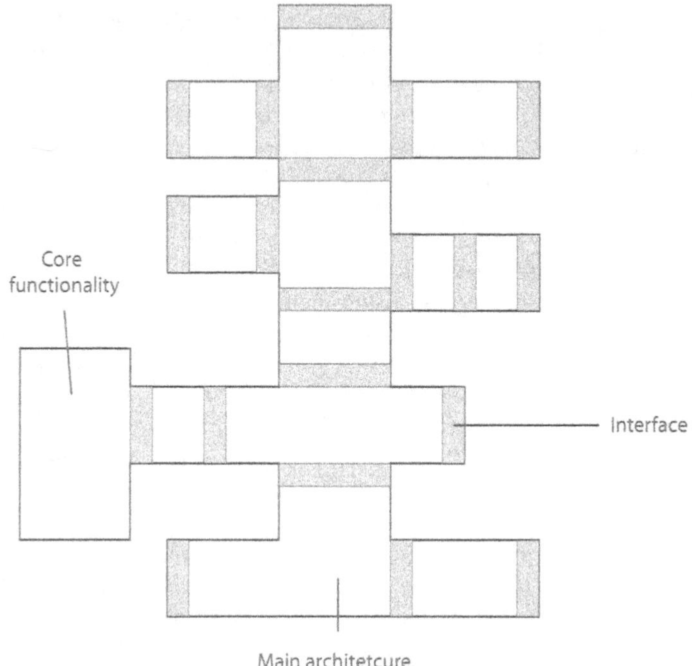

Figure 4.2 Conceptualizing an architecture.

4.1.4 Architecture Defined

In this section we will try to define what we mean by an architecture. A software architecture encompasses:

- *the* overall *plan for the structure of the system.* That is, it is the blueprint for the system (see Figure 4.2). It should be possible to read the architecture and gain an appreciation of how the system was structured (without needing to know the details of the structural elements).
- *the key structural elements and their interfaces.* That is, what elements make up the system, their interfaces and how they are plugged together.
- *how those elements interact (at the top level).* That is, when the various elements of the architecture interface, what they do and why they do it.
- *how these elements form subsystems and systems.* This is a very important aspect of the architecture. Early identification of the core systems and subsystem of the design not only helps organize future design (and implementation), it helps promote reuse and the comprehensibility of the system.
- *the architectural style* that guides this organization.

The intent is that within this architecture, designers are then free to work in the "spaces" left for them by the architecture. However, this is not the end of the story. The software architecture also involves:

- How the system will be used.
- What the functionality of the final system is expected to be.
- Any performance issues which need to be addressed (these may involve more detailed development of the software architecture's implementation to assess performance constraints).
- Resilience to further development.
- Economic and technology constraints and trade-offs. The architecture can consider different solutions to the same problem, allowing different technological solutions to be aired and the most appropriate adopted (for example, CGI scripts versus Java servlets on a Web server).

4.1.5 Characteristics of a Good Architecture

It is easier to specify what makes a good architecture than to actually produce a good architecture, and in many cases it is not possible to maximize all of the following. However, we present the guiding characteristics which all software architects should bear in mind when developing an architecture:

- *Resilience.* The architecture should be resilient to change. That is, changes in functionality or additional functionality should have a minimal effect on the architecture (although they may have a major effect on the design). Thus subsystems should have clear and specific interfaces. Indeed, it is almost true to say that the very first thing an architect should do is to identify the interfaces which will be used within the architecture and then identify the subsystems which will realize the interfaces etc.
- *Simplicity.* The architecture should be simple. Remember that as a rule of thumb the architecture should only be about 10% of the size of the overall design, and is supposed to be comprehensible on its own and in its entirety. Avoid making the architecture complex just for the sake of it.
- *Clarity of presentation.* As the architecture will be used not only as the base reference for the remainder of the design but also for future iterations of the system, it should be easily accessible and devoid of ambiguity (this is critical!), and should avoid assuming current project knowledge.
- *Clear separation of concerns.* The architecture should clearly separate out different aspects of the system. For example, in the case of a house, plumbers probably don't want to know about the wiring of the house except where it might impinge on what they are doing. Therefore a plumber's plans should not have a great deal of detail about the wiring harness for the house.
- *Balanced distribution of responsibilities.* The responsibilities of the subsystems should be appropriate and balanced. That is, if a subsystem is identified for dealing with general application security, don't then make it also responsible for user login. Instead, provide a user login subsystem (which may well make use of the security subsystem).
- *Balances economic and technological constraints.* The architecture may well need to justify why one approach was adopted over another – partly to explain the overall choices to those working within different aspects of the design. This is important, as it may impose restrictions on what the elements of the design can and cannot do (or the technologies or solutions they may adopt).

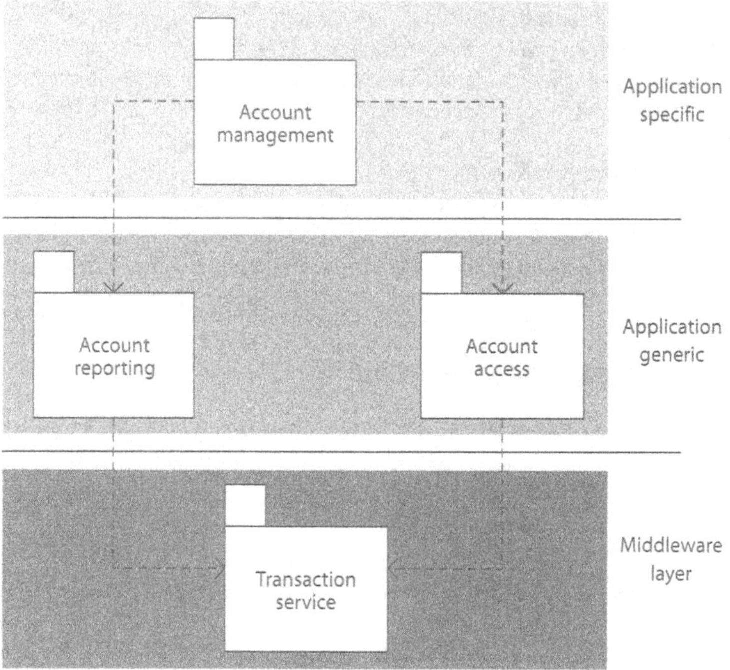

Figure 4.3 Layering the architecture.

4.1.6 Layering the Architecture

Layering the architecture can be useful in helping to simplify the architecture to ease the understanding and organizing of the development of complex systems. It is also a good way of ensuring that subsystems in different layers are loosely coupled. That is, subsystems in lower levels should not be aware of subsystems in higher levels that may use them. Subsystems should only access subsystems in lower layers or in their own layer. Figure 4.3 illustrates an architecture with three layers and four subsystems.

Identifying layers can also be useful for identifying reusable subsystems. For example, in Figure 4.3 the top layer is application-specific, the middle layer is application-generic (in that these subsystems may be useful to other applications in the same domain), and the bottom layer is generic to a wide range of applications.

4.1.7 Use Cases and Architecture

At the beginning of this chapter we stated that merely working from the requirements (of functionality) of a system could be fraught with danger and that an architecture could help to mitigate this danger. However, there must be a relationship between the functionality of the system and its software architecture. In the case of object-oriented design this means that there needs to be a relationship between the use cases in the use case model and the software architecture.

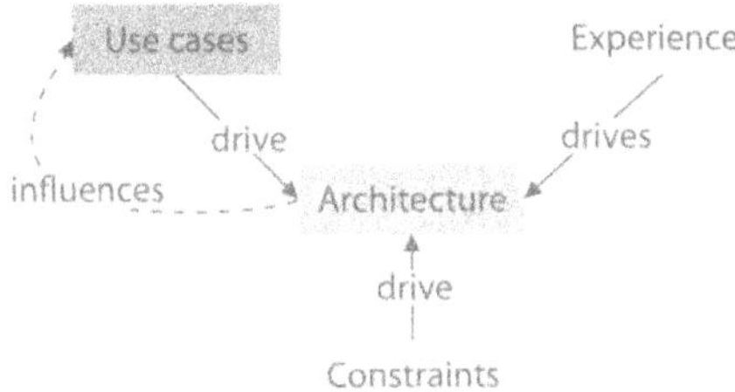

Figure 4.4 Major influences on architecture.

Essentially, the use cases and the architecture have a direct influence on each other (Figure 4.4); you could almost say that they are two sides of the same coin.

4.1.8 So What Is an Architecture?

Let us now go back to the question of what a software architecture actually is. In essence, it is a number of things. Earlier discussions have indicated that it is more than just a set of diagrams, and here we will consider that in more detail:

An Architecture Baseline

The software architecture contains an architectural baseline which will provide both a proof of concept and the basic skeleton of the system. This is a "small, skinny" system which captures the essential functionality of the final system. It is a working prototype which proves the concepts and the architectural structure.

An Architecture Description

This is a detailed description of the architecture containing information about the systems, subsystems, classes and interfaces which comprise the architecture. It should also contain discussions of architectural design decisions, constraints, required behaviour etc.; indeed, everything that is necessary to understand the architecture. The information should be sufficient to guide the whole development team throughout the lifetime of the system. As has already been said, this description may evolve over time.

Format of the Architecture Description

The format of the architecture description should really be chosen as appropriate for the team, project and company involved. It is likely to contain at least:

- A use case model of architecturally significant use cases.
- An object model of the classes and objects in the architecture.
- A component model of the subsystems and their interfaces.
- Dynamic models of the behaviour of the architecture described in terms of sequence and collaboration diagrams.

- A glossary of classes and interfaces.
- Additional descriptions supporting the above.

These elements are often broken down further into different views. These views focus on different aspects of the analysis and design of the software architecture:

- The *analysis view*, which describes the internal requirements of the system given the specified functionality.
- The *design view*, which presents the set of classes, interfaces and subsystems which will meet the requirements.
- The *component view*, describes how the implementation will be broken up into components that may execute different processes.
- The *implementation view* presents the implementation detail of the design view.

It is also worth considering the nature of the software architecture description. This is something which may well change over time; however, these changes should be small and should be limited to aspects such as:

- new classes and interfaces
- new functionality
- new versions of components (this may be due to new versions of operating systems, Java or releases of third-party components etc.)

By their very nature, some elements will be treated in a very superficial manner within the software architecture. This is not a problem, as that is exactly how they should be treated. The detail of such elements should be found elsewhere in the analysis or design models. Also, all elements within the architectural description should be architecturally significant. If they are not, then they should not be part of the software architecture.

Finally, the architectural description is primarily produced during the elaboration phase (see Figure 4.5) of the Unified Process. This illustrates that it is essentially part of the process of determining what features the system requires internally to match the external requirements and precedes the process of determining how those requirements will be met.

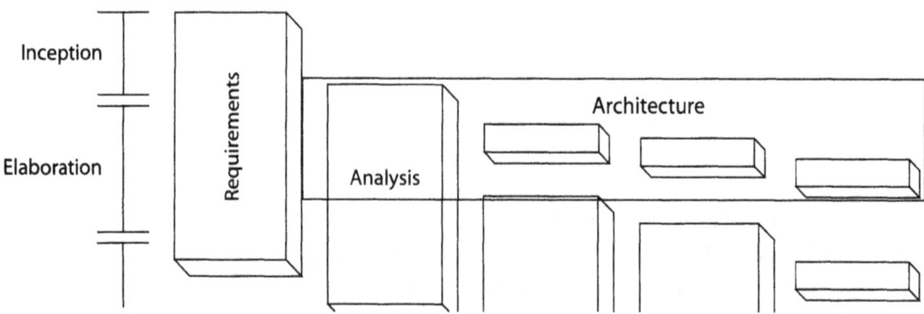

Figure 4.5 How the architecture fits in.

4.2 Software Patterns

Software patterns can be a great help in identifying the structure of parts of the architecture. They are discussed in more detail later in the book.

4.2.1 What Are Design Patterns?

A design pattern captures expertise describing an architectural design to a recurring design problem in a particular context (Gamma *et al.*, 1993; Johnson, 1992; Beck and Johnson, 1994). It also contains information on the applicability of a pattern, the trade-offs which must be made, and any consequences of the solution. Books are now appearing which present such design patterns for a range of applications. For example, Gamma *et al.* (1995) is a widely cited book which presents a catalogue of 23 design patterns.

Design patterns are extremely useful for both novice and experienced object-oriented designers. This is because they encapsulate extensive design knowledge and proven design solutions with guidance on how to use them. Reusing common patterns opens up an additional level of design reuse where the implementations vary but the micro-architectures represented by the patterns still apply.

Thus patterns allow designers and programmers to share knowledge about the design of a software architecture. They capture the static and dynamic structures and collaborations of previous successful solutions to problems that arise when building applications in a particular domain (but not a particular language).

Most systems are full of patterns that designers and developers have identified through past experience and documented good practice. The patterns movement has essentially made these patterns explicit. Thus the programmatic idioms that have previously been used are now documented as behavioural patterns. In turn there are design patterns which express some commonly used design structures and architectural patterns which express structural patterns.

4.2.2 What They Are Not

Patterns are not concrete designs for particular systems. This is because a pattern must be instantiated in a particular domain to be used. This involves evaluating various trade-offs or constraints as well as detailed consideration of the consequences. It also does not mean that creativity or human judgement has been removed, as it is still necessary to make the design and implementation decisions required. Having done that the developer must then implement the pattern and combine the implementation with other code (which may or may not have been derived from a pattern).

Patterns are also not frameworks (although they do seem to be exceptionally well suited for documenting frameworks). This is because frameworks present an instance of a design for solving a family of problems in a specific domain (and often for a particular language). In terms of languages such as Smalltalk and Java, a framework is a set of abstract cooperating classes. To apply such a framework to a particular problem it is often necessary to customize it by providing user-defined subclasses and to compose objects in the appropriate manner (e.g. the Smalltalk MVC framework). That is, a framework is a semi-complete application. As a result, any given framework may contain one or more instances of multiple patterns, and in turn a pattern can be used in many different frameworks.

4.2.3 Architectural Patterns

Architectural patterns are patterns that describe the structure of a system (or part of a system). For example the Model–View–Controller (or MVC) pattern describes how a user interface, the associated application and any event handlers should be structured. They can be used to help you structure your architecture as well as to explore different possible architectures. There are a whole range of architectural patterns which have been documented, including:

- *Distributed*, in which various parts of the system reside in different processes, potentially on different processors.
- *Layered*, in which a system is decomposed along application-specific vs. application-generic lines.
- *Model–View–Controller*, in which the display, the application and the control of user input are separated.
- *Blackboard*, in which a central "blackboard" acts as a communications medium for a number of cooperating agents.
- *Subsumption*, in which high-level components can subsume the role of those lower down in the architecture.
- *Repository-centric*, in which a central repository is used.

4.3 Constructing the Architecture

The primary steps involved in creating an architecture are presented below. Having presented the main steps we will go on to look at each step in more detail:

- Find architecturally significant use cases.
- Identify systems and subsystems.
- Identify/extract classes for the architecture. As part of this process, identify the structure of the classes and their relationships to subsystems.
- Identify the potential for concurrency and distribution.
- Manage the data stores used by the system.
- Deal with additional architectural concerns.
- Implement one or more architectural prototypes.
- Derive tests from the use cases.
- Evaluate the architecture.

Note that not only is this process iterative (in that it is unlikely that, for a system of any real size, this process will be completed in one pass), but also that it is not as sequential as may be suggested from this list. Rather, the identification of classes may lead to the identification of subsystems, which in turn may lead to the need for concurrency etc.

4.4 Find Architecturally Significant Use Cases

4.4.1 Architecturally Significant Use Cases

The software architecture contains the architecturally significant use cases. These use cases can be summarized as those that involve:

- some important and critical functionality
- functionality at the extremes of the system
- some important requirement that needs to be implemented/tested early in the project lifetime
- importance to users
- highest risk of failure

Identifying such use cases is not trivial. It is suggested that the best way to approach this is first to generate the complete (at least as far is both possible and reasonable) set of use cases via the Use Case Analysis discipline (described in the next chapter). Having done this, you should then consider each use case against the points presented above. This initial set of use cases should then be checked for duplication of intent (remember that this is the architecture, not the complete design, so we don't need duplicate use cases with related behaviour – unless of course both are critical to the operation of the system). Generating these use cases is likely to be an iterative process and should involve a team of people.

4.4.2 Use Case Description

The use case description contains the architectural view of the use case model. That is, it contains the architecturally significant use cases. Related use case realizations should appear in the architecture description during analysis and design. A use case realization is a description of how the use case will be implemented given the elements within the architecture. Each use case should have at least one use case realization. If any use cases do not have a use case realization then they are not supported by the architecture.

4.5 Identify Key Classes

During the architecture generation it is necessary to identify the key classes which will be included in the architecture. These classes must provide the realizations of the architectural use cases. Note that the use cases appear to be driving the architecture, but remember that the architecture influences which use cases can be included.

Identifying an appropriate set of architectural classes is neither simple nor straightforward. You should use your experience, intuition, design patterns and any constraints to do this. A good starting point is to identify the entity classes in the *Analysis Model* that should be part of the architecture. These are the key data holding classes identified during the Analysis discipline. These classes may later become design classes, or may be broken down into subsystems, composite classes or a variety of classes. However, they are likely to be important "concepts" in the architecture, whatever they map into in the design.

As the full design progresses you may find that new classes need to be added to the architecture, particularly if new use cases are identified and added to the system. You need to ensure that the concepts captured within the architecture are sufficient to support all (reasonable) communications between the various "modules" in the system while leaving the option open for future change or extension.

Note that a natural by-product of this is the actual structure of the classes, or the relationships between the classes. As you develop the set of classes you should be developing the relationships between the classes in exactly the same way as you would do for the remainder of the design (see the appropriate chapters for discussions of this process).

It is also necessary to assign classes (and objects) to subsystems and to group classes together into new subsystems (this actually illustrates the iterative nature of this whole process).

As the identification of classes is a complex and in-depth subject in its own right, we will defer such a discussion to a later chapter.

4.6 Breaking the System into Subsystems

This stage is primarily concerned with the identification of the overall architecture of the system. It is from this architecture that the structure of the actual design will be hung. That is, the subsystem architecture provides the context within which the more detailed design decisions, made during the rest of the design discipline, will be performed.

The subsystem decomposition defines an architecture which can be used as the basis on which the detailed design can be partitioned among a number of designers, thus allowing different designers to work independently on different subsystems. This is because it specifies the *goals*, *strategies* and *policies* within which each section of the system must be designed.

The steps used to generate this architecture are:

1. Organizing the system into subsystems.
2. Identifying major system interfaces.
3. Identifying concurrency inherent in the problem.
4. Allocating subsystems to processors and tasks.
5. Choosing an approach for management of data stores.
6. Handling access to global resources.
7. Considering generic design issues.
8. Handling boundary conditions.
9. Setting trade-offs between competing priorities.

Of course, not all these steps are important for all applications. For example, a batch-oriented, purely serial process probably cannot have much concurrency imposed on it. Equally, the precise ordering of these steps will vary according to the domain, type of application and problem being solved. You should therefore attempt to use this list in the most appropriate manner for your particular situation.

4.6.1 Breaking the System into Subsystems

Most systems comprise a number of subsystems. For example, a payroll system might possess a file subsystem, a calculation subsystem and a printing subsystem. A subsystem is not an object or a function, but a package of use case realizations, interfaces, classes, associations, operations, events and constraints that are interrelated and that have a reasonably well defined and (hopefully) small interface with other subsystems. Subsystems can, of course, also contain other subsystems. The UML package notation can be used to represent subsystems (Figure 4.6 illustrates a set of subsystems from a Java system presented using the UML package notation.)

A subsystem (or package) is usually characterized by the common (or associated) set of services that it provides. For example, the file package would provide a set of services to do with creating, deleting, opening, reading and writing files. The use case model may be useful in identifying such common services.

Each package therefore provides a well-defined interface to the remainder of the system which allows other packages to use its facilities. Such an interface also allows the internals of the package to be defined independently of the rest of the system (i.e. it encapsulates the package). In addition, there should be little or no interaction between objects within the package and objects in another package (except via the specified interfaces).

In simple systems it is quite possible that there will only be a single tier to the package hierarchy. However, for most real-world systems it is likely that the packages will be hierarchical. You therefore need to identify sub-packages and the most appropriate architectures for these packages.

Packages can be involved in client–server or peer-to-peer relationships with other packages. Client–server relationships are easiest to implement and maintain, as one package responds to requests from another package and returns results. In peer-to-peer relationships,

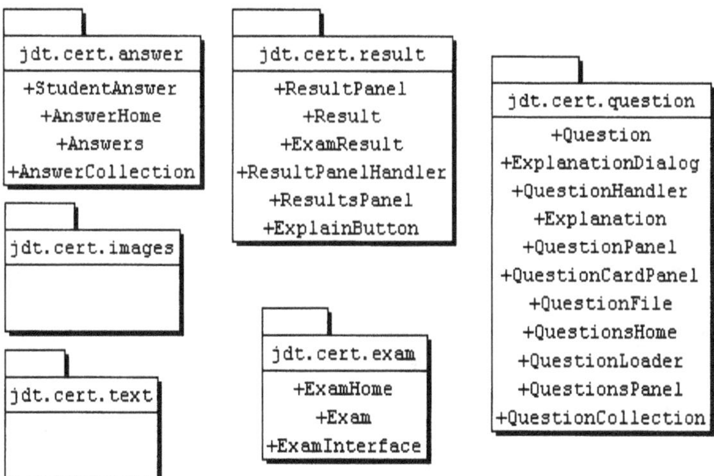

Figure 4.6 UML package notation.

both packages must be capable of responding to requests from the other. This can result in unforeseen circularities.

The above description implies that the identification of these packages is straightforward and that you should be able to do it in a methodological manner. However, for complex systems it is unlikely that the most appropriate architecture for every package will be immediately obvious. You therefore need to consider different alternative architectures and evaluate these alternatives against some criteria.

The process of identifying subsystems involves first identifying a candidate set of subsystems. This is best done by a number of different people, with different backgrounds, all of whom need to analyze the goals of the system as well as the results of the analysis phase in detail. Personally, I have found that brainstorming sessions can be a particularly effective way of coming up with different potential architectures. The process of identifying subsystems is considered in more detail below.

4.6.2 Identifying Subsystems

The following steps help in identifying subsystems:

- Look at the analysis model (as a starting point).
- Look for separation of design concerns.
- Look for functionally related classes and interfaces (and sub-subsystems).
- Look for classes, interfaces and subsystems with many dependencies.
- Look for large-grained components (i.e. information management system).
- Look for reusable components.
- Look for interfaces.
- Look for software products that need to be wrapped up as a subsystem (e.g. using a JDBC-based subsystem to access a DBMS).
- Look for legacy systems which need to be wrapped up as a subsystem (e.g. using JNI).
- Look for service subsystems based on Java technologies (such as JavaMail). Represent such a service subsystem using a <service subsystem> stereotype.

4.6.3 Assessing the Subsystems

The primary steps followed in this process are:

- *Consider design criteria and assess subsystems against them.* Considering the needs of various actors against the advantages and disadvantages of each candidate subsystems can help determine whether subsystems are appropriate or not. The following criteria are often used: cost, ease of use, development effort, deployment effort, performance, reliability, extensibility, integrity and security. However, the most significant criteria include:
  - *Cohesion,* that is, a subsystem should have strongly related contents.
  - *Loose coupling.* Subsystems should be loosely coupled, with few dependencies on the contents of other subsystems. If subsystems have very many links between them, it may be that they are really part of the same subsystem.
  - *Fulfilment of a purpose.* It should be possible to specify the purpose of the subsystem directly and without the need for lengthy "and" clauses!

- *Quantify the compliance of the architectures against the decision criteria.* That is, assess the architectures against the criteria you have identified. This can be done in many ways; however, be careful of assigning quantitative values to such compliance and using a simple function to sum the values, as this may be misleading – only use any such method as a guide.

You should also attempt to take into account the package structure of your application. That is you should consider looking for:

- *Application subsystems* which fall naturally out of your application.
- *Middleware subsystems* which you may exploit in your design. For example, utilizing the Remote Method Invocation (RMI) facilities of Java, JavaIDL, servlets or applets may well affect how you decompose you application into subsystems.
- *Legacy systems.* You should consider any legacy systems with which you need to interface as another subsystem (and how you link to these legacy systems may affect other subsystem choices).
- *System software.* If you integrate or use any other system software these should be considered to be subsystems.

4.6.4 Identify Major System Interfaces

You should also attempt to identify the interfaces between subsystems as early as possible (although remember that these are likely to evolve over time). This can be done by considering the relationships between packages, how one package uses another, what you expect a package to do and what you expect it to provide etc. By explicitly specifying the interfaces up front and using them to link packages together you will both improve the cohesive nature of the architecture and ensure that subsystems are loosely coupled. It will also force you to consider how two subsystems are related if their interface does not support the operations required.

4.6.5 Layering the Subsystems

As was stated earlier, it can be a good idea to layer your architecture. You should attempt to identify subsystems that are at the same layer. This can be done by examining their use of lower level subsystems and by considering whether the subsystem is specific or generic to an application, or whether it represents some middleware etc. This is illustrated for a simple Web-based employee search engine in Figure 4.7.

4.7 Identifying Concurrency and Active Classes

Concurrency (or distribution) is an important issue for the design of the architecture, as it may affect the design of classes and their interfaces, the Java technology used (such as RMI or JavaIDL) and how the system is broken down into subsystems.

Concurrency can be very important for improving the efficiency of a system. However, to take full advantage of concurrency, the system must be designed around the concurrency

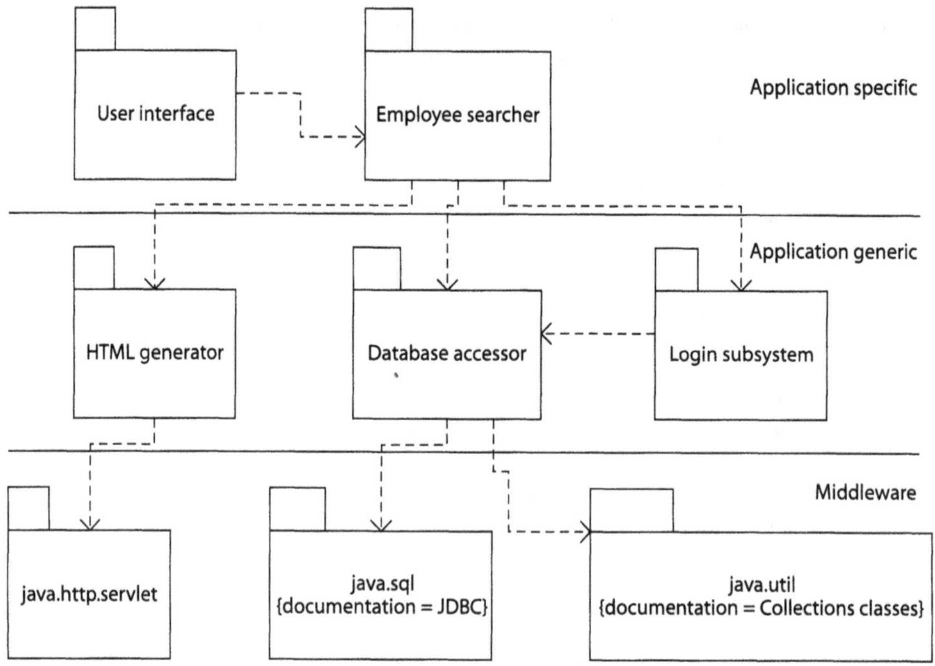

Figure 4.7 A three layer architecture example.

inherent in the application. You can do this by examining the dynamic model for objects that receive events at the same time or perform any state transitions (and associated actions) without interacting. Such transitions are concurrent and can be placed in separate execution threads without affecting the operation of the system.

Active classes are classes that will need to execute within their own process. This may be within a lightweight thread in Java or as a native process (green threads in Java). However, like subsystems which must be on separate nodes or within separate process, they will have a significant impact on the architecture (they are therefore architecturally significant). The following steps help in identifying active classes:

- Look at performance issues.
- Look at resource issues and access to resources.
- Distribution implies multiple active classes.
- Reliability issues.
- Two processes calculate a result simultaneously.
- Need to consider dynamics of active classes.

Active classes or subsystems can be documented using a UML deployment diagram. The relationships between the different nodes can be indicated via stereotype links. For example, if a client node (holding an active classes) will communicate with a server node via RMI then this can be denoted via an <rmi> stereotype (as illustrated in Figure 4.8).

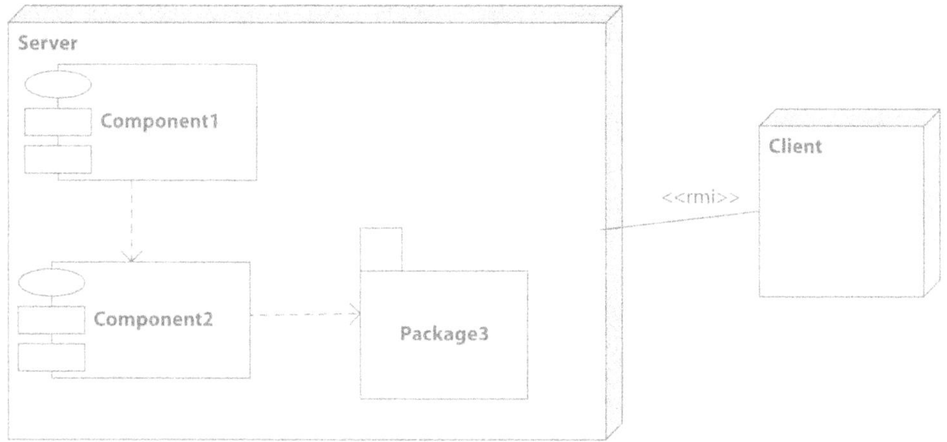

Figure 4.8 Using an <rmi> stereotype.

4.7.1 Allocating Subsystems to Processors and Tasks

Each concurrent package should be allocated to an independent process or processor. The system designer must therefore:

- estimate performance needs and the resources needed to satisfy them
- choose hardware or software implementations for packages
- allocate packages to processors to satisfy performance needs and minimize interprocessor communication
- determine the connectivity of the physical units that implement the packages
- consider the connection between nodes and the communications protocols to use
- consider the need for redundant processing
- identify any interfaces implied by deployment

You can use a UML deployment diagram to illustrate the results of this step.

4.7.2 Deployment Diagrams

A deployment diagram illustrates how the system will be physically distributed on the hardware. A simple single-user PC-based system will have a trivial deployment diagram. However, with the advent of Java, applets and the Java database interface JDBC, as well as facilities for enterprise development (such as the Java Message API and Java Transaction Service, as well as the Java Naming Directory Interface) all three tiers in a "web-deployed" client–server system may need to be designed. The deployment diagram for such a system might resemble that in Figure 4.9.

The elements in Figure 4.9 are called nodes. They represent processors (PCs and Server) and devices (Printer and Fax). A node is thus a resource in the real world upon which we can distribute and execute elements of the (logical) design model. A node is drawn as a three-

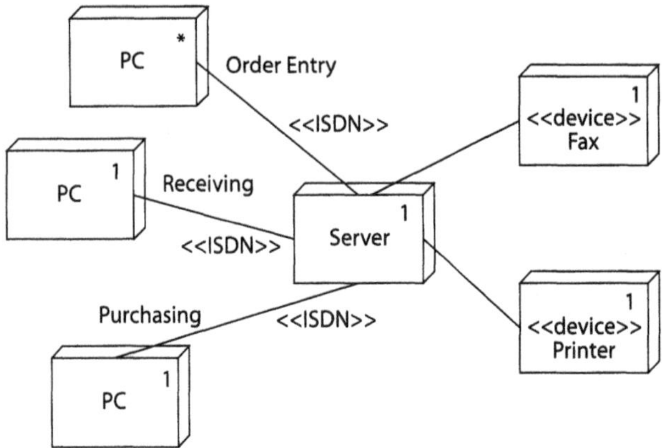

Figure 4.9 A deployment diagram.

dimensional rectangular solid with no shadows. The <device> stereotype designation of the Fax and Printer indicates that these nodes are not processors. That is, they do not have any processing ability (from the point of view of the model being constructed). You can also show how many nodes are likely to be involved in the system. Thus the Order Entry PC is of order * (0 or more), but there is exactly one server, printer, fax, etc. Finally, the diagram also shows the roles of the associations between nodes and their stereotype. For example, the *Receiving* association on one PC uses a type of ISDN connection (which has yet to be specified).

4.8 Managing Data Stores

You must identify appropriate data stores for both internal and external data. This involves identifying the complexity of the data, the size of the data, the type of access to the data (single or multiple users), access times and portability. Having considered these issues, you can make decisions about whether data can be held in internal memory or on secondary storage devices, and whether it should be held in flat files or in relational or object database systems. Such considerations are not specific to object-oriented systems and so are not considered in detail here. The following issues should be considered when selecting an appropriate approach to data storage:

- *Data persistence.* Does data need to be persistent? If so then files, serialization or a database must be considered.
- *Purchase cost.* If your system requires a database system then it is likely that this will increase the cost of the system. It may also involve licensing agreements in order that you can redistribute the DBMS to your users' systems.
- *Life cycle cost.* This reflects costs such as purchase, development, deployment, operating and maintenance costs. For example, files have no purchase cost but may have high develop-

ment and maintenance costs. A database system, by contrast, may have a high purchase cost but lower development and maintenance costs.

- *Amount of data.* The more data you have the more carefully you need to think about how it should be stored, access times etc.
- *Performance.* In-memory storage will provide the fastest data access, while files are likely to provide the poorest performance for all but the smallest amounts of data. Note that techniques such as serialization make life easy for the programmer but provide poor performance.
- *Extensibility.* How easy will it be to extend your application in the future given the method of data storage selected?
- *Concurrent access.* If you need to take concurrent access into account then you may need to consider the use of a database system.
- *Crash recovery.* If this is important, you need to think about how you will recover from a system crash (for example, by providing back up files or by using the crash recovery facilities of a database system).
- *Distribution.* Will the data need to be distributed among a number of sites? If so, careful thought needs to be given to this issue. Some database systems provide facilities for replicating data across multiple sites.

4.8.1 Handling Access to Global Resources

The system designer must identify what global resources are required and how access to them can be controlled. Global resources include processors, disk drives, disk space and workstations, as well as files, classes and databases.

4.9 Additional Architectural Concerns

There are a variety of other architectural concerns which need to be addressed. These include choosing the implementation control to be used in the software, identifying generic design mechanisms, deciding how to handle boundary conditions, setting trade-offs between competing resources and specifying default policies for the rest of the design.

4.9.1 Choosing the Implementation of Control in Software

The choice of the internal control mechanism used by the system is mediated by the facilities provided by the implementation language. For example, Ada supports concurrent tasks, but Visual Basic does not. Smalltalk and Java support lightweight processes and can be said to mimic concurrent systems. The choices available for implementation of control are:

- *Procedure-oriented systems.* Such systems represent a procedure-calling mechanism in which the flow of control is passed from one procedure or method to another when the first calls the second. This type of control tends to be favoured for applications that lack a substantial user interface (or for parts of an application that are remote from the user interface).

- *Event-driven systems.* This is the approach taken by the dynamic model of the analysis phase. Essentially, operations are triggered by events that are received by objects. Many window-based interfaces operate in this manner. This type of control tends to be used for applications that require a polished user interface (and is the control used by Java's GUI facilities and for JavaBeans).
- *Concurrent systems.* Here, the system exists in several processes that execute at the same time. Some synchronization between the processes may take place at certain times, but for the majority of the time they are completely separate. This approach tends to be used across applications (for example in client–server architectures) rather than within a single application.

4.9.2 Identify Generic Design Mechanisms

This step deals with issues such as:

- *Persistence of information and objects.* If information or objects persist this is architecturally significant and may affect your design.
- *Object distribution philosophy.* Will there be duplicate objects, will objects be "sent around the network" or will they be made available remotely? Each of these will affect your overall architecture (for example, if objects are to be sent around the network, then JavaIDL is not an appropriate solution).
- *Security features,* including communications security. For example, do you need to ensure that all communications are secure or only that some communications are secure?
- *Error detection and recovery.*
- *Transaction management.*

4.9.3 Handling Boundary Conditions

There are three primary boundary situations that the designer should consider:

- *Initialization* involves setting the system into an appropriate, clean, steady state.
- *Termination* involves ensuring that the system shuts down in an appropriate manner.
- *Failure* involves dealing cleanly with unplanned termination of the system.

4.9.4 Setting Trade-offs Between Competing Resources

In any design, there are various trade-offs to be made. For example, the trade-off between speed of access and data storage is a common one in database systems. The larger the number of indexes used, the faster data retrieval can be (however, the indexes must be stored along with the data). Such design trade-offs must be made with regard to the system as a whole (including non-software issues) as sub-optimal decisions are made if they are left to designers concentrating on a single package.

4.9.5 Specifying Default Policies for the Object Design

Some of the issues that should be considered include:

- *Associations.* Choose a basic approach to designing associations that should only be deviated from for specific and justifiable reasons.
- *Null values.* Ensure that common values are used to indicate a null value. For example, in Java the null value of an integer instance variable is 0, while that for a reference variable (one containing an object) is the special value *null*.
- *Role names.* What a role name is converted into in the design is open to interpretation. Specify the approach to be taken, e.g. instance variable names.
- *Attribute names.* Specify any conventions to be used with attribute names.
- *Derived data.* Specify a policy for computing derived data (for example, when needed or cached in advance). This policy can specify the conditions for either a lazy or future approach.

4.10 Plan Incremental Build of Software

Once you have put an architecture in place you are in a position to plan the remainder of your analysis, design and (to some extent) implementation. The development of the architecture should have helped to identify the appropriate subsystems, active classes, interfaces etc., which can be used as the starting point for distributing the work involved in the project among teams or developers (depending upon the size of the project).

The approach advocated by the Unified Process is to build your system in iterations. Each iteration adds some of the functionality required by the system, but not all of it. The end result should be that all the required functionality is included. This is a very good approach, as you always have a version to fall back on and you can involve users at an early stage in the development process by giving them (limited functionality) alpha releases to explore. It also helps to detect any other defects or unidentified problem areas at intermediate stages rather than at the end of the project.

The key to doing this successfully is to ensure that each iteration represents a manageable build within the time-scales set and that each build incorporates an appropriate subset of the functionality required by the system. This may need careful analysis of the use cases to identify appropriate functionality for each iteration.

4.11 The Online ATM Architecture Design

In this section we consider the architecture design of the online ATM. Not all of the issues identified above are relevant to this system, particularly as we are actually designing a prototype system rather than a fully operational system. For this reason, a number of issues are not considered, for example deploying the system on distributed hardware.

4.11.1 Identifying Architecturally Significant Use Cases

Architecturally significant use cases fall into three categories: those that relate to key functionality, those that relate to risks that are important to the overall system, and those which are at the extremes of the system. In the case of the online ATM system, these relate to being able to withdraw and deposit money.

4.11.2 Organizing the System into Subsystems

As the online ATM system is relatively straightforward there is really only one subsystem: the ATM system. However, we will separate the GUI from the body of the main system. This is because the GUI part of the system will represent a substantial implementation in its own right. In reality there might also be a storage package to handle the maintenance of customer and employee records. However, we will ignore this issue in our example. Instead, we will separate the main application-specific parts of the system into three packages, one for the GUI, one for the main business logic of the ATM and one to act as an interface to the back-end database used by the ATM (in essence this is a layered three-tier architecture – Figure 4.10). Note that we will adopt a layered approach to the design of the architecture in which application-generic packages are identified. These application-generic packages link our top-level application-specific packages to the underlying Java technologies which support them.

4.11.3 Identify Key Classes

The key classes would be identified by following the use cases into the analysis and design models. It is therefore likely that classes such as Account, Customer, Transaction and possibly Statement would be part of the architecture. Along with these classes, the architecture would include classes to support the key deposit and withdraw activities. In the case of withdraw this would also involve checking whether a particular amount can be withdrawn; this might therefore also involve an Overdraft class.

4.11.4 Identifying Concurrency

In a real online ATM, concurrent access would be an issue. However, in this simple prototype we do not consider concurrency.

4.11.5 Allocating Subsystems to Processors

Again, for the simple prototype we will assume that the whole system is running on a single processor within a single process.

4.11.6 Managing Data Stores

We can consider each of the issues identified above for data storage:

- *Data persistence.* Data does need to be persistent. If a deposit is made into a customer's account, this needs to be recorded so that that money is available at a later date.

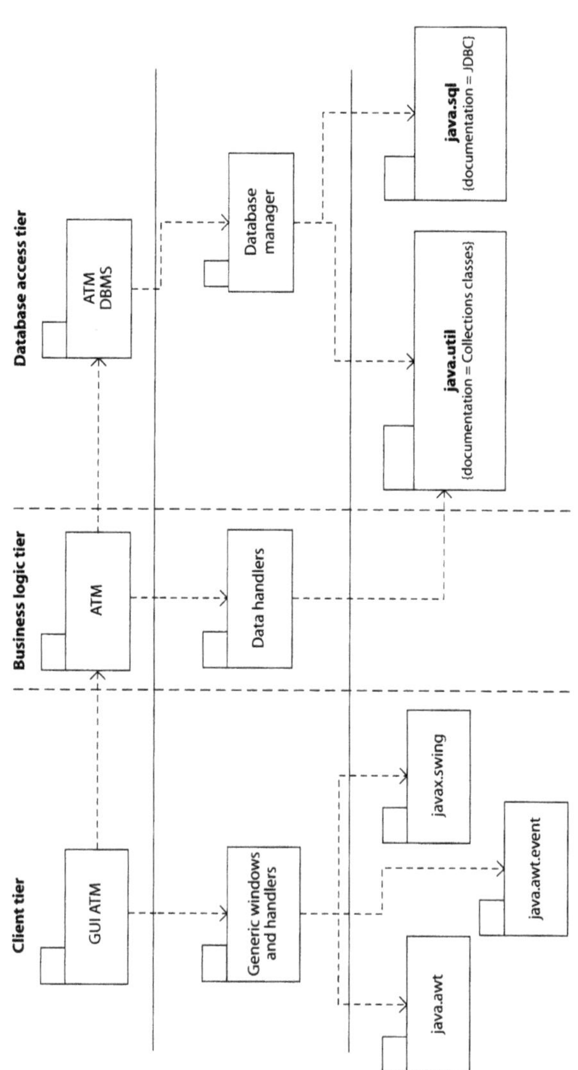

Figure 4.10 The layered subsystem architecture.

- *Purchase cost.* As this is a prototype system this is a significant issue. We therefore wish to keep the purchase cost to a minimum. For a real system a budget for purchasing a suitable data storage system might well be available.
- *Life cycle cost.* Again, as this is a prototype system we are not concerned with life cycle cost. For a real-world system, such as that of an online ATM, it would be a significant consideration.

The remaining issues can all be treated in the same manner at the life cycle cost. That is, for our prototype system they are not an issue, but for a real-world system they would all require careful analysis.

The conclusion we can make from this is that JDBC via the ODBC bridge to a simple database (such as Access or mSQL) will probably be sufficient for our current needs.

4.11.7 Handling Access to Global Resources

The only global resource in our prototype online ATM is the ATM system itself. In this system only one user can be logged on at a time. Thus the resource is only available when no user is logged on.

4.11.8 Choosing the Implementation of Control

The primary choices available are procedure calling, event-driven or concurrent. We have already dismissed concurrency, leaving us with procedure calling and event-driven. As we intend to implement the system in Java, it is a good idea to consider any constraints imposed on us by the language. By default, a Java GUI exploits an event-driven control mechanism, as exemplified by the delegation event model introduced in the JDK 1.1 specification of Java. However, once the appropriate event listener calls a method on a particular object a method (for this, read procedure) calling form of control is instigated. Therefore, in our online ATM system we are likely to employ both the event-driven mechanism (for the user interface package) and a method-calling mechanism (for the main ATM package).

4.11.9 Boundary Conditions

We shall consider two boundary conditions for the online ATM, as, for a prototype, we are not concerned with a failure condition. For the initialization condition, the system must load information about its customers and users from a file. If no file is available, default test data will be used.

For the termination condition, the system must save up-to-date data on its customers and users. Before doing this, it should make a backup of any existing data files.

The data files should exist in the same directory as the class files of the online ATM and should be called `customers.data` and `users.data`.

4.11.10 Default Policies for the Object Design

For the object design these guidelines are provided:

- *Associations.* These will be treated as references from one object to another unless an association is expected to possess data or operations. In this latter case the association will be treated as a link object.
- *Null values.* All variables should be initialized to their appropriate (Java) null value. Note that instance variables are automatically initialized; however, local variables are not.
- *Role names.* These will be treated as the names of instance variables in the appropriate objects that hold the associated reference.
- *Attribute and operation names.* Standard Java conventions will be used for these.

4.11.11 Implement a Skeleton Architecture

It is essential that (for any large system) you implement the skeleton architecture. This is important, as this acts as a verification of the feasibility of your architecture. It can also be useful in helping to identify active classes and to deploy these on "physical" nodes to ensure that your deployment model is effective.

It can also provide the software skeleton on which the remaining system will be constructed. This can be done explicitly by moving the architecture forward or implicitly by using the architecture as a base reference and reimplementing from scratch. Essentially the remaining steps in the analysis, design and implementation phases put the muscle and skin on this skeleton. The muscle is the additional functionality required to meet all the functions, while the user interface is the skin.

In general, implementing a skeleton architecture up front helps to identify any inherent implementation problems as early as possible. This allows you to deal with them when there is sufficient time in the project to consider alternative solutions and to redesign any affected areas. If no such architecture is implemented, then typically such problems come to light late in the implementation phase when there is great pressure to just finish the project rather than to "get it right".

4.12 References

Beck, K. and Johnson, R. (1994). Patterns generate architectures, *Proc. ECOOP'94*, pp. 139–149. Springer-Verlag, Berlin.

Gamma, E., Helm, R., Johnson, R. and Vlissades, J. (1993). Design patterns: abstraction and reuse of object-oriented design, *Proc. ECOOP'93*, pp. 406–431, Springer-Verlag, Berlin.

Gamma, E., Helm, R., Johnson, R. and Vlissades, J. (1995). *Design Patterns: Elements of Reusable Object-Oriented Software.* Addison-Wesley, Reading, MA.

Johnson, R.E. (1992). Documenting frameworks with patterns, *Proc. OOPSLA'92, SIGPLAN Notices* 27(10), 63–76.

For further information on all aspects of software architectures refer to:

Bass, L., Clements, P. and Kazman, R. (1998). *Software Architecture in Practice.* Addison-Wesley, Reading, MA.

Buschmann, F., Meunier, R., Rohnert, H., Sommerlad, P. and Stahl, M. (1996). *Pattern-Oriented Software Architecture – A System of Patterns.* John Wiley & Sons, Chichester.
Hofmeister, C., Nord, R. and Soni, D. (1999). *Applied Software Architecture.* Addison-Wesley, Reading, MA.
Kruchten, P. (1995). The 4+1 view model of architecture, *IEEE Software,* 12(6), November; http://www.rational.com/support/techpapers/ieee/.
Rechtin, R. Maier, M. (1997). *The Art of System Architecting.* CRC Press, Boca Raton, FL.
The World-Wide Institute of Software Architects. http://www.wwisa.org/.

Requirements Discipline: Use Case Analysis

5.1 Introduction

This chapter provides an introduction to the requirements discipline of the Unified Process. It is based heavily upon the use case analysis that originated in the Objectory design method (Jacobson *et al.*, 1992). Subsequent chapters discuss the analysis and design as well as implementation disciplines of the Unified Process.

The remainder of this chapter introduces the use case analysis process, the notation used to represent use cases and the steps performed to generate a use case. A worked example is presented at the end of the chapter.

5.2 Requirements Discipline

The requirements discipline attempts to express the systems requirements in terms of use cases. Thus the output of this discipline is a Use Case model. A Use Case model comprises a set of:

- use cases describing particular interactions with the system
- actors who interact with the system
- other artefacts including GUI prototypes and non-functional requirements

Use cases attempt to capture the functional requirements of the system by describing the different ways in which an *actor* (essentially a type of user) can interact with the system. The intention is that the focus should be on the value added to each type of user by a use case. If a use case does not add value, then it is not required.

Use cases are very important from the point of view of the Unified Process, as they are the key drivers of the whole process. That is, not only do the use cases help to identify what the system should do, but from this the key elements of the system are generated, test cases devised, classes defined etc. This is illustrated in Figure 5.1.

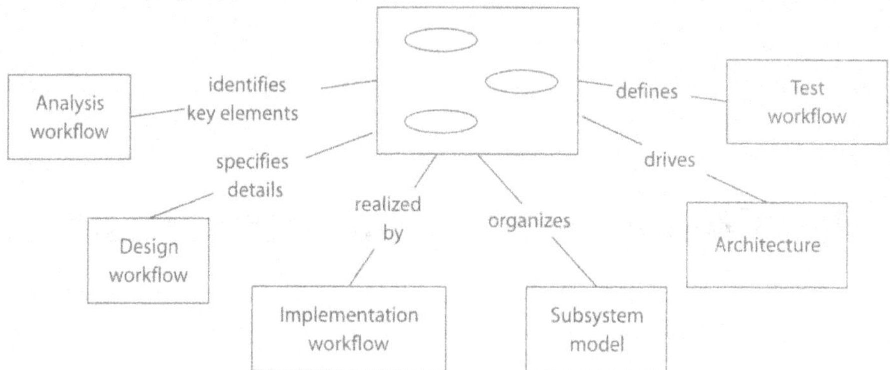

Figure 5.1 The use case relationships with disciplines.

5.3 Use Case Analysis

There are five primary steps to use case analysis; these are:

- Find and describe the actors in the system.
- Find the use cases.
- Describe the use cases as appropriate.
- Describe the use case model as a whole.
- Prepare a glossary of terms.

This process is unlikely to be completed in a single iteration; rather, it is likely that you will need to iterate and refine the model. In fact, it is usually the case that by the end of the use case analysis only about 80% of the use cases will have been uncovered. The remaining 20% will come to light during the analysis and design disciplines. In addition, the process is by no means as sequential as might be expected from the above list. Rather, it is likely that you will be jumping between identifying actors, identifying use cases and describing each in turn.

5.4 The Use Case Model

Figure 5.2 illustrates the contents of a use case model. It illustrates that the use case model comprises the actors (and their specifications), the use cases and their descriptions, prototype graphical user interfaces (if appropriate) plus any other interfaces (for example with legacy systems), and the glossary of terms. In addition, this figure also illustrates that sequence diagrams, activity diagrams and statecharts may also be used to express the behaviour of a use case. Indeed, any appropriate format may be used, including pseudocode or natural language. If the use case model is complex enough, it may also be necessary to partition it into packages that divide the use cases up into more manageable chunks. If this is done, the packages should attempt to group related use cases.

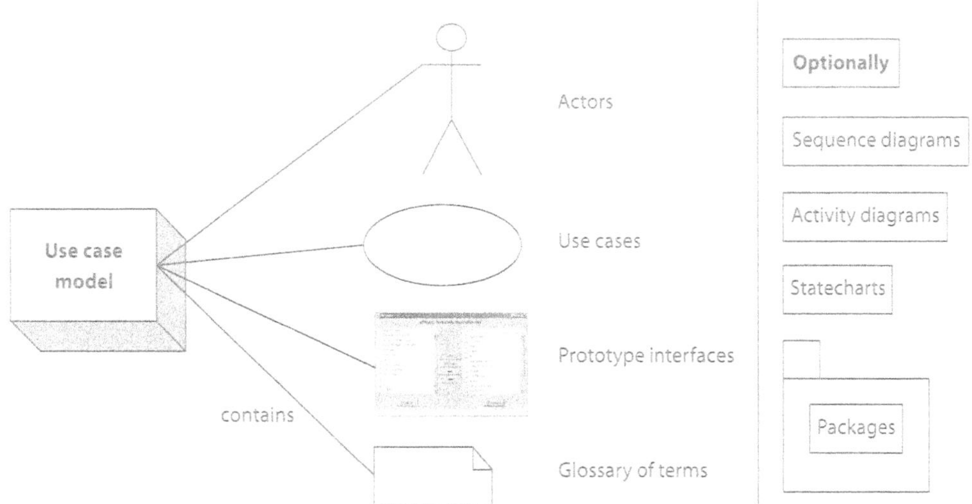

Figure 5.2 The constituent elements of a use case model.

5.5 Use Case Diagrams

Use case diagrams explain how a system (or subsystem) is used. The elements that interact with the system can be humans, other computers or dumb devices that process or produce data. The diagrams thus present a collection of use cases which illustrate what the system is expected to do in terms of its external services or interfaces. Such diagrams are very important for illustrating the overall system functionality (to both technical and non-technical personnel). They can act as the context within which the rest of the system is defined.

The large rectangle in Figure 5.3 indicates the boundaries of the system (an online banking system). The stick figures on either side of the system indicate external actors (in this case, an Account Holder, a Cashier and a Manager) which interact with the system. An actor represents a specific role played by a user. The ovals inside the system box indicate the actual use cases. For example, both the Account Holder and Cashier actors need to be able to "Check a Balance".

The notation for actors is based on "stereotypes". An actor is a class with a stereotype: <actor> indicates the actor stereotype and the stick figure is the actor stereotype icon. We will return to discuss the stereotype concept in Section 6.4.

Each individual use case can have a name, a description explaining what it does, and a list of its responsibilities, attributes and operations. It may also describe its behaviour in the form of a statechart. The most appropriate form of description for a use case differs from one domain to another, and thus the format should be chosen as appropriate. This illustrates the flexibility of the UML; it does not prescribe the actual format of a use case.

You can use sequence diagrams and collaboration diagrams with use case diagrams to illustrate the sequence of interactions between the system and the actors (see next chapter),

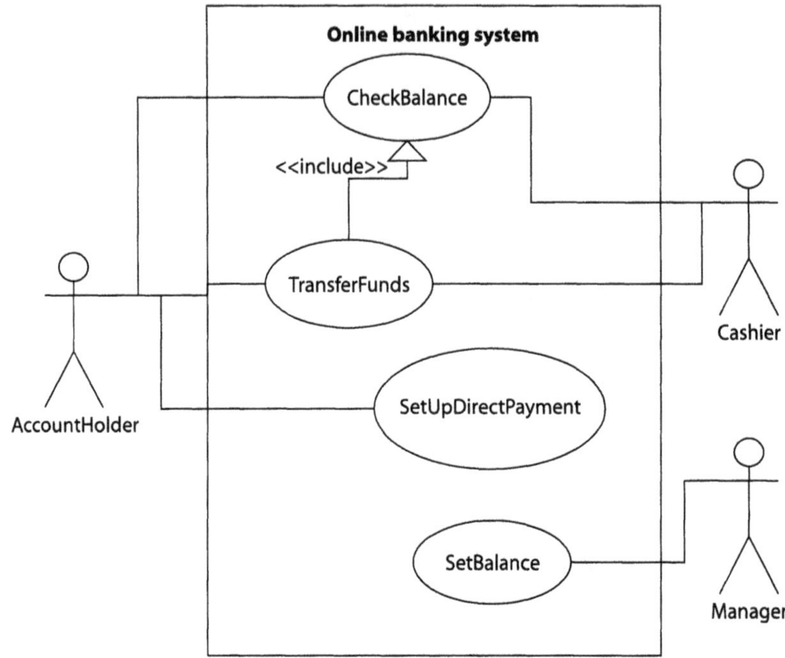

Figure 5.3 A use case diagram.

or you can use natural language, as will be done here. You should also annotate use cases with a statement of purpose, to place the use case in context.

Finally, the relationship between use case diagrams and class diagrams is that use cases are peers of classes. Depending on the size of the system, they can be grouped with the object model in a package or remain totally independent.

A note of caution is probably appropriate at this point. First, if you are using a tool such as Together or Rational Rose you may find that some of the notational elements presented for Use Cases (and indeed other parts of the UML) may not be supported. For example, the version of Rose that I use does not support the concept of the system boundary box (presented in Figure 5.3). The second point is not to get too carried away with Use Case diagrams. This is a subject I will return to at the end of this chapter.

5.6 Actors

An actor can be anything that interacts with the system: a human user, another computer system, a dumb terminal, a sensor, a device to be controlled, etc. However, an actor not only represents the user, but also the role that the user plays at that point in time. For example, in a small company, the accountant might act as the data entry clerk at one time, the internal auditor at another and as the payroll administrator at yet another time. A different actor could represent each of the roles, although the same person might perform them all. To stress the difference between actors and users, Jacobson *et al.* (1992) says that they think of an actor as "a class, that is, a description of a behaviour", while a user is described as playing "several roles" which are "many actors".

An actor should have a description that clearly specifies the role of the actor in the system. Actors can also, optionally, have:

- *Attributes*, such as name and address
- *Operations*, such as closeAccount
- *Tagged values*, containing extra information as appropriate
- *Constraints* on their behaviour

Actors may also input and/or receive information from a system. A description of an actor is shown in Figure 5.4.

Identification of the actors in the system is not trivial, and, as Jacobson *et al.* (1992) point out, "all actors are seldom found at once". Jacobson goes on to state that a "good starting point is often to check why the system is to be designed?". Having done this it should be possible to identify the main users of the system and what they need to do with it. From these users and their needs you can identify actors. Identification of human actors is usually relatively straightforward, but it is often much more difficult to identify non-human actors. In general, as the rest of the use case model develops these actors "come out in the wash". For a simple online ATM system the actors may be the *customer*, the *bank clerk* and the *bank manager*.

The UML notation for an actor is used in this book.

Figure 5.4 An example actor.

5.6.1 Steps in Finding Actors

In order to find the actors in your system you need to consider whatever information you have available to you. This information may be some form of problem statement, a wish list of requirements made by a user, a formal requirements specification or a business model. Using all the information available to you, you need to ask the following questions:

- Who is interested in the system?
- Who is likely to use the system?
- Who will benefit from the system?
- Who will supply information to the system?
- Who will receive information from the system?
- Who will maintain information in the system?
- Where in the organization is the system to be used?

Answering these questions will help to identify an initial set of users for the system. You then need to convert these users into actors. Remember that actors represent a role played by a user in the system rather than specific users. For example, a user may play many roles; equally, an actor may be representative of a variety of users.

To identify the actors you should group the users into categories, thus helping to find related users (i.e. those playing the same or similar role). There are two rules of thumb to bear in mind when doing this:

1. There should always be at least one user for each actor.
2. There should be a minimum of overlap in the roles played by actors.

Once again this is an iterative process. The first cut is likely to produce too many actors, many of which may be thrown away at a later date. It is also unlikely to identify all the actors (except for relatively small or very familiar systems).

Finally, all actors should be named to indicate their role in the domain. That is, they should be given semantically meaningful names (such as "customer") rather than names such as user.

5.7 Use Cases

A use case represents one way in which the system can be used by an actor. The definition for a use case given in Jacobson *et al.* (1999) is:

> a use case specifies a sequence of actions, including variants that the system can perform and that yields an observable result of value to a particular actor.

Thus a use case describes how the user interacts with the system for a specified purpose (see Figure 5.3). The achievement of this purpose involves following one or more steps. If there are multiple steps, they may be in a specific sequence to achieve the desired purpose. For example, to obtain money from a cash dispenser (ATM), you must "insert your card, type in your PIN, select the type of transaction you require, specify the amount of money required, take the card and then take the money". If you attempt to change this sequence (e.g. you type in your PIN before inserting your card), you cannot obtain your money. The combination of the purpose and the specified sequence of steps forms a use case.

An individual use case can be represented in a number of ways: the two most common are as natural language descriptions and as state transition diagrams. Whichever approach is adopted, the same information should be captured. The most appropriate form may depend on the availability of support tools for the state machine notation.

Use cases possess:

- a sequence of actions performed
- an optional set of one or more alternative sequence(s) of actions
- a brief description of the purpose of the use case
- communications with one or more actors
- constraints on their use

In addition, use cases can be related to one another via the <extends> and <includes> relationships (the latter is a little like a uses relationship). Use cases can also possess non-functional requirements, such as "the user's current balance should be displayed within 30 seconds". Figure 5.5 shows an example of a use case.

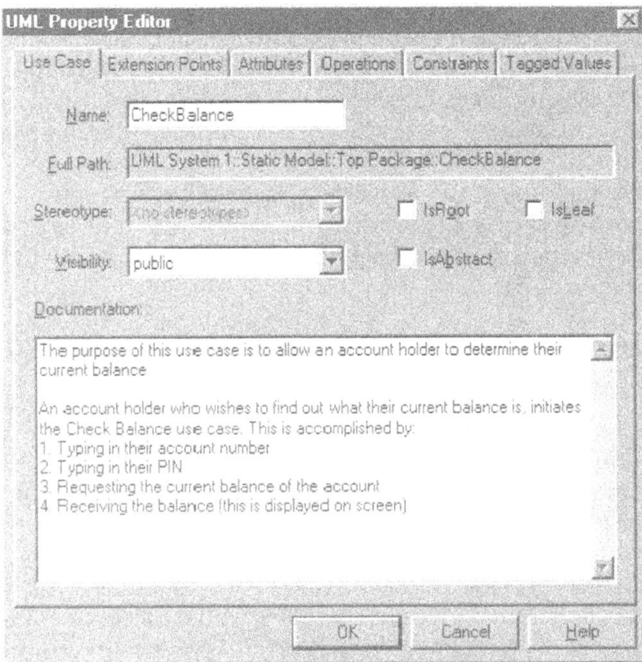

Figure 5.5 An example use case.

5.7.1 Identifying Use Cases

The collection of all the use cases for a system defines the functionality of that system. The identification of use cases is based on the identification of actors. Each actor does one or more things to the system, each of which is a use case. Each actor must have at least one use case (and may be involved in many use cases). Whether each use case is unique (or merely a duplication of another use case) may only be determined once all the use cases are identified and defined. To help in identifying the use cases, you can ask the following questions (Jacobson *et al.*, 1992; Quatrani, 1998):

- What are the main tasks of each actor?
- Will the actor have to read/write/change any of the system information?
- What use cases will create, store, change, remove or read system information?
- Consider each actor in turn:
    - Will the actor have to inform the system about outside changes?
    - Does the actor wish to be informed about outside changes?
- What use cases will support and maintain the system?
- Can all functional requirements be performed by the current set of use cases?

As well as relying on information sources available it is often a good idea to include:

- interviews with those who will be using the system to find out what they need to do,
- storyboarding to describe how the system will operate,
- workshops to brainstorm different scenarios relating to the system.

Early in the analysis process it is often enough just to identify the possible use cases and not worry about their details. Once a reasonable set of use cases has been identified, you may be able to analyze the systems requirements in greater detail in order to flesh out the use cases. Use case identification tends to be iterative and should not be treated as a single-step process for any but the simplest of systems.

Having identified the use cases, we can identify the steps performed within each use case. In many cases this can help to identify omissions and over-generalizations in the problem statement or domain understanding. For a simple online ATM system mentioned above, a typical use case might be (see Figure 5.5):

A Customer who wants to find out what his or her current balance initiates the Check account use case. This is accomplished by:

1. *Typing in the account number*
2. *Typing the PIN*
3. *Requesting the current balance of the account (this may be on-screen or a printout)*
4. *Receiving the balance*

Notice that the first element of the use case is a statement of its purpose. This is then followed by the sequence of steps performed by the use case. The steps described above are referred to as the *basic course* of the use case. That is, it is the normal way in which the use case executes. In general, use cases only possess a single basic course, but they may possess one or more *alternative courses*.

These alternatives deal with exceptional situations or errors. For example, what if the customer does not have a current account? What happens if the customer does not log off from the system?

Use cases are normally named relative to their actions. Thus a use case which describes how a user logs into the system should be called Login, or one in which a users checks the account balance should be called CheckBalance.

5.7.2 Identifying Use Case Events

A use case possesses at least one set of events (sequence) that describes its operation (and possible multiple sets). These events describe what the system does in response to an actor interacting with it. Note that these events describe the steps performed and how they are achieved/implemented by the system. Such sequences should include:

- Any preconditions on the use case (i.e. the user must be logged on).
- When and how the use case starts and terminates.
- What interaction the use case has with the actors.
- What data is needed by the use case.
- The normal sequence of events.
- Any alternative or exceptional sequences.
- Any post conditions.

Actually identifying these sequences is, like the identification of the use case itself, reliant on the information you have available. Again, interviews, storyboarding and the like may be valuable tools. Usually, the sequences are only brief descriptions that are filled out as the analysis progresses and your understanding of the system increases. Thus this in itself is an iterative process. Often exceptional or alternative sequences are added at a later stage as they become clear. Note that you should not expect to capture every single possible path that an actor might take within a use case. Nor should you expect to be able to identify the basic course and significant exceptional courses in one go. Which you include will depend on the application etc. It is also difficult to say when a branch in a sequence of events should become an alternative sequence in its own right. Essentially it should do so when it is either big enough or significant enough to document separately!

5.8 Refining Use Case Models

The identification of the actors and the use cases helps to specify the limits of the system. That is, anything that is an actor is outside the system, whereas anything that is a use case is within the system boundaries. This means that you can draw a line around the use cases to indicate the boundary of the system in terms which both a developer and a user can understand. This can help to clarify misunderstandings between users and developers over what is the system's responsibility and what is not. A partial use case model for the simple account system is presented below.

Producing a set of use cases is not hard; however, producing an appropriate well-formed use case model is a great deal harder. This involves determining what is a "good" use case and what is a poor or "bad" use case for the current system. Some of the issues to consider include:

- Use cases should not be too small or too large. You should aim for comprehensibility in your use case model.
- A use case should be self-contained and complete. You should not need to refer to a great deal of additional material (including other use cases) in order to determine what the use case does.
- Use cases should provide "added value" to the users of the system (i.e. the actors).
- Each use case should relate to at least one actor. Any use case without an actor is never going to be used.

5.9 Additional Documents

The use case model should also possess a glossary of all the important or commonly used terms that have been adopted in the use case model. This glossary is not fixed and will evolve during the lifetime of the project. The use case model should also include additional documentation covering any non-functional requirements which could not be directly linked to a use case. These requirements can be documented in whatever manner is appropriate, although natural language is the most common format.

5.10 Interface Descriptions

Having defined the actors in the system and the uses they make of the system, the next step is often to specify the interfaces between the actors and the system. For human users of the system, these interfaces may well be graphical user interfaces (GUIs). You can draw them with a drawing tool or develop a mockup using some form of interface simulation software. These interfaces can be very useful in confirming the users' needs and their anticipated use, as well as helping to keep them involved in the development.

As the use cases specify the sequences of operations to be performed, the GUIs can mimic the desired system behaviour. This is a good way of confirming that the use case is correct. For non-human interfaces any proposed communications protocols can be defined and checked (for example, that the interacting system is capable of sending and receiving the appropriate information).

5.11 Online ATM Use Case Analysis

The system to be analyzed is a (very) simple online ATM system (Figure 5.6). Such a system maintains information on customers, their current accounts, and the deposits and withdrawals they make, as well as any direct debits they have set up (a direct debit is a regular direct payment from one bank account to another). There are two types of user of the systems: bank clerks and bank managers. Each has access to different parts of the online ATM system. Note that this does not

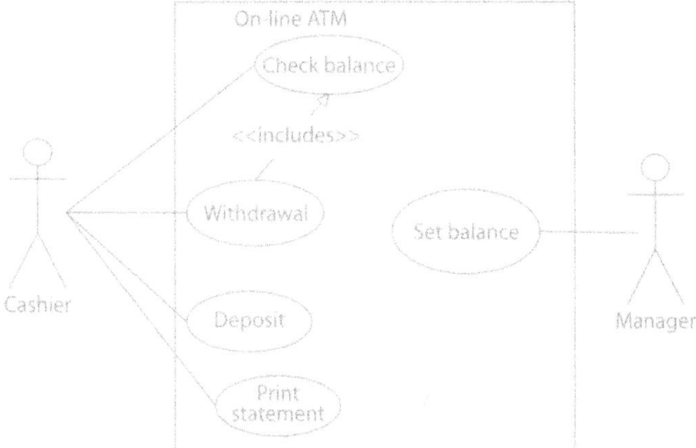

Figure 5.6 The On-line ATM use case diagram.

mean that a bank manager cannot act as a bank clerk – remember that actors represent roles played by potential (in this case human) users.

Having identified the actors in the system we are now in a position to identify what they do, and hence the use cases. As noted earlier we can consider a number of questions that will help in identifying the use cases. We shall do this for the clerk actor as an example of how the process works. Each of the questions is considered below:

- *What are the main tasks of the clerk actor?* Bank clerks will wish to find out the amount of money in a bank account. They will also want to be able to deposit and withdraw money for customers. In the case of withdrawing money they should be able to do so if there are sufficient funds in the customer's account. This indicates that at least three use cases for *balance checking*, *deposits* and *withdrawals.*
- *Will the clerk have to read/write/change any of the system information?* As this is a banking system, we do not want the clerks to be able to directly change customer account details (only a manager is allowed to do that). However, we do want them to be able to deposit and withdraw funds that will indirectly change a customer's data. We do not want clerks to be able to change a customer's balance, but we do want them to be able to access it. All of this supports the three use cases identified by the previous question. In addition, we want a clerk to be able to print a customer's bank statement. We therefore need a fourth use case for the clerk: "print statement".
- *Will the clerk have to inform the system about outside changes?* In this particular system the answer is no. However, in a real banking system we might identify information such as change of address, employer or martial status that we would like the clerk to be able to change on the customer's behalf.
- *Does the clerk wish to be informed about unexpected changes?* Again, due to the simplicity of this application the answer is no; however, in the real system the answer might not be so clear-cut.

This leaves us with the three use cases for the clerk that must be analyzed in further detail. The basic course for the *check balance* use case was presented earlier in this chapter. We shall therefore present the basic course for the remaining use cases.

5.11.1 Deposit Use Case

The *deposit* use case is started by a clerk in response to a customer who wishes to place additional funds into their current account. This is accomplished by:

1. Typing in the account number
2. Typing in the PIN
3. Placing funds in an appropriate receptacle
4. Receiving acknowledgement of the deposit

5.11.2 Withdrawal Use Case

A customer who wishes to obtain funds from his or her current account causes the clerk to initiate the withdrawal use case. This is accomplished by:

1. Typing in the account number followed by the PIN
2. Typing in the PIN
3. Requesting a specified amount from the account
4. The online ATM system confirming availability of funds
5. Receiving the specified amount of money

For the withdrawal use case we shall also consider an *alternative course* of steps. This course will present the series of steps that should be performed when the customer does not have sufficient funds in their current account to meet the withdrawal requested:

1. Typing in the account number
2. Typing in the PIN
3. Requesting a specified amount from their account
4. The online ATM system rejects the request due to lack of funds
5. Receiving the notification of failure

The identification of the remaining use cases and their basic courses (as well as any additional alternative courses) is left as an exercise for the reader due to space constraints.

5.11.3 Interface Descriptions

The interface for this system is quite straightforward. The user is presented with the *main logon screen* that allows the selection of one of the four use cases (presented as options). This is illustrated in Figure 5.7. Note that the bottom options have their associated buttons greyed out, as no user has yet logged on. Depending upon the option selected by the user, the logon, deposit and withdrawal, check balance or set balance screens are presented.

The logon screen is illustrated in Figure 5.8. The result of an authorized user of the system logging on is that the "check balance", "withdraw and deposit" and "set balance" options are enabled. The check balance screen is illustrated in Figure 5.9. This interface

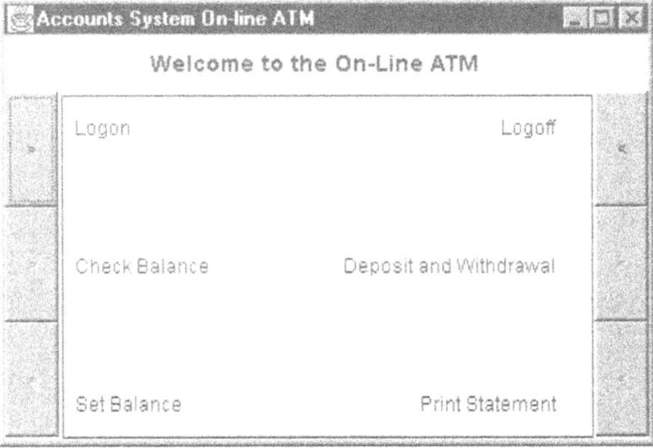

Figure 5.7 Main logon screen.

requires information such as the account number and PIN to allow access to a customer account.

The deposit and withdraw (transaction) screen is presented in Figure 5.10. Note again that an account number is required. The amount specified can then be withdrawn or deposited, depending upon the option selected.

The set balance screen is presented in Figure 5.11. Note that a security code is required as well as the account number and new balance. The security code is checked against the current user. If the current user is not a manager or if the security code is not correct an error message is displayed. If the security code is correct, the account specified by the account number has its balance reset to that specified in the new balance field.

Finally, the print statement screen is illustrated in Figure 5.12. This screen accepts the customer's account number and then prints the associated statement into the scrollable text area below.

Figure 5.8 The logon screen.

Figure 5.9 The check balance screen.

Figure 5.10 The transaction screen.

Figure 5.11 The set balance screen.

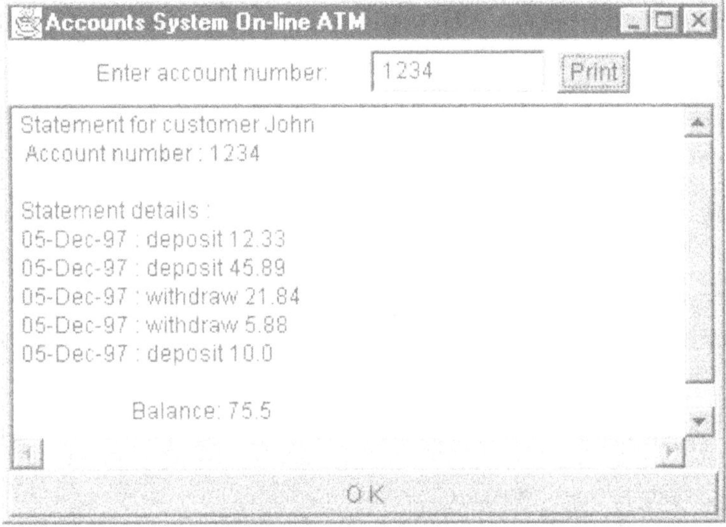

Figure 5.12 The print statement screen.

5.12 Structuring the Use Case Model

As well as using packages to structure the use case model, you may also find it useful to include additional use case diagrams. These can be used to focus on a particular aspect of the functionality of the system, for example by focusing on:

- all the use cases for one actor,
- all of the actors for one use case,
- one particular way in which the system can be used (i.e. directly related use cases).

This approach can be particularly useful, as you can show a particular user all the use cases that relate to them, rather than all the use cases in the whole system etc.

In some situations what you want to do is generate a hierarchy between your use cases. This allows a high-level use case to be broken down into a more detailed analysis if appropriate. This can be extremely useful where you wish to be able to present a high-level view of the overall functionality of the system, but also be able to burrow down into the more detailed functionality. For example, let us say that your application centres on being able to search large amounts of data. The "search" use case would probably be central to the whole system. However, there are perhaps five or six versions of search available. You might wish to expand the "search" use case to be able to explore each of the options. Thus the "search" use case may refer to "simple search", "name search", "search deleted records", "advanced search" and so on.

5.13 Are Use Case Diagrams Useful?

Use cases *per se* are extremely useful. They provide a view of how actors will interact with the system, the sequence of steps they expect to go through and the anticipated outcomes. However, an important question is "Are use case diagrams useful?". I have seen, on several projects, detailed use case diagrams created that are then never used or referred to. On questioning this can be put down to a number of reasons:

- Lack of familiarity of those analyzing and designing the systems with use case notation.
- The density of the use case diagrams – the "I can't see the wood for the trees" problem. That is, there are so many use case diagrams that I don't know where to start.
- Use case diagrams are not requirements – they are scenarios describing aspects of the interactions of the system with external entities (humans and other systems).
- Many requirements are hard to capture and harder to present in a pure use case diagram.

Personally, I find that some aspects of use case modelling are extremely useful. However, they are really part of a wider picture that involves the documentation of system requirements. In general, a use case diagram can be a very useful tool for highlighting system interactions. It can be used as the basis of a set of "how the system will be used" sections. These are, however, sections in a requirements document, not the actual requirements.

As an example, consider the structure of a requirements document that was created by JayDee Technology Ltd for a recent client. This document had the following structure (generalized for this book):

Section 1.   INTRODUCTION
Section 2.   INTENDED AUDIENCE
Section 3.   CURRENT SITUATION
        3.1. Current working method and processes
        3.2. Data sheet structure
Section 4.   DISCUSSION OF DOMAIN CONCEPTS
Section 5.   NON-FUNCTIONAL REQUIREMENTS
Section 6.   NEW WORKING METHODS
        6.1. Assumptions
        6.2. Basic discipline
        6.3. Consideration of new methods
Section 7.   DETAILED DESCRIPTION OF THE REQUIREMENTS
        Detailed descriptions of the various activities that the software needs to cover.
Section 8.   WHAT IS NOT IN THE REQUIREMENTS
        Description of operations, procedures, behaviour etc. that are outside the scope of the system.
Section 9.   DISCIPLINES AND DIAGRAMS
Section 10.   OUTPUT ISSUES AND PROPOSED SOLUTIONS
Section 11.   SECURITY ISSUES AND PERMISSIONS
Section 12.   BASIC GUI REQUIREMENTS

Section 13.   SCREEN DESIGNS
              Details of each screen, fields, options and behaviour
Section 14.   USE CASES
Section 15.   SUMMARY
Section 16.   GLOSSARY OF TERMS

One of the things to take from this table of contents is that the use cases are just one element of the document. Indeed, this element is just one of 16 different sections. The other sections capture extremely important information from the point of view of the resulting software system. In addition, in this case, the use cases were not presented as diagrams. Instead they were presented in a scenario-based manner. Each use case was described in terms of the actors involved. Next, a set of steps were provided that described the scenario represented by the use case. For example, one such use case description is reproduced below.

Make CC and Link
Actors: Bibliographer
Scenario:

1. Do a search. Refine and redo the search if necessary. Able to do an additional search if appropriate.
2. Browse the results and select one or more citations.
3. Press the right mouse button and select Make CC and Link.
4. The CC Review Window is displayed, containing the selected citations in the same order as they were displayed in the search results screen. At this stage the citations are automatically locked to prevent other users editing them. If any of the citations are locked, the process is aborted and the user informed by an error dialog box. Ideally, the user holding the (first encountered) lock will be displayed.
5. The user has the option at this stage of removing citations from the CC Review Window (i.e. they are not to be linked). The citations that are removed from the list are unlocked immediately.
6. The user then selects a single citation that is to form the basis of the CC (the selected citation has no special status or behaviour – it is effectively copied to create a starting point for the CC).
7. Press the right mouse button and select one of:
    7.1.   `Edit and make CC`
           If `Edit and make CC` is selected, then CAPs/TED is displayed, containing a copy of the selected citation (excluding local data). The user makes changes as necessary, and when finished exits CAPs/TED as normal.
    7.2.   `Make CC`
           If `Make CC` is selected, then no editing is needed.
8. The Edit Confirmation Window will be displayed (following both 7.1 and 7.2). The user can review the before/after formatted copies of the citation, and override the new CC's default status. The user can edit the new CC again if necessary, or OK the changes, or CANCEL the changes. The buttons are:

`Edit Again`	go back to CAPs/TED (go back to Step 7.1)
`OK and Link`	confirm the changes, and link the citations in the CC Review Window to the new CC
`CANCEL`	lose the edits and do not create a CC yet, and return to the CC Review Window

9. Assuming that a CC has been created (`OK and Link`), the citations in the CC Review Window are automatically linked to the new CC. The original versions of the citations (pre-CC link) are kept in the database. *Ideally*, the window is refreshed to display the citations after the link operation (i.e. the CC is displayed many times with each citation's local data).

10. The linked citation's statuses are NOT altered.

11. The user can optionally sort the citations based on local data (so that the citations with local data are displayed at the top).

12. The user can, for any or all citations or selected citations, call up the Local Mend Editor to review a citation using before/after formatted copies of the citation, and to edit the citation's local data. The user can edit the citation and then press the following buttons:

`OK`	Confirm the local changes and move onto the next selected citation
`CANCEL`	Lose the local data edits and move on to the next selected citation
`CLOSE`	Close the mend window, keeping any edits made thus far, and return to the CC Review Window
`UNLINK`	Unlink this citation from the CC and lose any local data edits to it. Move on to the next selected citation

13. The user can now close CC Review Window, either by exiting as normal, or by aborting all the changes made. Both options remove all the citations' locks. If exiting normally, all the changes are made permanent (i.e. committed).

So where does that leave you? Well, if you must take the use case diagram approach (either for political reasons or because of management intransigence), there are a few guidelines to bear in mind:

1. Don't get carried away with the diagrams – they are easy to produce but don't necessarily provide that much added value. Instead, focus on use cases that actually provide value to what you (or your colleagues) will be doing next.

2. Don't lose the message in the detail – use cases are very good at providing general interaction paths that illustrate system interaction – they are less good at being the requirements.

3. Do support the use case diagrams with other types of documentation, such as a more traditional requirements document, screen designs, non-functional requirements etc.

4. Try not to produce very large use case models. If you do find your use case diagrams growing, try to structure them into meaningful "packages" as you would software.

5. Don't assume that use case diagrams are a "natural means of communication" to all project stakeholders. If you are going to present use case diagrams to analysts, designers, developers or testers, then train them in the use case notation and approach.

6. Focus on the software to be built (that is the end product) and not on the use cases *per se* – keep in mind the goal of use case modelling.

5.14 Further Reading

Bittner, K. and Spence, I. (2002). *Use Case Modeling*. Reading, MA: Addison-Wesley.
Cockburn, A. (2000). *Writing Effective Use Cases*. Reading, MA: Addison-Wesley.
Bramble, P., Cockburn, A., Pols, A. and Adolph, S. (2002). *Patterns for Effective Use Cases*. Reading, MA: Addison-Wesley.
Kulak, D. and Guiney, E. (2000). *Use Cases*. Reading, MA: Addison-Wesley.

5.15 References

Jacobson, I. *et al.* (1992). *Object-Oriented Software Engineering: A Use Case Driven Approach*. Addison-Wesley, Reading, MA.
Jacobson, I., Booch, G. and Rumbaugh, J. (1999). *The Unified Software Development Process*. Addison-Wesley, Reading, MA.
Quatrani, T. (1998). *Visual Modeling with Rational Rose and UML*. Addison-Wesley, Reading, MA.

The Analysis Discipline: Finding the Entities

6.1 Introduction

The aim of the analysis discipline is to analyze the requirements identified in the use case analysis (the requirements discipline) and to structure them in terms of the internals of the system. That is, the requirements are converted from the external users view into "what the system needs to do to support the user's requirements". This does not mean how the system will do it, merely what it must do. For example, users may be unaware that they have an internal *profile* which specifies what they can and cannot do; however, an *internal* requirement on the system might be to check the user's actions against the user's profile.

The intention is that this will provide a better understanding and a more maintainable form for the (internal effects of) the requirements. The issue here is that the requirements (as described in the use case model) are in the language of the customer, not the language of the developer. The analysis discipline therefore attempts to move the requirements into the language of the developer and to identify what the key elements/concepts/entities of the system will need to be in order to support the user's requirements. In particular, the analysis discipline aims to identify the important entities in the system. These entities are likely to form important aspects in the architecture. They may become classes, collections of classes, or even subsystems within the final design.

The analysis model is thus expressed in terms of analysis classes, packages and collaborations. It is useful to note that the primary resources produced by the analysis discipline are the important entities in the system. These entities should be the key concepts for the remainder of the design and implementation of the system. Table 6.1 presents a simple comparison of the output of the requirements discipline versus the analysis discipline.

The analysis discipline actually produces more than just the analysis model. It also defines a set of use case realizations which describe how the use cases map into the analysis model and an evolving data dictionary which defines all the interfaces and classes, as well as subsystems in the analysis model, and has an input into the software architecture. This is illustrated in Figure 6.1.

Table 6.1 Comparison between the requirements discipline and the analysis discipline.

Requirements discipline	Analysis discipline
Language of customer	Language of developers
External view of functionality	Internal view of system w.r.t. functionality
Structured by use cases	Structured by stereotypical classes and packages
Used to understand what the system should do	Used to understand what the system needs to do to support the user requirements
May contain redundancy and inconsistency	Should not contain redundancy and inconsistency
Captures functionality of the system	Outlines the key concepts (entities) which are important to the system
Defines use cases	Defines use case realizations

The analysis discipline tries to rephrase the system requirements in terms of the software system (rather than the terminology of the user). As such, use cases and the analysis model are two sides of the same coin. Note that, as mentioned above, the analysis model rephrases all the system's requirements, not just the use cases, as there may well be additional requirements on the system which are not easily expressed via the use cases (such as security, performance and up time).

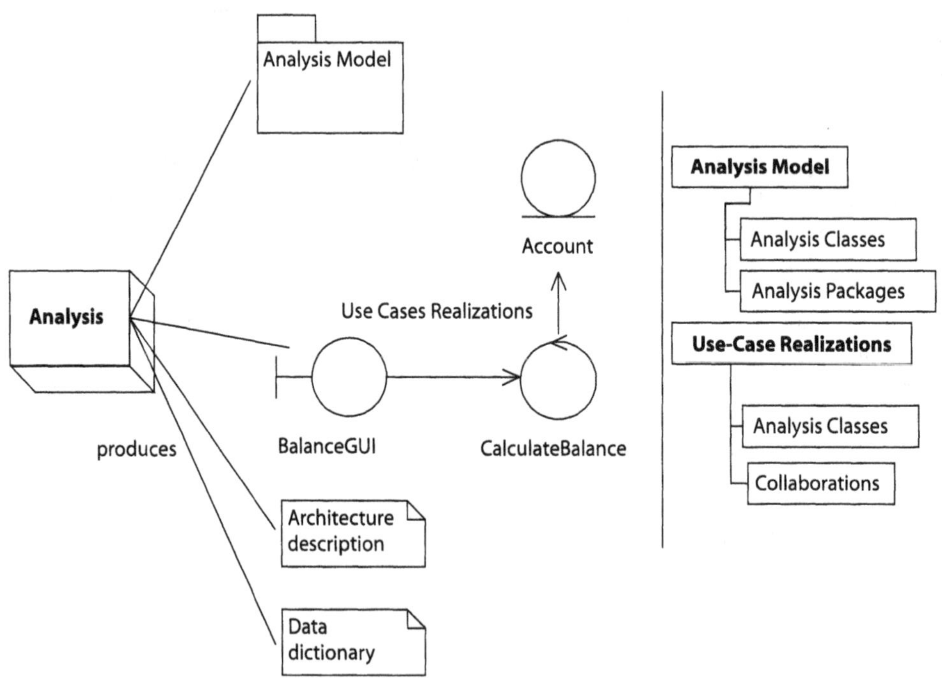

Figure 6.1 The products of the analysis discipline.

6.2 Analysis Discipline Activities

Four primary activities comprise the analysis discipline. These activities are:

- architectural analysis (covered in Chapter 4)
- generation of analysis classes
- generation of analysis packages
- analysis of use cases for the generation of use case realizations

Once again this process is not as sequential as this list might suggest; rather, it is iterative. In addition each activity may effectively be carried out in parallel. Thus there may be feedback loops between activities.

6.3 The Analysis Model

The analysis model is the key element of the analysis discipline. It is the first step in understanding how the system should be formed. The analysis model essentially comprises the analysis class diagrams. These diagrams illustrate the static structure of a system via the important analysis classes in the system and how they relate to each other. The UML documentation currently talks about class diagrams (and within this about object diagrams), stating that "class diagrams show generic descriptions of possible systems and object diagrams show particular instantiations of systems and their behaviour". It goes on to state that class diagrams contain classes while object diagrams contain objects, but that it is possible to mix the two. However, it discusses both under the title *class diagrams*. To avoid confusion, we use the term *analysis model* to cover both sets of diagrams (following the approach adopted in both the Booch and OMT methods).

The information for the analysis model comes from:

- the problem statement (possibly written in natural language),
- a requirements analysis process such as OOA,
- the domain experts,
- general knowledge of the real world,
- and in particular the use case model.

The analysis model should be viewed as elucidating the requirements as described in the use case model. It can be viewed as a first cut at a design model, but this should not be treated as its primary purpose. Indeed, a warning is in order here. The analysis model simplifies the set of classes available to just three: the boundary class (essentially the interface between the system and an actor), the control class (which expresses the events in a use case) and the entity class. The control classes are very simple and essentially procedural and are merely intended as a placeholder for the actions to be performed during the users' interaction with the system. It is all too easy, however, merely to transfer these classes from the analysis model into the design model. To do this is to lose sight of the object-oriented nature of these systems: that behaviour and functionality reside together in appropriate classes. Placing the functionality in a control class is simple but non-object-oriented!

The identification of the entity classes, however, may well affect the structure of the architecture and will certainly help to highlight the important concepts in that architecture.

The important thing about the analysis model is that it makes an abstraction and avoids solving some of the problems that the design discipline will need to deal with. It also leaves the handling of some requirements and in particular non-functional requirements to the design or indeed the implementation disciplines. It also does not attempt to consider issues such as performance or algorithm choice, leaving these instead for the later disciplines. Thus the analysis model should be simpler and easier to understand than the design model or the complete software architecture.

6.3.1 Why Have an Analysis Model?

You may very well be asking yourself at this stage: why bother with an analysis model? Indeed, for simple systems it may not be necessary to go to the lengths of generating an explicit analysis model; however, it is still a useful exercise to consider what it is intended for.

The analysis model helps you to think about what will happen inside the system in response to an actor interacting with that system (i.e. carrying out a use case). It is intended to be much smaller than the design model (indeed Jacobson *et al.* indicate that there should be a ratio of about 1:5 in the size of the analysis model versus the design model). Thus the analysis model should be a great deal more comprehensible than the design model. It should thus allow a reader to get familiar with what the system should do and the key entities of the system.

Thus the most important aspect of the analysis model is the identification of the entities. In many respects, identifying the boundary and control classes is almost (although not quite) automatic. However, the real task is in identifying the entities, and if this is taken as the focus of the analysis discipline, it has both an important role and a clear place within the overall design process.

The analysis model can also be used to help understand how legacy systems and other components relate to the requirements and to the new elements of the system being constructed, as they can be represented by entity objects. As such information will be buried deep in the design model, this may be the only place where it is clearly described.

In addition, any particular analysis model may have more than one design model. This might be the case where it is necessary to provide more than one implementation of a system to ensure failsafe behaviour etc.

6.3.2 Analysis Model Classes

Analysis model classes represent an abstraction of one or more classes or subsystems (in the final design model). This is because the level of detail expected in the design model is explicitly not required nor appropriate for the analysis model. The focus here is on handling functional requirements at a high level of abstraction. Thus analysis classes are distinguished from design classes in the following ways.

- *They have responsibilities, not operations.* These responsibilities should be documented in textual form. In addition, a textual description of the purpose of the class should also be provided.
- *They have high-level attributes described in domain terms.* That is, an attribute in the analysis model may represent a complex concept which will need to be expanded in the design model. For example, an invoice can be treated as a simple attribute in the analysis but not in the design. Another example would be that an amount in a bank account can be treated as currency without worry about how currency should be represented.
- *They have relationships,* but these relationships are concept- rather than implementation-oriented. They thus express the abstract relationship between two classes rather than how two classes should be linked in order to be implemented.
- All analysis classes should be *directly involved in one or more use case realizations.* No analysis classes should exist which are not directly used to explain how a use case could be implemented (in terms of the analysis model).
- *They are all of one of three types of class.* These classes are entity, boundary or control classes.

As analysis classes are quite distinct from design classes they have been given their own stereotype, with a stereotype icon to illustrate them. These stereotypes are illustrated in Figure 6.2. The three types of analysis class are described below:

- *Entity classes.* Such classes represent data that tends to exist over a period of time (such as a customer's bank account), important concepts in the system, and major components or significant elements in the system (such as a fundamental subsystem). If an entity class represents some data, then in many cases this information is persistent and may be stored in some form of long-term storage (such as a database). Entity classes most often model information, concepts or real-life objects or events. In many cases entity classes are an abstraction of some more complex concept that will need to be expanded on and explored in the design model. These are the real nuggets of gold which the analysis model is attempting to mine. It is these classes we need to identify in order to have a chance of creating a robust, reusable, stable architecture.

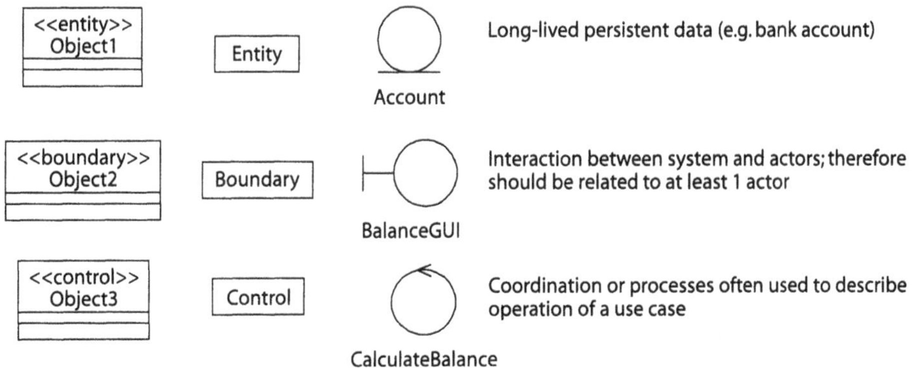

Figure 6.2 Types of analysis class.

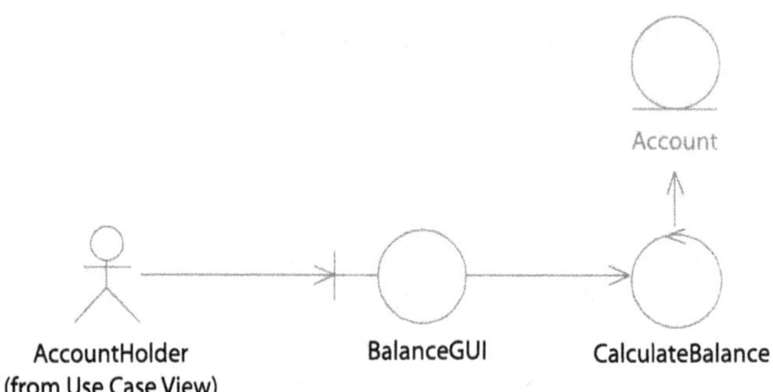

Figure 6.3 An analysis class diagram for part of the Online Bank Account.

- *Boundary classes.* These are classes that are used to model the interaction with the actors (i.e. the users of the system). This interaction involves sending and receiving (or both) information. Thus boundary classes often represent abstractions of graphical user interfaces or external APIs, or indeed protocols such as HTTP or FTP. Each boundary class should be linked to at least one actor (and vice versa).
- *Control classes.* A control class represents the functionality required to manage the interaction between the user (via the boundary class) and the data in the entity class (i.e. it is the set of events in the user case restated in the terminology of the system). That is, control classes encapsulate the coordination and sequencing of the interactions between other classes. Note that a single user-oriented event in a use case might map into a number of actions within the control class. Thus it is not necessarily a one-to-one mapping between the events in the use case and the actions described by the control class.

It is interesting to compare the use of the boundary, entity and control classes with the model–view–controller pattern. If this comparison is performed it is clear that a boundary class is an abstraction of a view, an entity is an abstraction of the model (or application data) and the control class represents the controller.

The result of combining these three types of class in an analysis diagram is presented in Figure 6.3. This diagram shows the relationship between the BalanceGUI boundary class, the CalculateBalance control class and the Account entity class. Note that it simply shows the relationships (links) between them and (at this point) little else.

6.3.3 Use Case Realizations

Use case realizations link the use cases identified in the use case analysis of the requirements discipline with the analysis classes in the analysis model. A use case realization expresses which class will participate in implementing the use case and the interactions which will occur between them.

A use case realization is therefore a collaboration within the analysis model which "implements" a use case. However, it focuses on determining the functionality or behaviour required of the system and not the actual implementation (this is deferred until the design discipline).

The primary elements of a use case realization are:

- *class diagrams*, illustrating relationships between classes for this use case realization
- *collaboration diagrams*
- *textual descriptions of collaboration* to help clarify or elucidate detail within the diagrams

The key new feature here is the collaboration diagram. This is used to represent the interactions between the analysis classes. Indeed, analysis objects may be created, modified and destroyed within a collaboration diagram. In particular:

- *Boundary objects* are often created and terminated within a singe use case realization. That is, a window is generated, presented to a user and destroyed.
- *Entity objects*, by their very nature, tend to be long lived and exist between use case realizations. However, they may still be created in one use case realization (e.g. new customer) and deleted at some later stage by another use case realization (e.g. close customer account).
- *Control objects* often represent the functionality associated with a single use case (i.e. a particular set of events in that use case) in which they are created and subsequently destroyed.

An example of a collaboration diagram is presented in Figure 6.4. In this figure the links between the three analysis classes have been annotated with the messages which are sent between the objects. Note that in this diagram the names of the three entity classes are underlined; in UML this notation indicates that these are actually objects rather than the classes. Also note that an event generated by the actor triggers the messages which are sent. Each message is then assigned a number that indicates its position in the collaboration taking place.

Associated with any diagram such as that presented in Figure 6.4 should be a textual description of what is taking place. For example, this diagram should have a description associated with it, such as:

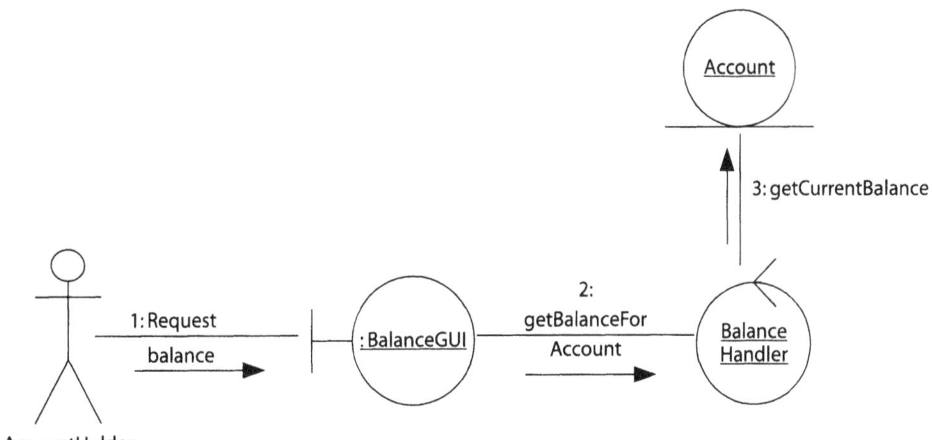

Figure 6.4 A collaboration diagram for the CheckBalance use case.

In the collaboration diagram, the `AccountHolder` requests the current balance on a particular current account (indicated by the `Account` entity). To do this the `AccountHolder` requests the balance through the balance GUI represented by the `BalanceGUI` boundary object. This then sends a `getBalanceForAccount` request to the control object (`BalanceHandler`). This object then checks that the `AccountHolder` has authority to access the `Account` entity. If the `AccountHolder` has this authority, it obtains the balance using the `getCurrentBalance` event.

6.3.4 Constructing the Analysis Model

The analysis model may be constructed by following these steps:

- Identify objects and classes. An approach such as that proposed by the CRC method may be appropriate here to help in identifying objects and classes.
- Generate use case realizations.
- Prepare a data dictionary.
- Identify associations (including aggregations) between objects.
- Identify attributes of objects at an abstract (probably textual) level.
- Organize and simplify object classes using inheritance.
- Iterate and refine the model.
- Group classes into modules.

You should not take the sequence of these steps too strictly; analysis and design are rarely completed in a truly linear manner. You are likely to perform some steps to a greater depth as the process goes on. In addition, some steps may lead to revisions in other steps and, once an initial design is produced, it will doubtless require revisions. You should consider these steps as a set of processes, the order of which may be influenced by the domain, the expertise available, the application etc. However, you should probably always start with the process of identifying objects and classes.

In the remainder of this chapter we shall consider each of these steps in turn.

6.4 Generating Analysis Classes

This section considers how classes are represented as well as how they are identified.

6.4.1 Representing Classes

A class is typically drawn as a solid-outline rectangle with three components (see Figure 6.5); however, three stereotypes are used for the analysis discipline. A class *stereotype* tells the reader what "kind" of class it is (exceptions, controllers, interfaces etc.). The stereotype is shown as a

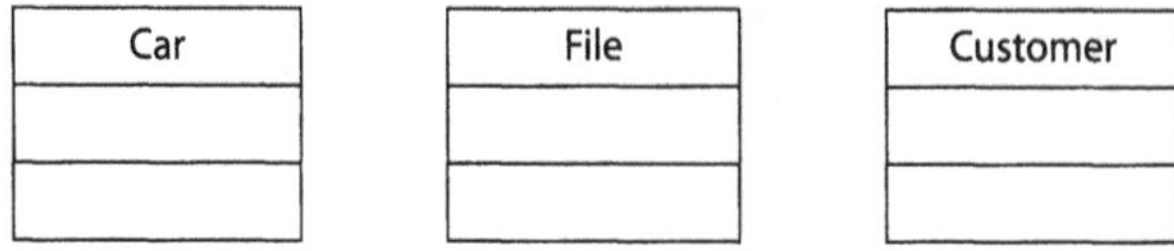

Figure 6.5 Example classes.

Figure 6.6 Alternative notation for entity classes.

normal font text string between < > centred above the class name or using a predefined icon (such as the circle with a line underneath for an entity class). In fact, the notation we have been using for the analysis classes is really a shorthand form of using the rectangle icon for a class with the stereotype written in angle brackets (as illustrated in Figure 6.6).

Interestingly, the UML makes no assumptions about the range of stereotypes that exist, and designers are free to develop their own. Other (language-specific) class properties can also be indicated in the class name compartment, although this is not really appropriate for the analysis discipline.

6.4.2 Representing Objects

An object in the UML is drawn as a rectangle divided into two sections. The upper section contains the *objectName : className* underlined. The object name is optional, but the class name is compulsory. In Figure 6.7, the object is repMobile1 and the class is Car.

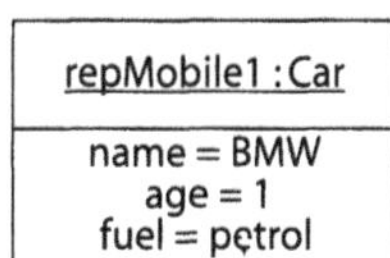

Figure 6.7 An object.

You can also indicate how many objects of a particular class are anticipated by entering the maximum value, range etc. in the top compartment. The lack of any number indicates that a single object is intended. The lower compartment contains a list of attributes and their values in the format *name type = value* (although the type is usually omitted). You can suppress the bottom compartment for clarity, which is normally done in the analysis discipline as we are focusing on abstract (textual) descriptions of the types of attributes an analysis object may possess.

In the analysis discipline, we use the three stereotypes to represent objects. In this case, the name of the stereotype is still underlined, but it is displayed within the stereotype icon (see Figure 6.8).

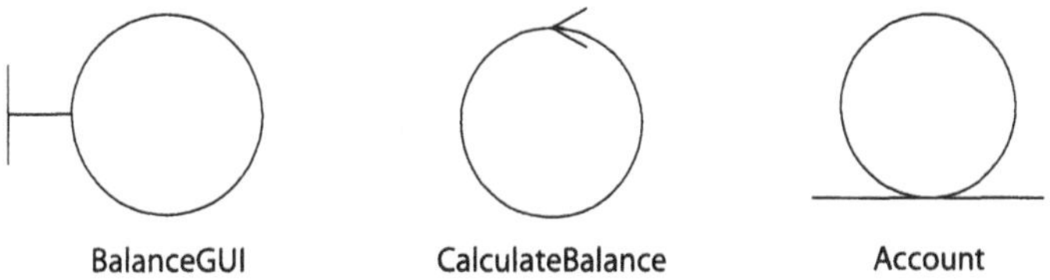

Figure 6.8 Analysis stereotype objects.

6.4.3 Generating Objects and Classes

A major step in constructing the analysis model is to identify the objects in the domain and their classes. These may be generated during the process of creating the use case realizations and in fact as part of the identification of the software architecture. However, the overall process of identifying the analysis classes is also a task in its own right. The aim is to identify a set of classes and their responsibilities (maintained in the data dictionary) such that every class participates in at least one use case realization and all use cases are implemented by a use case realization. Any class that you identify which does not participate in a use case realization is not a suitable analysis class.

Identifying the boundary and control classes is (as has already been mentioned) relatively straightforward. That is, every use case will have at least one boundary class and one control class. However, the identification of the entity classes is much harder and by far the more important (although identifying the others can help identify the entity classes). As has already been stated, finding the correct entity classes is the key to understanding the system and the important concepts in the architecture. Get the entity classes right and much of the rest of the design process will be that much easier.

In order to help with the process of identifying analysis classes you can adopt any technique which is appropriate. For example, the CRC or Class Responsibility Collaboration technique discussed in Chapter 15 is well suited to this task. Much of the philosophy behind what is in the CRC technique has actually been absorbed in the following presentation, as it is a natural way to explore the candidate set of classes which will eventually result in the set of actual classes in the analysis model.

To identify analysis classes identify:

- one boundary class for each actor and use case combination,
- one control class for each use case,

This may have already been done during the process of generating use case realizations (or may occur in parallel).

You then need to look for entity classes. To do this you need to look in depth at your application, your domain, and indeed anything that has gone before (e.g. paper systems), and consider:

- *physical entities* such as petrol pumps, engines and locks
- *logical entities* such as employee records, purchases and speed
- *soft entities* such as tokens, expressions or data streams
- *conceptual entities* such as needs, requirements or constraints

As long as an item makes sense for the application and the domain, then it is a candidate object or class. The only things you should avoid are objects that relate to the proposed computer implementation.

Do not worry about getting it right at this point or about identifying classes that should not be there. Inappropriate classes are filtered out later on; for the moment, attempt to find anything that could be a class. Remember that we start off by identifying a *candidate* set of classes, some of which are very likely to be irrelevant or wrong, but we are going to refine this candidate set as our understanding of the domain improves.

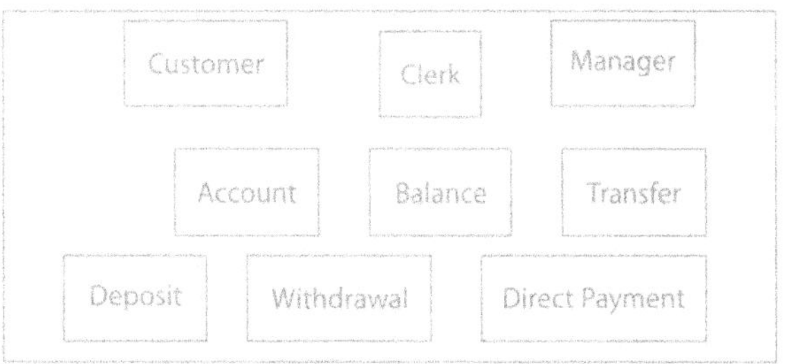

Figure 6.9 Initial set of classes.

Once you have a comprehensive list of candidate classes, you can discard any unnecessary or incorrect ones by using the following criteria:

- *Are any of the classes redundant?* If two or more classes express the same information then one is redundant. For example, customer and user may be different names for the same thing.
- *Are any of the classes irrelevant?* A class may be outside the scope of the system to be built even if it is part of the domain. For example, although porters work in a hospital, they are probably not relevant to a hospital bed allocation system. It may also be a design-oriented concept, so remove it from the analysis model.
- *Are any of the classes vague?* Some classes may represent ill-defined concepts. For example, *history provision* is vague – of what is it a history? Remember that although analysis classes are abstract in terms of the final system they should still have a clear and precise role in what the system is required to do.
- *Are any of the classes really attributes of other classes?* For example, name, address, salary, and job title tend to be attributes of an employee object rather than objects in their own right. This can be tricky, as it is often possible to represent something as both a class and an attribute, but remember that we are in the analysis discipline and thus our models should be less complex rather than more complex. In addition, attributes should be described textually, and thus breaking attributes down into programming level detail is both time-consuming and ultimately unlikely to be particularly useful (as the analysis classes may be abandoned in the design discipline).
- *Does the name of the class represent its intrinsic nature and not its role in the application?* For example, the class Person might represent an object in a restaurant booking system, but the class Customer is a better representation of its role in the system. This is particularly important with entity classes, where we really do want to identify their role in the application.
- *Is a class really an implementation construct?* Processes, algorithms, interrupts, and exceptions are implementation concepts and tend not to be related to the application domain. Remember that this is the analysis discipline; we should be a million miles away from anything resembling an implementation construct or concept!

Remember that the aim is to identify important entities.

6.4.4 Identifying Classes for the Online ATM System

The first step is to identify all candidate classes (even if later they may be identified as super-fluous). In addition, a customer can only have one account and we will assume an account is association with just one customer. For example, in our online ATM system (this may be done directly from the use case analysis) we might identify customer, clerk, manager etc. directly. Notice that these are all entities. We may go on to question what classes are required to support the use cases. For example, we might identify Account, Balance, Transfer, Deposit, Withdrawal, Direct payment. This would result in the initial set of classes illustrated in Figure 6.9.

Other classes may then be identified, such as Account History, Statement, Transaction, Amount, Account Number and PIN. This would result in the extended set of classes, illustrated in Figure 6.10. Note that we have not attempted to rationalize these classes, merely to identify potential classes.

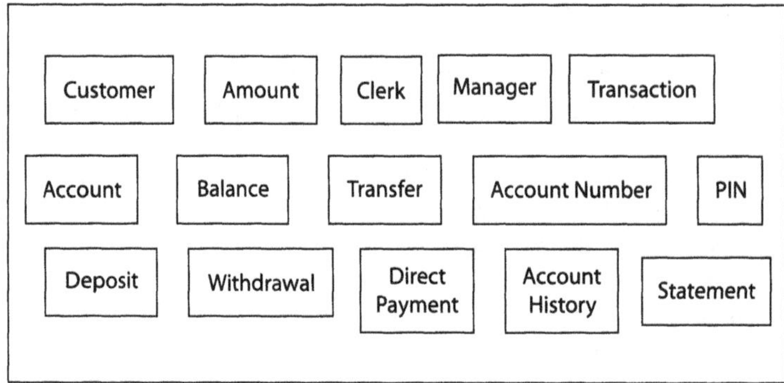

Figure 6.10 Additional classes.

6.4.5 Rationalizing Classes

We shall consider each of the questions presented earlier for removing unnecessary or incorrect classes. Notice that most of these questions are particularly relevant to entity classes, but are much less likely to be relevant to boundary or control classes.

- *Is the class cohesive?* That is, does the class act as a single concept (at the appropriate level of abstraction)? Does it represent a unified role within the application? If not, then the class may actually represent more than once concept. This is most often the case with entity classes.
- *Are any of the classes redundant?* If we examine Figure 6.10 it would appear that the Account history class and the Statement class are representing essentially the same information – historical data relating to the bank account. We can therefore remove the more generic and potentially less semantically meaningful Account history. There may also be duplication between Account and Balance, but this is not yet clear.
- *Are any of the classes irrelevant?* None of the classes identified so far appears to be outside the scope of this system.

- *Are any of the classes vague?* It is not clear what the Amount class represents. However, we will leave the renaming of this class until we have completed the rationalization of the classes, as the role may then become clearer.
- *Are any of the classes really attributes of other classes?* This is a tricky question, as it may be unclear whether a particular class will possess more than one item of information in the final design. However, in our system it is possible to identify some classes as being attributes of another class. For example, the Balance is probably just a numeric value and should be an attribute of the Account class. In turn, the Account Number and PIN are merely sequences of digits, and should be attributes of the Customer class.

  At this point it is unclear whether the Amount should be a class or an attribute of the Deposit or Withdrawal classes. We will therefore leave the Amount class for now.
- *Are any of the classes really operations?* If we consider the classes in Figure 6.10, there are a number of classes that appear to be operations; for example, Deposit, Withdrawal and Transfer. These might well evolve into classes for the implementation; however, here we are trying to represent the application domain. They are therefore inappropriate and need to be removed.
- *Does the name of the class represent its intrinsic nature and not its role in the application?* If we consider the classes in Figure 6.10 all the classes appear to fit the application. However, if we consider the role of clerk and the manager it may be argued that the manager is actually a privileged user (as the manager doesn't actually manage the application). However, to allow the semantics of the system to remain clear we will leave the manager class alone for now.
- *Is a class really an implementation construct?* None of the classes in our system appears to fall into this category.

This leaves us with the classes presented in Figure 6.11. Of course you might well have produced a completely different set of classes. Remember that design such as that being described here is still more of an art than a science, and rarely is there a single correct answer.

Also note that all these classes represent entities. None are boundary or control classes – again emphasizing the importance of entities in the analysis workflow.

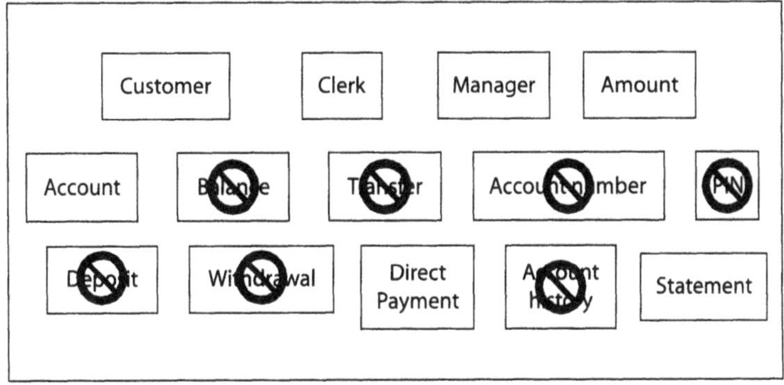

Figure 6.11 The refined set of classes.

6.5 Generating Use Case Realizations

In order to generate the analysis use case realizations it is necessary to examine each of the use cases in turn. It is likely that this is where the boundary and control classes will be identified. Additional entity classes may also emerge. For each use case you need to:

- Start by considering the event generated by the actor which triggers the use case realization. This should be sent to a boundary class and is the starting point for finding classes.
- Move through the flow of events, identifying the classes involved in the flow of events and the messages and links between the classes.
- Identify all the analysis classes involved in the use case sequence of events.
  - Each time you need to find a class examine those already in the data dictionary to see if there is one which matches your requirement.
  - If new classes are found then they need to be added to the use case realization and to the data dictionary. Note that it is often very useful to appoint a librarian who will be responsible for the data dictionary, for maintaining it, for updating it and for managing the identification and acceptance of new classes.
- Distribute the use cases behaviour among the classes.
  - Record the responsibilities of the classes in the data dictionary (and with the class itself).
  - Classes can have more then one responsibility (as they are abstractions of what will be in the design model). However, the responsibilities should be related to keep the class consistent.
- Note any special requirements from the use cases or identified during the analysis discipline with the use case realization.
- Record interactions between classes.
- The basic path associated with all use cases should produce one collaboration diagram.
- Alternative paths may produce one or more collaboration diagrams. A useful rule of thumb is to break the alternative paths into multiple collaboration diagrams if they become too complex to explain in one sentence.

Do not be too shaken by this description. You are not expected to find all the classes first time, nor just by considering the use cases. Generating the use case realizations and the process of generating the analysis classes themselves is really a very iterative process in which many different techniques come into play. We will look in more detail at how you might find analysis classes in the next section.

6.6 Identifying Attributes

Remember that this is the analysis discipline and that in general attributes really represent information-holding responsibilities of entity classes. As such, natural language is generally the most convenient way of representing attributes. Most (all) UML diagramming tools will allow you to annotate your classes with additional documentation, thus allowing you to describe both the data and operation responsibilities of analysis classes in natural language.

6.6.1 Identifying Attributes of Objects

Attributes often correspond to nouns followed by possessive phrases, such as "the colour of the car" or "the position of the cursor" in the domain under analysis. If you have used a method such as OOA, you may already have identified the key attributes. Luckily, attributes can (usually) be easily added to objects as and when they are identified; it is rare that the addition of a new attribute causes the structure of the system to become unstable.

To find an initial candidate set of attributes, look at the class's responsibilities as well as any domain information that you have available. Entity attributes should be associated with real-world entities (such as a customer's name and address). Boundary attributes should represent properties of the interface. Control classes are unlikely to have attributes as they express functionality and behaviour and not state-based information. Remember that we are dealing with the analysis classes here, so you do not need to represent the attributes explicitly. Indeed, as mentioned earlier, it is probably best to stick to textual descriptions of attributes and not to get bogged down in formally specifying the attributes and their types/visibility etc. at this stage.

An important point to note is that you should only be trying to identify analysis domain attributes. This means that attributes that are needed during the implementation of the system should not be included at this stage. However, link attributes (which might appear to be implementation attributes) may be identified at this stage as they have an impact on the architecture (although they may also be deferred to the design discipline). A link attribute is a property of the link between two objects, rather than a property of an individual object. For example, the many-to-many association between Stockholder and Company has a link attribute of "number of shares".

Having identified the set of candidate attributes for each object, you should then challenge these attributes using the following criteria:

- *Should the attribute be an object?* Earlier we said that a telephone call should not be an object; however, if you are constructing a telephone call billing system, then perhaps it *should* be an object. You need to think carefully about the domain when deciding whether something is an attribute or an object. Do not worry about getting it wrong: you can come back to it later and refine the model.
- *Is an attribute really a name?* Names are often selectors used to identify a unique object from a set of objects. In such situations, a name should really be a qualifier.
- *Is an attribute an identifier?* Here, *identifier* means a computer-based identifier and is an implementation issue and not part of the application domain. For example, `objectId` is an identifier that is probably not in the application's domain.
- *Is an attribute really a link attribute?* Link attributes are often mistaken for object attributes. Link attributes are most easily identified when it becomes difficult to identify to which of two (or more) classes the attribute should belong. In such situations, it is an attribute of the link between the two classes.
- *Does the attribute represent an internal state of the object that is not visible outside the object?* If it does, remove the attribute. It is an internal implementation issue and not part of the domain problem (note that you may wish to push it forward into the design model).

- *Does the attribute represent fine detail?* If the attribute represents some aspect of the object that is relatively low-level, then omit it. It does not help with the overall understanding of the domain and increases the complexity of the object model.
- *Are any of the attributes unlike the others in their class?* Such discordant attributes may be misplaced (this may indicate that one class should actually be two or more), or the attribute may not be part of the current application (although it may be part of the overall domain).
- *Is there any duplication of attributes?* If a class contains the same information but in different ways, is it necessary to hold each of them.
- *With all the attributes in place is a class too big?* If so, break it up into more than one class.
- *Are all the attributes at the analysis level?* Avoid the temptation to slip down into the design or implementation levels.

6.6.2 Identifying Attributes in the Online ATM System

We are now ready to start identifying the attributes of the objects represented by the classes we have been defining. This can be done by returning to the use case analysis to see what information is provided or required. However, you will also have to rely on additional domain information. For example, nowhere in the descriptions of the online ATM system have we seen a reference to a customer's name. However, it is reasonable to assume that every customer will have a name (even if it is a business customer and the name is the name of a business). Table 6.2 illustrates the attributes identified for the classes we are defining.

In Table 6.2 we have introduced a number of attributes which may not have been obvious from our previous analysis of the online ATM system. These become important when the responsibilities of the classes were considered. For example, a direct debit object must record when the debit occurred, how much was involved and to whom the payment was made. In turn, it was necessary to record the name of a clerk or manager and their department to identify them uniquely. For a manager an additional security code was identified as a way of indicating that they had access to the "set Balance" operation. Note that the Account system class has no attributes. This is not a problem at the moment, as we introduced it to give meaning to the associations. However, we will need to come back to this class as it may be an implementation class rather than a design class.

Having identified the attributes we must now analyze their validity. In this case we do not need to remove or alter any of the attributes identified.

Table 6.2 Attributes identified for classes.

Name	Customer	Account	Statement	Transaction
Attributes	name address account no. PIN	balance	period	date amount type
Name	Direct Debit	Clerk	Manager	Accounts system
Attributes	date amount recipient	name department	name department security code	customers

6.7 Preparing a Data Dictionary

A data dictionary provides a definition for each of the terms or words used in the evolving analysis models. Each entry precisely describes each object class, its scope, any assumptions or restrictions on its use and its attributes and operations (once they are known).

6.7.1 The Online ATM Data Dictionary

We are now in a position to start to extend our data dictionary for our simple online ATM application. Given the remaining classes presented in Figure 6.11, our data dictionary will resemble that presented in Table 6.3.

As a result of producing the data dictionary we have removed the Amount class and added it as an attribute of the Transaction class. The data dictionary should be updated as and when attributes, operations and new classes are identified.

Table 6.3 The data dictionary.

Name	Description	Assumptions	Attributes
Customer	Client of bank with a current account		Account Number PIN
Clerk	User of system		
Manager	Privileged user of system	Can change balance directly	
Account	Holds information on a customer's account		Balance
Statement	Historical record of deposits, Withdrawals and direct debits To and from the account	Is an ordered record	
Transaction	This represents the amount deposited, withdrawn or debited. It therefore represents a transaction.	Can represent type of transaction	Amount
Direct Debit	Records the details of the direct debit payment	Works with a transaction	

6.8 Identifying Associations

6.8.1 Representing Associations

An association is represented as a link between two analysis classes. It can be given a directional arrow and a name; however, for the analysis discipline it is usual just to show that there is a relationship between two classes. This is illustrated in Figure 6.12, which was originally presented earlier in this chapter.

Note that all analysis classes will have at least one association with another class. For example, the structure in Figure 6.12 is typical of analysis class relationships. There is an association between a boundary class and at least one control class. In turn, there is an association between the control class and at least one entity class. Remember that it is the entity classes we are really interested in here, so any associations between entity classes might be architecturally significant and may warrant more detailed scrutiny.

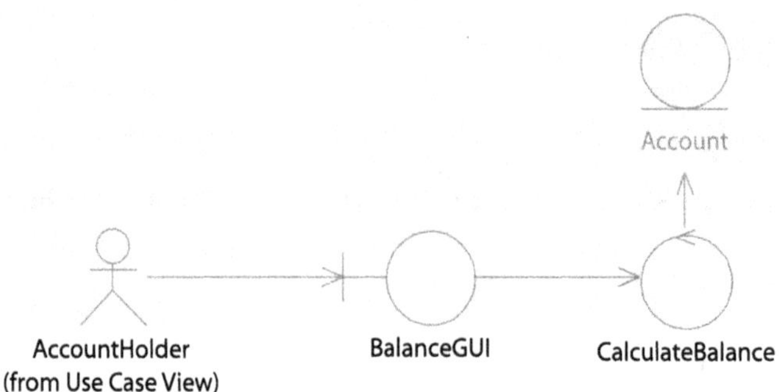

Figure 6.12 Illustrating associations between analysis classes.

6.8.2 Identifying Associations Between Objects

The next step is to identify any (and all) associations between two or more analysis classes. This is done by looking for references between two classes. A good place to look for these relationships is to examine the problem description for verbs or verb phrases between known objects. In particular, it identifies the following types of relationships:

- physical location (next to)
- physically contain each other (water in kettle, contained in)
- composed of each other (computer systems)
- form a conceptual collection (students in a class)
- directed actions (drives), related actions
- communication (talks to)
- ownership (has, part of)
- satisfaction of some condition (works for, married to, manages)
- relate objects (works for)
- apply some operations to all parts

Again, it is a good idea to identify all possible relationships and not to worry at this point about getting it right. If you have constructed a business model you may already have some knowledge about the relationships between the classes in the domain. The CRC technique discussed in Chapter 15 is also an excellent way of identifying collaborations between classes (indeed, that is one of its fundamental aims).

If you have not used a method, then consider which classes are likely to need to work with which other classes (e.g. the accounts clerk may need to work with the salaries clerk). A good place to look for this type of information is in the collaboration diagrams associated with the use case realizations. However, do remember that we are working with the analysis model and that you should not try to go to the level of detail expected in the design model.

Once you have a set of candidate associations, the following set of criteria can be used to help in refining them:

- *Is the association between eliminated classes?* If one of the classes involved in the association has been eliminated then the association should be eliminated.

- *Are any of the associations irrelevant or implementation associations?* Eliminate any associations that are outside the scope of the application domain (including implementation-related associations).
- *Are any associations transient?* An association should be a structural property of the application's domain. For example, *interacts with customer* is a temporary association in a hotel booking system.
- *Are any of the associations ternary?* Although the OMT and UML notations allow ternary associations, they are not encouraged. You should decompose these associations into binary ones (they are easier to implement, maintain and understand!).
- *Are any of the associations derivable?* It is suggested that you should remove any associations that can be derived from other associations. However, you should be wary of removing such associations, as they may be critical to understanding the domain relationships. That is, if two existing associations can replace an association, only do so if the semantic meaning of the two associations can be combined to provide the same semantic meaning as the one to be removed. For example, a *GrandparentsOf* relationship can be replaced by two *ParentOf* relationships.
- *Are there any missing associations?* Check that all reasonable associations are present. You may need to do this in consultation with the domain expert.

6.8.3 Identifying Associations in the Online ATM System

To identify the associations we refer back to the use cases and determine which classes need to work with which other classes in order to achieve the use case. For example, consider the "check balance" use case. This use case had four steps, which were:

1. Typing in the account number followed by the PIN
2. Requesting the current balance of the account
3. Receiving the balance
4. Logging off

The whole of this use case relates to the customer. We are therefore considering the classes Customer and Account and their relationship. In this situation a customer *has an* account. Thus there is an association between the Customer and Account classes which can be labelled as *has*. In addition, a customer can only have one account, and we will assume that an account is association with just one customer. If this process is applied to all the use cases we can obtain the set of associations illustrated in Figure 6.13. Note that we have omitted the boundary classes for clarity.

You may note that this diagram has introduced a new class: Accounts system. This is because it was necessary to define the relationship between a Clerk and Customers. It did make sense to associate these classes together as customers do not have clerks, nor do clerks have specific customers. Instead, a class was added to represent the overall system. This allows the concept of authorization to be introduced to show that a particular clerk can be authorized to use the system.

We are now ready to refine the associations. We can do this by considering the questions identified earlier. For example, one of the questions asks "are any of the associations transient?". In Figure 6.13 at least one of the associations may be transient. These are the association between the Clerk and Account classes and that between the Manager and Account

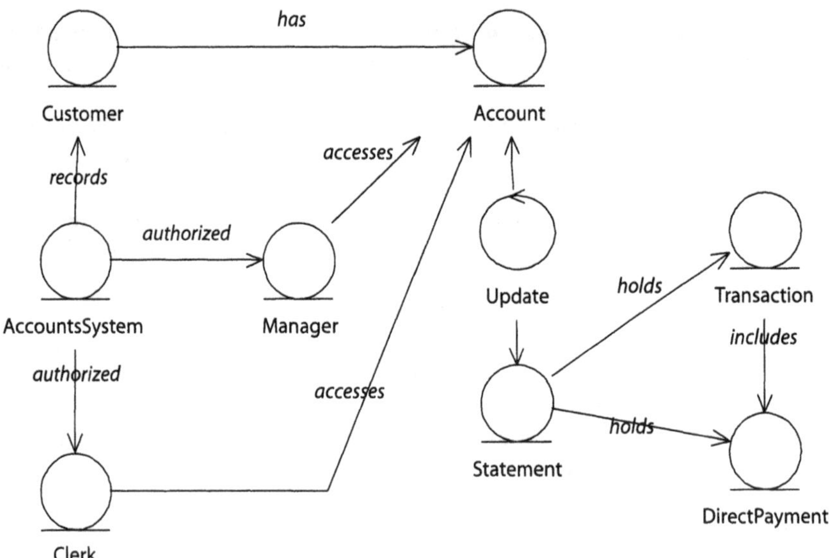

Figure 6.13 Basic class associations.

classes. These associations are labelled accesses. However, this is a temporary association as a clerk does not permanently reference each and every customer account. Therefore this association should be removed. Having removed any inappropriate associations we are now in a position to refine the remaining associations.

The next set of questions for refining associations relate to the semantics of the associations, for example checking the naming of associations, adding names where appropriate etc. For instance, does a Statement hold a Transaction? Does it record a Transaction? What role does a Transaction play in a Statement and vice versa? There is no single answer to any of these questions. Finally, we must identify the multiplicity of the associations. Figure 6.14 illustrates the result of these refinements.

6.9 Identifying Inheritance

Inheritance (or generalization) involves the identification of shared or common behaviour. The aim in the analysis model is to keep to as high and conceptual a level as possible. That is, you should attempt to promote the clarity of the analysis model by indicating inheritance relationships rather than worrying about implementation reuse.

6.9.1 Representing Inheritance

A solid line drawn from the subclass to the superclass with a large (unfilled) triangular arrowhead at the superclass end (see Figure 6.15) indicates inheritance of one class by a subclass. For

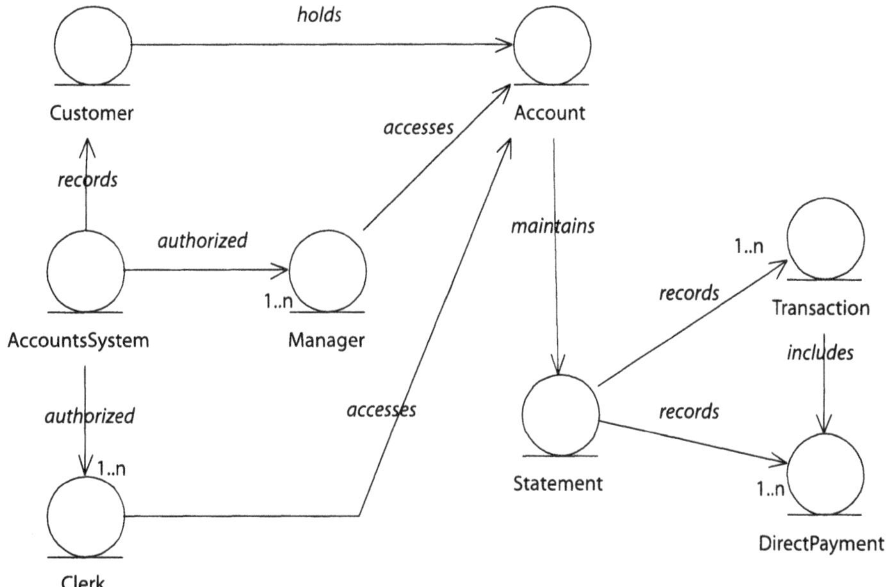

Figure 6.14 The associations after refinement.

compactness, you can use a tree structure to show multiple subclasses inheriting from a single superclass.

You can also model multiple inheritance, as languages such as the Common Lisp Object System (CLOS) and C++ support it. Multiple inheritance is represented by inheritance lines from a single subclass to two or more superclasses, as in Figure 6.16. In this figure, the class

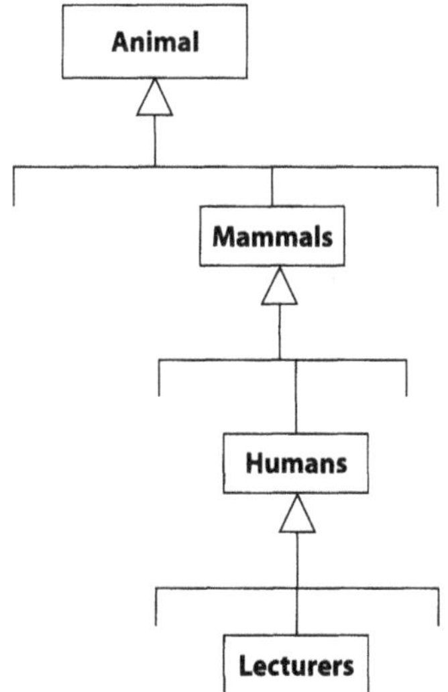

Figure 6.15 The inheritance hierarchy.

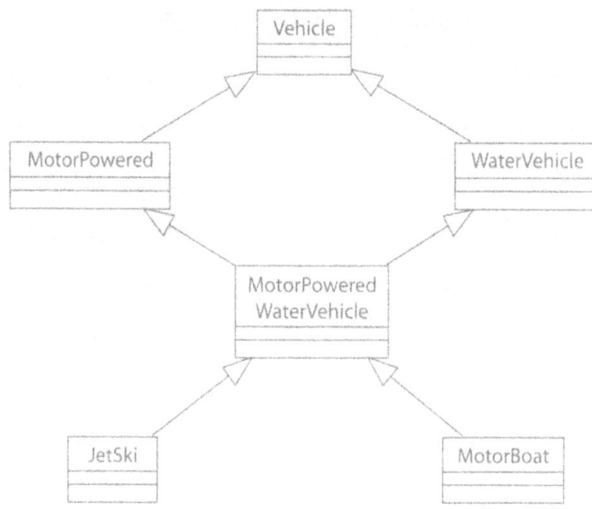

Figure 6.16 Multiple inheritance.

Motor powered water vehicle inherits from both *Motor powered* and *Water vehicle*. However, it should be noted that Java does not support multiple inheritance. We will therefore not use it in the remainder of this book.

6.9.2 Organizing and Simplifying Analysis Classes Using Inheritance

You can refine your classes using inheritance in both directions. That is, you can group common aspects of existing classes into a superclass, or you can specialize an existing class into a number of subclasses that serve specific purposes.

Notice that you are not doing this with a view to implementing the generated class hierarchy; rather, you are trying to understand the commonalities in the domain.

Identifying potential superclasses is easier than identifying specialized subclasses. To find potential superclasses, you should examine the existing classes looking for common attributes, operations or associations. Any common patterns you find may indicate the potential for a superclass. If you find common features, then you should define the superclass with an appropriate name (i.e. one that encompasses the generic roles of the classes that inherit from it). Then move the attributes, associations and operations that are common up into this superclass.

Do not try to force unrelated classes to become subclasses of a superclass just because they happen to have similar attributes (or associations or operations). When you group a set of classes together under a superclass, try to ensure that the grouping makes sense in the application domain. For example, grouping the classes car, truck and bus under a superclass vehicle makes sense. However, adding the class student, just because they all share the attribute *registrationNumber*, does not make sense!

Identifying specializations can be more difficult; however, if you find a class playing a number of specific roles then specialization may be appropriate. You should be wary of

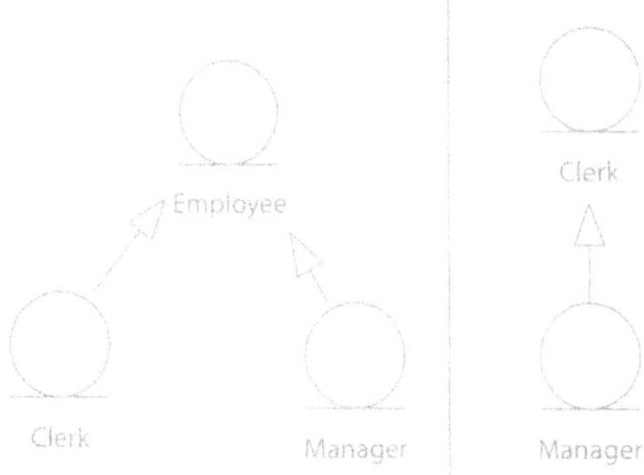

Figure 6.17 Alternative inheritance.

specialization, as you do not want to overspecialize the classes in your object model. You may be talking about separate instances of the same class, rather than subclasses.

6.9.3 Identifying Inheritance in the Online ATM System

We are now ready to identify any inheritance in the simple online ATM system. If we examine the classes illustrated in Figure 6.9 and Table 6.2 it quickly becomes clear that there are two situations in which common attributes and associations would suggest that inheritance may be used. These are in the classes Clerk and Manager and in the classes Transaction and Direct Debit.

There are two ways in which we may exploit inheritance. The first is to define a generic abstract class (for example, Employee) and allow the appropriate classes to inherit from this class. The other is to say that one class is a specialization of another existing domain class. These two options are presented in Figure 6.17 for the Clerk and Manager classes.

Which of these approaches is adopted depends on which is the more meaningful in the context of the application. Figure 6.17(b) implies that managers are actually a special type of clerk – which may not be meaningful. In this case we will adopt the approach illustrated in Figure 6.17(a).

For the Transaction and Direct Debit classes we will adopt the style of approach indicated in Figure 6.17(b). This is because it does make sense to say that a direct debit is a type of transaction. This results in the object model illustrated in Figure 6.18.

The remaining steps in this process involve checking the design and iterating and refining it. The resulting classes are then grouped into packages.

6.10 Grouping Analysis Classes into Packages

The final step associated directly with the analysis model is to group classes into packages to improve the clarity of a large model. A package may contain analysis classes, use case realizations and other packages. You should identify packages by looking for classes that work together/are

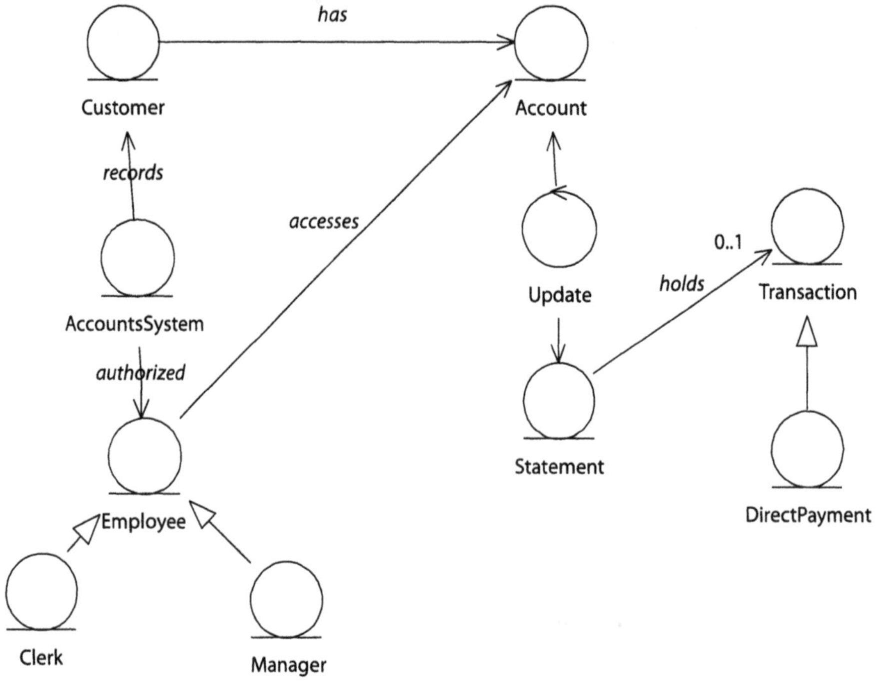

Figure 6.18 The final online banking analysis class diagram.

strongly (functionally) related and the use case realizations that they are involved with. Do not base the packages purely on system functionality, as this is likely to change and result in inappropriate packaging. You should also attempt to ensure that the packages are loosely coupled, promoting low dependency between the packages.

Many people suggest that you should ensure that a package can be fitted onto a single drawing surface (be that paper or the screen), as this aids comprehensibility. This is actually true for any UML diagram. In addition, packages can be hierarchical and can be a very useful way of partitioning the design of the system among a number of designers.

6.10.1 Identifying Analysis Packages

To identify analysis packages follow these steps:

- Allocate use cases to a package based on
  - same actors, similar business processes
  - relationships between use cases (such as extends and uses).
- Include in the package all classes and collaborations associated with the use cases.
- Identify all dependencies between packages.
- Attempt to localize modifications due to changes in processes/actors.
- If you identify common functionality used in multiple packages, extract this functionality into a new package.

Additional service packages can be identified by looking for optional services or potentially optional services which may be provided (for example, a direct payment package or transaction management package for the online bank account system).

6.10.2 Representing Packages

Packages group associated modelling elements, such as classes in the analysis model. They are drawn as tabbed folders in the UML.

Figure 6.19 illustrates five packages called *Clients*, *Business Model*, *Persistent Store*, *Bank* and *Network*. In this diagram, the contents of *Clients, Persistent Store, Bank* and *Network* have been suppressed (by convention, the package names are in the body) and only *Business Model* is shown in detail (with its name in the top tab). *Business Model* possesses two classes, Customer and Account, and a nested package, *Bank*. The broken lines illustrate dependencies between the packages. For example, the package *Clients* directly depends on the packages *Business Model* and *Network* (i.e. at least one element in the *Clients* package relies on at least one element in the other two packages).

A class may belong to exactly one package but make reference to classes in other packages. Such references have the following format:

```
packageName :: className
```

For example:

```
Business Model :: Customer
```

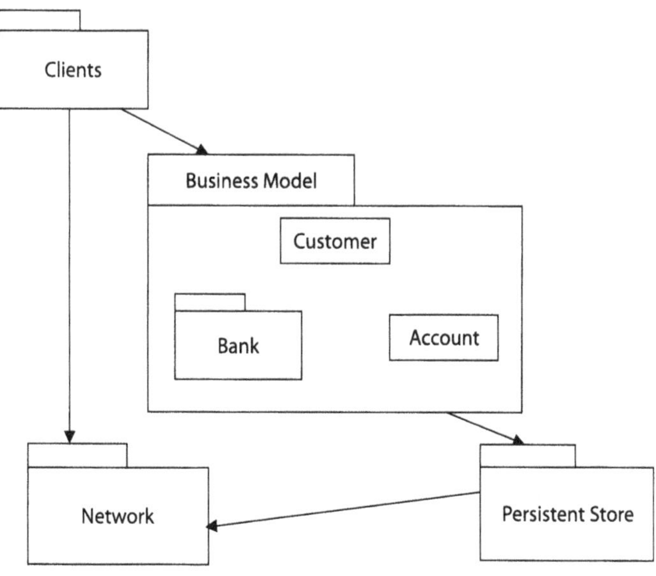

Figure 6.19 Figures with dependencies.

Packages allow you to structure models hierarchically; they organize the model and control its overall complexity. Indeed, you may use a package to enable top-down design of a system (rather than the bottom-up design typical of many object-oriented design methods) by allowing designers to specify high-level system functionality in terms of packages which are "filled out" as and when appropriate (for example in the design discipline).

6.10.3 Analyzing Analysis Packages

You should ensure that all packages are as independent of the other packages as possible. Each package should also fulfil a purpose (for example, a package should implement a use case or define a domain concept or entity). You should also test that any changes relating to the internals of one package have a minimal effect on other packages. Finally, you should ask yourself whether the packages you have defined maintain a cohesive structure. At this point, identifying the *generic* types of interfaces you require between the different packages is extremely useful. Do not worry about the exact operations (methods) which will be listed on the interfaces. This is the analysis model: we are merely trying to determine what interfaces are needed to support the analysis view of the system's requirements. This should help in identifying the actual interfaces needed later in the design.

6.11 Iterating and Refining the Model

Object design is still more of an art than a science and (unless the problem is trivial) the first version of the analysis model is probably not correct (or complete). Object-oriented design is far more iterative in nature than some other design methods, and it therefore acknowledges that you need to repeat the above process a number of times to get a reasonable object model. Indeed, some changes are initiated by the development of the design model that you have not even considered yet. However, you can ask yourself the following questions about the object model:

- Are there any missing analysis objects (does one class play two roles)? In particular, can you identify any further entity classes (and where they are used)?
- Are there any unnecessary classes (such a class may possess no attributes)?
- Are there any missing associations (such as a missing links between entity objects)?
- Are there any unnecessary associations (such as those that are not used by anything)?
- Are all attribute descriptions in the correct class?
- Are all associations in the correct place?
- Do all operation descriptions fit with the role of the class within which they have been defined?

Cross-referencing the object model with the use case model may help answer some of the above questions.

6.12 Identify Common Special Requirements

You should identify all the special requirements or deferred decisions produced during the analysis discipline. To find these requirements, examine the use case analysis, use case realization generation and class analysis. Document the special requirements together to ensure that none are missed during the design stage. Examples of such special requirements include:

- persistence
- distribution and concurrency
- security features
- fault tolerance
- transaction management

The Design Discipline: System and Class Design

7.1 Introduction

The primary inputs to the design discipline come from the use case analysis and the analysis discipline. That is, the inputs to the design discipline are the use cases, the analysis use case realizations, and the analysis classes and packages identified in the analysis discipline. If, however, you have not carried out the analysis discipline then you must go back to using only the use case analysis, and use that as your starting point.

The design discipline differs from the analysis discipline as it is aimed at implementation abstraction, i.e. how the system should be built, rather than trying to rephrase the system requirements (at a high level of abstraction). That is, it provides the means to enable developers to visualize and reason about the implementation. It identifies major subsystems and their interfaces and deals with implementation-oriented constraints, classes and their responsibilities and operations, and inter-class relationships and their structures. Table 7.1 compares the analysis and design disciplines.

7.2 Design Discipline Activities

There are four primary activities in the design discipline, these are:

- *Architectural/subsystem design.* This was discussed in Chapter 4 on software architecture.
- *Generation of design classes.* We are now interested in all the details required to design the system. Thus there will be many more classes required to support the use case realizations than was the case in the analysis workflow.
- *Identification of design interfaces.* To reduce the dependency between classes, we will also identify the key interfaces in the system. Indeed, architecturally speaking, the interfaces are

Table 7.1 Comparing the analysis and design disciplines.

Analysis workflow	Design workflow
Conceptual model	Physical model
Describes functional requirements	Determines how system will meet requirements
Only uses 3 types of class	Classes as appropriate
Less complex (1:5)	More detailed (5:1)
Less formal descriptions	More formal descriptions (e.g. visibility of attributes)
Created by workshops, interviews etc.	Created by prototypes, visual analysis, engineering

more important than the classes that they implement. This is because, if we get the interfaces right, the dependencies between the classes will be less and thus a change to one class should have less of an impact on another class.

- *Generation of design use case realizations.* We now need to consider how the design implements the use cases identified during the requirements discipline (this ensures traceability from the use cases right through the design).
- *Generation of subsystems.* We are also interested in producing actual subsystems, rather than subsystems that help us understand the system.

Remember that the whole of the design process is far more iterative and incremental than can easily be expressed on paper. Thus you should not take the sequencing of the above list literally. For example, it is difficult to identify the interfaces between subsystems, between classes etc. without knowing what the classes need to do; however, once an interface has been identified more than one class may then be used to implement that interface (remember that in Java a class can implement zero or more interfaces). Thus it is by nature an incremental process.

The design discipline is actually broken down into two stages, just as the other disciplines have been. The two stages are the architectural design (which we have already looked at and which will be performed at a much earlier point in the analysis) and the class design. Be careful of assuming that these two stages are completely independent – they are not. One will influence the other. For example, the structure of the architecture will influence how the remainder of the system is designed. In turn, as new classes, interfaces, operations and attributes are identified, the architecture may evolve to meet unforeseen requirements.

This chapter focuses on the class design. The class design concentrates on identifying the classes, interfaces and subsystems required to implement the system and their associated behaviour with reference to the structures put in place by the architecture. The behaviour is captured using a number of different diagrams that combine to represent a dynamic model of the system under analysis. Note that the same notation is used, but to describe the underlying architecture and to describe the subsystems, classes and interfaces which *plug into* the architecture. This means that it can be difficult, if not confusing, to see what is part of the architecture and what is part of the rest of the system. The best advice I can give here is to make sure that all things are documented clearly. If the UML tool you are using directly supports the separation of a design into different *models* which are clearly labelled, then place all the architectural components in the *architecture* model.

For both the class design and the architecture design the dynamic behaviour of the system can be captured using interaction diagrams and the statechart diagrams. These together comprise the dynamic model(s) of the design. The dynamic model describes the behaviour of the application and the objects that comprise that application. The UML sequence and state diagrams described in this chapter are the main components of the dynamic model. The aim of the dynamic model analysis is to identify the important events that occur and their effects on the state of the objects.

7.3 Class Design Stage

The primary steps in the class design activity are:

- Analyze use cases.
- Identify design classes, interfaces and subsystems.
- Identify the dynamic behaviour of classes.
- Identify attributes and operations.
- Design algorithms to implement operations.
- Optimize access paths to data.
- Implement control for external interactions.
- Adjust class structure to increase inheritance.
- Design associations and aggregations.
- Produce the deployment model.

The primary products of the design discipline are presented in Figure 7.1. These form the design model itself. This is made up of the packages, classes, interfaces and their associations that comprise the design of the system. It should also include sequence diagrams and statecharts for describing the dynamic behaviour of the classes (both of these are described in further detail later in this chapter). The design discipline also produces the deployment model. This describes how the system will be deployed in terms of components and subsystems on nodes (processors) etc. It also possesses a set of design model-oriented use case realizations. These use case realizations describe how the associated use cases are implemented in the design model. Every use case should have at least one use case realization. Finally, the design discipline should also produce an updated data dictionary describing all the elements of the design model.

Note that much of the notation which was introduced in the last chapter for the analysis discipline will be reused in this chapter (with the exception of the analysis class stereotypes) we shall therefore introduce only new notation and assume familiarity with that already presented.

7.4 The Design Model

The design model describes the physical realization of use cases. That is, it describes those classes, interfaces and subsystems that will move forward to be implemented in order to

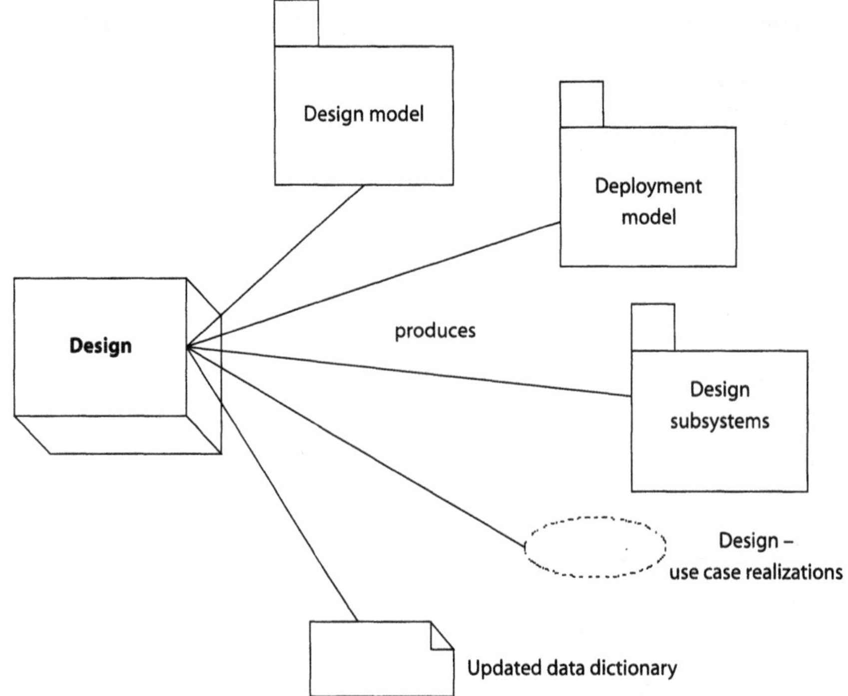

Figure 7.1 The products of the design discipline.

provide a system which implements the functionality described in the use cases. Thus the design model needs to take into account both the functional requirements (as expressed by the use cases) and any non-functional requirements, although some of these may still be deferred to the implementation discipline. The design model also needs to take into account the implementation environment and language to be used etc. We shall assume that we are using Java with the Java 2 platform. This means that to some extent we are hidden from any specific operating system issues (see Chapter 13 for a discussion of the language independence of an object-oriented design).

In the design model, design-oriented use-case realizations ensure that design classes implement the functionality required of the system. As we are moving towards the implementation, the design model is also described using the terminology of the implementation environment (e.g. the classes, packages, interfaces and visibility facilities of Java). This also means that the relationships between classes are mapped to the implementation features of the language. Thus we can use concepts such as the ability of a class to implement an interface in Java to indicate that a design class implements an interface directly. In addition, aggregation (i.e. one class being contained within another) may imply the use of inner classes etc. Obviously some implementation details will be left until the implementation discipline (e.g. which sorting algorithm to use) as this is the design discipline. However, we will try to move the design towards something which can be implemented.

7.5 Design Classes

7.5.1 Design Class Notation

The design class notation does not use the three stereotype classes presented in the analysis discipline. This is because we are now interested in the classes which will actually form part of the system, rather than an abstraction of what the system needs to do. Thus we use the standard box notation with the attribute and operation compartments fully documented.

Note that you may well decide to define your own stereotypes for your own project (remember that the UML does not limit the range of stereotypes that can be defined). For example, if the concept of an Asset is fundamental to your application, then you might decide that there are lots of different types of asset, such as maps, files, disks, tapes and folders, and that all of these are classes that are a type of asset. You could even create an icon for your asset stereotype (if your UML tool will allow it). This can increase the clarity of your designs and reduce clutter on a diagram (as you don't have to have so many inheritance links to some generic class).

The primary difference, however, between the design classes and the analysis classes is the amount of information provided and the need to be very specific when we define attributes and operations. For example, in the analysis discipline we left attributes as textual descriptions; in the design model we will need to be more precise (see below). We will also need to include information on operations (methods), their parameters and return types. Both attributes and operations should be specified in the implementation language (in this case Java). Thus we will be filling in the details in the middle and lower boxes of the class rectangle.

Representing Attributes

An attribute is a data item defined by a class. Attributes can be associated with a class (e.g. a static or class variable) or with instances (e.g. an instance variable). They are not variables *per se* but may well be implemented as such in the actual system (in our case, attributes map directly to either instance of class (static) variables in Java). An attribute has a name and a type specified in the following format:

```
name: type = initialValue
```

The name and type are strings that are ultimately language-dependent. The initial value is a string representing an expression in the target language. Thus, for example, we might define the following in a design class:

```
title: String = Question
```

which would map onto the following Java:

```
String title = "Question";
```

You can hide the attribute compartment from view to reduce the detail shown in a diagram. If you omit a compartment, it says nothing about that part of the class definition.

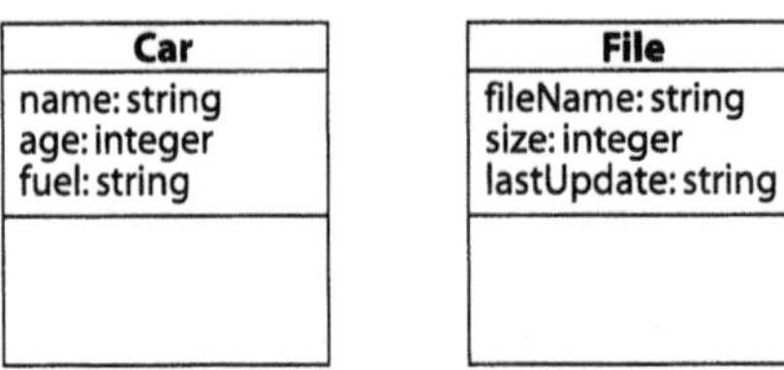

Figure 7.2 Classes with attributes.

However, if you leave the compartment blank, there are no definitions for that part of the class. Additional language-dependent and user-defined information can also be included in each compartment in a textual format. The intention of such additions is to clarify any element of the design in a similar manner to a comment in source code.

Figure 7.2 illustrates two classes: Car and File. The Car class possesses three attributes: name, age and fuel are string, integer and string types, respectively.

You can also indicate the intended scope of attributes in the class definition. The absence of any symbol in front of an attribute indicates that the element is public for that class. The significance of this depends on the language. The symbols currently supported are shown in Figure 7.3. You can combine symbols to indicate, for example, that an attribute is a class-side public value (such as +$defaultSize).

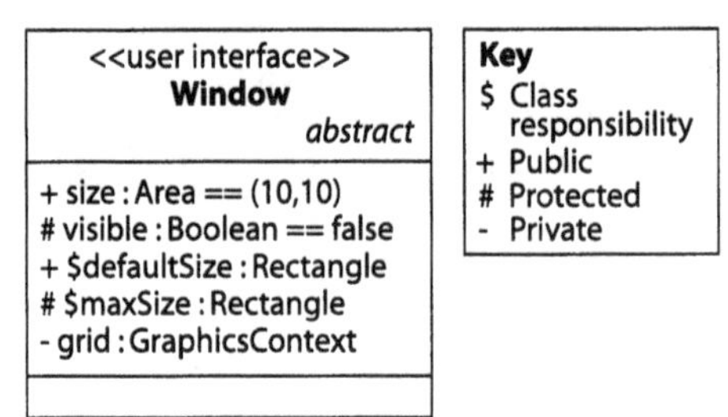

Figure 7.3 Class with additional annotations.

A derived value can be represented by a slash ("/") before the name of the derived attribute (see Figure 7.4). Such an attribute requires an additional textual constraint defining how it is generated; you indicate this by a textual annotation below the class between curly brackets ({}).

Representing Operations

Figure 7.5 illustrates two classes: Car and File. The Car class possesses three attributes (name, age and fuel are string, integer and string types, respectively) and four operations (start, lock and

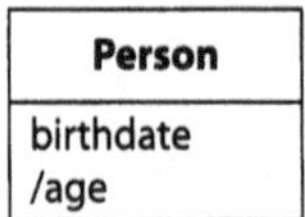

{age = currentDate − birthdate}

Figure 7.4 Derived values.

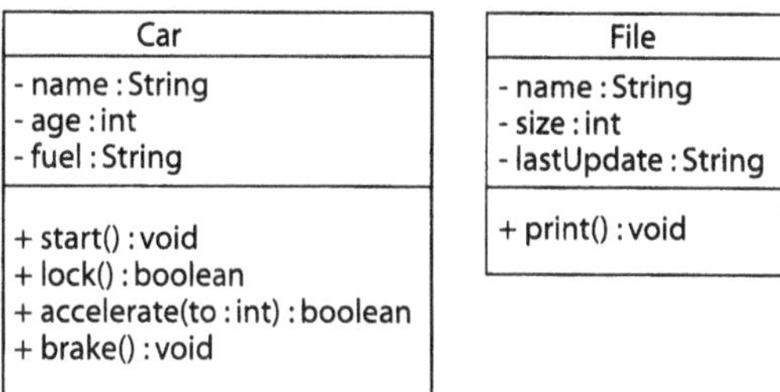

Figure 7.5 Classes with attributes and operations.

brake take no parameters; accelerate takes a single parameter, to, which is an integer that represents the new speed). We have already seen the definition of attributes above, so we will concentrate on the operations.

An operation has a name and may take one or more parameters and return a value. It is specified in the following format. The constituent parts are language-dependent strings:

name (parameter : type = defaultValue, ...): resultType

You can hide the attribute and operation compartments from view to reduce the detail shown in a diagram. If you omit a compartment, it says nothing about that part of the class definition. However, if you leave the compartment blank, there are no definitions for that part of the class. Additional language dependent and user-defined information can also be included in each compartment in a textual format. The intention of such additions is to clarify any element of the design in a similar manner to a comment in source code.

Other (language-specific) class properties can also be indicated in the class name compartment. For example, in Figure 7.6, the Window class is an abstract class.

You can also indicate the intended scope of attributes and operations in the class definition. This scope can be public, private, default or protected (which can be used to map onto the Java visibility modifiers of the same names). This can be useful even for languages, such as Smalltalk, which do not support concepts such as public, private and protected attributes and operations. The absence of any symbol in front of an attribute or operation, for Java

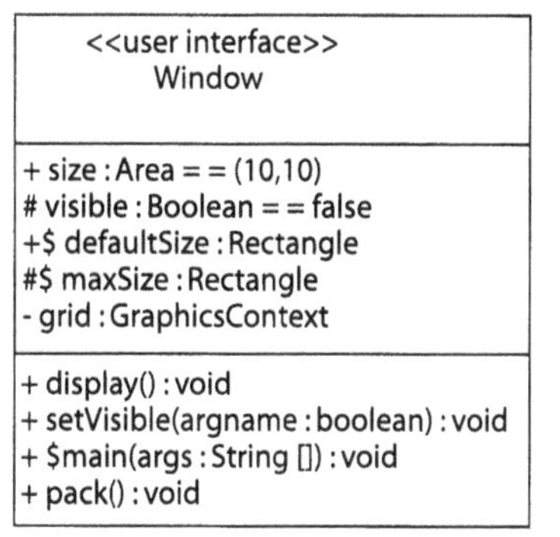

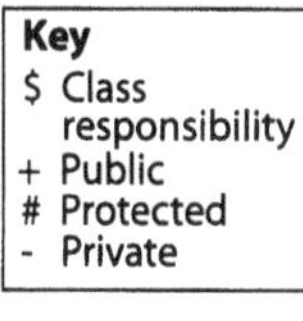

Figure 7.6 Class with additional annotations on operations.

Table 7.2 Visibility modifier notation in UML for Java.

Symbol	Meaning
–	Private
+	Public
#	Protected
<blank>	Package
$	Static or class side

applications, should be considered to indicate package visibility (i.e. the default visibility). The notation used for public, private and protected in Figure 7.6 is presented in Table 7.2 (note that the UML tool you use may well have icons that are intended to be easier to remember, such as a padlock for private).

The $ symbol indicates that the element is part of the class (as opposed to being part of the instance). The significance of this depends on the language; in the case of Java, it implies that the attribute or operation is a class side (or static) element. The symbols currently supported are shown in Figure 7.6 and Table 7.2. You can combine symbols to indicate, for example, that an operation is a class-side public method (such as +$main(String[]):void).

Design Class Stereotypes

Design classes are often given stereotypes that in our case indicate a Java class or type. This helps to link the design class to the actual implementation class and forces the designer to take into account the facilities provided by the target language. However, take care not to try to do this too soon. Normally the earlier in the design you are, the less likely you are to be able to specify particular classes. However, as the design progresses it is far more likely that you will want to link the design to your implementation language.

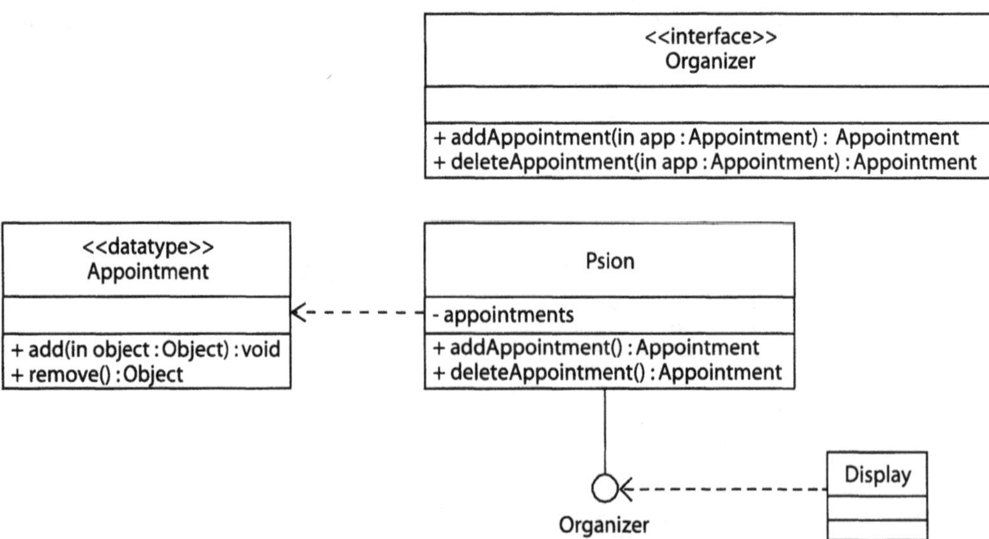

Figure 7.7 Design class annotations.

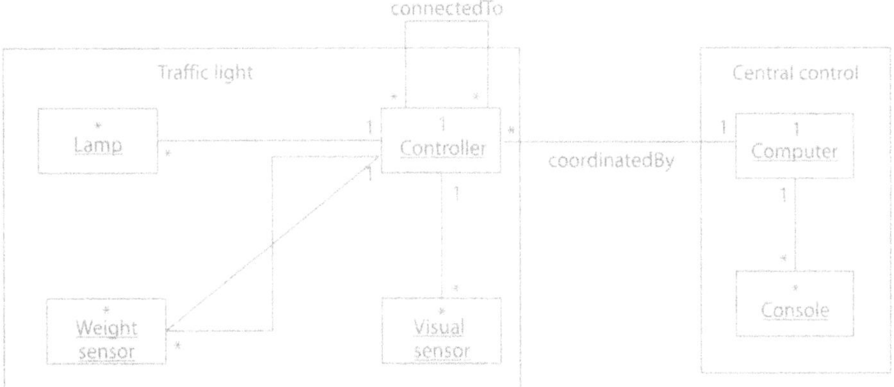

Figure 7.8 Composite classes.

One stereotype which is provided with the UML is the interface stereotype. This means that for Java we can define explicit interfaces, with operations specified, which the implementing classes must provide. We can specify that a class implements an interface or provides an interface. We can also identify active classes as being types of thread etc. Note that all design classes should also clearly document their role in the system. Figure 7.7 illustrates the use of interface and datatype stereotypes (note that the datatype could be implemented by one of the collection classes, but we have deferred that decision until later). In this figure are shown both the interface stereotype (the line with a circle on the end of it) and the interface definition (as the standard class box with the <interface> stereotype show in the top compartment). Remember that in Java interfaces can possess not only operations but also final static constants that can be presented in the attribute compartment. But the UML does not know this and will allow you to define any type of attribute!

Composite Classes

A class may define a pattern of objects and links that exist whenever it is instantiated. Such a class is called a composite, and its class diagram contains an object diagram. You may think of it as an extended form of aggregation where the relationships among the parts are valid only within the composite. A composite is a kind of *pattern* or *template* that represents a conceptual clustering for a given purpose. Composition is shown by drawing a class box around the embedded components (see Figure 7.8) which are prototypical objects and links. That is, a composite defines a context in which references to classes and associations, defined elsewhere, can be used.

7.6 Identifying and Refining Design Classes

7.6.1 Identifying Classes

First look at the analysis classes in the analysis model:

- For *boundary* classes you should "implement" then with appropriate interface classes. For example you may need to identify design classes which are stereotypes of <<Frame>>, <<JFrame>> or <<JPanel>> etc. Or you may need to specify a design class that provides a particular protocol etc.
- For *entity* classes you will need to determine what classes, files, database etc. will "implement" these classes. It is often the case that one entity class will result in multiple design elements, even to the extent of representing a design subsystem, and care needs to be taken with this analysis. Remember that the entity classes described the key concepts in the system; thus whatever they evolve into in the design will be key elements in the design!
- *Control* classes. Essentially the behaviour encapsulated in the analysis control classes needs to be divided between the various design classes that will implement that behaviour. This is not straightforward, but can be done by considering the objects associated with each step and determining which objects should "own" that step. To do this it is useful to consider the role of each class involved in the interactions originally described by the control class. Then try to place the behaviour such that it fits with the role of the classes. Particular care needs to be taken if there are likely to be any distributed behaviour or transactions involved in the behaviour abstracted by the analysis control class. In some case you may find that you need to provide a control design object to complete the "implementation". However, you should treat this as a last resort rather than the norm. Otherwise you will be slipping into a procedural approach for your system.

It is also likely that you will need to consider additional support classes above and beyond what might have been identified straight from the use cases and the analysis classes. Again supporting techniques such as that advocated by the CRC method may well be useful here. You should not expect to get these classes right first time, and indeed the result of your first cut at finding classes should be viewed as a candidate class set which will require refinement. In general, as your understanding of the design improves the set of classes in the design will be modified, updated and improved.

It is also useful to consider design patterns at this stage. (Design patterns are discussed in more detail in Part 2). These are essentially useful recurring solutions to problems within designs. For example, "I want to loosely couple a set of objects: how can I do this?", might be a question facing a designer. The Mediator design pattern is one solution to this. If you are familiar with design patterns you can use them to solve problems which occur. Typically, early in the design process the problems are more architectural/structural in nature, while later in the design process they may be more behavioural. Design patterns actually provide different types of pattern, some of which are at the architectural/structural level and some of which are more behavioural. They can thus help at every stage of the design process.

7.6.2 Refining the Set of Classes

Once you have an initial set of classes you will need to start refining them (just as you did in the analysis discipline). The issues you will need to consider will include:

- Do any subsystem interfaces imply classes?
- Do any other interfaces need classes?

- Are any of the classes redundant?
- Are any of the classes irrelevant?
- Are any of the classes vague?
- Are any of the classes really attributes of other classes?
- Are any of the classes really operations?
- Does the name of the class represent its intrinsic nature and not its role in the application?
- Is a class really an implementation construct?
- Do any of the classes map directly to Java classes?
- Does the class represent more than one role?
- Are classes just data?
- Are classes just operations?
- Are any classes extensions of existing classes (either application or Java)? This implies inheritance.
- Are any of the classes really objects? If so, what is the class?
- Is the class cohesive – does it represent a coherent concept?
- Is it too big – would it benefit from being broken down into a number of different classes?

Instead of using inheritance, can you identify any component-based reuse which will allow you to modify the class's behaviour by "plugging in" another class to provide that behaviour (in the way that sorted collections can be in the Java collection API)?

However, don't forget that this process is iterative and incremental; do not expect to get a final set of classes the first time round the loop.

7.6.3 Identifying Attributes for Design Classes

As you are identifying your classes, you should also be thinking about the attributes they possess. This is important, as it will not only help you to identify other classes (when an attribute is a composite of a grouping of information) but also help you to identify classes that are really the same – just with different names. For example, Customer and Account Holder may well be different, but if all their attributes are the same they may well be the same concept – do you really need a class for each?

To identify the attributes, consider the attributes that were textually described and the associated analysis classes. These may help you to identify key attributes for the design classes. Remember that the analysis attributes could be an abstraction of a more complex concept that will need to be expanded upon in the design model. Also examine the information required by the class to fulfil its role. For example, a bank account class will need to include a variety of information, including the account holder's name, address, occupation, account number, related account numbers and overdraft limit. Finally, as our target language is Java we can also take into account whether an attribute should be associate with an instance or with the class (i.e. a class or static variable).

7.6.4 Refining Attributes for Design Classes

Once you have an initial set of attributes for a class you are ready to refine them. The refinement process and the attribute discovery process are really tightly coupled and should be treat as parts of the same activity. They should also be treated as iterative and you should not expect to find all

Table 7.3 Online bank account system attributes.

Name	Customer	Statement	Transaction	Direct Debit	Clerk	Manager
Attributes	name address account no. PIN occupation overdraft	balance period entries	date amount type	date amount recipient	name department	name department security

the attributes for a given class in one pass. To refine the attributes you have identified for a design class you can apply the following:

- Should the attribute be an object?
- Is an attribute really a name?
- Is an attribute an identifier?
- Is an attribute really a link attribute?
- Does the attribute represent an internal state of the object and should thus not be visible outside the object?
- Does the attribute represent implementation detail?
- Are any of the attributes unlike the others in their class?
- Has the class become too complicated due to its attributes? If so, break it down.

Table 7.3 illustrates the revised set of design classes identified for the online bank account system and the attributes that have been produced.

7.6.5 Representing Operations

An operation has a name and may take one or more parameters and return a value. It is specified in the following format:

```
name (parameter : type = defaultValue, ...): resultType
```

The constituent parts are language-dependent strings.

You can hide the operation compartment (as well as the attribute compartment) from view to reduce the detail shown in a diagram. If you omit a compartment, it says nothing about that part of the class definition. However, if you leave the compartment blank, there are no definitions for that part of the class. Additional language-dependent and user-defined information can also be included in each compartment in a textual format. The intention of such additions is to clarify any element of the design in a similar manner to a comment in source code.

7.6.6 Describing Operations

Operations can be described in whatever form is appropriate. This could be natural language, it could be in the form of pseudocode (although this has a tendency to end up being very close to actual code!), or it could be via activity diagrams. Activity diagrams are another way in which the

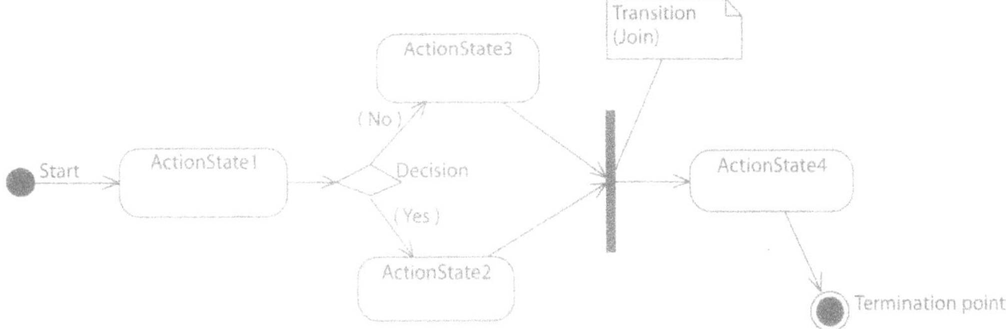

Figure 7.9 An activity diagram.

dynamic behaviour of the system can be represented. They are typically used for small operations. An activity diagram is presented in Figure 7.9. As you can see from this diagram, for a method of any complexity these diagrams would become extremely complex. Note that even if you use activity diagrams to represent the behaviour of an operation, you should still document the purpose and role of the operation explicitly.

7.6.7 Identifying Operations

When searching for the operations that an object should perform, you should look for:

- Operations implied by the responsibilities documented on analysis classes.
- Operations implied by the steps performed by the analysis discipline control classes (and where they should be located).
- Operations implied by events and particularly interactions with actors.
- Operations implied by interaction diagrams such as collaboration or sequence diagrams. The messages in these diagrams usually map onto operations.
- Transitions implied by statecharts (which we will consider below).
- Interfaces implemented by a class.
- Operations implied by state actions and activities (which are part of the statecharts for the object).
- Application or domain operations.
- Special requirements on analysis classes.

Each of these will be considered in more detail below.

Operations from Analysis Classes

There are actually three places to look for operations from the design classes. The first are the entity classes. During the analysis discipline, the entity classes should have been documented with their responsibilities. Some of these responsibilities may map onto data or information that the entity needs to hold; others may map onto the operations that the entity needs to provide. By examining these responsibilities an initial set of operations can be identified and located with the design classes which have evolved from the entity (note that this is a first cut and that the operations may be relocated at a later stage).

The second place to look for operations is within the control class itself. The steps performed by the control class (which should have been documented with the control class) will need to be mapped to operations in the design. These operations need to be located with the appropriate classes, and care needs to be taken with this. Consider the roles of each class and whether one or more operations fit with that role. Also consider the data that the class represents, and again ask whether the operation is related to that operation (remember that data and methods reside together in an object-oriented system).

The third place to consider in the analysis model is where the events are sent between the various entity classes. These may well map onto operations between design classes.

Operations Implied by Events

All the events in the object model correspond to operations (although a single operation may handle multiple events and vice versa). The old OMT method suggests that during analysis "events are best represented as labels on state transitions and should not be explicitly listed in the object model". However, if you find it clearer to list the operations corresponding to the events in the object model, then do so.

Operations Implied by State Actions and Activities

The actions and activities in the state diagrams correspond to operations. These can be listed in the corresponding classes in the object model.

Operations from Interaction Diagrams

Each message on a sequence or collaboration diagram usually corresponds to one or more operations. The messages should be organized into operations on objects. This is not as straightforward as it might at first seem, since a message may actually be an abstraction of a set of related operations.

Domain Operations

There may be additional domain operations that are not immediately obvious from the problem description. These should be identified from additional domain knowledge and noted. For example, although a cash dispenser (ATM) system does not allow you to open and close accounts, such operations are appropriate within the domain and may be important for understanding the domain or for aspects of the application which have yet to come to light.

Simplifying Operations

Examine the object model for operations that are essentially the same. Replace these operations with a generic one. Notice that earlier steps may well have generated the same operation but with different names. Check each object's operations to see whether they are intended to do the same thing even if they have very different names. Adjust the other models as appropriate.

7.6.8 Refining Operations

Once you have identified an initial set of operations you can begin to refine them. Once again the process of discovering operations and refining them is an iterative and incremental one. The things to consider when refining the operations include:

- Look for simplifying operations. For example, view the description associated with the operation. Does the operation attempt to fulfil more than one role? If so can it be broken down?
- Visibility of operations.
- Every operation should be traceable to a use case realization.
- Ensure that all roles played by the class are supported by the operations.
- All operations should be documented, with:
  - functionality performed, pre and post conditions
  - meaning of inputs, return value etc.
  - dependencies implied by parameters or return types.

7.7 Identifying Operations for the Online ATM System

To identify the operations in the online ATM System we can consider each of the points noted above.

7.7.1 Operations Implied by Events

There are a number of events (which are not considered elsewhere – e.g. in the functional model) which imply operations. For example, the closeAccount event identified in the last chapter is certainly an operation on a Customer, but one which may not have generated a functional model (because it is not a functional entity – it merely changes the state of the associated object).

7.7.2 Operations Implied by State Actions and Activities

It is quite possible that these will have been explored in the online ATM system functional model. However, if they have not, then they should be registered as operations. For example, the actions identified in the "registered" sub-state diagram may not have been included; however, they will be operations on the customer object. In particular, actions such as recordAccountAccess need to be registered as operations.

7.7.3 Application or Domain Operations

In the case of the online ATM, only a few application operations have been identified. These are operations such as being logged onto and off the system, which were not explicitly identified by the use case analysis but which are essential to the safe operating of the system.

7.7.4 Simplifying Operations

A couple of simplifying operations have been identified for the online ATM. These are operations such as newTransaction which are used in a similar manner to a constructor in Java (indeed, in the implementation they will probably be replaced by Java constructors).

7.7.5 The OBA Operations

The full set of operations produced by the analysis phase for each of the classes is presented in Table 7.4. You should add these operations to your evolving data dictionary and to your object model. In addition you should identify the parameters they accept, the values they return as well as their visibility. You should also identify which operations are class-side (or static) operations and which are instance operations. In the following we use $ to indicate a class-side operation, "+" to indicate a public operation and "–" to indicate a private operation (in line with the UML).

Note that many of the operations in Table 7.4 come from the complete analysis of the Online ATM, which has not been presented here due to lack of space. However, it is hoped that enough of the analysis has been presented to allow you to obtain a feeling for how the

Table 7.4 OBA operations.

Customer	Account
+checkAccountNo(accountNumber : int) : boolean +checkPIN(PIN : int) : boolean +requestBalance() : double +closeAccount() $setUpCustomer(name : String, accountNumber : int, PIN : int, initialBalance : double) +resetPIN(PIN : int) +deposit(trans : Transaction) +withdraw(trans : Transaction) +printStatement() +setBalance(amount : double) -recordAccountAccess()	+requestBalance() : double +addTransaction(trans : Transaction) +setBalance(newBalance : double)

Transaction	Direct Debit
+$newTransaction(type: String, amount : double)	+recordRecipient(name : String)

Statement	AccountSystem
+addTransaction(trans : Transaction) print()	+logon() +logoff() +checkBalance(accountNumber : int, PIN : int) : double -findAccount(accountNumber : int) : Customer +transaction(accountNumber : int, type : String, amount : int)

Employee	Clerk	Manager
+checkUser(name : String) : boolean		+checkSecurityCode(code : int) : boolean

process progresses. You should consult a variety of object-oriented design books as well as practising the design process yourself.

We should now return to our data dictionary and add the above operations. Note that we should examine the classes in the data dictionary to see if there are any attributes, implied by the operations, which are not present in the appropriate class. Having done this we should update the object model and examine the dynamic model to ensure that it is complete, repeating all design steps as appropriate.

7.8 Analyzing Use Cases

A parallel process, carried out during the identification of the classes and their operations, is the generation of the use case realizations. In this activity the use cases originally identified are "implemented" in terms of the design classes being defined (this is done with reference to the use case realizations produced in the analysis discipline).

7.8.1 Generating Design Classes from Use Cases

As was indicated earlier, the whole process being described in this chapter is far from sequential, and the act of identifying classes (and interfaces) is particularly incremental. One of the inputs to identifying classes will be analysis of the original use cases (and the analysis use case realizations). These will also contribute to finding an initial candidate set of classes as well as refining the set of classes as the design progresses. Remember that the whole unified process is incremental and iterative; we may therefore be attempting to identify the classes for a subsystem of the whole system which needs to fit into the architecture already in place as well as any other subsystems also in place). Thus there are many influences on the identification of a set of classes. Whether we are considering the first or last subsystem, for example, the set of use cases which describe the behaviour that affects that subsystem need to be considered.

The process of generating a set of design classes from the use cases is done by following these steps:

1. Look for classes in use cases:
    - by considering the analysis entity classes associated with the use case produced when generating the analysis model use case realizations
    - from the evolving design. As new classes are identified elsewhere in the design, they may be able to support the current use case.
2. Consider the implications of the use case for system interfaces. Do you need to implement any protocol handlers for specific protocols or legacy system APIs etc.? What effect will the use of these systems have on your design? What about other graphical user interfaces?
3. Examine control classes and consider where their functionality should be located – does this imply a new class?
4. If no existing class is found define a new one and add its definition to the data dictionary.
5. Consider any non-functional requirements which were associated with the use case or the analysis model use case realization.

It is necessary to consider how the design will handle these requirements, as they may affect your design. In some cases you may need to defer consideration of the non-functional requirements until the implementation discipline as it is an implementation issue. However, if you do this you need to make it very explicit.

7.8.2 Design Use Case Realizations

You should now consider the design equivalents of the use case realizations that you produced for the analysis discipline. These are necessary so that you can be sure that all use cases are supported by your design. You may start this process up front, but may not complete it until you have identified all the classes and interfaces in your design. Of course, the classes in your design model are influenced by the use cases and the use case realizations, so these processes are likely to be iterative, incremental and tightly coupled. The reality is therefore that you will explore classes and use case realizations iteratively and incrementally.

The use case realizations therefore relate the design classes and functionality of the system as expressed by the use case model. Design use case realizations are made up of:

- A textual flow of events description.
- Class diagrams depicting the interacting classes from the viewpoint of the use case. These class diagrams may only list those class elements that are relevant to the use case.
- Interaction diagrams (you may find it necessary to include collaboration diagrams at this point as well as sequence diagrams). The Unified Process does not see collaboration diagrams as being particularly useful in the design discipline, however, personal experience suggests that seeing the messages and the objects and their relationships in a collaboration diagram can be as useful in the design discipline as it is in the analysis discipline.
- The subsystems and system interfaces involved in use cases.

You may also wish to document any non-functional requirements which are either annotated on the use cases or analysis realizations or that are identified during the generation of the design use case realizations. It is also useful to include a list of implementation issues which should be dealt with during the implementation discipline.

7.9 Identifying Dynamic Behaviour

The dynamic behaviour of the system and the classes in the design model is very important. In the analysis model we hid most of this by specifying control classes, which were expected to handle most of the operation of the system, leaving us to work with simple user interface (boundary) and data (entity) objects. Although this was useful for expressing the key data and interfaces in the system, but is not really very object-oriented. Normally, in an object-oriented system the behaviour of the system is distributed among the classes that comprise that system. We therefore need to identify where this behaviour should be and what the classes should do. This is the job of the dynamic elements of the design model. There are two key diagramming techniques that support this in the design discipline (plus the collaboration diagrams from the analysis discipline that are augmented with additional design information). The two techniques are sequence diagrams and statecharts. Sequence diagrams capture the interactions between the objects and (optionally) the focus of control and lifetime of the objects, whereas statecharts capture the state-based behaviour of classes and subsystems.

7.9.1 Design Collaboration Diagrams

As described in the previous chapter, collaboration diagrams illustrate the sequence of messages between objects based around the object structure (rather than the temporal aspects of sequence diagrams). A collaboration diagram is formed from the objects involved in the collaboration, the links (permanent or temporary) between the objects and the messages (numbered in sequence) that are exchanged between the objects. Design-oriented collaboration diagrams can include far more information than their analysis counterparts. An example design collaboration diagram is presented in Figure 7.10.

The label *new* before the object name (e.g. the Line object in Figure 7.10) indicates objects that are created during the collaboration. Links between objects are annotated to indicate their type, permanent or temporary, existing for this particular collaboration. These annotations are placed in boxes on the ends of the links and can have the following values:

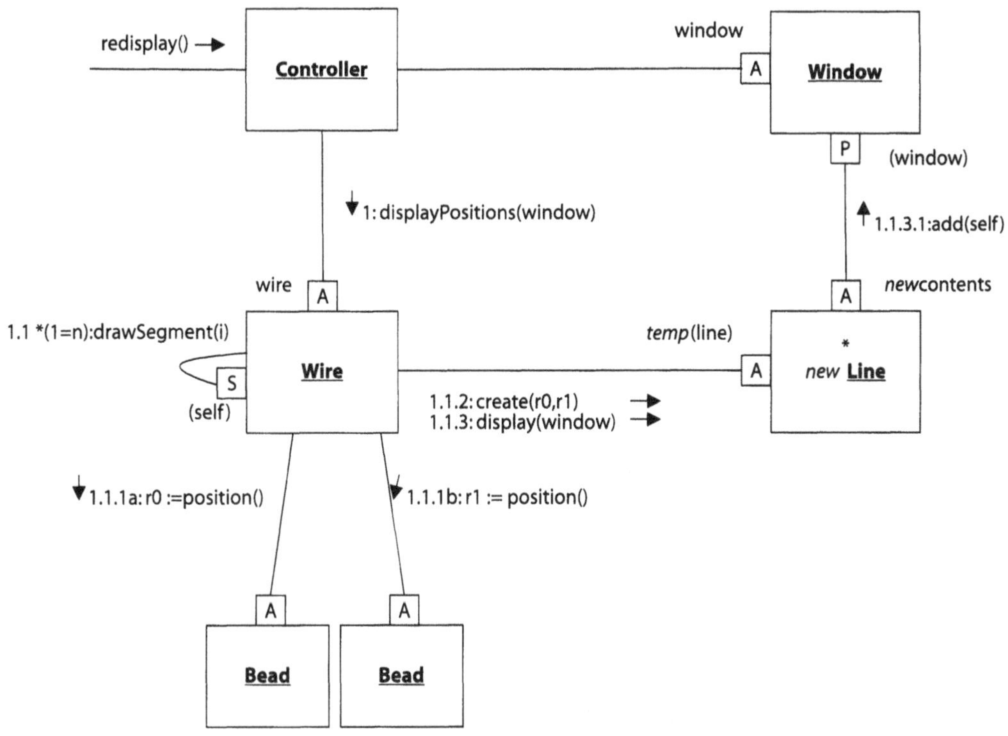

Figure 7.10 An example collaboration diagram.

A   Association (or permanent) link
F   Object field (the target object is part of the source object)
G   Global variable
L   Local variable
P   Procedure parameter
S   Self (this in Java) reference

You can add role names to distinguish links (e.g. self, wire and window in Figure 7.10). Role names in brackets indicate a temporary link, i.e. one that is not an association.

Labels next to the links indicate the messages that are sent along links. One or more messages can be sent along a link in either or both directions. The format of the messages is defined by the following (some of which are optional):

1. *A comma-separated list of sequence numbers in brackets, e.g. [seqno, seqno]* which indicate messages from other threads of control that must occur before the current message. This element is only needed with concurrency.

2. *A list of sequence elements separated by full stops,* "", which represent the nested procedural calling sequence of the message in the overall transaction. Each element has the following parts:
   - A letter (or name) indicating a concurrent thread. All letters at the same level of nesting represent threads that execute concurrently, i.e. 1.2a and 1.2b are concurrent. If there is no letter, it usually indicates the main sequence.
   - An integer showing the sequential position of the current message within its thread. For example, message 2.1.4 is part of the procedure invoked by message 2.1 and follows message 2.1.3 within that procedure.
   - An iteration indicator (*), optionally followed by an iteration expression in parentheses, which indicates that several messages of the same form are sent either sequentially (to a single target) or concurrently (to the elements of a set). If there is an iteration expression, it shows the values that the iterator assumes, such as "(i=1..n)"; otherwise, the details of the iteration must be specified in text or simply deferred to the code.
   - A conditional indicator (?), optionally followed by a Boolean expression in parentheses. The iteration and conditional indicators are mutually exclusive.

3. *A return value name followed by an assignment sign,* ":=", which indicates that the procedure returns a value designated by the given name. The use of the same name elsewhere in the diagram designates the same value. If no return value is specified, then the procedure operates by side effects.

4. *The name of the message* which is an event or operation name. It is unnecessary to specify the class of an operation since this is implicit in the target object.

5. *The argument list of the message* which is made up of expressions defined in terms of input values of the nesting procedure, local return values of other procedures and attribute values of the object sending the message.

You may show argument values and return values for messages graphically using small data flow tokens near a message. Each token is a small circle, with an arrow showing the direction of the data flow, labelled with the name of the argument or result.

7.9.2 Sequence Diagrams

Sequence diagrams are used to describe the effect of use cases on the design model elements (in design-oriented use case realizations) and for describing the interactions between objects within a subsystem in response to external interactions (which will have been originated by an event on a use case).

They capture the sequence (ordering) of events between the participating objects. Optionally they can take into account the amount of time an event takes to be processed and the focus of control (i.e. which objects have the focus of control at any one time – remember that this may be a distributed system utilizing multiple processors).

Depending on the level being represented the sequence diagrams may represent objects or subsystems or a combination of the two. If the sequence diagram represents a use case, then the originating actor may be included on the diagram.

The information passed between the sequence diagrams is in the form of messages, although they may be abstracted into events. However, events can have parameters and return values and as we are now dealing with the design model we may well wish to include this information on the sequence diagram.

7.9.3 Preparation of Sequence Diagrams

An analysis-oriented use case realization shows a particular series of interactions among analysis objects in a single execution of a system. That is, it is a history of how the system behaves between one start state and a single termination state. This differs from an envisionment, which describes all system behaviours from all start states to all end states. Envisionments thus contain all possible histories (although they may also contain paths that the system is never intended to take).

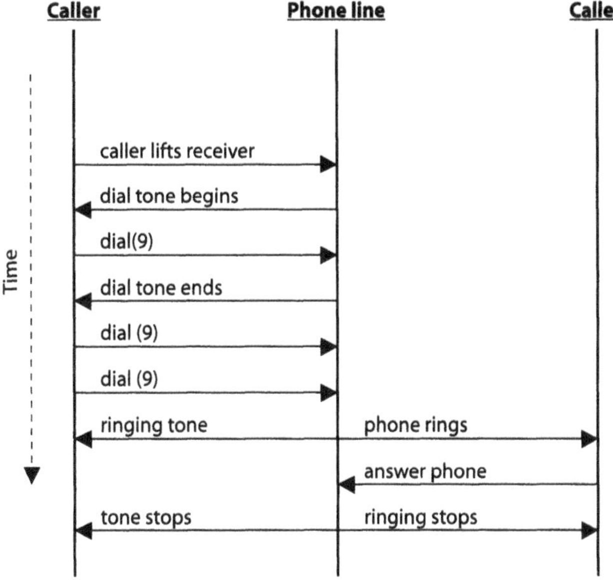

Figure 7.11 A sequence diagram.

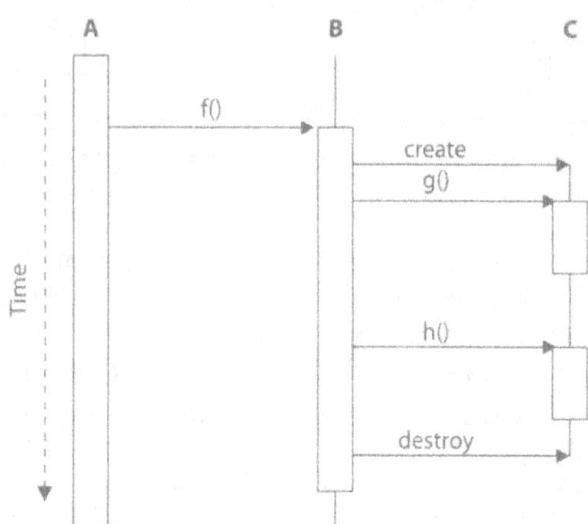

Figure 7.12 Sequence diagram with focus-of-control regions.

Sequence diagrams are another way of presenting the interactions that occur between classes. They take into account temporal ordering and (optional) focus of control issues, whereas the collaboration diagrams used in a use case realization focus on the messages and the objects which send the messages.

Figure 7.11 illustrates the basic structure of a sequence diagram. The objects involved in the exchange of messages are represented as vertical lines (which are labelled with the object's name). Caller, Phone Line and Callee are all objects involved in the scenario of

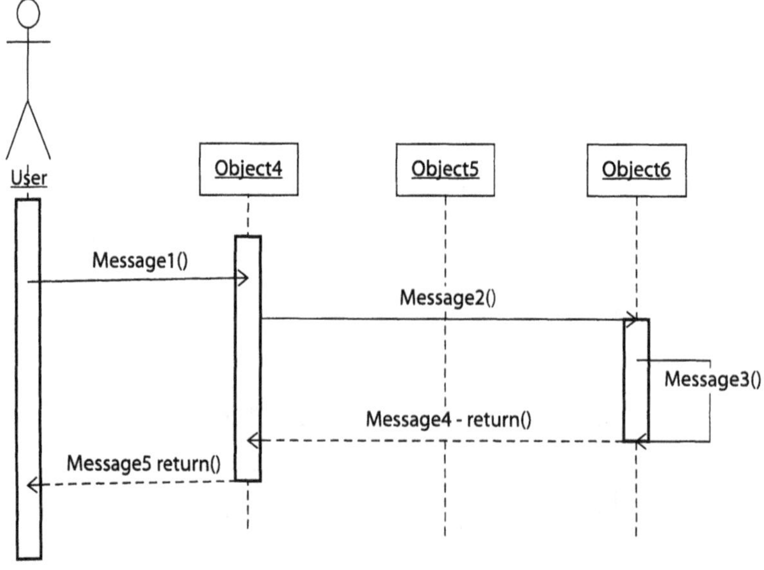

Figure 7.13 A sequence diagram for a use case.

dialling the emergency services. The horizontal arrows indicate an event or message sent from one object to another. The arrow indicates the direction in which the event or message is sent; that is, the receiver is indicated by the head of the arrow. Normally return values are not shown on these diagrams. However, if they are significant you can illustrate them by annotated return events.

Time proceeds vertically down the diagram, as indicated by the broken line arrow, and can be made more explicit by additional timing marks. These timing marks indicate how long the gap between messages should be or how long a message or event should take to get from the sender to the receiver.

A variation of the basic sequence diagram (called a focus-of-control diagram) illustrates which object has the thread of control at any one time. A fatter line shows this during the period when the object has control (see Figure 7.12). Notice that the bar representing the object C only starts when it is created and terminates when it is destroyed.

As was mentioned earlier a sequence diagram for a use case may include the actor which initiates the use case and the "boundary" object which the actor interacts with (note here we do not mean a boundary analysis class!). This is illustrated in Figure 7.13.

7.9.4 Dealing with Complexity in Sequence Diagrams

It is very easy to make your sequence diagrams too complex and to end up with diagrams which are almost meaningless to anyone but yourself (and you may not find them so clear at a later date). You should therefore aim to keep your sequence diagrams simple. Try to illustrate only one interaction per sequence diagram. If your interaction needs to have branches in it, either clearly annotate the branch (there is no easy way of indicating a branch on a sequence diagram) or define a separate sequence diagram if this will be clearer. Note that with this second option you will still need to document the fact that the sequence diagrams are related, and annotation on the actual diagrams may well be the best way of doing this. You should aim to ensure that the reader of your sequence diagram has no trouble in identifying the objects, the functionality presented, and the interactions and messages sent.

7.9.5 Generating a Sequence Diagram

There are a variety of ways in which you could generate a sequence diagram, the following presents a series of steps which can act as a guideline relating to how to do this:

- Identify all the classes involved in a particular sequence. You may notice that this statement assumes that all the classes are already defined; however, as with much of the design process this is really an iterative process in which, as the classes become clearer, so the sequence diagrams may evolve.
- Determine the life line of the objects, that is when they are created and when they are destroyed. If the sequence diagram creates or destroys the object then you will need to make this clear.
- Identify the initiating event (you should look to the use cases for this).
- Determine the subsequent message(s). What does the "boundary" object do when the actor initiates the event? Then consider the behaviour of the receiving object and what messages it might send etc.

- Identify the focus of control for the object.
- Identify any returned messages (returned values).
- Identify any deviations (either annotate them on the sequence diagram or generate separate sequence diagrams for each deviation).

7.9.6 Sequence Diagrams for the Online Bank Account System

As suggested above, we will start by looking at a use case in order to produce a sequence diagram for the online bank account system. We shall use the results of the use case analysis as the basis of the scenarios and the events. To illustrate this we will consider the "Check Balance" use case. The basic course for this use case is presented below:

1.   Typing in the account number
2.   Typing in the PIN
3.   Requesting the current balance of the account (this may be on screen or a printout)
4.   Receiving the balance

The users' actions will be used as the initiating events. These events must be sent somewhere and the most logical place for them to be received is the Account System object. Having identified these events it is then necessary to identify the events triggered by these initial events and the receiving object. In this case the identification of subsequent events is fairly straightforward. For example, if the Cashier needs to find out what balance a particular account holder current has, then they need to enter the customers account number, this number needs to be checked against those account numbers currently on the system. Checking each Customer object until the correct Customer object is identified does this. In Figure 7.14, this is indicated by the condition and the iteration symbol "*" on the event. Once the correct customer is identified, the account object is requested to provide the current balance, which is returned to the customer object then to the user interface object and finally back to the Cashier.

Sequence diagrams should be produced for all use cases and for each course defined by the use case. Once this has been done, collaboration diagrams can be generated.

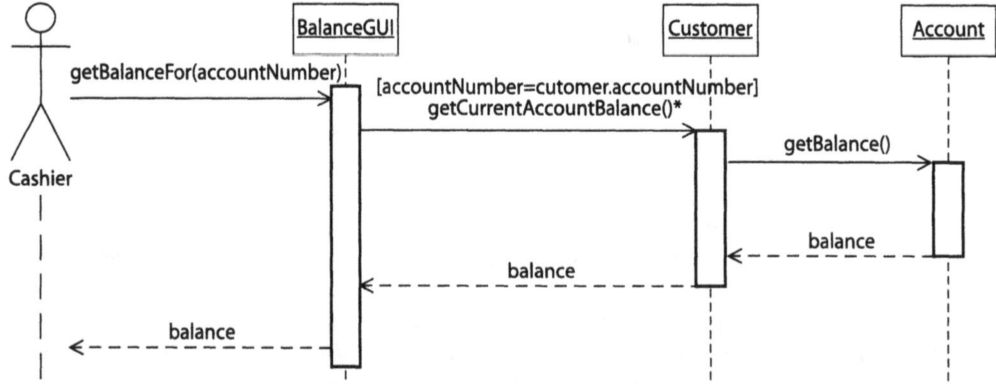

Figure 7.14 Sequence diagram for checking a balance.

7.9.7 Describing an Object's Behaviour

The process of describing the behaviour of an object can be done at the method or at the whole object level. In many cases, if you describe the operation of a single method in isolation (for example, using an activity diagram) you do fail to capture the interactions between the state of the system and the method(s) involved. Thus statecharts have been developed to try to describe how methods and the state of the object interact. Essentially, a statechart describes all the states of the object and how the methods cause the state transitions. Note that the state of the object is a combination of the values (states) of the attributes (instance variables) of the object.

7.10 Statechart Diagrams

Collaboration diagrams and sequence diagrams are used to help understand how the objects within the system collaborate, whereas state diagrams illustrate how these objects behave internally. State diagrams relate events to state transitions and states. The transitions change the state of the system and are triggered by events. The notation used to document state diagrams is based on *statecharts*, developed by Harel (Harel *et al.*, 1987; Harel 1988).

Statecharts are a variant of the finite state machine formalism, which reduces the apparent complexity of a graphical representation of a finite state machine. This is accomplished through the addition of a simple graphical representation of certain common patterns of finite state machine usage. As a result, a complex sub-graph in a "basic" finite state machine is replaced by a single graphical construct.

Statecharts are referred to as state diagrams in UML. Each state diagram has a start point at which the state is entered and may have an exit point at which the state is terminated. The state may also contain concurrency and synchronization of concurrent activities.

Figure 7.15 illustrates a typical state diagram. This state diagram describes a simplified remote control locking system. The chart indicates that the system first checks the identification code of the handheld transmitter. If it is the same as that held in the memory, it allows the car to be locked or unlocked. When the car is locked, the windows are also closed and the car is alarmed.

A state diagram consists of a start point, events, a set of transitions, a set of variables, a set of states and a set of exit points.

7.10.1 Start Points

A start point is the point at which the state diagram is initialized. In the figure, there are four start points indicated (`Start`, `lock`, `close` and `unlock`). The `Start` start point is the initial entry point for the whole diagram, while the other start points are for substate diagrams.

Any preconditions required by the state diagram can be specified on the transition from the start point (for example, the `transmittedID` must be the same as the `memoryID`). It is the initial transition from which all other transitions emanate. This transition is automatically taken when the state diagram is executed. Notice that the initial `Start` point is not equivalent to a state.

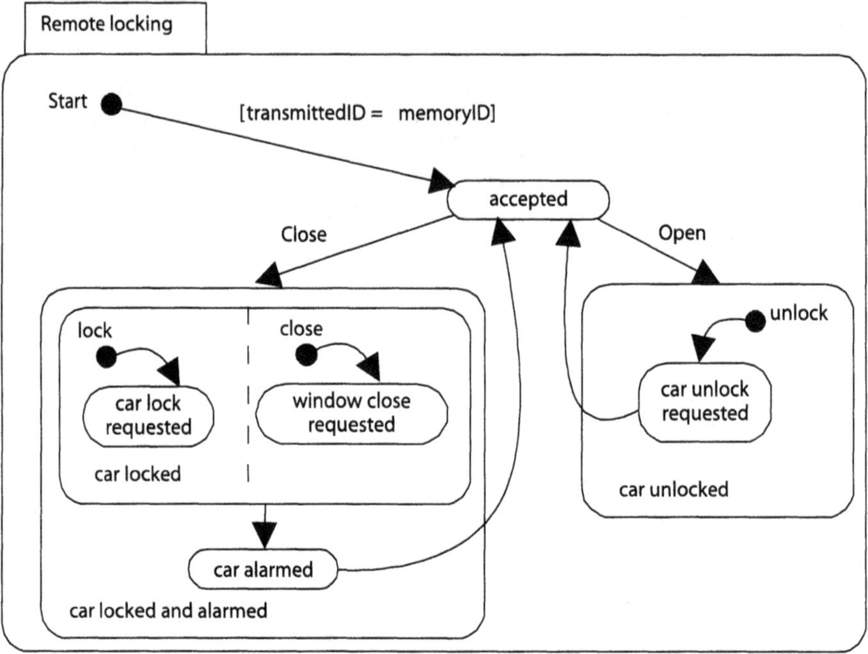

Figure 7.15 An example statechart diagram.

7.10.2 Events

Events are one-way asynchronous transmissions of information from one object to another. The general format of an event is as follows:

```
eventName (parameter:type, ...)
```

Of course, many events do not have any associated parameters.

7.10.3 A Set of Transitions

These are the statements that move the system from one state to another. In a state diagram, each transition is formed of four (optional) parts:

1. An event (e.g. `lock`) which can have parameters.
2. A condition (e.g. `transmittedID = memoryID`).
3. The initiated event (e.g. `^EngineManagementUnit.locked`), which can also possess parameters.
4. An operation (e.g. `/setDoorToLock`).

The event is what triggers the transition; however, the transition only occurs if the condition is met. If the event occurs and the conditions are met, then the associated operation is performed.

An operation is a segment of code (equivalent to a statement or program or method) which causes the system state to be altered. Some transitions can also trigger an event that should be sent to a specified object. The above example sends an event *locked* to the *EngineManagementUnit*. The process of sending a global event is a special case of sending an event to a specified object. The syntax of an event is as follows:

```
event(arguments) [condition]
    ^target.sendEvent(arguments) /operation(arguments)
```

7.10.4 A Set of State Variables

These are variables referred to in a state diagram, for example, memory ID. They have the following format:

```
name: type = value
```

7.10.5 A Set of States

A state represents a period of time during which an object is waiting for an event to occur. It is an abstraction of the attribute values and links of an object. A state is drawn as a rounded box containing the (optional) name of the state. A state may often be composed of other states (the combination of which represents the higher level state). A state has a duration; that is, it occupies an interval of time.

A state box can contain two additional sections: a list of state variables and a list of triggered operations (see Figure 7.16).

An operation can be of the following types:

- *Entry* operations are executed when the state is entered. They are the same as specifying an operation on a transition. They are useful if all transitions into a state perform the same operation (rather than specifying the same operation on each transition). Such operations are considered to be instantaneous.
- *Exit* operations are executed when the state is exited. They are less common than entry actions and indicate an operation performed before any transition from the state.
- *Do* operations are executed while the state is active. They start on entry to the state and terminate when the state is exited.

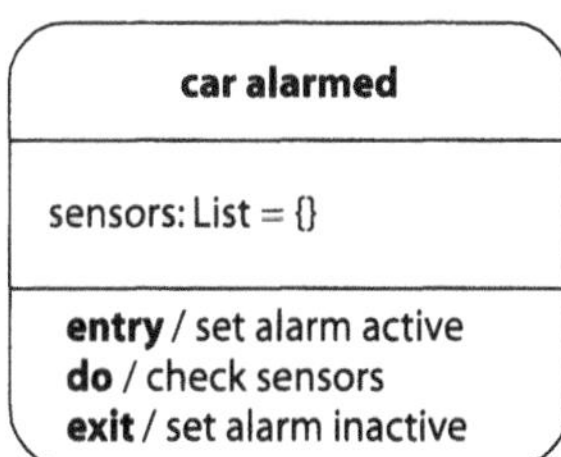

Figure 7.16 State box with state variables and triggered operations.

- *Events* can trigger operations while within a particular state. For example, the event *help* could trigger the *help* operation while in the state *active*.

Each operation is separated from its type by a forward slash ("/"). The ordering of operations is:

1. Operations on incoming transitions
2. Entry operations
3. Do operations
4. Exit operations
5. Operations on outgoing transitions

State diagrams allow a state to be a single state variable or a set of substates. This allows for complex hierarchical models to be developed gradually as a series of nested behaviour patterns. This means that a state can be a state diagram in its own right. For example, *car alarmed* is a single state and *car locked* is another state diagram. Notice that the transition from *car alarmed* to *accepted* jumps from an inner state to an outer state.

The broken line down the middle of the *car locked* state indicates that the two halves of that state run concurrently. That is, the car is locked as the windows are closed.

A special type of state, called a history state, represents a state which must be remembered and used the next time the (outer) state is entered. The symbol for a history state is an H in a circle.

7.10.6 A Set of Exit Points

Exit points specify the result of the state diagram. They also terminate the execution of the state diagram.

7.10.7 Building a Statechart Diagram

You should construct a state diagram for each object class with non-trivial dynamic behaviour. Every sequence diagram (and thus collaboration diagram) corresponds to a path through a state diagram. Each branch in control flow is represented by a state with more than one exit transition. The procedure for producing state diagrams, as described by the OMT method (which still holds for the Unified Process), is summarized below by the following algorithm:

1. Pick a class.
2. Pick one sequence diagram involving that class.
3. Follow the events for the class; the gaps between the events are states. Give each state a name (if it is meaningful to do so).
4. Draw a set of states and the events that link them based on the sequence diagrams.
5. Find loops, repeated sequences of states, within the diagram.
6. Choose another sequence diagram for the class and produce the states and events for that diagram. Merge these states and events into the first diagram. That is, find the states and events that are the same and find where they diverge. Now add the new events and states.

7. Repeat Step 6 for all sequence diagrams involving this class.
8. Repeat from Step 1 for all classes.

After considering all normal events, add boundary cases and special cases. Also consider events which occur at awkward times, including error events.

You should now consider any conditions on the transitions between states and any events that are triggered by these transitions. Notice that we still have not really considered the system's operations.

Matching Events Between Objects

Having produced the state diagrams, you should now check for completeness and consistency across the whole system. Every event should have a sender and a receiver, all states should have a predecessor and a successor (even if they are start points or exit points) and every use case should have at least one state diagram which explains its effect on the system's behaviour. You should also make sure that events that are the same on different statecharts have the same name.

An Example State Diagram

In this section we follow the guidelines presented above. Therefore we select a class, in this case a class Customer. We then pick a sequence diagram and identify the required states and transitions. For example, if we select the Check Balance sequence diagram then we can see that that:

1. The customer must be in a state that allows the user to check the balance. We shall call this state "registered" (Figure 7.17).
2. Although there is a lot of interaction with the customer object, none of that interaction changes the state of that customer (although the state registered may be expended to represent states such as "Account Number Accepted", "PIN Accepted", "Balance Provided" etc. See Figure 7.18 for an example of this).
3. Part of the "check balance sequence diagram" results in the Customer object sending an event to the Account object. This must therefore be reflected in the state diagram.

Figure 7.19 illustrates the state of the state diagram at this point. As can be seen it captures the information identified above, but does not take into account any other events or states implied by any other sequence diagrams – this is quite normal.

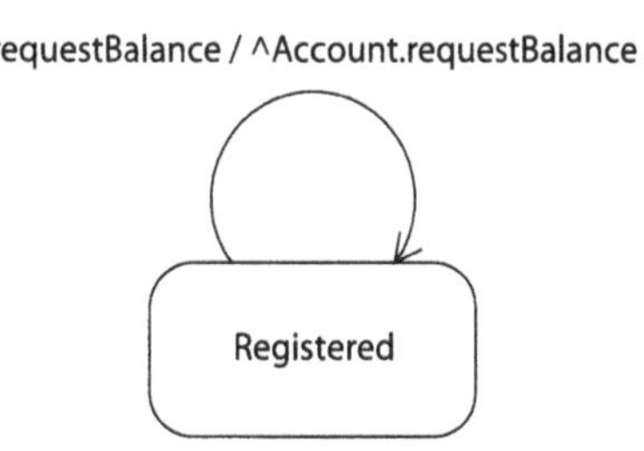

Figure 7.17 A partial state diagram.

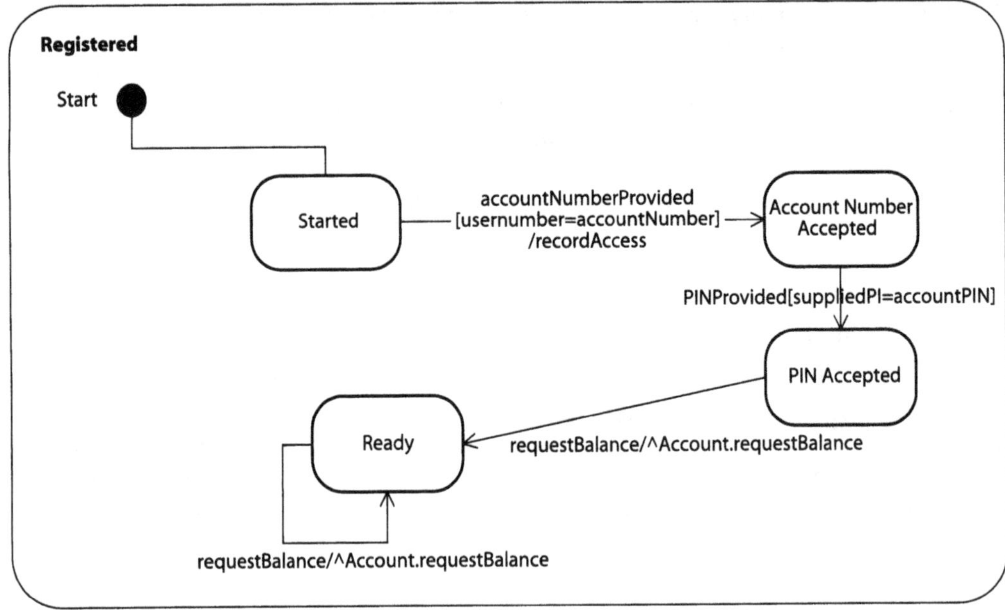

Figure 7.18 A state diagram for the "Registered" state.

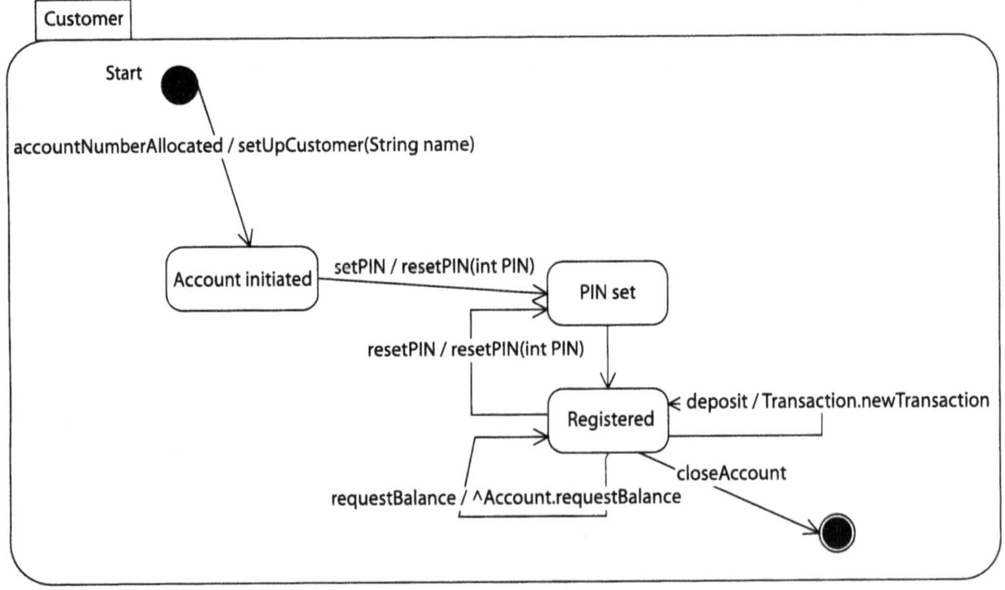

Figure 7.19 The customer state diagram.

We are now ready to consider another sequence diagram. Essentially we need to repeat the above steps, attempting to identify any duplicate states or transitions. The results should then be merged with the evolving state chart. The result for the Customer object is illustrated in Figure 7.19. As you can see, this is a far more complex state diagram and has introduced a number of states indicated by sequence diagrams derived from use cases with alternative courses (such as being overdrawn).

As a comparison we present below the statechart for the Accounts System itself (see Figure 7.20). This statechart indicates the states that the overall system can be in. These states are primarily derived from the use case analysis. For example, a user logs onto and off the system. Additional states were identified from the analysis of the object model. This shows that at some point it is necessary to obtain the employees and customers associated with the Accounts System (i.e. they are objects referenced by the Accounts System object but which are likely to be persistent – i.e. held in a database or on file). It is therefore necessary to identify the acquisition of this data as a specific system state (how the data is actually stored will be considered later in the design process). Also note that once a user is logged on there are three events which do not cause a change of state and thus return the user to the logged on state.

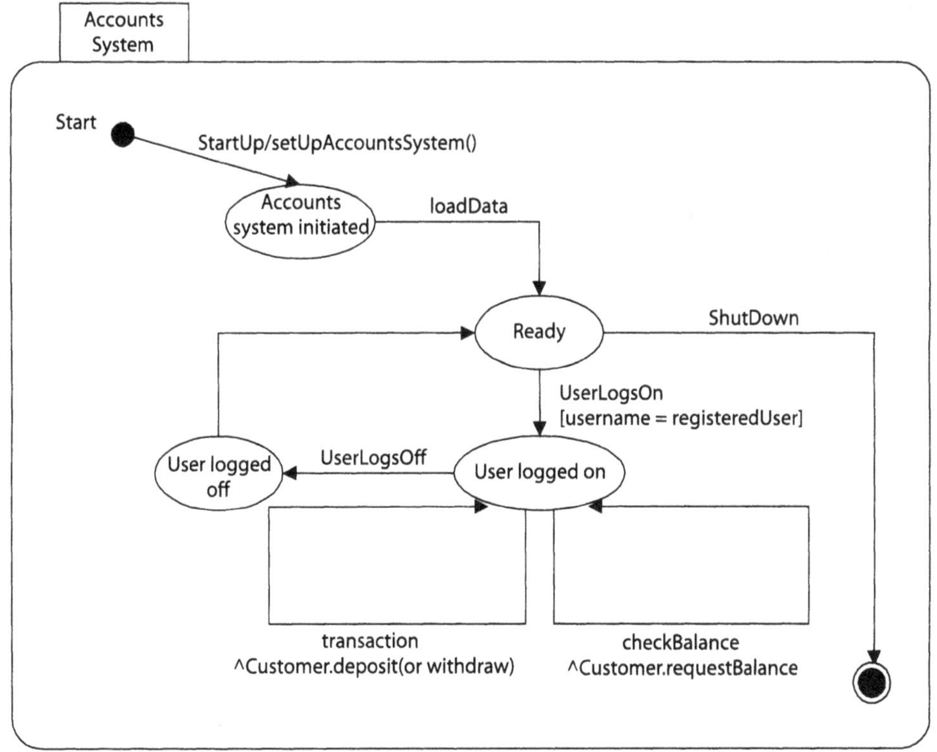

Figure 7.20 The Online Bank Accounts System state diagram.

7.11　Associations

7.11.1　Representing Associations

Just as in the analysis discipline an association is drawn as a solid line (see Figure 7.21); however, the association can now be annotated with a name, the ends can be given roles etc. A design association between classes may have a name and an optional direction arrowhead that shows which way it is to be read. For example, in Figure 7.21, the relationship called hasEngine is read from the Car class to the Engine class. In addition, each end of an association is a *role*. A role may have a name that illustrates how its class is viewed by the other class. In Figure 7.21, the engine sees the car as a name and the car sees the engine as a specified type (e.g. Petrol, Diesel, Electric, etc.).

Figure 7.21　Association between classes and links between objects.

Each role (i.e. each end of the association) indicates the multiplicity of its class, which is how many instances of the class can be associated with one instance of the other class. This is indicated by a text expression on the role: * (indicating zero or more), a number or a range (e.g. 0..3). If there is no expression, there is exactly one association (see Figure 7.22). You can specify that the multiple objects should be ordered using the text {Ordered}. You can also annotate the association with additional text (such as {Sorted}), but this is primarily for the reader's benefit and has no meaning in UML.

In some situations, an association needs attributes. This means that you need to treat the association as a class (see Figure 7.23) These associations have a dashed line from the association line to the association class. This class is just like any other class and can have a name, attributes and operations. In Figure 7.23, the associations show an access permissions attribute which indicates the type of access allowed for each user for each file.

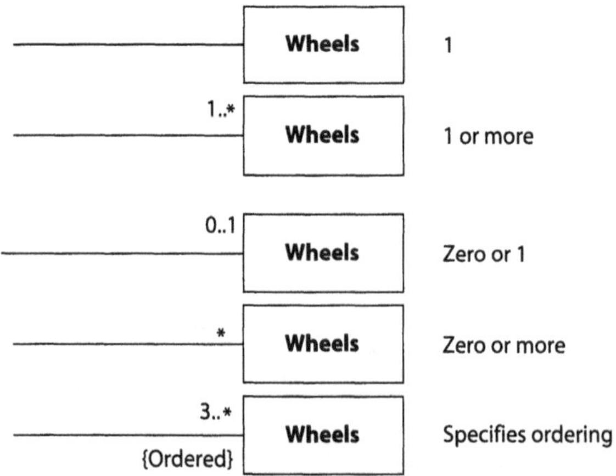

Figure 7.22　Annotated associations.

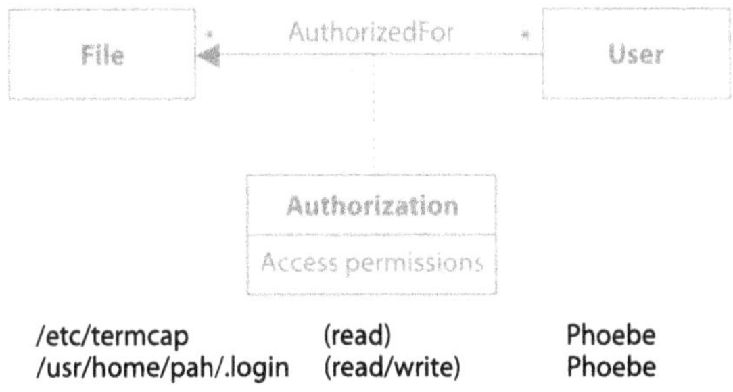

Figure 7.23 Associations with attributes.

Aggregation indicates that one or more objects are dependent on another object for their existence (*part-whole* relationships). For example, in Figure 7.24, the microcomputer is formed from the Monitor, the System box, the Mouse and the Keyboard. They are all needed for the fully functioning microcomputer. An empty diamond shows aggregation on the role attached to the whole object.

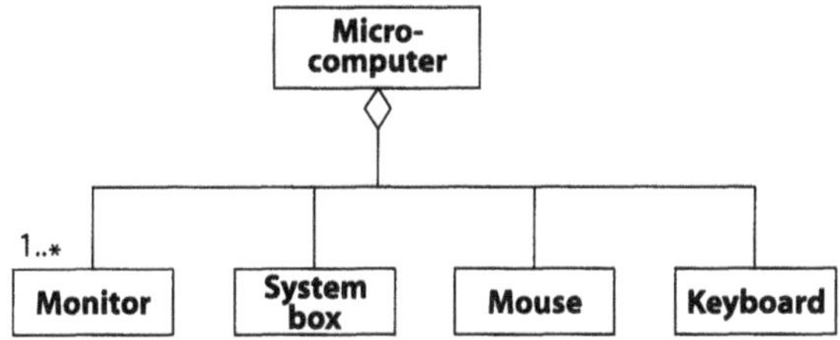

Figure 7.24 Aggregation tree notation.

It is sometimes useful to differentiate between a reference and a part of relationship (see Figure 7.25). If the aggregation symbol is not filled, it indicates a by-reference implementation (i.e. a pointer or other reference); if the aggregation symbol is filled, it indicates a direct part of implementation (i.e. a class that is embedded within another class). The latter can be implemented in Java using inner classes, although this does limit future reusability of that class.

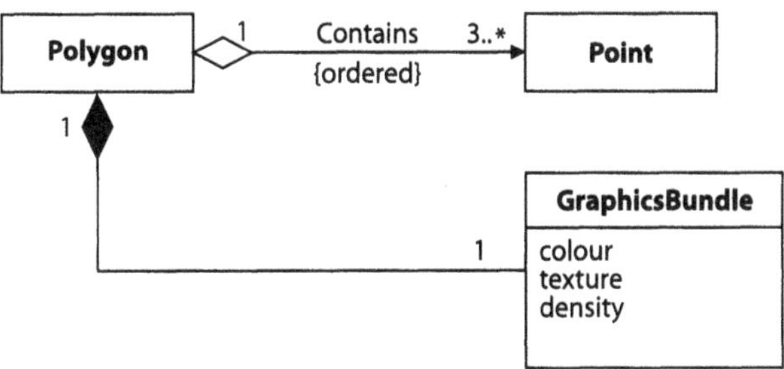

Figure 7.25 Aggregation links.

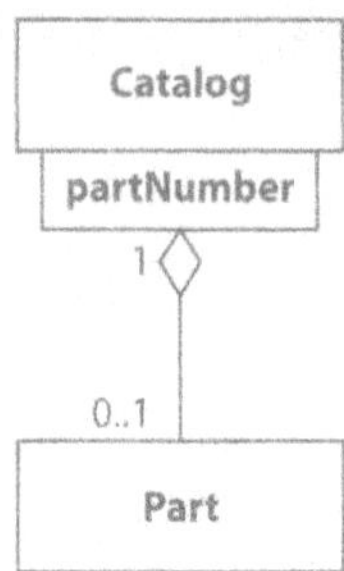

Figure 7.26 Qualified associations.

A qualified association is an association that requires both the object and the qualifier to identify uniquely the other object involved in the association. It is shown as a box between the association and the class. For example, in Figure 7.26 you need the catalog and the part number to identify a unique part. Notice that the qualifier is part of the association, not the class.

A ternary (or higher order) association is drawn as a diamond with one line path to each of the participating classes (see Figure 7.27). This is the traditional entity–relationship model symbol for an association (the diamond is omitted from the binary association to save space). Ternary associations are very rare and higher order associations are almost non-existent. However, you can model them if necessary.

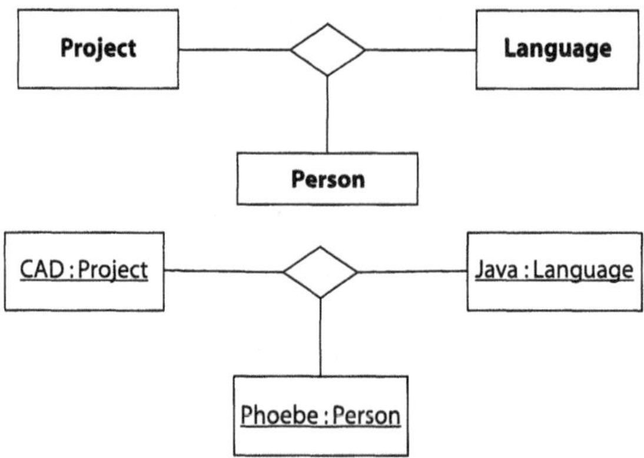

Figure 7.27 Ternary associations.

7.11.2 Identifying Associations

We have already touched on this briefly; that is, when considering the classes in the analysis discipline we needed to consider the associations between classes. Also, by the very fact that we have been exploring the classes in the design, it will have been necessary to consider which classes *collaborate* with other classes. These collaborations represent associations, whether they are permanent associations (for example, as represented by an instance variable in one class referencing another class) or temporary associations (as represented by objects being passed into methods). As this suggests, the identification of the associations between the classes is closely tied up with actually identifying the classes, and techniques such as CRC can be very helpful in starting this process off. Thus, once again, the actual design process is very incremental and iterative and far from being as sequential as the ordering of the topics in this chapter suggests.

Where then do you look for potential associations? There are actually numerous places in the evolving design which can suggest associations. The following list summarizes these places.

- *Look at the analysis entity class associations.* This will highlight associations between the important concepts in the design. Exactly how these concepts have been translated into the design may vary, but there is still likely to need to be some form of relationship between the design versions of these concepts.
- *Look at messages in interaction diagrams.* Every time an event or operation is sent between two objects in an interaction diagram there needs to be an association place. If one does not exist then the objects involved cannot communicate. However, be wary of merely adding the associations automatically; some of the associations may well be transient, and thus will not need to be made into permanent associations.
- *Look at the use of interfaces.* If one class implements an interface and another class uses that same interface, then there is an implied association between the two. Is this association in fact used? How should it be documented? etc.
- *Look at access paths.* Make sure that any collaborations which are required to support all use cases are supported by appropriate associations. Thus if the accomplishment of one use case requires three particular classes to work together, then it is likely that there needs to be a set of associations between those three classes.
- *Consider association multiplicity, role names, association classes, ordering etc.* The more information you can identify during the design phase, the less likely it is that the implementors will misinterpret what you mean in terms of the associations. Remember: although the UML directly supports concepts such as multiplicity, ordered and sorted associations, association attributes, and qualified associations, the Java programmer will have to map all of these into Java in some way (see Chapter 13 for a more detailed discussion of this).
- *Consider whether association is aggregation (inner class).*

7.11.3 Refining Associations

Having identified an initial set of associations, it is still necessary to refine them. Indeed, it is likely that you will continue to refine, add to, modify and generally evolve the associations in your design throughout the design process. Some of the questions to consider when refining your associations include:

- Is the association between eliminated classes?
- Are any of the associations irrelevant or implementation associations?
- Are any associations transient? That is, are they really representing a short-term link between two objects as represented by parameters to a method? These should only occur in interaction diagrams, or class diagrams which represent a particular moment in time.
- Are any of the associations ternary? You should try to break all ternary associations down into their constituent parts (it's easier to implement them then).

- Are any of the associations derivable?
- Refine the navigability of the associations.
- Are there any missing associations?
- Attempt to minimize associations

Having removed inappropriate associations, you can now consider the semantics of the associations you have left:

- *Are any of the associations misnamed?* Associations should reflect what they represent. They should be named after their use or the relationship they indicate.
- *Add role names where appropriate.* Role names describe the role that a class plays in the associations from the point of view of the other class.
- *Are there any qualified associations?* That is, are there any associations that require a qualifier to identify a unique object?
- *Specify multiplicity on the associations?* That is, indicate how may objects are involved in the association. By default all associations are 1-to-1 associations. Where no multiplicity is specified, check that they really are 1-to-1 links.

7.12 Identifying Interfaces

We have already indicated how important interfaces are within a Java system. As UML provides an interface stereotype you should attempt to identify as many interfaces as possible to increase the loosely coupled nature of code, while still retaining high cohesion. That is, one class is not directly dependent on another class if they both refer to an interface, but we are guaranteed that they will work together at compile time (by the interface). Places to look for interfaces include:

- Interfaces between subsystems, as these are considered architecturally significant.
- Dependencies between:
    - classes
    - classes and subsystems
    - subsystems and subsystems.
- Dependencies between layers

In each case, consider the behaviour being presented and the operations being used and group these operations into logical units. If all the operations are part of the same unit, then this implies a single interface. If there are multiple units, then define multiple interfaces. This allows different parts of the system to treat the element under consideration in different ways. It also allows only one interface to change, thereby not affecting any system elements which rely on the other interfaces.

Also remember that in Java interfaces can inherit from other interfaces. Thus if you find that you have forgotten some operations at a later date, rather than modifying an interface which is already in use (and has possibly been implemented and tested) you can merely extend the interface and use the new interface where you need the extra operation.

7.13 Identifying Inheritance

Inheritance is the one thing which really makes object-oriented systems stand apart from other systems. Many systems have concepts such as encapsulation, but inheritance is unique. As your design is evolving you should try to identify any natural inheritance in it. But be careful, remember that you inherit all the features of the parent class, whether you want them or not. Thus a subclass of the `java.util` class `ArrayList`, which only holds `Strings`, may make sense, but a subclass which implements a queue may not. This is because the `Queue` subclass inherits all the methods from the `ArrayList` class, which include add, but also `set(int index, Object obj)`, `get(int index)` and `removeRange(int fromIndex, int toIndex)`, all of which may or may not be appropriate for a queue (and probably are not). Thus for a queue I would use a component-based approach, in which my `Queue` object held an `ArrayList`, and only made available methods such as `add(Object obj)`, `get()` and `isEmpty()`. This is discussed in more detail in Chapter 16.

Places to look for inheritance include:

- Common operations and attributes between classes (generalization).
- Special cases of classes (specialization).
- Functionality provided by Java classes (e.g. `JFrame`, `RemoteInterface`).
- Common associations and dependencies – may imply a package.
- Move functionality and attributes up the hierarchy as high as possible.

7.14 Remaining Steps

7.14.1 Optimizing the Design

The analysis model only described the application and its requirements, and did not attempt to take into account efficient access to information or processing. You must consider the following issues:

- Adding redundant associations to minimize access cost and maximize convenience.
- Rearranging the computation for greater efficiency.
- Saving derived attributes to avoid recalculation of complicated expressions.

You may also wish to start to identify attributes which were not part of the analysis model but which will be needed for the implementation. Do not go as far as specifying implementation detail attributes (these should be left to the implementation phase).

7.14.2 Testing Access Paths

This step involves checking that paths in the model make sense, are sufficient and are necessary. It is often suggested that you trace access paths through the object model to see if they yield sensible results. You may wish to consider the following issues:

- Where a unique value is expected, is there a path yielding a unique result?
- For multiplicity, is there a way to pick out a unique value when needed?

Are there any useful (domain-specific or application-specific) questions that cannot be answered?

7.14.3 Implementing Control

During the system design, an approach for handling the internal control of the system must have been identified. That approach is fleshed out here. This includes determining how to implement the selected approach and identifying any constraints that this choice imposes on the design. Essentially, in Java this means deciding which of the approaches that can be used to communicate that something should happen should be adopted. These include method calling, event handling, observers and observable dependency, as well as issues such as whether to use RMI or JavaIDL or some event broadcast mechanism.

7.14.4 Adjusting Class Structure

As the design progresses, the class hierarchy is likely to change, evolve and become refined. It is quite common to produce a design and then rearrange it in the light of commonalities that were hidden at an earlier stage. You should:

- Rearrange and adjust classes and operations to increase inheritance.
- Abstract common behaviour out of groups of classes.
- Use delegation to share behaviour when inheritance is semantically invalid.

7.14.5 Designing Associations

Associations are an important aspect of the analysis object model. However, they are conceptual relationships and not implementation-oriented relationships. You need to consider how the associations can be implemented in a given language. The choices made for representing associations may be made globally for the whole system, locally to a package or on an association-by-association basis. The criteria used for determining how associations should be represented in the design are based on how they are traversed. If they are traversed in only one direction a pointer representation may be sufficient. However, if they are bidirectional an intermediate object may best represent the association.

7.14.6 Object Representation

In most situations, it is relatively straightforward to identify how to represent an object if you are using an object-oriented programming language such as Java. However, even when using a language such as Java there are some cases in which you must consider whether to use a system primitive or an object. For example, Java has the basic types int and char, but it also has classes Integer and Character.

7.15 Applying the Remaining Steps to OBA

7.15.1 Optimizing the Design

As this is a prototype online ATM no attempt was made to optimize the design for performance etc. Clarity was considered more important.

7.15.2 Implementing Control

Given the decision made in the system design to allow the GUI to use an event-driven mechanism and the ATM to use a method-calling mechanism, it is necessary to determine how these two control mechanisms interact. We shall adopt an approach based on the model–view–controller model and treat the GUI as the view and controller element and the accounts system as the model. Thus the model is unaware of what is calling its methods, while the GUI is not expected to do anything other than call the appropriate methods on the account system object and display the result.

7.15.3 Adjusting the Class Structure

If we examine the classes in the online ATM there are only a few places in which additional inheritance could be employed. For example an abstract class Person could be defined. This class could define that a person has a name and methods to get and test the name of a person. This class could then be the parent class of Customer and Employee. The only other area in which the structure of the system could be modified is the GUI. In here the controllers could be made inner classes of the main GUI class, thus simplifying the access of date and methods. However, for the simple online ATM we will make no changes, as we wish to adopt clarity as our overriding design principle.

7.15.4 Designing Associations

In the online ATM all link associations will be implemented by references as no link variables or methods have been identified. The inheritance associations will be implemented by the "extends" inheritance mechanism in Java.

7.15.5 Determining Object Representation

In the online ATM the object instantiation mechanism in Java will be used to create instances. Primitive types will be used where possible, as they are more efficient than their object counterparts. Otherwise everything else will be an object.

7.16 Iterating and Refining the Model

Once you get to this stage, whether you are dealing with the architecture as a whole or a subsystem within that architecture, you need to iterate over your design, refining it as you go. You should continue to do this until you are sure that what you have produced is stable, reasonably resilient to change and (given the time and resources available) an acceptable design solution. To help you in this task, the following questions can be asked of the design:

- Are there any missing objects (does one class play two roles)?
- Organize and simplify object classes using inheritance.
- Verify that access paths exist for operations.
- Are there any unnecessary classes (such a class may possess no attributes)?
- Are there any missing associations (such as a missing access path for some operation)?
- Are there any unnecessary associations (such as those that are not used by anything)?
- Are all attributes in the correct class?
- Are all associations in the correct place?

7.17 References

Harel, D. (1988). On visual formalisms. *Communications of the ACM*, **31**(5), 514–30.
Harel, D. *et al.* (1987). On the formal semantics of Statecharts. *Proceedings of the 2nd IEEE Symposium on Logic in Computer Science*, pp. 54–64.

Implementation Phase

8.1 Introduction

This chapter considers the implementation discipline of the Unified Process. This discipline is concerned with implementing the design produced by the design discipline (that is, in terms of Java, it concentrates on implementing classes and interfaces, creating packages and producing class files). It also deals with the remaining non-functional requirements and the deployment of the "executable" modules (in our case Java class files) onto nodes (such as specific processors). It must therefore deal with any implementation issues that have been left as too specific during the design discipline.

However, implementation still tends to pose unexpected design problems which you must solve. These decisions should be subject to, and determined by, the processes described in the remainder of this book.

You should treat the implementation of an object-oriented system in just the same way as you would treat the implementation of any software system. This means that it should be subject to, and controlled by, the same processes as any other implementation.

This chapter does not try to present the concepts behind current thinking in software engineering best practice for software implementation (that could take a whole book in itself); rather, it focuses on those aspects that are specific to the Unified Process.

In the remainder of this chapter the artefacts and activities of the implementation discipline are presented.

8.2 Implementation Discipline Artefacts

The primary artefacts produced by the implementation discipline are:

- *Implementation model.* This describes how the design has moved forward into the implementation. That is, it describes how design elements have been implemented in terms of the software system (in this case Java).

155

- *Deployment model.* This describes how the implemented software should be deployed on the physical hardware.
- *Architecture description.* This is the implementation view of the architecture, illustrating the architecturally significant elements in the implementation. This usually refers to the breakdown of the implementation into subsystems and their interfaces and key components identified in the design of the architecture.
- *The actual implementation.* This is the implemented software (Java code) that realizes the requirements outlined during the requirements discipline. It comprises source code files (in the case of Java), class files, archive files, and potentially databases and middleware technologies such as CORBA or RMI.
- *Integration build plan.* This plan describes how the various elements of the system, potentially constructed at different times, should be brought together into a single system.

8.3 Implementation Discipline Activities

The implementation of an object-oriented system in Java is really just like the implementation of any other system. Care needs to be taken with the realization of the design in the implementation language, testing must be carried out thoroughly, decisions made need to be documented etc.

However, the implementation is structured in the Unified Process into four "primary" steps. These are:

1. Implement skeleton architecture.
2. Define implementation model.
3. Implement subsystems, classes and interfaces in Java.
4. Integrate systems.

In addition, classes, frameworks and combinations of objects all need to be tested appropriately, the results analyzed and appropriate actions carried out. One task which many developers prefer to avoid should also be completed, and that is the generation of the necessary documentation. This documentation should explain how the design has been translated into the implementation. It should also, of course, document the implementation.

8.3.1 Implementing the Skeleton Architecture

The design and implementation of the architecture have been discussed a number of times in this book (and particularly in Chapter 4). However, one key to thinking about the implementation of the architecture is to view it as a thin skinny system in which the emphasis is on reuse. If at all times the reuse element is kept in mind (and thus liberal use of interfaces is adopted) along with the fact that this is really just a complete (if limited functionality) system, then it should be implemented in the same way as the remainder of the system.

8.3.2 Define the Implementation Model

One of the key products of the implementation phase is the implementation model. This model describes the implementation.

- The implementation model documents the structure of the implementation. It describes the design of important operations (i.e. it specifies algorithms to be used to implement operations).
- The implementation model may also describe how the class structure has been modified to increase inheritance, maximize performance or minimize implementation problems.
- The implementation model also describes how components, interfaces, packages and files all relate. To do this it indicates how various aspects of the design map onto the target language – in this case Java (for example, a design subsystem is a Java package and a design interface is a Java interface). This aspect is discussed later in this book.

Above we have mentioned something called a component, but what is a component? A component is a Java class, a data file, a document or anything else which makes up the final delivered system.

The implementation model is important, as the implementation of Java classes from the UML-defined design classes is not just an automatic thing. For example, operations may not have specified how they are to be implemented or what algorithm should be used, or may not have taken into account the limitations of the Java language. It is therefore necessary to design and implement the required algorithms. This in turn may identify new classes, with their own variables and methods, or may cause the design class to acquire new methods.

Indeed, at this stage it will be necessary to identify existing Java classes which either map onto the design classes or will be needed to work with the design classes in order to meet their responsibilities. This may be simplified if the designers took into account the Java language during design; however, the decision to implement using the Java language may not have been taken until late on in the design process, or may just have been ignored by the designers.

It is often the case that during implementation additional inheritance becomes clear. This inheritance was not obvious prior to this due to the more abstract nature of design. In some cases it may identify a new common class from which the existing classes inherit or whose instances are used by existing classes.

Of course, an important point here is that any changes made to the design should be fed back into the design to ensure that the design remains relevant and any knock-on effects of the changes can be identified.

The implementation model uses much of the UML notation already presented in this book plus a few additional forms for describing the relationships between components (see Figure 8.1).

Note that in this figure a package is used to indicate that all the elements are part of the system. The elements within the diagram are components. Stereotypes are used to indicate what type of component they are. The arrows between the components indicate dependency. That is, the Java class file `Accounts.class` is dependent on the `Accounts.java` source file. Components are discussed in more detail below.

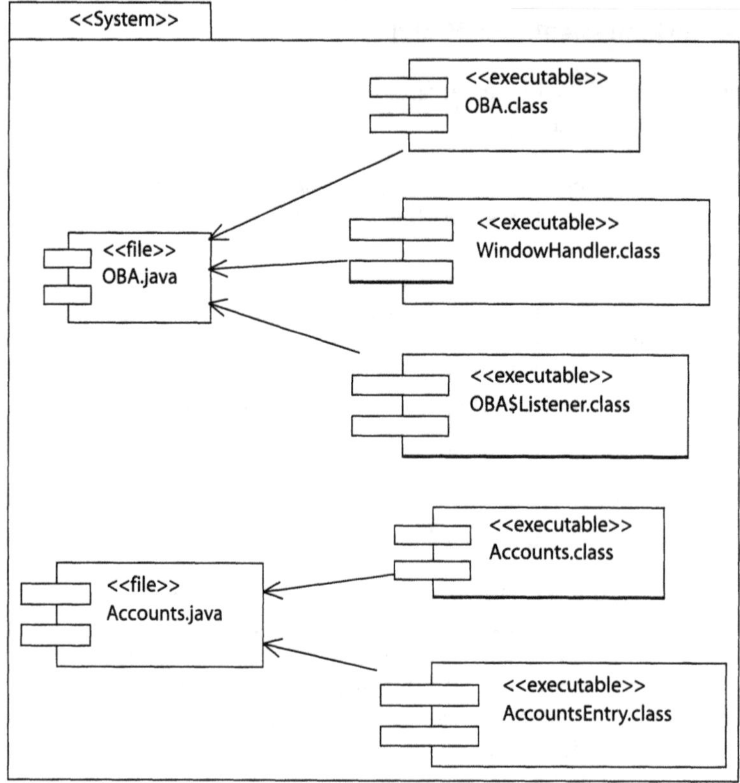

Figure 8.1 The elements of a component diagram.

Components

Each component in a component diagram is denoted by a stereotype. Examples of standard stereotypes used in many UML tools are:

- Data file <<file>>
- Source file (`.java` files) <<java file>>
- Byte code files (`.class` files) <<executables>> or <byte codes>
- Executables (e.g. `.exe`) <<executables>>
- DLL <<library>>
- Document <<document>>

A component may implement more than one design element. That is, the file `Account.java` may define multiple Java classes and interfaces (only one of which may be public). Such a component would result (in the case of Java) in generating (or having dependent on it) multiple executable components. Therefore component diagrams are very useful for mapping design elements to actual physical components, such as source and class files.

Of course, any component must provide the same protocol as the design element (or elements) which comprises it. That is, the implementation model should not suddenly spring new methods/operations on you. They should have been fed back up to the design. Therefore if you examine a design element and then the source code which implements that design element, the external protocols of each should be the same (within the limitations of the implementation language used).

It is important to note that there may well be additional components in the implementation model which do not map to any particular design element. This is because, in the implementation, issues which are too low level for the design need to be addressed. Therefore additional classes or interfaces may be identified to support the design. If they are hidden from the external view of the design elements they do not necessarily have to be reported back to the design level. However, they do need to be clearly documented so that anyone maintaining the system understands what has happened.

8.3.3 Implement the System

As was stated at the beginning of this chapter, implementing the system is very similar to implementing any other system in any programming language. It should thus be subject to all the usual software engineering practices adopted for any implementation. However, there are a number of additional issues for an object-oriented system whose design has been created using the Unified Process. These are:

- *Implementation model.* This has already been discussed, but is a crucial element is describing how the design has been realized in the implementation.
- *Components versus classes, interfaces etc.* As was mentioned in the previous section, an implementation component may actually implement more than one design element. This needs to be documented in the implementation model.
- *Packaging in Java.* UML supports many concepts and ideas which are not supported directly in all programming languages. In particular there are a number of UML concepts that are not supported in Java such as template classes, packages with interfaces and inheritance between packages. Care needs to be taken with such constructs and how they are mapped into Java (see Chapter 13 for a detailed discussion of this issue).
- *Reusing existing (Java) classes.* Unless the design takes into account that the implementation language will be Java, it is not possible for the designers to consider specific Java classes. It is therefore necessary to map the design elements to either standard Java classes or user-defined classes – you do not want to have to reinvent the wheel if there is already a class available which does what you want!
- *Coping with new (implementation) components.* In the Java platform there are a number of different types of new component emerging which you might wish to exploit within your implementation. Such components include Enterprise JavaBeans, Servlets and Java Server Pages. These can be packaged up into different types of archive file, such as Java Archive (JAR) files (for Enterprise JavaBeans and standard Java classes), Web Archive (WAR) files (for HTML pages and servlets) or Enterprise Archive (EAR) files for the Java 2 Enterprise Edition. New stereotypes will need to be defined to ensure clarity within the implementation models. Indeed, the inclusion of such components may in fact impact on the actual design (for example, Enterprise JavaBeans may suggest a particular type of architecture).

8.3.4 Refining the Implementation Model

Just as with the preceding disciplines, it is unlikely that the implementation model (and its associated diagrams and implementation) will be completed in one iteration without any modification or refinement. In fact, this discipline may be involved in numerous iterations throughout the software development process.

The implementation model itself is likely to proceed through successive refinements before being completed. To guide this refinement the following questions are provided:

- *Does the implementation match the model?* It is important to try to keep the actual software implementation, the implementation model and the design model synchronized. That is not to say that everything you place into the actual Java software must be described in the design (if you do this the design will become too detailed – remember that the design is an abstraction of the actual software you implement). However, any major changes should be reflected. It is the job of the implementation model to map anything else from the source code through to the design model.
- *Does a class still provide a single role?* During implementation it is easy to forget all the criteria you applied to the design, not least because it is easy to think that issues such as "Should a class be one class or two classes?" have already been dealt with. However, during implementation new behaviour may arise, and it is important to assess your Java classes with as much rigour as you assessed your design classes. Thus asking questions such as "Does the class still provide a single role?" are just as valid. If the answer is "no", then it is possible that the class should be split or that you have misplaced some of the functionality being implemented.
- *Does a method implement one function?* This is really the same issue as the previous point applied to the method level rather than the whole class level, and is still as important.
- *Are you increasing the dependency between classes?* It is easy once you start coding to find that it would be much easier to add in some extra links to get hold of data or methods. This may be the case because during the implementation issues arise or requirements become clearer which were hidden due to the more abstract nature of the design. However, by doing this you may be evolving your carefully crafted clear design into a bird's nest implementation (I know that I have done this myself without meaning to). Having available systems which will take your source code and generate UML diagrams of your source can be very useful in highlighting such problems.
- *Have you overdone inheritance?* Inheritance is a good thing – yes? Sometimes inheritance is not what you want, and you may be restricting further expansion, reusability or indeed the integrity of your software system by trying to overutilize it. Don't force inheritance – if it doesn't fit, don't use it. In some situations plugging objects together using interfaces can be a much better option. In others, duplication of functionality can actually have benefits in terms of reusability or maintainability.
- *Are you using existing classes?* Again, "don't reinvent the wheel if you don't have to". So get to know your Java classes.
- *Are you reusing patterns?* This is a very important question. When you come to implement your design there are usually a number of ways in which you could implement the same requirement. Some are better than others and most will involve a number of collaborating classes. In many situations others have faced that same problem, and over time common so-

lutions have been created. These common solutions have become known as frameworks and have been documented as what are called patterns. One advantage of using patterns is that patterns represent a shared awareness of the intention, trade-offs and design for a particular problem. That is, if you say you are using the Observer pattern for part of your system, many others will already know what you are taking about. You should therefore look to see whether any existing software patterns can be applied – for further details on software patterns see Chapter 11.

8.3.5 Integrate the Systems

Finally, you need to bring all the disparate parts of your system together and present a working system. This may go through a number of test releases, such as various alpha releases, before it reaches the point where you feel comfortable with releasing a beta release into the heady world of your users. The test workflow should be examined to help you generate your test plan and test cases.

The Test Discipline: How It Relates to Use Cases

9.1 Introduction

This chapter briefly outlines the test discipline and highlights the relationship between test cases and use cases. As testing and quality assurance are very large subjects in their own right we do not try to produce an exhaustive description here (see Hetzel, 1998). Instead we highlight the structure of this discipline.

9.2 The Purpose of the Discipline

The purpose of the test discipline is:

- To plan the tests to be performed for each iteration of the system as well as the final deliverable.
- To design and implement the test cases by creating executable test cases (which include any test harnesses required).
- To systematically perform the tests and analyze the results obtained.

9.3 Aims of Discipline

The aim of the test discipline is to ensure that the system provides the required functionality. As the required functionality was originally captured in the form of the use cases in the use case model there is obviously some form of relationship between the two. In fact, the use cases are an ideal place to start looking for potential test cases. That is, the use cases specify what inputs a user will provide to the system, what actions they expect to happen in what order (they even specify what should happen if something goes wrong) and what the end result is expected to be. In some cases non-functional requirements may also have been documented with the uses cases (and may certainly have been identified during the requirements discipline).

Therefore the system as implemented should be tested against the use cases as originally identified. You should therefore start to build your test plan based on your use cases. However, you should not be blind to other sources of test information, as use cases are just one source of test information (albeit a very important one).

The artefacts produced by the test discipline are:

- A test model which describes how executable components are tested by integration and system test. It is comprised of test cases.
- Test cases. Each test case specifies one way of testing the system being developed.
- A test plan, which describes the testing strategies, resources and schedule to be followed.

9.4 Test Discipline Activities

There are six activities to the test discipline:

- Plan tests
- Design tests
- Implement tests
- Perform integration tests
- Perform system tests
- Evaluate tests

9.4.1 Plan Tests

The purpose of this activity is to plan how the system will be tested, how iterations will be tested, what the testing strategy will be, what resources will be required and when the tests will occur. The primary product of this activity is the Test Plan.

9.4.2 Design Tests

The next activity in this discipline is the design tests activity. This activity identifies and describes the test cases as well as how the tests will be performed. There are primarily two types of test being designed, integration tests and system tests. Integration tests will be performed as and when parts of the system are being brought together. System tests should be performed each time a new "release" of the system has been created. This could be at the end of an iteration or of the whole design and implementation process. We will consider the two types of test separately below.

Integration Testing

We have already mentioned use cases as a very good source of test information for the system as a whole. However, what about integration testing. In such situations we might not have enough of the system available to support a whole use case. In such situations sequence diagrams may a very good source of test cases. They specify how the various objects in the system interact in response to some event or initiating message. They indicate what information is passed and potentially (with statecharts) the changes in the system. It is therefore possible to use the sequence diagrams (supported by statecharts) to generate tests and to compare the test results with the predicted behaviour. That is, you can trace the sequence diagram against test results. This will help to ensure that the correct messages are sent, in the correct sequence, between the correct objects (note the changes due to implementation) with the expected result.

Design System Tests from Use Cases

Each system test represents one or more use cases. Of course, it is likely that one particular use case will support (or generate) multiple test cases. This is because the test cases may need to be applied to the system when it is in different states, to test different paths through the use case, to test different options within the use case etc.

If more than one use case is tested in a single test case then it is important to consider the order in which the use cases are considered. This is necessary, as some use cases may impact on others, some may have interactions with others and some may run in parallel with others. These are all very important issues and need to be considered carefully when designing test cases. However, in all cases the results obtained from the test case should match the associated use case's post conditions. If they do not, analysis of both the use case and the system must be carried out. There could be a fault in the software or the design; there could also be an omission or error in the use case.

9.4.3 Implement Tests

This activity implements the test cases that have been identified. This may involve implementing test harnesses that set the system up into the desired state. In many cases the test harnesses are much larger than the actual tests themselves. However, it is critically important to ensure that the test is performed with the system in the correct state.

9.4.4 Perform Integration Tests

This activity actually carries out the integration tests that have been implemented. The results of the integration tests should be captured and analyzed. This analysis should highlight any changes needed to the design or the implementation thus far.

9.4.5 Perform System Tests

This activity carries out the test of the system as a whole. This activity can begin once the integration tests have indicated that the integration of the system is stable enough. Note that integration tests may have identified problems in the system which may have necessitated various rewrites of the design and/or implementation. The integration tests should then be re-performed and only once the results obtained are satisfactory should system testing take place.

9.4.6 Evaluate Tests

This activity checks and monitors the results of the various tests performed through the current iteration. The results obtained may modify plans and affect which tests they will carry out in future, and indeed may affect the design of the whole system. For example, it may be clear that there were many "faults" within a certain part of the system: is this because of the team involved, because of weak specifications or because this is a particularly "risky" part of the product?

9.5 Summary

The primary artefact produced by the test discipline is the test model. This model contains the test plan and the test cases. It should also contain the results of carrying out the tests and the analysis of those test results.

9.6 Reference

Hetzel, B. (1998). *The Complete Guide to Software Testing*, 2nd edn. Wellesley, MA: QED Information Sciences.
Kit, E. (1995). *Software Testing in the Real World*. Reading, MA: Addison-Wesley.

The Four Phases

10.1 Introduction

This chapter examines the relationship between phases and, in particular disciplines. It also considers iterations and how they fit into the Unified Process life cycle. It concludes by briefly discussing cycles and how they drive successive applications of the four phases.

10.2 The Unified Process Structure

The primary focus in this book so far has been on the disciplines that direct the designers and developers during the production of the software system. However, these disciplines are organized into iterations (of course there may only be a single iteration!). In turn, the iterations are organized into phases. The four phases were discussed back in Chapter 3; however, it is worth returning to the phases and considering them in more detail here. In turn, the phases are organized into cycles which lead to successive releases of the product (see Figure 10.1).

As has been shown, disciplines determine the order in which activities are carried out, while activities determine how things are done and how artefacts are produced. So where

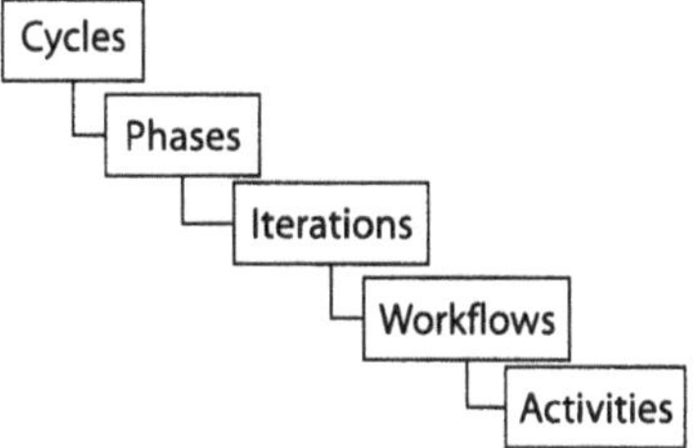

Figure 10.1 The hierarchical structure of the Unified Process.

do the phases fit in? Essentially they highlight what the current emphasis should be at any particular point in the project. We will consider this in greater detail below.

10.3 Relationship Between Phases and Iterations

So phases highlight what the emphasis in the project should be at any particular point in time? What does that mean? Let us first consider the more traditional view of software development. In this view:

- Many projects only have one cycle.
- Many projects only have one iteration per phase.
- Many projects follow the waterfall model, carrying out requirements, analysis, design, implementation and then ongoing maintenance.

In such an approach it is not too difficult to see what the primary aim at any one time is. During the requirements process the emphasis is on deciding what the system should do, what its scope is, and any non-functional requirements such as performance criteria.

However, object-oriented system development tended to be more iterative and incremental even before the Unified Process came into being. If you study the way in which many designers and developers applied the earlier methods such as OMT you will find that there was a blurring of distinction between the requirements process, the design process and even the implementation process.

The Unified Process explicitly acknowledges this and accepts the problems and weaknesses inherent in such an approach. To overcome these (such as not completing the requirements sufficiently before implementing the system!) four phases have been introduced. These four phases give guidance on what should be happening during that phase. For example, during the elaboration phase both the design and implementation disciplines are in evidence. However, this does not mean that the bulk of the system is being designed and implemented before the requirements have been fully formalized. Rather, the elaboration phase highlights that at this point the design and implementation which are being carried out should either be helping to clarify requirements or should be attempting to produce the initial baseline architecture. The four phases are considered in more detail below.

10.3.1 The Four Phases

The four phases of the Unified Process are the inception phase, the elaboration phase, the construction phase and the transition phase (see Figure 10.2). Table 10.1 summarizes the role of each of these phases.

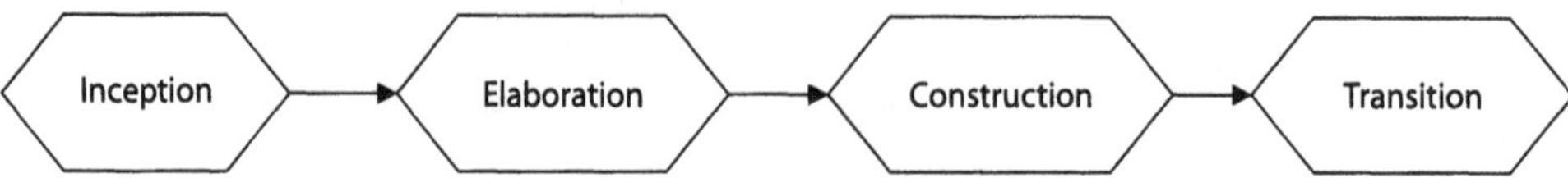

Figure 10.2 The four phases of the Unified Process.

Table 10.1 The role of each phase.

Phase	Role
Inception	Define the scope of the project and develop the business case. Establishes feasibility.
Elaboration	Capture functional requirements, specify non-functional requirements, create architecture baseline.
Construction	Build the product.
Transition	Move the product into user environment.

The relationships between the phases and the disciplines are illustrated in Figure 10.3 and are discussed in more detail below.

Inception

The inception phase primarily focuses on the generation of the business case; that is, whether it is feasible and worthwhile to produce the system under consideration. This involves identifying the core use cases for the system and the actual scope of the system, as well as identifying the new, risky or difficult parts of the system, all of which will have an impact on the success (or otherwise) of the project. This phase also involves the first tentative cut at the architecture (but at the highest level), just to start to get a feel for what will be involved. Part of this is to prove the feasibility of the project as well as to determine the complexity involved, in order to provide reasonable estimates to clients, managers etc. The primary discipline used here is the requirements discipline,

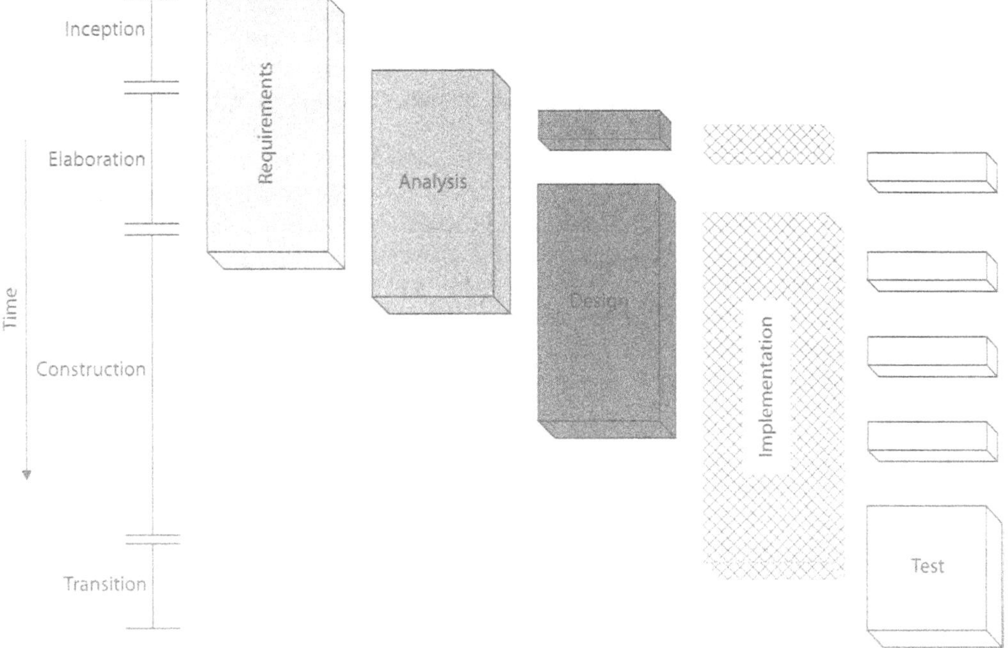

Figure 10.3 The relationship between phases and disciplines.

however, in order to examine the architecture it is inevitably necessary to analyze, design and possibly carry out some implementation at this stage. However, these should not be excessively large exercises; the intention is only to gain an understanding, not to design and implement the whole architecture!

Elaboration

The primary aims of the elaboration phase are to understand how the requirements are translated into the internals of the system and in particular to produce the baseline architecture for the remainder of the project. This means that during this phase the majority of the use cases will be captured. This phase should also explore further the risks identified earlier, and in particular should identify the most significant risks. These should help identify what should be part of the architecture or at least considered in early iterations during this or the construction phase. It will also be important to consider reliability and performance levels during this phase, as both may have an impact upon the architecture as well as the approach taken during the remainder of the project. The key disciplines used in this phase are the requirements and analysis disciplines. The design discipline is important for producing the architecture, as is the implementation discipline for implementing that architecture. Obviously the test discipline is necessary to test the architecture. Later in the phase additional elements may be designed and implemented to confirm design decisions, determine risks etc.

Construction

The result of this phase is the full beta release of the system. That is, it is a fully functional product ready for beta testing. It may contain some defaults (bugs) and further enhancements may be made (however, these are expected to be minor and not affect the major functionality of the system). It is usually the largest phase by some way (see later). In addition it tends to have the most iterations (indeed, the previous two phases may only have a single iteration, whereas this phase may have a number of iterations).

This phase will focus on the design and implementation of the majority of the system. It is the phase which puts the muscle and skin onto the skeleton of the architecture. However, note that it will also need to maintain the integrity of the architecture in the light of any modifications imposed as the design and implementation progress.

An important aspect of the success of this phase is to monitor the critical aspects of the project, in particular the significant risks identified earlier in the project.

This phase concentrates on the design and implementation disciplines (although some requirements and analysis may still be performed). In fact, some additional use cases may be identified at this stage (and this is quite normal).

Transition

The transition phase often begins with the release of the beta system. It focuses on the deployment of the beta system, monitoring user feedback and handling any modifications or updates required. This may involve further design and implementation (and potentially even new use cases etc., although this should be avoided at this late stage). This phase is completed with the formal release of the software. This phase primarily involves the test and implementation disciplines.

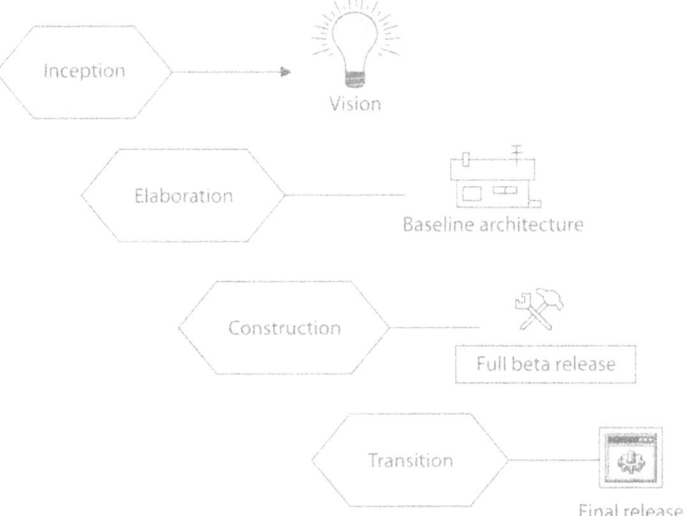

Figure 10.4 Major milestones for each phase.

Major Milestones

As has been indicated above, each of the phases has a major milestone that has to be met before the project can move on to the next phase. These milestones are:

- *The inception phase* produces the business case and basic requirements (indicated by the vision milestone in Figure 10.4).
- *The elaboration phase* produces the architecture and a more detailed understanding of the requirements.
- *The construction phase* produces the full beta release of the software.
- *The transition phase* produces the actual final release that has been beta tested by prospective users.

10.4 Effort Versus Phases

It is worth considering the amount of effort which is put into each phase within a typical project to help understand how the phases relate to the time taken by a project. This is illustrated in Figure 10.5. As can be seen by this diagram, the biggest effort by far is put into the construction phase. This term "effort" refers to both the amount of straight time spent and the amount of resources applied during that time. However, a significant amount of time is also spent on the elaboration phase, and indeed a significant amount of the resources available is also spent on this phase. Essentially, the elaboration phase accounts for about a quarter of the total resources used and 30–40% of the time on the project, while the construction phase takes between 40 and 50% of

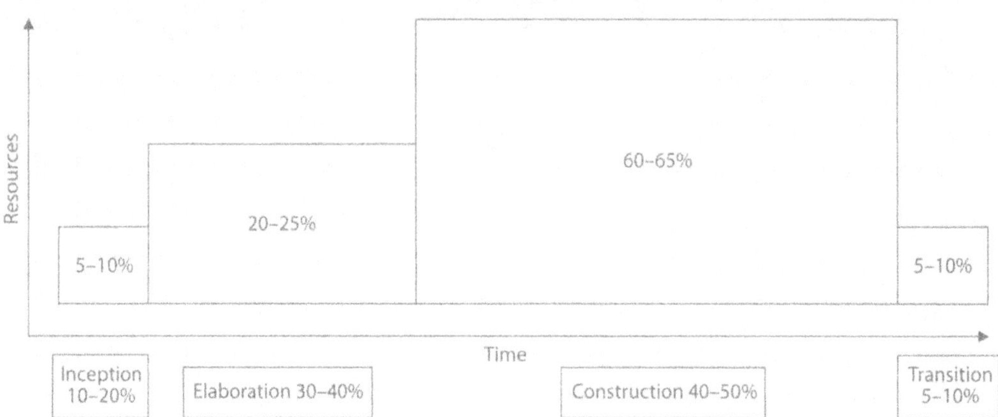

Figure 10.5 Effort versus phases.

the time available and from 60 to 65% of the total resources used on the project. Thus between 70 and 90% of the time on a project is spent on the elaboration and construction phases alone. Note that this does not mean that the other phases are insignificant (they are not, as the transition phase, for example, is very important). It is also important not to confuse phases with disciplines and think that testing will only occur in the transition phase (when the system is being beta tested). It does not: the construction phase will exploit the test discipline very thoroughly before allowing the system to get to beta test stage.

10.5 Phases and Iterations

We have now discussed the relationship between phases and disciplines, but where do iterations come in? If we look back to Figure 1 we can see that iterations sit between phases and disciplines, why then have we not mentioned them until this point in time? It is because iterations apply disciplines one or more times during a phase. For example, a moderately complex project might have the following organization:

- *Inception phase*. One iteration, primarily applying the requirements discipline.
- *Elaboration phase*. Two iterations, one identifying the use cases and an outline architecture and a second refining the architecture further.
- *Construction phase*. A number of iterations (three, four or even five) depending on the risks identified and the complexity of the system. Each iteration will run through at least the design, implementation and test disciplines (and may involve the analysis discipline as well).
- *Transition phase*. One or two iterations depending on how successful the beta testing is.

Thus each phase may have one or more iterations; however, the important point to note is that the iterations should be planned at the start of the phase and should not be invented as you go along. Note that this means that producing a firm plan of exactly what you will be doing for the whole project right at the beginning of the project is not now feasible (you plan each phase in detail just before starting that phase). You can, of course, produce an outline plan in which you fill out the details as you go along. However, many managers may find this disconcerting at first.

Each iteration should deal with a "manageable" chunk of work. That is, it may focus on a particular aspect of a system. It may focus on producing a minimal system or it may focus on dealing with a particular risk. However, you plan the iteration based on the resources and time available. That is, you:

- identify some requirements
- implement part of the functionality

Each iteration should then produces a "release", even if that release is merely to prove that some approach will or will not work. Of course, a "release" may represent an increment in the system, but equally it may not.

Thus iterations allow you to plan and arrange the work done within a phase into chunks which are doable and which may move the system forward. Of course, one of the great things about this approach is that at any particular time you may have a (limited) system to demonstrate to clients and managers, as each "release" may provide you will a (limited) functional system. This also has the advantage that if an unforeseen problem arises you still have the last "release" to fall back on.

10.6 Phases and Cycles

The final part of the hierarchy presented in Figure 10.1 comprises cycles. They sit above phases and are essentially major iterations of the whole life cycle of the development of the software system. That is, a single cycle will produce a full release of a system (for example, release 1.0). The next cycle will produce the next full release of the system (and depending on the numbering system used this may be release 1.2 or release 2.0 or even release 200!).

This reflects the fact that many products often have a lifetime during which they evolve. Take the Java environment itself: it has gone through a number of releases, including 1.0, 1.1 and now the Java 2 platform. In between there have been a (large) number of maintenance releases (for example, JDK 1.1.8). Each release is made up of a cycle.

Each cycle produces a new release and is made up of all four phases. In this case the inception phase looks at what is required in each cycle; this may be done by identifying gaps in the product or examining user wishes as a result of feedback from extended use of the product. Whatever the source of the requirements, they are then fed through the remaining three phases in exactly the same way as the original requirements were fed through.

The JDSync Case Study

11.1 Introduction

This case study describes the analysis and design of a simple standalone Java application. This application will illustrate some of the aspects of the Unified Process, the UML and their application to Java-based systems. However, it is a very simple system and therefore cannot explore all the possible aspects of the Unified Process. Indeed we will not deal with the issue of the architecture, partly because this system is simple enough not to warrant it. It is hoped, instead, that the very simplicity of the system will allow a full analysis and design to be performed and for the steps involved to be described.

11.2 Problem Statement

The aim of this system is to provide an application that will:

1. Back up one directory to another.
2. Bring two directories in line with each other ensuring that the latest version of any file or directory is available in both locations. The program should also ensure that any new files or directories found in either directory are copied to the other directory.
3. Allow direct copying of files and directories from one directory to another.

11.3 The Requirements Discipline: Use Case Analysis

As this system is relatively straightforward, the use case analysis is not complicated. However, we shall step through each of the activities you would normally perform to illustrate what actually happens.

We will start by identifying the actors involved in the system; we will then go on to identify uses cases and to look at their definition.

11.3.1 Actors in JDSync

The process of finding the actors involves looking in "whatever has gone before". In this case we have a (very) simple problem statement. This problem statement does not say anything about who will use the system. We must therefore go on to consider the questions that can be used to help identify the actors. These are questions such as who is interested in the system? Who is likely to use the system? Who will benefit from the system? And so on. In this case the answer to all these questions is the same – the user of the JDSync program. We do not, however, have different categories of user, as the same user will use it to perform all three of the primary activities outlined in the problem statement. This is primary because the system is so simple. Thus, the user of the program will be interested in what it can do, the user will be the one who actually uses it to synchronize two directories, and it is the user who will benefit from this synchronization. We have chosen the name "User" for our actor, as this is exactly who that is: the "person using JDSync". The person is not a customer, an administrator, a client etc.

The outcome of this is that we have a single actor whom we are calling "User" (this actor is illustrated in Figure 11.1).

Of course, merely naming the actor is not enough we must consider the various different information elements which are associated with actors. These are discussed below:

Figure 11.1 The "User" actor specification.

- *Description*: The role of this actor is as the user of the system. That is, a person who wishes to synchronize their directories. Such users are expected to be familiar with file selection dialogs, the file structure of their computer systems and WIMP style interfaces.
- *Attributes*: This actor does not possess any attributes.

This actor will both give and receive information to and from the system.

11.3.2 Use Cases

We are now ready to consider the use cases for the JDSync application. Again we must consider the guidelines provided for identifying use cases. We shall list each of the questions presented below and address them in turn:

- *What are the main tasks of each actor?* As there is only one actor this is quite straightforward. The tasks of the actor are to synchronize two directories and to copy files and directories from one directory to another.
- *Will the actor have to read/write/change any of the system information?* Yes, the actor will need to copy files from one directory to another, either directly using the copy operation or indirectly using the synchronizing operation. This implies that the user must specify the source and sink directories for such operations.
- *What use cases will create, store, change, remove or read system information?* We will leave this for a moment as it is really the sort of question we would ask in a subsequent iteration of the use case identification process.
- *Consider each actor in turn*:
  - *Will the actor have to inform the system about outside changes?* Yes, if new directories are created which need to be backed up or synchronized.
  - *Does the actor wish to be informed about outside changes?* No.
- *What use cases will support and maintain the system?* We do not need any special support or maintain activities in this system, as there are no defaults, no persistent data, no options etc.
- *Can all functional requirements be performed by the current set of use cases?* Again we will leave this for a moment as it is really the sort of question we would ask in a subsequent iteration of the use case identification process.

We have also been exhorted to consider methods such as interviews of those who will be using the system, storyboarding to describe how the system will operate or workshops to brainstorm different scenarios relating to the system. In this case the system is simple enough to do without such techniques.

So where does that leave us? Well if we consider the answers to our questions above, three things become clear:

1. The actor must specify the directories involved in any operations.
2. The actor must be able to copy files from one place to another.
3. The actor must be able to request that two directories are synchronized.

Given these three functional requirements we can begin to define three separate use cases. In doing this we will have to consider the sequences of events involved. As this system is straightforward we will rely on natural language for this description. To help identify the events it is useful to consider what information is required:

- Pre-conditions on the use case. Here you must look to see what is required before the use cases can execute.
- When and how the use case starts and ends.
- What interaction the use case has with the actor.
- What data the use cases need.
- The normal sequence of events.
- Any alternatives or exceptional sequences of events.
- Post-conditions. These are useful to indicate what the final effect of the use should be. This information is particularly helpful is test generation.

Use Case 1: Select Directories

This use case will express the first the of primary functions we identified above. That is, it will express the need for the user to be able to specify which directories they wish to work with. This means that other than starting the system up (an implied pre-condition!) there will be no pre-conditions on this use case – it is the first thing the actor must do. However, we will specify two attributes for this use case called `directory1` and `directory2` to indicate the directories selected by the actor. Here is the use case specification.

Brief Description
This use case is started by the user. It allows the user to select the two directories to be synchronized.

Pre-conditions
None

Main Flow
This use case begins when the user starts to run the "JDSync" program. Initially the system will present two blank directory windows (see Figure 11.4). The user can then select each of the directories to be synchronized. The user can do this either by entering the directory name directly or by using the "Browse" button.
   If the user selects the "Browse" button, `BrowseSubflow` is performed.

SubFlows
BrowseSubFlow
The system displays a directory selection dialog (see Figure 11.3). This dialog presents the current directory's contents, and buttons which allow the user to select a directory or cancel the interaction. The user should navigate through the file system in order to select the desired directory.

Alternative Flows
If the user selects or enters a file instead of a directory, the directory within which the file resides is selected.

Post-condition
`directory1` and `directory2` are selected.

Use Case 2: Synchronize Directories

This use case represents the core functionality of the system. It specifies how the user will initiate the synchronization of the two directories selected in the previous use case. As such, it possesses a pre-condition which specifies that that use case must have completed. Its post-condition will be that the two directories contain the same information. The events described in the use case illustrate how the actor expects to interact with the system. Here is the use case specification; notice that the use case includes an example. This is natural and will not only help to clarify the operation of the use case but also the generation of test cases.

Brief Description
This use case is performed by the user to bring the contents of two directories in line (i.e. up to the same version of all files and subdirectories). The newest version of all files will be copied from their original location to the other directory (whichever that might be). For example, let us assume that the two directories are called Data and Mobile, and that their contents are as presented below:

Data	Mobile
D1 23.03.99	D1 20.02.99
D2 10.03.99	D2 11.03.99
D3 01.01.99	D3 01.01.99
M1 11.02.99	M2 14.04.99

The result would be that D1 and M1 would be copied from Data to Mobile and D2 and M2 would be copied from Mobile to Data.

The process recurses down any subdirectories. Any files or directories not in both locations are copied from their location into the other directory.

Pre-conditions
The Select Directories use case must have executed to complete before this use case begins (that is both directory1 and directory2 must have been set).

Main Flow
The use case begins when the user select the "Sync" button on the main JDSync window (see Figure 11.4). The contents of the two directories are then copied as required.

Alternative Flows
None.

Post-condition
The two directories will have the same versions of all files and directories.

Use Case 3: Copy Files and Directories

Brief Description
This use case allows the user to copy a single file or directory from one selected directory to another.

Pre-conditions
The Select Directories use case must have executed and completed before this use case begins (that is both `directory1` and `directory2` must have been set).

Main Flow
Users select a file or directory in one of the two directory listings, in the main JDSync interface (Figure 11.4). They then select the appropriate "Copy" button in the main JDSync interface (see Figure 11.4). These buttons appear as arrows from one directory to the other. This copies the select file or directory from the source directory to the sink directory.

Alternative Flows
If the user selects the "Copy" button with the arrow pointing at the directory in which a file or subdirectory has been selected, an error message is displayed saying that the wrong copy button or the wrong directory has been selected. This is because the copy button's arrowhead indicates the destination of the copy operation: if the arrow points to the same directory as the selected file or directory then the user would be trying to copy the file or directory onto itself.

Post-condition
The file or directory is copied from the source directory to the sink directory (replacing any existing files or directories of that name).

11.3.3 The Use Case Diagram

The use case diagram for our three use cases and one actor is presented in Figure 11.2.

In a larger system we would now attempt to rationalize and refine the set of use cases we had identified. For example, we could test the use cases against such criteria as size, self-containment and providing added value. We could also look to see where there should be a *uses* or *extends* link between any use cases. In our example, all three use cases are about the

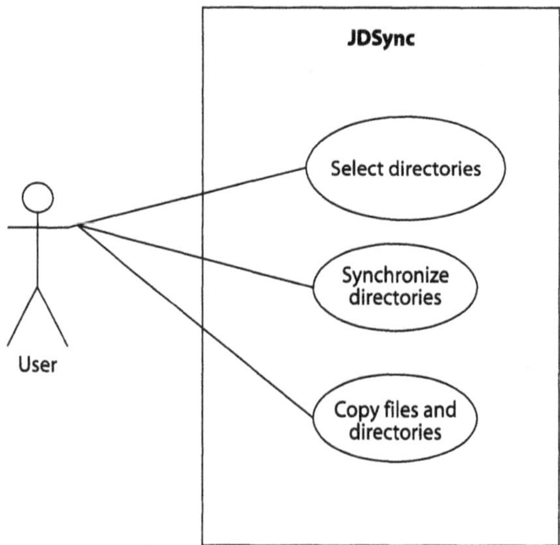

Figure 11.2 The use case diagram for the JDSync application.

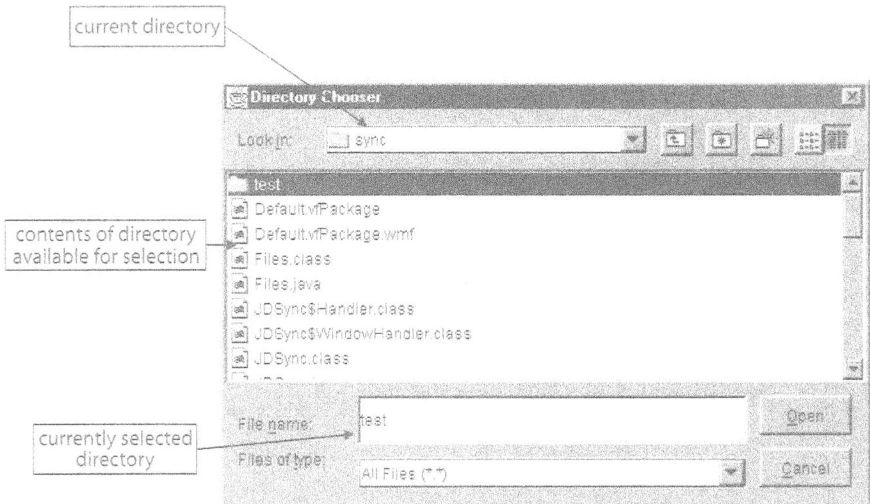

Figure 11.3 The JDSync graphical user interface.

same size, they are clearly distinct and there are no *uses* or *extends* relationships. You may think that there is a *uses* relationship between the Select Directories use case and the other two use cases, but you would be wrong. The other use cases have a pre-condition that relates to the first use case, but they do not directly use it.

11.3.4 Example User Interfaces

Having defined our use cases and the actor we are ready to present some sample user interfaces. Notice that we would probably have developed these in conjunction with the use cases, as the use cases refer to them. However, for clarity we are presenting the interfaces in a separate section.

The use cases refer to an interface which allows the user to input two directories and to either copy or "sync" their contents. The first use case also refers to a dialog which allows the directories to be selected interactively. Of course, we could produce many different user interfaces to match these requirements. However, in consultation with our users we have design the user interfaces presented in Figures 11.3 and 11.4. These user interfaces have been annotated for clarity. Such user interfaces do not need to be annotated; however for users this information can be useful. This can, in addition, help users to clarify that the user interfaces is suitable or not.

As both user interfaces are relatively simple we will leave out a detailed description of the their presentation and operation. However, for more complex applications such information may well be required.

11.4 The Analysis Discipline

Once we are happy with the set of use cases, actors and interfaces we can move on to consider the analysis discipline. Remember that you may well find out information during this discipline

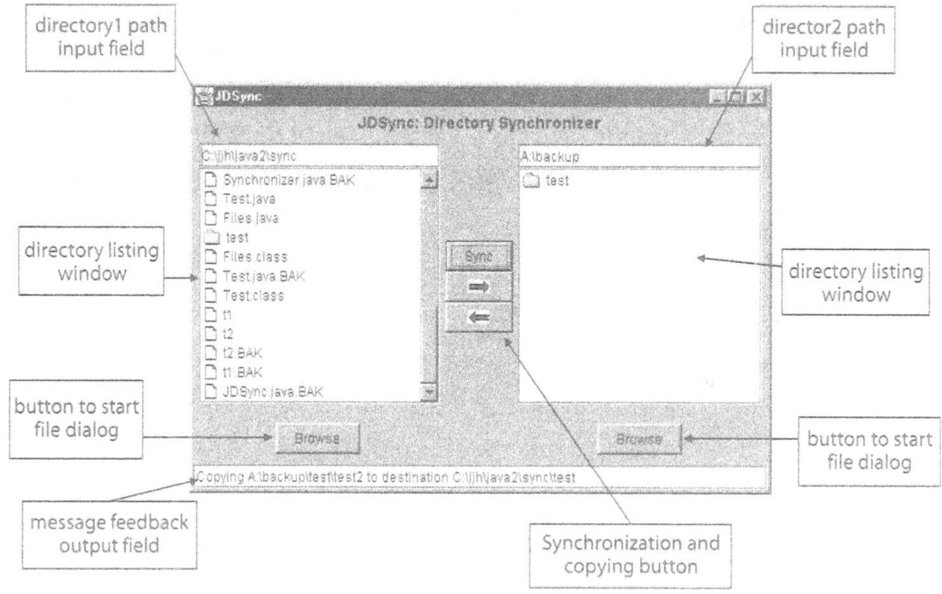

Figure 11.4 The directory selection dialog.

which causes you to go back to the requirements discipline! In this case our application is simple enough that we will not need to do that.

11.4.1 Identifying the Analysis Classes

We will start off by identifying the core analysis classes for the JDSync system by examining the use cases. We will first attempt to identify the classes implied by the use cases and then to consider the interactions between these classes suggested by the use cases. Due to the nature of paper we will present these two steps sequentially, but in reality they would be closely interwoven. We will then return to the class diagrams to construct a single class diagram which will bring what we have learnt together.

If we turn our minds back to the guidelines provided for identifying analysis classes, we will find that the guidelines state:

To identify analysis classes identify:

- One boundary class for each actor and entity in a use case
- One control class for each use case

This may have already been done during the process of generating use case realizations (or may occur in parallel). You then need to look for entity classes (remember that this is the key to the analysis phase); to do this consider:

- physical entities, such as petrol pumps, engines and locks

- logical entities such as employee records, purchases and speed
- soft entities such as tokens, expressions or data streams
- conceptual entities such as needs, requirements or constraints.

Therefore we can expect at least one boundary class and three control classes. If we follow the guidelines for looking for entity classes, then at least directories present themselves as the logical entities involved in this system.

We will consider each of the use cases separately.

Use Case 1: Select Directories

This use case describes an interaction between the actor (user) and the system. There will therefore need to be at least one boundary object in place for them to do this. As this is the analysis discipline we are not too concerned with the number of windows displayed or their content, merely that there is such an interface. We will therefore treat both of the windows identified in the use case analysis as part of the same boundary analysis object. We will call the class representing this object the "JDSync Interface". This name is both descriptive and generic enough to cover both the main window and the directory dialog.

The use case then describes how the user specifies two path names indicating which directories should be involved in the remaining use cases. This use case defines two attributes, directory1 and directory2. These directories could be attributes of the some entity object or they could be entity objects in their own right. In this case we will assume that they are entity objects in their own right, as this will make it easier to see what is happening in the collaboration diagrams. Note this says nothing about how we should implement the directories.

Finally we need a control object which will handle the interaction between the boundary object and the directory entities. We will call this control object "Selector". For the time being we do not worry too much about what it should do other than to document its role.

The resulting class diagram is illustrated in Figure 11.5. Note that in this case we are using the stereotype label to indicate that the classes are analysis type classes (we could have used the icons defined for these stereotypes, but have chosen not to do so).

Use Case 2: Synchronize Directories

This use case describes how the user requests the JDSync application to synchronize the two directories selected in the previous use case. Again we need a boundary class and classes to represent the two directories to be synchronized. The main difference is that we need a control class

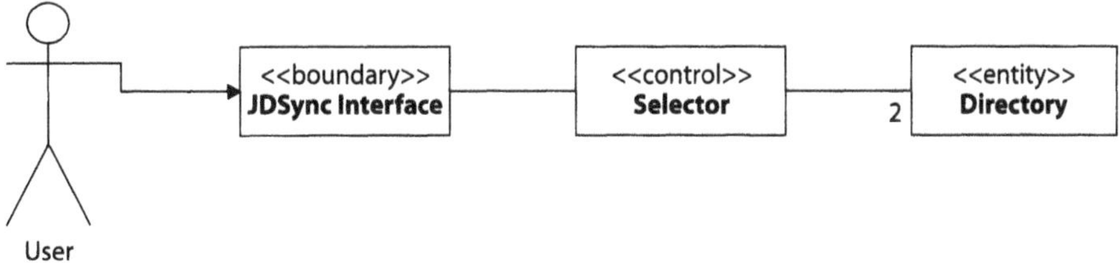

Figure 11.5 The class structure implied by the "select directories" use case.

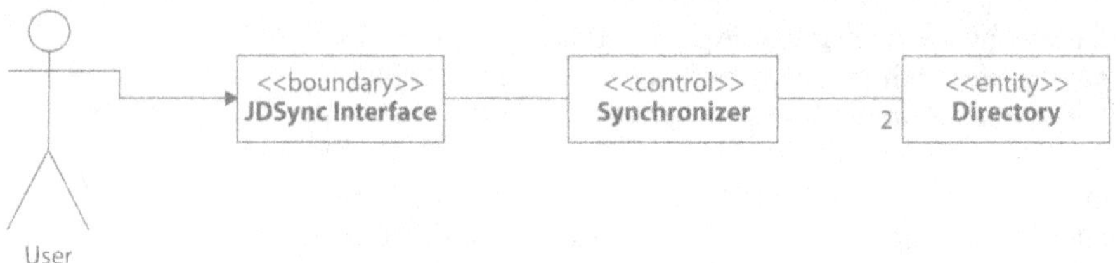

Figure 11.6 The class structure implied by the second use case.

which will perform the synchronization operation, rather than the selection operation. We will call this class the "Synchronizer" class. The resulting class structure is presented in Figure 11.6.

Use Case 3: Copy Files and Directories

As with the previous use cases, this use case requires a boundary object and two directory entity objects. However, the control class must this time describe the process of copying files and directories. We will call this control class the "Copier". This is illustrated in Figure 11.7.

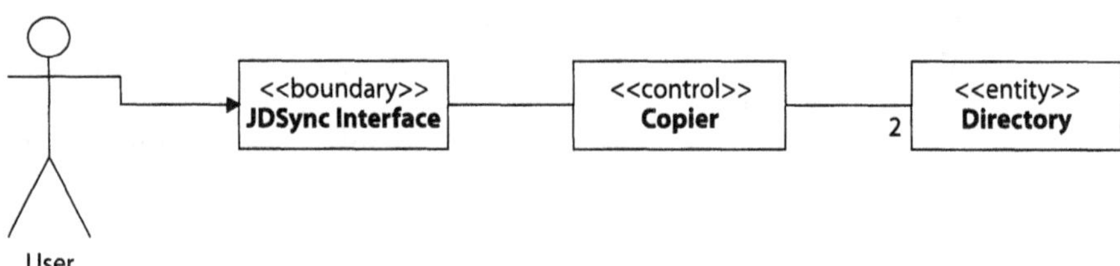

Figure 11.7 The class structure implied by the third use case.

11.4.2 Generating the Collaboration Diagrams

Having obtained a first cut at the classes implied by the use cases we can now produce a set of collaboration diagrams that describe how the classes "implement" the use cases. Note that this would be done in parallel with the class identification step. These collaboration diagrams will form the set of use case realizations which ensure that the analysis model "implements" all the use cases.

The first thing to note about the collaboration diagrams is that they illustrate the objects (as opposed to the classes) involved in the collaboration. This means that we will illustrate both instances of the Directory entity class in our diagrams. Next we will need to identify the messages sent by the objects in response to an initiating event. The events will be the names of the use cases. This makes the relationships between the analysis model and the use model easier to follow. This is not a problem, even though the use cases represent a series of interactions; remember that this is the analysis discipline and we can treat all the interactions with the actor as a single abstract event! To find the messages sent between the objects we need to consider the event scenarios defined in the user cases.

We shall consider each use case individually again.

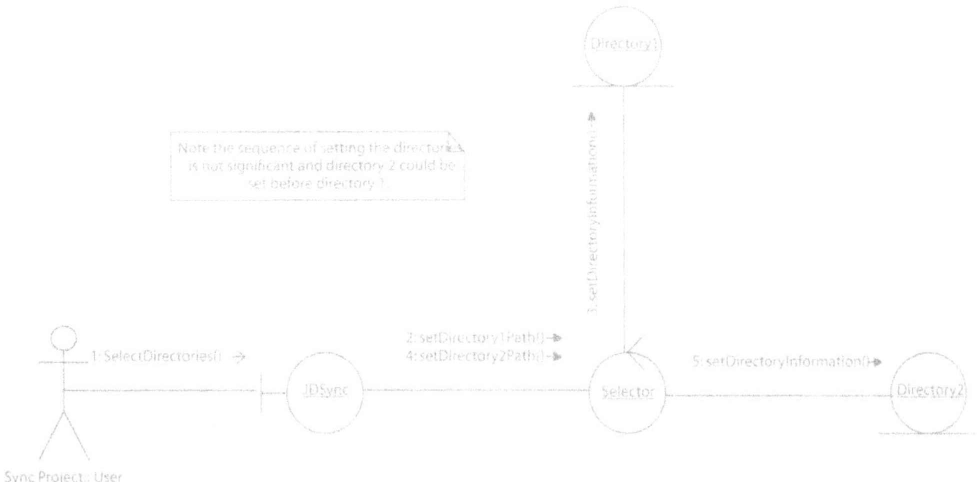

Figure 11.8 The analysis collaboration diagram generated from the select directories use case.

Use Case 1: Select Directories

We now have the three classes support this use case. These three classes will produce four objects. The four objects are the JDSync Interface, the Selector and the two Directory entity objects. The initiating event will be the "SelectDirectories" event. We must now decide what action(s) the JDSync Interface object should take in response. Again remember that we are aiming for clarity here, and not concerning ourselves with the detail. Essentially the boundary object needs to indicate to the select object that the user has selected one or other of the directory paths to be used with the directory entity objects. The name given to this message should be meaningful and we have chosen the names "setDirectory1Path" and "setDirectory2Path". In turn, the Selector object must send a message to the directory objects telling them to set themselves to the appropriate information. We have decided that this message should be called "setDirectoryInformation". Note that both directories have the same message, as they are instances of the same class. The resulting collaboration diagram is presented in Figure 11.8.

Use Case 2: Synchronize Directories

In generating the next collaboration diagram we must again consider the initiating event, in this case the "Synchronize Directories" event. This time the JDSync object should send a synchronize message to the Synchronizer object. This object must then initiate messages to the two directory objects requesting that they copy files and directories from one to another. This means that the two directory objects must be able to find out which files and directories that they possess are newer than the files and directories held by the other directory entity. At this point we now find that this means that it would be useful if the two directory entities directly knew about each other. There should therefore be a new reference between these objects. This reference must be added to the class diagrams describing the structure of the analysis model (we will come back to this later). We must also try to identify meaning names for the messages passed between the objects. Note

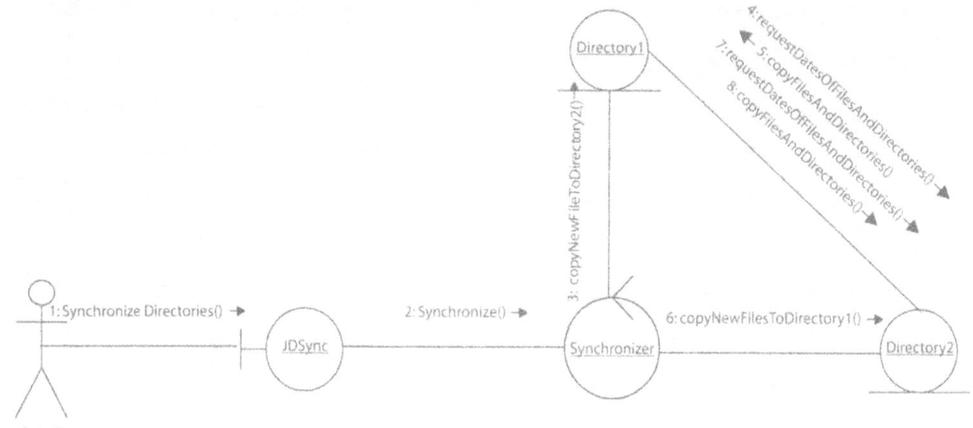

Figure 11.9 The collaboration diagram generated from the *synchronize directories* use case.

that any message can have supporting documentation provided which explains the message's role, any parameters or return values expected, whether it is synchronous or asynchronous, etc. The resulting collaboration diagram is presented in Figure 11.9. Note that even this simple collaboration diagram is actually the result of three iterations. The first iteration had no link between the two directory entities and the second did not include a request to find out the dates of files and directories!

Use Case 3: Copy Files and Directories

This collaboration diagram is triggered by the "Copy files and directories" event. This causes the JDSync boundary object to send a message to the Copier object requesting that it copy the files selected by the user. This object obtains the names of the files and/or directories selected by the user and the directories to copy from and to. It then sends a message to the source directory asking it to copy the specified files and/or directories to the destination directory. Figure 11.10 illustrates the collaboration diagram for the situation in which the user copies from directory 1 to directory 2. Of course, almost exactly the same collaboration diagram could be drawn for the process of copying from directory 2 to directory 1.

If we wished, at this point we could generate a second collaboration diagram to describe the alternative path defined for this use case. However, as this would merely send a message from the JDSync object to the Copier object and back again (the return message would state that there was a problem copying the file or directory) this has been omitted.

Rationalizing the Class Diagrams and Collaboration Diagrams

If we consider the three collaboration diagrams it is possible to see that the synchronizer's role and the copier's role have some overlap – both are copying files and directories. However, the synchronizer does more: it decides which files to copy and from which directory. Therefore we could combine the synchronizer and copier objects in one collaboration diagram, using the copier object to copy the files and the synchronizer to decide which files to copy. This would more accurately describe the func-

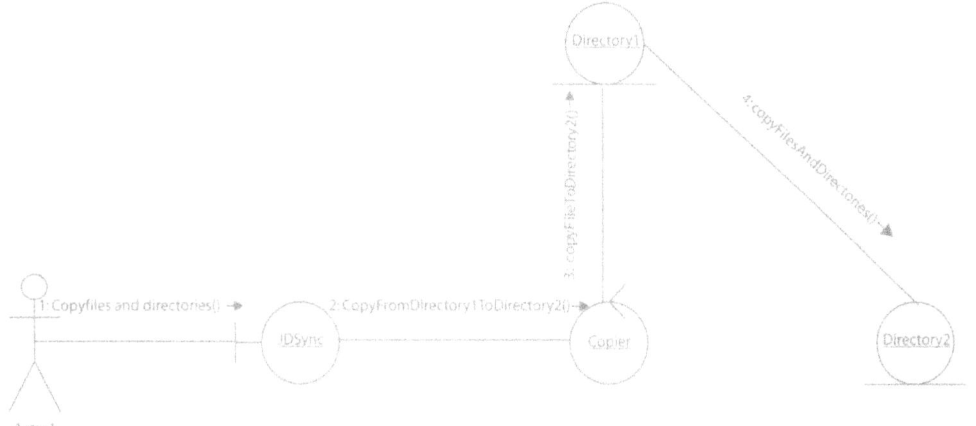

Figure 11.10 The collaboration diagram generated from the *copy files and directories* use case.

tionality of these two control classes. This also means that the class diagrams need to include a reference from the synchronizer class to the copier class. In Figure 11.11 we combine all three class diagrams together to present a single class diagram for the analysis discipline.

We leave the updated diagram for the "synchronize directories" collaboration as an exercise for the reader!

We should also consider what attributes the analysis classes require. However, at the level we are considering, few attributes are required. The directory class could have an attribute called "path" to indicate the directory it represents, and the synchronizer could keep a list of which files should be copied. Other than this, there appear to be few if any other attributes.

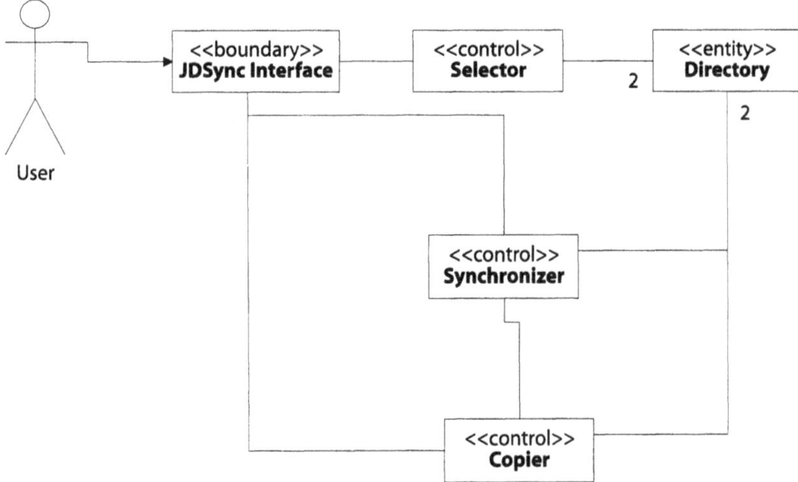

Figure 11.11 The updated and combined class diagram.

We could attempt to refine these classes further by considering issues such as: Are any of the classes redundant? Are any of the classes irrelevant? and Are any of the classes vague?, but with so few classes this would become clear early on and we are happy without five analysis classes. We could also look for additional associations; however, we believe that these have all been found via the collaboration diagrams. We could also consider inheritance, but there is no obvious inheritance in these analysis classes.

From the point of view of packaging this system up, as there are only five classes it does not make sense to separate them out into separate packages. We will therefore place them all in a package called "sync". In addition, as this application is relatively simple there are no additional special requirements, such as persistence, distribution or concurrency, to be examined.

11.5 The Design Discipline

11.5.1 Initial Identification of Classes

We will start the design discipline by considering what (initial) classes there may be in the design model. Note that this is merely a first cut at identifying the classes, and we do not expect to get them right.

The guidelines presented in the design discipline chapter indicate that you should start exploring the classes in your application by looking at:

- The boundary classes in the analysis model – they will map onto one or more interface classes in the design model.
- The entity classes – these will map onto one or more classes in the design model.
- The control classes – it is likely that these will need to be broken down, and the functionality that they represent spread between the classes in the system. However, this is by no means a for gone conclusion. It may well be that a control class in the analysis model will map to one or more control-style classes in the design model, particularly if the application is not particularly data oriented (as the JDSync is indeed not).

Let us first consider the JDSync Interface class. This class was used as the primary interface with the actor (the user) in the analysis model. This class will need to map to one or more classes in the design. If we look back at the requirements discipline, there are actually two interfaces presented there: the main JDSync interface and a dialog interface. Therefore the JDSync Interface boundary class will map to two separate classes in the design: one for the main interface and one for the dialog (see Figure 11.12). We could leave it at that; however, we know that we are targeting Java, and thus we can determine what type of classes these are. As the needs of the interfaces presented in the requirements discipline include icons and lists with icons in them, we will have to use the Swing set of components. Thus the JDSync class can be a type of JFrame. We could indicate this via inheritance or, as we are doing here, by specifying a stereotype called JFrame to indicate that the JDSync object will need to be a type of JFrame object.

Next let us consider the Directory entity object – how might this translate into the design model? This object represents the location of a directory. It should also be able to provide

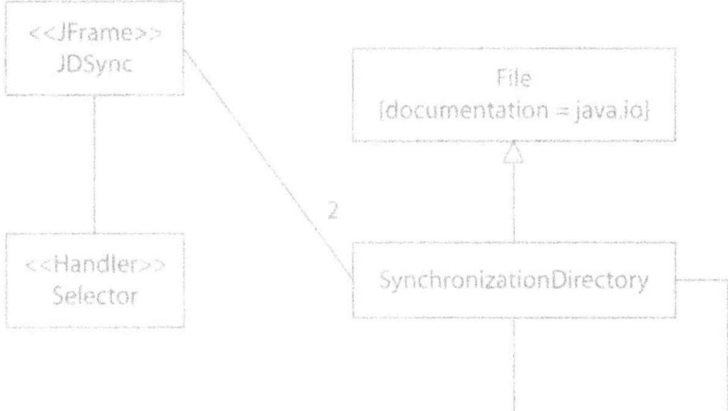

Figure 11.12 An initial design class structure diagram.

the contents of the directory. We could decide to design and implement our own class to do this; however, if we examine the Java class library, there is already a class which meets most, if not all our requirements – the java.io.File class. We will therefore initially assume that this class will be the design class that implements the analysis model's Directory entity class.

This leaves us with the three control classes: selector, synchronizer and copier. In this particular application there is nowhere immediately obvious to break these classes down into. For example, it does not appear to make sense to put the synchronizer functionality within a directory class, as that would imply that a directory can synchronize itself (when actually we need two directories). Herein lies one of the weaknesses of moving the analysis model forwards into the design model – it is easy to get procedural. If we decided to create three new classes:

- one to handle all user interaction, called "handler" (which encompasses all the behaviour of the selector and the appropriate elements of the other two classes), and
- two further control-oriented classes called synchronizer and copier,

then we would be implementing a very procedural system. Initially this might be appealing, as they will implement the analysis models of the same name. However, it is not really a good object-oriented design. Care must be taken that you are not defaulting to a procedural approach because this is the simplest for you to understand.

Let us go back to what these three control classes are actually doing. The selector control class is primarily aimed at allowing the selection of the two directories to be synchronized. As such, there doesn't (at present) appear to be anywhere obvious for this class to go. Indeed, if we consider how this control class might be implemented it becomes clear that it is likely that this will handle the events generated by the user interface. Such classes are often referred to as event handlers. To make this clear we have decided to use a stereotype for this class which indicates its nature.

Let us now consider the remaining control classes from the analysis mode. The synchronizer and copier control classes represent functionality that is associated with the two directory classes (now represented by the design element File). This suggests that we could place the functionality in these two classes within a subclass of File. For the moment this is the approach we are going to take. The selector control class will be used to initialize two instances of a new subclass of File (called SynchronizationDirectory for want of a better name; see Figure 11.12). The new SynchronizationDirectory subclass will implement the synchronization and copy operations implied by the analysis model classes.

Note that we have not provided a permanent link between the Selector class and the SynchronizationDirectory class. This is because the selector will be initiated in response to user input to instantiate these classes, but they will be associated with the interface class and not the event handler.

To find the initial associations between these classes (we could leave this till later; however, it is usually an integral part of identifying the classes) we can examine the collaboration diagrams which defined the analysis use case realizations. Each time there is a link between the analysis classes, we should determine which design classes these classes map to and provide the equivalent associations. Doing this for the JDSync application results in the links in Figure 11.12. We will come back to the classes and the association later in the design discipline as we understand more about the evolving design.

11.5.2 Sequence Diagrams

Sequence diagrams are the primary method used to describe the design use case realizations. The following section relies on the original use cases from the use case analysis performed in the requirements discipline and the analysis use case realizations generated by the analysis discipline. The aim of the design use case realizations is to consider how the design model implements the use cases. The sequence diagrams relate therefore to design classes rather than to the analysis classes of the analysis discipline. Note that you may find it useful to include collaboration diagrams to illustrate the collaborations between objects, as these diagrams can capture the interactions which are either too complex to present in a single sequence diagram or cover multiple sequence diagrams. As the JDSync application is relatively straightforward we will not present any collaboration diagrams here.

To generate a sequence diagram you should:

- Identify all the classes involved in a particular sequence – you can do this by looking at the analysis collaboration diagrams and their analysis classes and determining which are the associated design classes.
- Identify the lifeline of the objects of the classes (i.e. when they are created and when they are destroyed – you will see examples of both below).
- Identify the initiating event for the sequence (by examining the originating use cases).
- Determine the subsequent messages by exploring the collaboration diagrams.
- Identify the focus of control to determine when each object is active.
- Identify any returned messages (which will become return types on operations).
- Identify any deviations by looking back to the use cases for alternative paths.

Directory Selection Sequence Diagrams

This section will describe the sequence diagrams that are generated from the Select directories use case and the associated analysis collaboration diagrams. We start off by identifying all the classes that may be involved in any sequence diagrams related to this use case. This is done in a number of ways, but the starting point is to consider the design classes generated from the analysis classes involved in the analysis use case realization. This gives us an initial set of classes, namely:

- JDSync – implied by the boundary class
- SynchronizationDirectory – implied by the directory entity class
- Selector handler – implied by the selector control class

In a sequence diagram we do not present the classes themselves; rather, we present the objects involved in the sequence. Hence the sequence diagram will possess two instances of the class SynchronizationDirectory: one for each of the directories involved in the synchronization process.

We must now identify the initiating event. This is done by examining the initiating event for the analysis use case realization (the collaboration diagram). Thus the initiating event is "select directory" – notice that we now use the singular form here, as the user will need to follow this sequence diagram twice, once for each of the directories involved. Following the initiating event we must determine the messages sent between the objects. In the analysis collaboration diagrams we abstracted these into messages such as selectDirectory1Path; however, in the design we must consider how these messages will be generated and received. We do not yet wish to tie this too closely to any particular implementation (i.e. Java actually has two event-handling mechanisms and we wish to leave the selection of which to use open at this point). We shall therefore give the message the name "selectDirectoryAction" but annotate with information to indicate that this might be implemented as part of an actionPerformed(ActionEvent) event handler or similar. This message will need to be sent from the jdSync object (the interface object) to the event handler (called "selector" in the figure). The selector must then carry out the appropriate action.

The selector object must create two new instances of the class SynchronizationDirectory. This is illustrated in the sequence diagram by having the lifeline for the two files start at a later point in the sequence diagram. In addition, the message sent from the handler to the various file objects is preceded by the name of the class and is the new message. This message indicates that a new instance of the named class has been created (if you wish you can use the normal Java syntax here; however, we are following the UML notation).

The "select directories" sequence diagram is presented in Figure 11.13.

If we return to the original use case we may also note that there is the option of browsing the file structure to find the directories to synchronize (rather than entering them). This is illustrated in Figure 11.14's sequence diagram.

In the "browse" sequence diagram (see Figure 11.14) the user again initiates the sequence of messages; however, this time it is the "browse" event which triggers the interactions. This is again received by the jdSync object. This object then sends another action message to the selector. Again we are abstracting exactly how this would happen in the software system and refer to the action as the "browseAction" message. Note that we may wish to explicitly define these messages as operations on the selector class, which are then called by an appropriate event handler method (such as actionPerformed) or we may wish to implement the behaviour of the message in the actionPerformed event – again we are deferring this decision).

Once the selector receives the browseAction message we must decide what actions it performs and therefore what messages it sends to what objects. In this case it is fairly straightforward, and

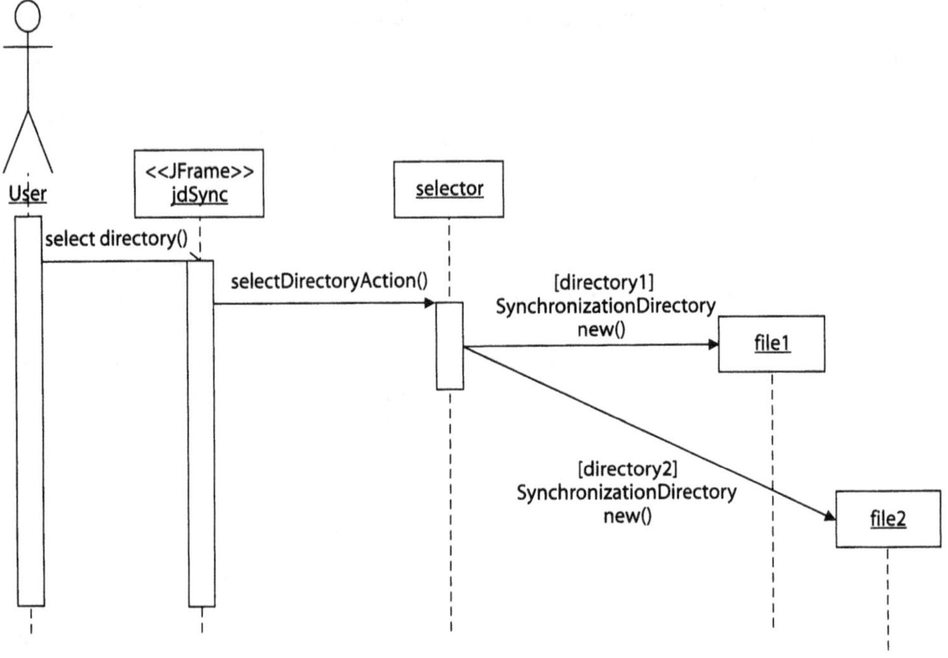

Figure 11.13 The sequence diagram for the "select directories" use case.

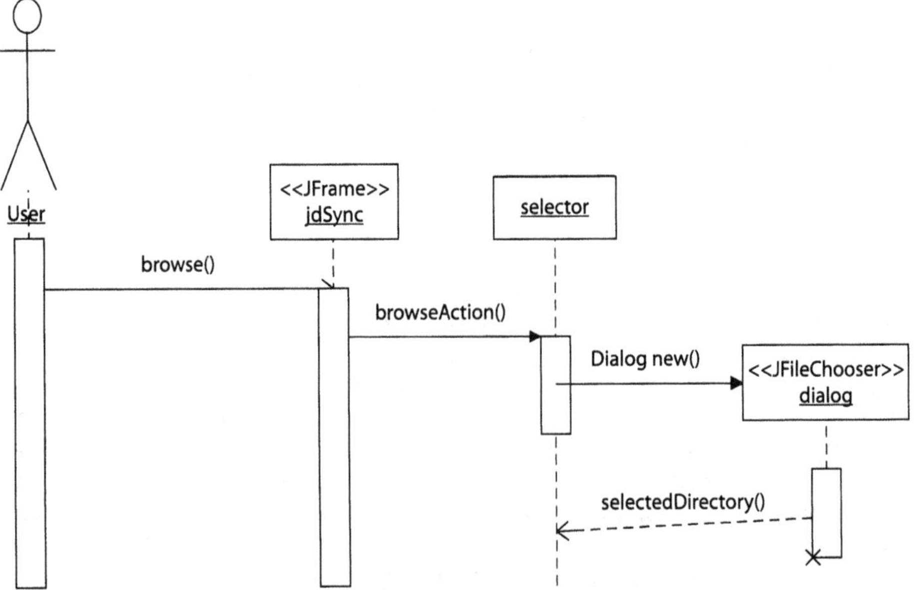

Figure 11.14 The browse sequence diagram.

the handler creates a new JFileChooser object which implements the dialog, allowing the user to select the actual directory to use. The selected directory is returned via a selectedDirectory return message. Notice that the JFileChooser is created in response to the new message sent by the handler and destroyed just after the selectedDirectory message returns the value to the handler. In the actual implementation we may decide to create the JFileChooser up front. We could then reuse it whenever it is needed. This is often a good idea because actually creating the dialog is a lot of work; however, this is an implementation issue which will be deferred to the implementation discipline (and documented as such in the design model). Note that we have not attempted to describe the sequence of events and messages that are initiated by the user interacting with the JFileChooser dialog, for two reasons:

1. It is quite complicated and would need at least one sequence diagram (if not more).
2. It is a system-supplied class that should have been documented by the suppliers of the Java environment we are using.

The Copy Files and Directories Sequence Diagram

This sequence diagram is produced in exactly the same manner as the previous sequence diagrams. That is, we study the analysis discipline collaboration diagrams for an initial set of classes and we determine the corresponding design classes. We must then determine when the objects are created and destroyed (in this case all objects will already be put in place before the sequence diagram executes), the initiating event and the messages sent between the objects. Remember that in doing this we may identify the need for additional classes. In turn, other steps in the design process may cause us to return to this sequence diagram and modify its structure or contents – the whole design process is very fluid and becomes confusing if the results of each activity are not appropriately documented and cross-referenced.

The three classes involved in the "copy files and directories" sequence diagram are JDSync, Selector and SynchronizationDirectory (one object of each class will need to be in place before the sequence executes). The jdSync object will need to send another action message to the selector, this time indicating that a copy should be performed. We will therefore call this message "copyAction". As before, we will need to document it with its purpose and role as well as any pre- and post-conditions that may apply to this message. Note that messages will become operations in the class structure diagram, and therefore it is useful to carry out the documenting steps for a message/operation when you identify them – of course you may come back to these definitions and refine them later.

The selector then needs to indicate to one of the SynchronizationDirectory objects (we will assume file1) that a copy operation should be performed. To do this we will use the "copyFromTo" message. This is because it is both descriptive and a generalization of the version presented in the analysis collaboration diagram.

You may notice that in Figure 11.15 the "copyFromTo" message has a condition placed on it (you can add conditions to sequence diagrams if you need to – indeed Figure 11.16 takes this further and uses it for a branch situation). The condition on the "CopyFromTo" message indicates that as well as having file1 in place another instance of the SynchronizationDirectory class (referred to as file2) must have already been set by the user. We could also add an annotation to this diagram indicating that the file object being copied could actually represent a file or directory but that the file object representing the target of the copy must be a directory.

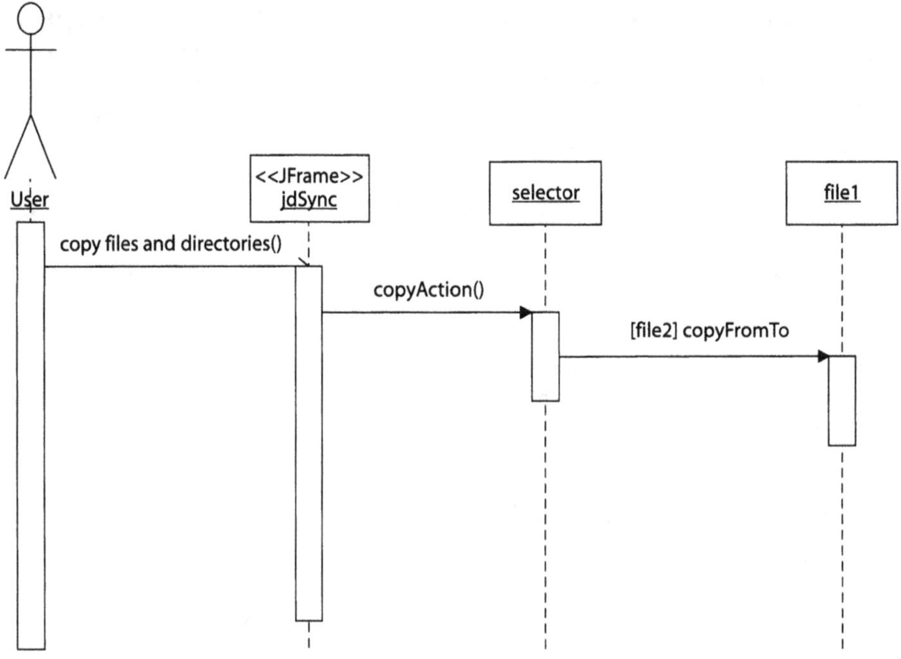

Figure 11.15 The sequence diagram generated from the "copy files and directories" use case.

The Synchronize Directories Sequence Diagram

The synchronize directories sequence diagram is the most complex sequence diagram in this simple system. It represents the sequence of messages, initiated by the user, that will be triggered in response to the "synchronize directories" event. In the analysis discipline we abstracted a great deal of what will happen within the synchronizer analysis class. However, in the design discipline we must extract more detail and identify the key messages to be sent, the objects to send them and the objects that will receive the messages. Note that we say key messages; in the implementation discipline we may identify further messages and related operations as we consider how these messages will be implemented.

The set of steps used to generate the sequence diagram in Figure 11.16 are the same as have been presented for the previous sequence diagrams; however, the set of messages sent between the objects is more complex (if we look back at Figure 11.9 we can see why that is – there is more happening in response to the event than before).

Once again, the jdSync object sends an action message to the selector object in response to an event sent to it by the actor. The message sent from the handler to the first instance of the SynchronizationDirectory class (called sync) then initiates the synchronization process. If we explore the analysis discipline collaboration diagram then we can see the steps we must perform; however, we are now constrained by the use of the methods inherited from the system class java.io.File. Thus we must determine what facilities the parent class provides and whether we can use them. This is to ensure that we don't try to reinvent the wheel! Notice that we have in effect chosen the instance SD1 at random in

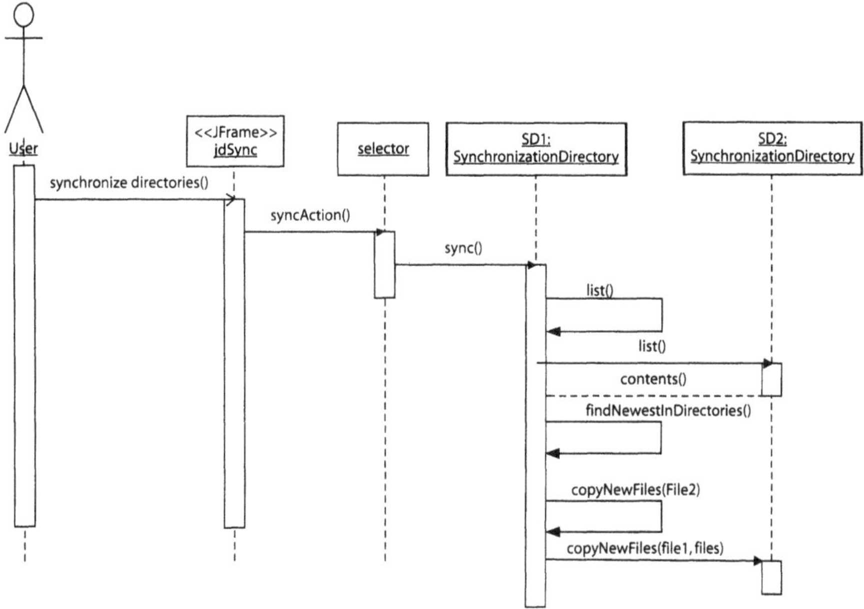

Figure 11.16 The sequence diagram generated by the "synchronize directories" use case.

Figure 11.16. We could just as easily have chosen SD2, as they are both instances of the same class and thus have the same set of methods etc.

To list the contents of a directory, the class File provides the list() method. We will therefore use this method's name as the message sent from file1 to itself and to file2. Of course in Java the method list() can return a value whereas in the UML a message cannot; we must therefore indicate the returned values via a return message (although we could annotate our list() message to indicate what is actually happening). These two messages must of course be used to obtain the contents of both directories involved in the synchronization process.

We then identify a new message called "findNewestInDirectories". This message represents the operation of identifying those files in each directory which need to be copied. The message is sent from the file1 object directory to itself. This allows this object to determine which of the files that it contains need to be copied to the second directory and which files that the second directory contains need to be copied to itself. We did not need to identify such a message, as it is really an internal operation to the file1 object (and could well be a private method in the actual implementation). However, it is a significant enough activity that will need to be performed that we have chosen to make it explicit in the sequence diagrams – this is intended to help the clarity of our design.

After finding all those files that are to be copied, the SD1 object must then send a message to itself to copy files to the second directory and to the SD2 object to ask it to copy files into the first directory. To separate out the two tasks, SD1 sends a copyNewFiles message to itself (with SD2 as the parameter). In turn it sends a copyNewFiles message to SD2 with itself as the parameter and a list of the files to copy).

We could have added an extra message to the sequence diagram to show that the two file objects could send themselves the copyFromTo message to perform the copy operation, but for simplicity we have left this out (although it should be described in the supporting documentation).

11.5.3 Identifying Attributes

We are now ready to revisit the design class diagram and add any attributes to this diagram which are either:

- implied by the use cases,
- indicated by the analysis classes,
- identified while generating the sequence diagrams.

The select directories use case specifies two attributes called directory1 and directory2. These attributes are effectively represented by the link from the SynchronizationDirectory back to itself (remember that this is a design, so we are not yet concerned with how these links will be implemented and are thus not interested in any attributes which may be used to hold a reference from one object to another).

The analysis classes identified only two attributes: the list of files to copy (and presumably where to copy from and where to copy to) in the synchronizer class and the path held by the directory entity classes. As has already been stated we have decided to use the Java class File as a superclass for the SynchronizationDirectory classes, and thus are relying on this built-in class holding the path (and indeed providing the required functionality). In addition, the list of files to copy is a list that may grow but which is going to hold elements which describe a file and where to copy it. This therefore suggests that in the design model we need a new class: one which is like a file but includes a destination attribute. Thus we will define a new subclass of File, called FileToCopy, which possesses an attribute called "destination" of type file. We will therefore replace the "list of files to copy" attribute with a List class which will hold zero or more FileToCopy objects. We will defer the decision about what type of class our List class actually is until the implementation discipline (it could be a class we define or a type of collection class from the Java 2 environment).

No further attributes were identified during the generation of the sequence diagrams. We are thus left with just one design attribute to add to our design class diagram. This is presented in Figure 11.17. Note that we have made the destination attribute of the FileToCopy class private – our default is always to make attributes private unless there is a good reason not to do so. We also need to determine what the FileToCopy class should do. This class must copy the file or directory it represents to the destination directory. It must therefore support a copy operation (see below). We should of course go back and update the sequence diagrams in which this class would be involved (i.e. the "synchronize directories" and "copy files and directories" sequence diagrams) – we shall instead leave this as a task for you the reader.

As there are so few attributes and we are fairly certain that these are fine we will skip the step of refining our attributes. Note that in a larger application or an application with more attributes this would be very important.

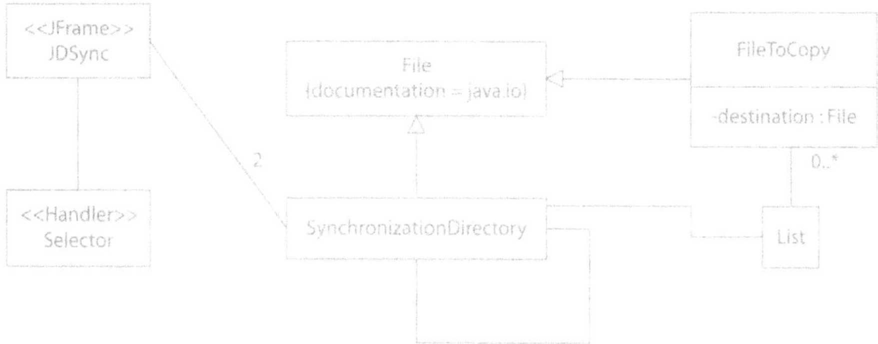

Figure 11.17 The evolving design class diagram with attributes.

Remember that each attribute should be documented with its intended type, visibility and its purpose or role in the application. For example:

11.5.4 Identifying Operations

We now need to take into account the operations we require to provide the behaviour described in the sequence diagrams. We will not concern ourselves with listing operations for Java classes (such as File), but will do so only for those classes we are providing.

The guidelines provided for identifying operations were described in the design discipline. Here we consider each guidelines in turn and consider its impact on the operations for the JDSync application:

- *Operations from analysis classes.* The control classes defined in the analysis model will need to be translated into operations on the handler, synchronize and copier classes in the design model. The sequence diagrams we have already produced will help with this and in identifying the operations required.
- *Operations implied by events and particularly interactions with actors.* Again it is the sequence diagrams which will help us to do this.
- *Operations implied by interaction diagrams such as collaboration or sequence diagrams.* The messages in these diagrams usually map onto operations. This is where we will find most of the operations we require for our design classes.
- *Transitions implied by statecharts (which we will consider below).* In fact, none of these classes is particularly state-based (a feature of the type of application we are building); we will therefore produce only minimal statecharts, merely to indicate that the directories must be selected prior to synchronizing or copying.
- *Interfaces implemented by a class.* We have two classes which implement different interfaces, and these will have an impact on the operations to be specified.
- *Operations implied by state actions and activities* (which are part of the statecharts for the object). See the comment on statecharts above.
- *Application or domain operations.* None.
- *Special requirements on analysis classes.* None.

Table 11.1 The messages sent to each object in the sequence diagrams.

Class	Messages
Selector	selectDirectoryAction
	sequenceAction
	copyAction
	browseAction
SynchronizationDirectory	sync
	FindNewestInDirectories
	copyFromTo (this is a generalization of the two copy messages used)
FileToCopy	copy (note that this message was not on any sequence diagram; however, we have added it after considering what the FileToCopy class should do)

From the above, it is clear that we should consider the messages sent to objects in the sequence diagrams used to describe the design use case realizations. Table 11.1 lists all the messages sent to each object in the four sequence diagrams presented earlier.

If we relate these operations back to the classes (and consider how Java might support these operations) then the design class diagram now resembles that presented in Figure 11.18. You may note that we have generalized all the action messages on the handler to one single actionPerformed operation. This is because we are giving a "nod" here to how the delegation event-handling mechanism in Java works. All of the action messages will be implemented using the delegation event method and thus all will be sent as ActionEvents to the actionPerformed method. The actionPerformed method will then be responsible for determining which of the actual actions to execute. This should be noted in the documentation for the actionPerformed operation.

Note that each operation should possess information on:

- any pre-conditions
- inputs/parameters and their meanings

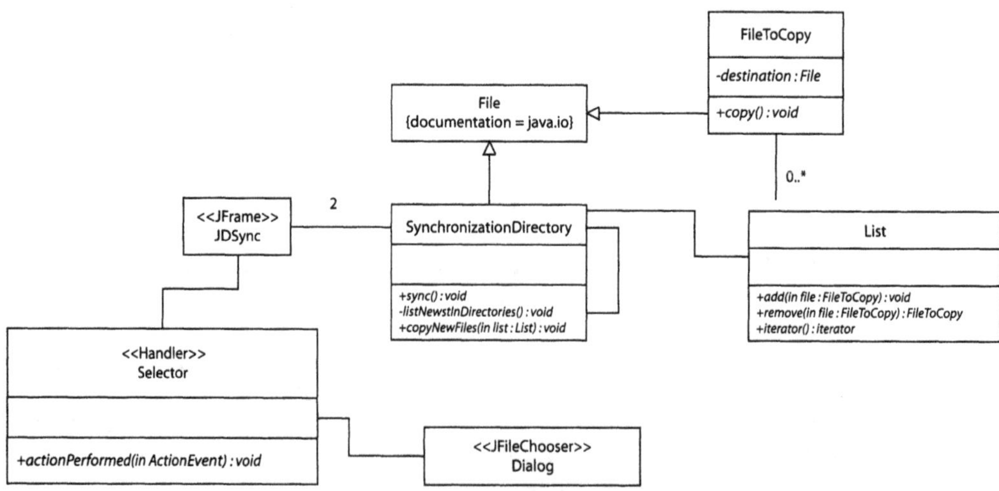

Figure 11.18 The design class diagram with attributes and operations (needs updating).

- its role and the functionality it performs
- return values and their meanings
- post-conditions

Rather than provide this for all operations we will present a single example to illustrate the idea. The operation presented is the sync operation on the SynchronizationDirectory class.

The Sync Operation

Preconditions: the two directories involved in the synchronization must have been set.
Inputs/parameters: None.
Role: the role of this method is to synchronize the two directories (represented by two SynchronizationDirectory objects – i.e. the current object and a second instance).
Functionality: The functionality of the method is (note that we can use more formal mechanisms for representing this functionality if we wish):
  - Obtain a list of all the files and subdirectories in both directories.
  - Generate a list of which files should be copied (including from where and to where). This will also involve descending into subdirectories.
  - The list should contain any files or directories not held in both directories and any files which are newer than their corresponding files in the other directory.
  - It should then request that the current object copy all the appropriate files into the destination directory.
  - Next it should request the second object to copy all the appropriate files into the current object's directory.
  - It should provide feedback to the user once this is complete.
Return values: None.
Post-condition: The two directories should be synchronized.

One of the interesting effects of introducing the FileToCopy and List classes and considering the operations on the various classes is that the copy operation can be decoupled from the two SynchronizationDirectory objects representing the two directories. Indeed, it now only needs to be presented with the list of files to copy. Each file will know where they should be copied to as well as where the original file is kept. This could make the SynchronizationDirectory class simpler; however, it really highlights that we have been misplacing this particular operation. This operation takes an instance of the List class and runs through all the elements in that list – why isn't it held within the List class? Primarily because we have been moving forward from the analysis classes, which tend to direct you towards a more procedural approach – that is, separating data and operations into different classes. However, in this case there is no good reason to do this. We shall therefore endeavour to correct this by moving the copyFiles method into the List class. This illustrates how you need to keep challenging your design as it progresses and as your understanding of the design grows (see Figure 11.18).

11.5.5 Describing the Overall Behaviour of an Object

It is often useful to describe the overall behaviour and the state changes that occur for significant classes in a design. In this case we will only look at a statechart for the whole system as this encompasses the behaviour of the classes which comprise it. Each individual class is relatively

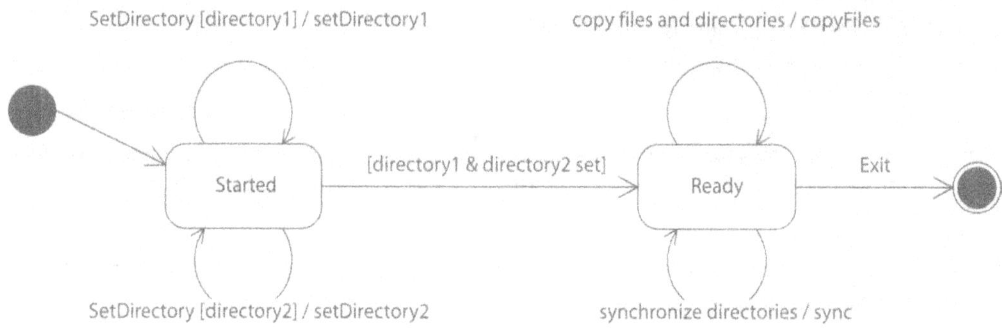

Figure 11.19 A simple statechart for the whole JDSync system.

simple and few possess any state-oriented behaviour. However, the system as a whole does have some state-oriented behaviour, as is indicated right from the use case analysis onwards. The system must be in the "two files set" state before any files can be copied or directories synchronized.

To generate the statechart we have followed the steps outline in the design discipline. We therefore examined the various sequence diagrams defined above and considered the messages sent between the objects and the effect on those messages on the state of the overall system (if you were doing this for an individual class you would only consider the effects on a single class). From this we noted that there were only two situations in which information was required (when the two directories are specified) and that until these two items of information are provided the system cannot perform a copy or a synchronization operation. It therefore appears that there are just two states in this system: "Started" (but not yet ready to copy or synchronize) and "Ready". We could have identified two states for the "Started" state (one for "no directories set" and one for "one directory set"), but this seemed to be moving to a level of detail which was below that required for the whole system. The final result is illustrated in the statechart presented in Figure 11.19 (note that in the modelling tool I am using I have had to link this to a particular class – I therefore linked it to the JDSync class).

11.5.6 Identifying Associations and Inheritance

We have been attempting to identify the associations between the JDSync class as we have gone along. If we had a larger application it would certainly be worth considering any additional links or inheritance at this stage. You should note that we are looking for design relationships, but inevitably you also need to think about your target environment. This is why we have indicated that the Selector will fit into the delegation event model, but have not yet said what type of interface it will implement – we shall leave this to the implementation discipline (having clearly documented this requirement on the implementation discipline). However, as there appear to be no further design-oriented association and inheritance to be found in JDSync we will not pursue this further. Instead we will annotate the associations with names, for example, the association between the JDSync class and the Selector class could be labelled with "view" and "controller" respectively. Do not go overboard with such labelling: only add these labels if it makes the model more meaningful – it is easy to end up with information overload.

11.5.7 Identifying Interfaces

Thus far we have not attempted to identify any interfaces, yet you have been told how useful they can be (particularly with reference to the software architecture). In this case the JDSync system was simple enough that we did not worry about specifying interfaces up front. However, they can still be a useful way of decoupling the classes. For example, we might well decide to specify an interface for the FileToCopy operations, thus allowing us to change the class used to represent the files to copy depending on whether it was a directory or a file. Thus encapsulating within a DirectoryToCopy class the functionality related to descending into subdirectories would simplify the SynchronizationDirectory class. In this case we will not do this, primarily in a bid to keep things simple.

11.5.8 A Complete Design Model

At this point we have a complete design model containing use case realizations in the form of the sequence diagrams, the design class diagrams, a list of operations for each class (and the associated documentation), a list of attributes for each class (and associated documentation) plus any additional non-functional requirements. In this case we require that the selector fit into the delegation event model architecture of the Java environment. Note that we should have been developing an explicit data dictionary which captures all the information relating to all classes and interfaces and their attributes and operations in the JDSync application.

11.6 The Implementation Workflow

The implementation moves the design model towards the actual implementation and carries out the physical implementation of the system in the target environment (in our case the Java environment). It is necessary to move the design model forward, as it does not take into account implementation details.

We will first develop the implementation model. This is really the design model moved forward to the implementation. You may wish to make a copy of the original design model so that you can return to that or you may wish to move that actual model forward to the implementation.

11.6.1 Updating the Class Structure

The first thing we will do is to look at the class diagram and consider how this diagram might be implemented in terms of the Java environment. This means taking into account:

- the delegation event-handling mechanism for the handler as well as other event-handling issues, such as the window events.

- the use of collection classes such as Vector or ArrayList for the List class.
- the GUI facilities in Java that will allow us to produce the interface first presented back in the requirements discipline.

We shall consider each of these below.

The Delegation Event Model

The Java delegation event model specifies that event handlers must implement the appropriate listener interfaces. The buttons on the JDSync user interface will generate the ActionEvent to be handled by objects which implement the ActionListener interface. Thus the Selector class must implement the ActionListener interface. The reference between the JDSync class and the Selector class is therefore one in which the Selector exposes the ActionListener interface and the JDSync class is dependent upon that interface (hence the addition of the interface association). In addition, a useful idiom in Java is that such event handlers can be implemented as inner classes; that is, directly as part of the GUI class. Thus we have modified the association between the JDSync class and the Handler class to use the composition aggregation symbol (a filled diamond).

The delegation event model also specifies a separate set of window events that must be handled by a class implementing the WindowListener. The WindowListener, however, lists seven different methods that must be implemented. As we are only interested in one of them, the windowClosing operation, we don't really want to have to implement all seven, six of which are empty. We will therefore define a class called WindowHandler, which is a subclass of the convenient WindowAdapter class. This convenience call provides seven null implementations for the WindowListener interface that it implements. Again we will make the WindowHandler class an inner class of the JDSync class.

Use of Collection Classes

The List class provides a very good match with the sort of functionality provided by the ArrayList class. However, what should the relationship between the ArrayList class and our List class be? If we make the List class a subclass of the ArrayList then all the methods defined in the ArrayList class that are public will also be available from the List class. This would allow a user of the List class to add any object to our List. Is this what we want? If we consider the operations defined for the List class, we find that we only want to add or remove instances of the FileToCopy class. Thus we don't really want to use inheritance here. Instead, we want the List class to contain an instance of the ArrayList and to add elements to that contained instance. In addition, the iterator operation can still be supported in this way by returning the iterator obtained from the contained ArrayList. Thus the relationship between the ArrayList and the List is one of aggregation.

The resulting implementation class diagram is presented in Figure 11.20.

Implementing the GUI

We can now turn our attention to how we might implement the user interface presented in the requirements discipline. As can be seen from the user interface presented, we are going to have to use the javax.swing set of components, including the JList class and JButtons with icons, and we must be able to have different icons for directories and files in the list. This is not as trivial as it may sound. If we study the documentation for the Swing set of components, although setting the

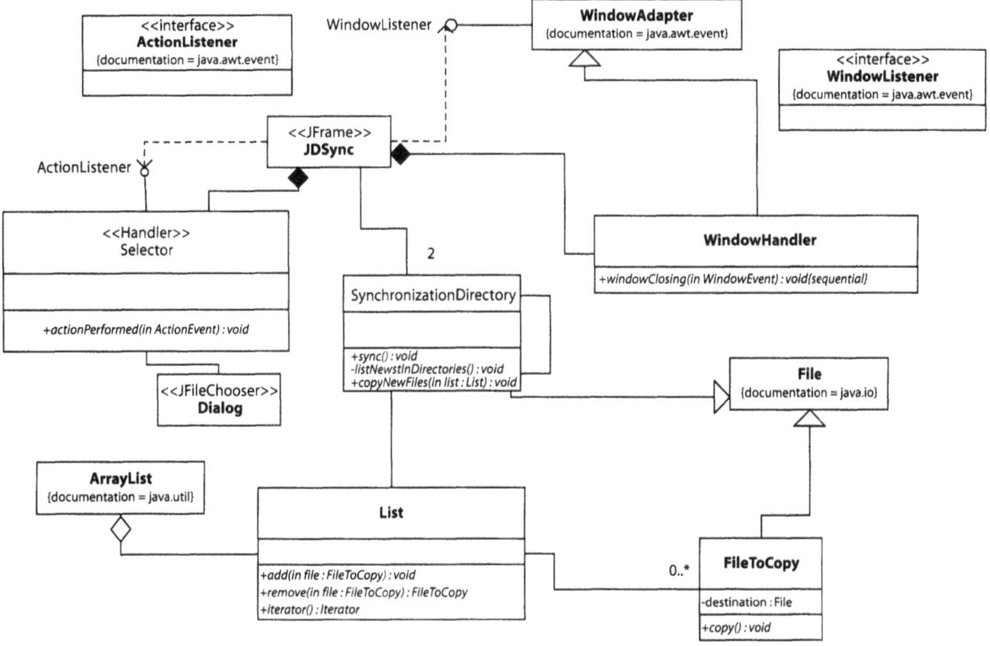

Figure 11.20 The implementation class structure for the "application" package (needs updating).

icon for a button (and indeed giving it some textual tool-tips is straightforward), if you wish to provide icons in a JList component you must define a cell renderer which will draw the icon in the list. This means that we will need a class to do this. This class must implement the ListCellRenderer interface and be able to display icons and text and decide how a user selection should be displayed. We will therefore need to subclass some type of Swing component (and in fact the JLabel class is the most obvious class).

However, this is not the end of the story. We will also need to provide a model for the JList component itself. This is because all Swing components possess an explicit model, which they display. For many Swing components this model is generated automatically (for example, those for a JButton) when that component is initialized (or the icons and text of the button are set). For a list item, the model has to be generated by the application. Once generated it must be registered with the application. The list will then display it. The list model can be modified at a later date by the application and the list can redisplay the modified list model.

A JList object expects its list model to be an object which implements the ListModel interface or subclasses a class which implements that interface. The DefaultListModel class is ideal for this, and thus our list model (to be called SyncListModel) will subclass the DefaultListModel. It must then obtain information from the two file objects to determine the contents of the two directories to display.

As the GUI part of the application has grown significantly we could now divide our application into two packages: the sync.application package and the sync.gui package. The

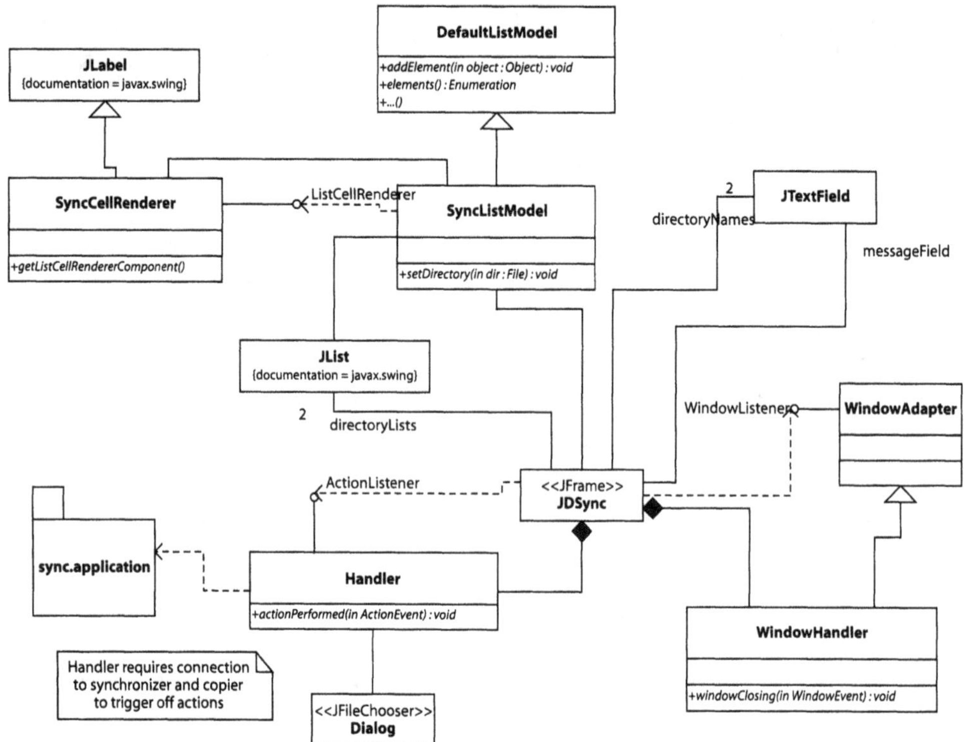

Figure 11.21 The sync.gui implementation class diagram.

contents of the sync.gui package are presented in Figure 11.21. We will assume that everything not in this package is in the sync.application package.

We do not present a package diagram for the two new packages, sync.gui and sync.application. This is because it would merely show two package icons with a dashed arrow from the sync.gui package to the sync.application package illustrating that the gui package is dependent upon the application package! Instead, we present the sync.application implementation class diagram as it now stands in Figure 11.22. As you will note, the separation of the gui element of the system from the actual application element has greatly simplified the application part. We could have done this earlier; however, until we started to examine how the user interface might be implemented it was not obvious that such a separation would be useful.

Also note that we have defined some new operations for the List class. This is because as we are drawing nearer to the implementation we are determining how the algorithms in the design model, which described the operation, might be implemented. Indeed, it might now be better to refer to the operations as methods to indicate the difference. When we came to analyze how the copyNewFiles method might be implemented, the need for a method in the List class to support the copy operation was identified. This method would action the copy method of the instances it holds. It is now listed in the figure. We should, of course, provide detailed documentation of any pre- and post-conditions, the role and purpose of the method, and any parameters and return types to ensure that each method is clearly specified.

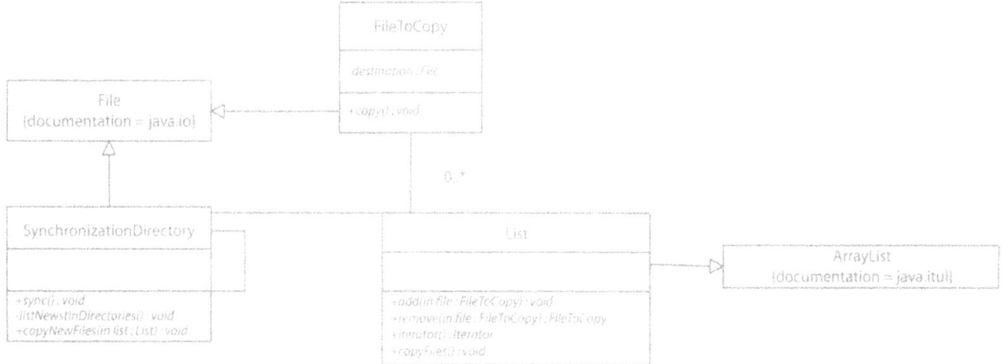

Figure 11.22 The sync.application implementation class diagram.

The Component Model

We must now define the component model for the implementation discipline. This model describes how files, classes, byte code files and the like relate. Essentially it should tell us which .java files define which .class file (and thus which classes). Remember that only public classes must be in a file with the same name as the class. The component model for the sync.gui package

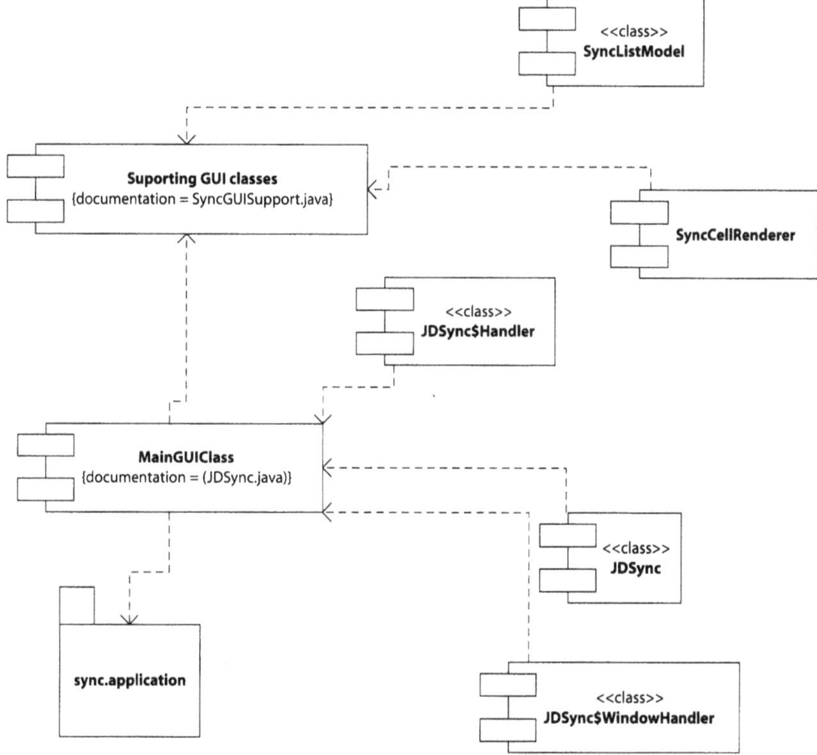

Figure 11.23 The component model for the sync.gui package.

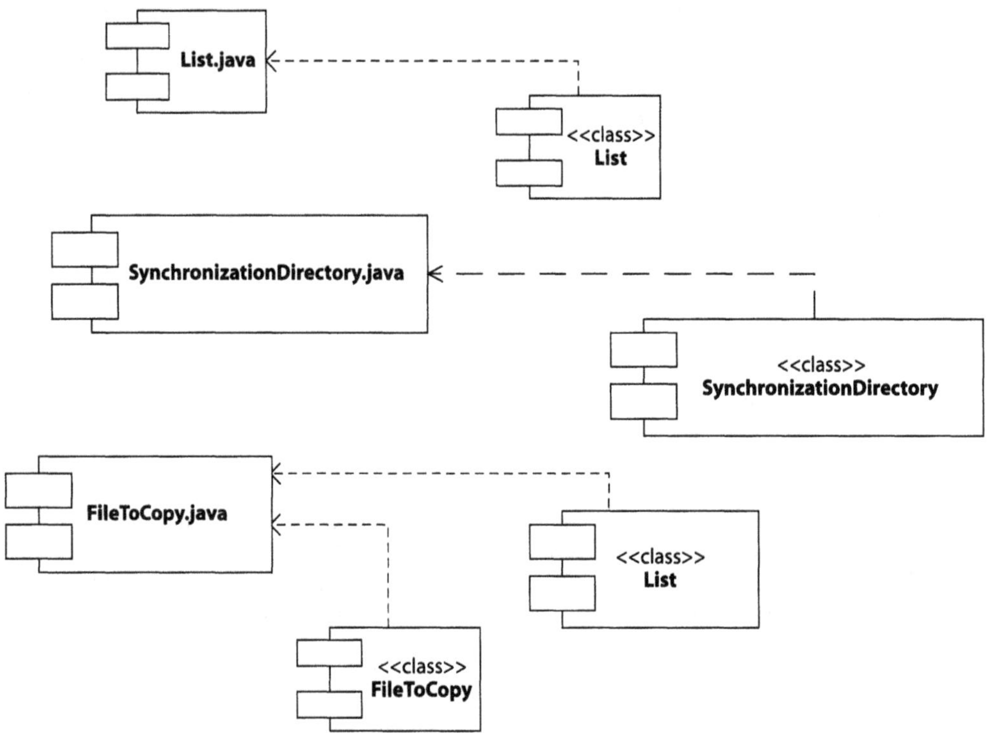

Figure 11.24 The component diagram for the sync.application package.

is presented in Figure 11.23. Note that the Selector class was renamed Handler when it became an inner class, reflecting its design stereotype.

The component model for the sync.application package is simpler as it contains fewer classes. This component model is presented in Figure 11.24.

11.7 Summary

We have now analyzed and designed a simple application. We have taken it from the initial problem statement right through to the implementation model. The only step left would be to actually implement it. This has been done (although it is not documented here), partly to prove that the design we evolved was feasible. Hopefully this has given you an idea of how the Unified Process is applied and will help you when applying it itself. It is also hoped that the incremental nature of object-oriented design was also brought out, even though, by its very nature, the paper medium is sequential.

Part 2

Design Patterns

Software Patterns

12.1 Introduction

There is a growing interest in what have become known generically as patterns; to be more precise, in design patterns. This is evidenced by the number of books now appearing on patterns (just try searching on "Patterns" and "Java" at amazon.com). One of these books in particular presents a very good introduction to the philosophy of patterns (Fowler, 1997). However, none of these attempts to present a sample pattern, highlight the many motivations behind the uptake of patterns or consider when they should be used. This chapter attempts to provide these along with a brief consideration of the strengths and weaknesses of patterns.

Historically, design patterns have their basis in the work of an architect who designed a language for encoding knowledge of the design and construction of buildings (Alexander *et al.*, 1977; Alexander, 1979). The knowledge is described in terms of patterns that capture both a recurring architectural arrangement and a rule for how and when to apply this knowledge. That is, they incorporate knowledge about the design as well as the basic design relations.

This work was picked up by a number of researchers working within the object-oriented field. This then led to the exploration of how software frameworks can be documented using (software) design patterns (for example, Johnson (1992) and Birrer and Eggenschmiler (1993)). In particular, Johnson's paper describes the form that these design patterns take and the problems encountered in applying them.

Since 1995 and the publication of the "Patterns" book by the *Gang of Four* (Gamma *et al.*, 1995), interest in patterns has mushroomed. Patterns are now seen as a way of capturing expert and design knowledge associated with a system architecture to support design as well as software reuse. In addition, as interest in patterns has grown their use and representational expressiveness has grown.

The remainder of this chapter is structured in the following manner: Section 12.2 considers the motivation behind the patterns movement and Section 12.3 considers what a pattern is and is not. As the focus of this book is primarily the Unified Process and the UML we have only a limited amount of space which can be devoted to the concept of patterns (see Fowler (1997) and Gamma

209

et al. (1995) for more details). Thus in this chapter only a brief introduction to the concept will be given, and greater emphasis will be placed on describing, documenting and illustrating patterns. Section 12.4 describes how patterns are documented. Section 12.5 briefly considers when patterns should be used and Section 12.6 discusses the strengths and limitations of patterns. Section 12.7 then presents an example pattern using Java. This pattern considers how you can use a mediator along with a set of associated objects to communicate in a loosely coupled manner.

12.2 The Motivation Behind Patterns

There are a number of motivations behind design patterns. These include:

- Designing reusable software is difficult. Finding appropriate objects and abstractions is not trivial. Having identified such objects, building flexible, modular, reliable code for general reuse is not easy, particularly when dealing with more than one class. In general, such reusable "frameworks" emerge over time rather than being designed from scratch.
- Software components support the reuse of code but not the reuse of knowledge.
- Frameworks support the reuse of design and code but not the knowledge of how to use that framework. That is, design trade-offs and expert knowledge are lost.
- Experienced programmers do not start from first principles every time; thus, successful reusable conceptual designs must exist.
- Communication of such "architectural" knowledge can be difficult, as it is in the designer's head and is poorly expressed as a program instance.
- A particular program instance fails to convey constraints, trade-offs and other non-functional forces applied to the "architecture".
- Since frameworks are reusable designs, not just code, they are more abstract than most software, which makes documenting them more difficult. Documentation for a framework has three purposes and patterns can help to fulfill each of them. Documentation must provide:
  - the purpose of the framework
  - how to use the framework
  - the detailed design of the framework
- The problem with cookbooks is that they describe a single way in which the framework will be used. A good framework will be used in ways that its designers never conceived. Thus a cookbook is insufficient on its own to describe every use of the framework. Of course, a developer's first use of a framework usually fits the stereotypes in the cookbook. However, once the developer goes beyond the examples in the cookbook, he or she needs to understand the details of the framework. However, cookbooks tend not to describe the framework itself. But in order to understand a framework, you need to have knowledge of both its design and its use.
- In order to achieve high-level reuse (i.e. above the level of reusing the class set) it is necessary to design with reuse in mind. This requires knowledge of the reusable components available.

The design patterns movement wished to address some (or all) of the above in order to facilitate successful architectural reuse. The intention was thus to address many of the problems which reduce the reusability of software components and frameworks.

12.3 Documenting Patterns

The actual form used to document individual patterns varies, but in general the documentation covers:

- The motivation or context that the pattern applies to.
- Prerequisites that should be satisfied before deciding to use a pattern.
- A description of the program structure that the pattern will define.
- A list of the participants needed to complete a pattern.
- Consequences of using the pattern, both positive and negative.
- Examples of the pattern's usage.

The pattern template used in Gamma *et al.* (1995) provides a standard structure for the information which comprises a design pattern. This makes it easier to comprehend a design pattern as well as providing a concrete structure for those defining new patterns. Gamma's book (Gamma *et al.*, 1995) provides a detailed description of the template; only a summary of it is presented in Table 12.1.

A pattern language is a structured collection of patterns that build on each other to transform needs and constraints into architecture. For example, the patterns associated with the HotDraw framework provide a pattern language for HotDraw. What is HotDraw? HotDraw is a drawing framework developed by Ralph Johnson at the University of Illinois at Urbana-Champaign (Johnson, 1992). It is a reusable design for a drawing tool expressed as a set of classes. However, it is more than just a set of classes; it possesses the whole structure of a drawing tool, which only needs to be parameterized to create a new drawing tool. It can therefore be viewed as a basic drawing tool and a set of examples that can be used to help you develop your own drawing editor!

Table 12.1 The design pattern template.

Heading	Usage
Name	The name of the pattern
Intent	This is a short statement indicating the purpose of the pattern. It includes information on its rationale, intent, the problem it addresses etc.
Also known as	Any other names by which the pattern is known.
Motivation	Illustrates how the pattern can be used to solve a particular problem.
Applicability	This describes the situation in which the pattern is applicable. It may also say when the pattern is not applicable.
Structure	This is a (graphical) description of the classes in the pattern.
Participants	The classes and objects involved in the design and their responsibilities.
Collaborations	This describes how the classes and objects work together.
Consequences	How does the pattern achieve its objective? What are the trade-offs and results of using the pattern? What aspect of the system structure does it let you vary independently?
Implementation	What issues are there in implementing the design pattern?
Sample code	Code illustrating how a pattern might be implemented.
Known uses	How the pattern has been used in the past. Each pattern has at least two such examples.
Related patterns	Closely related design patterns are listed here.

Essentially, HotDraw is a skeleton DrawingEditor waiting for you to fill out the specific details. That is, all the elements of a drawing editor are provided, including a basic working editor, which you, as a developer, customize as required. What this means to you is that you get a working system much, much sooner and with a great deal less effort.

HotDraw was first presented at the OOPSLA'92 conference in a paper entitled "Documenting frameworks using patterns" by Ralph Johnson (Johnson, 1992). This paper considers the problems associated with documenting complex reusable software systems, using HotDraw as a concrete example. Included with the paper are a set of appendices which act as very useful guides on how to change the default drawing editor. The appendices represent HotDraw's pattern language and comprise 10 different patterns. These 10 patterns explain how to define drawing elements, change drawing elements, add constraints between graphic objects, add lines etc.

I personally first used HotDraw in mid-1993 knowing nothing about patterns, and didn't really understand the paper. However, I found the appendices helped me to customize the drawing editor quickly and painlessly. I read only those patterns that I needed to understand what I wanted to do and ignored the other patterns. Over time I found that I read those other patterns as and when I needed them.

12.4 When to Use Patterns

Patterns can be useful in situations where solutions to problems recur but in slightly different ways. Thus, the solution needs to be instantiated as appropriate for different problems. The solutions should not be so simple that a simple linear series of instructions will suffice. In such situations patterns are overkill. They are particularly relevant when several steps are involved in the pattern which may not be required for all problems. Finally, patterns are really intended for solutions where the developer is more interested in the existence of the solution rather than how it was derived (as patterns still leave out too much detail).

12.5 Strengths and Limitations of Design Patterns

Design patterns have a number of strengths including:

- providing a common vocabulary
- explicitly capturing expert knowledge and trade-offs
- helping to improve developer communication
- promoting ease of maintenance
- providing a structure for change

However, they are not without their limitations. These include:

- not leading to direct code reuse
- being deceptively simple

- easy to get pattern overload (i.e. finding the right pattern)
- they are validated by experience rather than testing
- no methodological support

In general, patterns provide opportunities for describing both the design and the use of the framework as well as including examples, all within a coherent whole. In some ways patterns act like a hyper-graph with links between parts of patterns. To illustrate the ideas behind frameworks and patterns the next section will present the framework HotDraw and a tutorial HotDraw pattern example explaining how to construct a simple drawing tool.

However, there are potentially very many design patterns available to a designer. A number of these patterns may superficially appear to suit the designer's requirements, even if the design patterns are available online (via some hypertext-style browser (Budinsky *et al.*, 1996)) it is still necessary for the designer to search through them manually, attempting to identify the design which best matches their requirements.

In addition, once a design has been found that the designer feels best matches his or her needs, how to apply it to the application must be considered. This is because a design pattern describes a solution to a particular design problem. This solution may include multiple trade-offs which are contradictory and which the designer must choose between, although some aspects of the system structure can be varied independently (some attempts have been made to automate this process; for example, Budinsky *et al.* (1996)).

12.6 An Example Pattern: Mediator

This pattern is based on that presented in Gamma *et al.* (1995) on pages 273–282.

Pattern name: Mediator
Intent: To define an object that encapsulates how a set of objects interact. Mediator promotes loose coupling by keeping objects from referring to each other explicitly.
Motivation: Object-oriented design encourages the distribution of behaviour among objects. However, this can lead to a multiplicity of links between objects. In the worst case every object needs to know about/link to every other object. This can be a problem for maintenance and for the reusability of the individual classes.

These problems can be overcome by using a mediator object. In this scheme other objects are connected together via a central mediator object in a star-like structure. The mediator is then responsible for controlling and coordinating the interactions of the group of objects.

Applicability: The mediator pattern should be used where:
  - a set of objects communicate in well-defined but complex ways. The resulting interdependencies are unstructured and difficult to understand.
  - reusing an object is difficult because it refers to, and uses, many other objects.
  - a particular behaviour is distributed among a number of classes and we wish to customize that behaviour with the minimum of subclassing.

Structure: The class diagram for a mediator is illustrated in Figure 12.1.

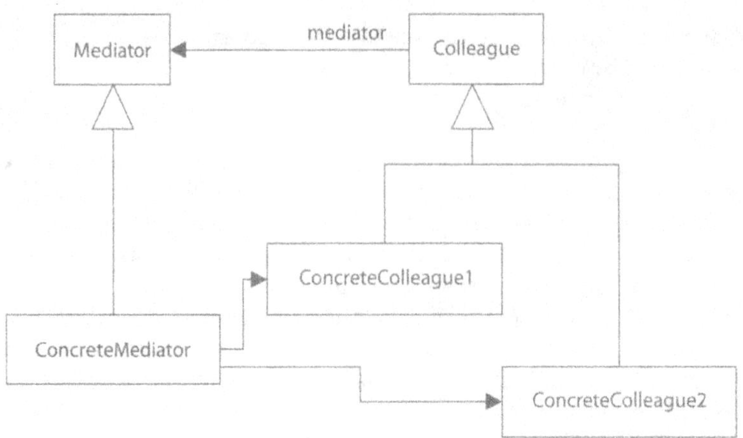

Figure 12.1 Mediator class diagram.

A typical object diagram for a mediator is illustrated in Figure 12.2.

Participants:
- *Mediator* handles communication between colleague objects.
- *ConcreteMediator* defines how the mediator should coordinate the colleagues' interactions. It knows and maintains its colleagues.
- *Colleague classes.* Each colleague knows its mediator object. It communicates with this mediator object in order to communicate with other colleagues.

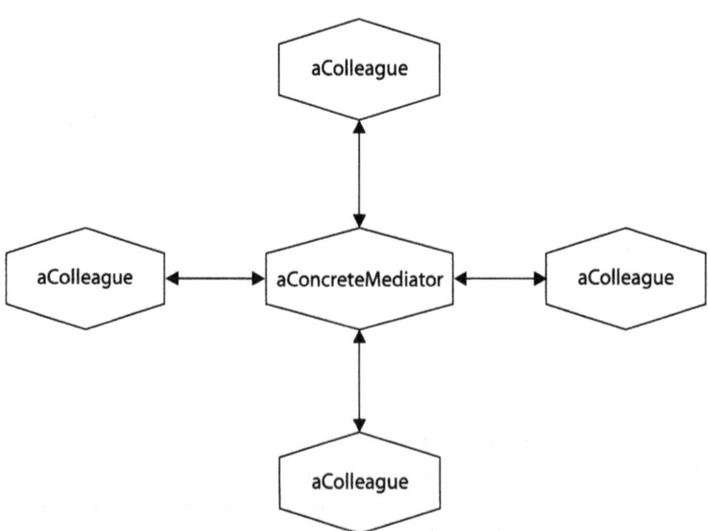

Figure 12.2 A mediator object diagram.

Collaborations: The mediator object receives messages from colleagues and relays them to other colleagues as appropriate.

Consequences: The mediator pattern has the following benefits and drawbacks:
- It limits subclassing to the mediator (e.g. by changing the routing algorithm in mediator you can change the system's behaviour).
- It decouples colleagues.
- It simplifies object protocols from many-to-many down to one-to-many.
- It abstracts how objects cooperate.
- It centralizes control.

Implementation: The following implementation issues are relevant to the mediator pattern:
- Omitting the abstract Mediator class. If there is only to be one mediator class there is no reason to define an abstract class.
- Colleague mediator communication. The colleagues need to tell the mediator when something interesting happens to them that they wish to relay to their colleagues. This could be handled via a dependency mechanism (see the Observer pattern) or by direct communication by the object. For example, the colleague could tell the mediator that something has changed and then allow the mediator to interrogate it to find out what. This is the approach taken in the sample code example.

Sample code: The following illustrates the basic structure for the classes used in a simple mediator-based system. The assumption used is that when colleagues need to communicate with the mediator, a colleague passes itself as an argument, allowing the mediator to identify the sender. The Mediator class (in Java) is:

```java
import java.util.*;
public abstract class Mediator {
  private Vector colleagues = new Vector();
  public void addColleague(Colleague col) {
    colleagues.addElement(col);
  }
  public abstract void changed (Colleague col);
}
```

Concrete subclasses of Mediator (such as CommunicationManager) implement the changed method to affect the appropriate behaviour. The colleague passes a reference to itself as an argument to the changed method to let the mediator identify the colleague that changed.

Colleague is the abstract class for all colleagues. A Colleague knows its mediator.

```java
public abstract class Colleague {
  private Mediator mediator;
  public void addMediator(Mediator med) {
    mediator = med;
  }
  private void changed() {
    mediator.changed(this);
  }
}
```

As an example, consider an application in which we wish to inform members of a software team whenever a meeting has been arranged (we will ignore the issue of checking that all the team members can make that meeting). Rather than construct a rigid set of links between the members we will use the Mediator pattern. We can then define a CommunicationsManager class (which inherits from Mediator) as follows:

```java
import java.util.Enumeration;

public class CommunicationsManager extends Mediator {
  public static void main (String args []) {
    CommunicationsManager c = new CommunicationsManager();
    c.setup();
    c.sampleMeeting();
  }

  public void setup () {
    int i;
    String teamMembers [] = {"John", "Denise", "Phoebe", "Isobel"};
    for (i = 0; i < teamMembers.length; ++i) {
      addColleague(new TeamMember(teamMembers[i]));
    }
  }

  public void sampleMeeting () {
  // This is just an example; the manager would
  // not normally initiate this.
    TeamMember aPerson;
    aPerson = (TeamMember)colleagues.firstElement());
    aPerson.meeting("9:00am 10/3/97");
  }

  public void changed (Colleague person) {
    TeamMember item;
    String theMeeting = ((TeamMember)person).currentMeeting();
    for (Enumeration e = colleagues.elements();
      e.hasMoreElements(); ) {
      item = (TeamMember)e.nextElement();
      if (item != person)
        item.newMeeting(theMeeting);
    }
  }
}
```

This class sets up the colleagues to be linked to the CommunicationsManager. In this case the colleagues are all instances of a class TeamMember (see below). It then uses an example method to trigger communications between the teamMember objects. To achieve this the

CommunicationsManager implements its own changed() method. This method merely passes details of the current meeting on to the other team members.

The TeamMember class extends the Colleague class and (for this simple example) can be defined as:

```java
import java.util.Vector;
public class TeamMember extends Colleague {
  // Instance variables
  String name, meeting;
  Vector meetings = new Vector();
  // A Constructor
  public TeamMember (String aName) {
    name = aName;
  }
  public void meeting(String aTimeAndDate) {
    meeting = aTimeAndDate;
    System.out.println("Generating a meeting " +
                       aTimeAndDate + " for " + name);
    changed();
  }
  public String currentMeeting () {
    return meeting;
    }
  public void newMeeting (String aTimeAndDate) {
    meetings.addElement(aTimeAndDate);
    System.out.println("Adding " + aTimeAndDate + " for " + name);
  }
}
```

This class defines the functionality of the TeamMember objects. It inherits all the functionality it needs to work with any form of mediator. The only detail that needs to be incorporated is a call to the changed() method when appropriate (in this case in method meeting()).

An example of this application running is presented in Figure 12.3.

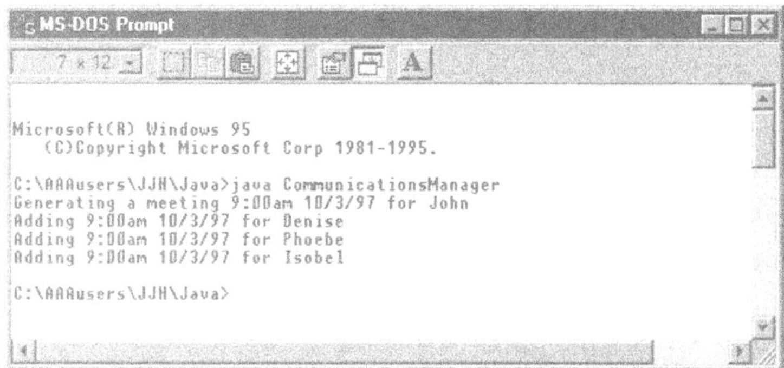

Figure 12.3 The CommunicationsManager application.

- *Known uses*: ET++ and the THINK C class library use director like objects in dialogs as mediators between widgets. Smalltalk/V uses it as the basis of its application architecture.
- *Related patterns*: Facade differs from Mediator in that it abstracts a subsystem of objects to provide a more convenient interface. However, its protocol is unidirectional where as mediator is multidirectional. Colleagues can communicate with a mediator using the Observer pattern.

12.7 Summary

In this chapter we explored the concepts of patterns as a method of documenting the design of reusable software architectures. Such patterns have a great deal of potential; however, online support for browsing and applying patterns is required. In addition work on methodologies which consider how to define and apply patterns is required.

12.8 Further Reading

A number of books and a great many papers have been written about patterns in recent years. The most influential of these is Gamma *et al.* (1994) by the so called "Gang of four", who are Erich Gamma, Richard Helm, Ralph Johnson and John Vlissides. There are also a series of conferences on Patterns referred to as PLoP (for Pattern Language of Program design). Two proceedings are available: Coplien and Schmidt (1995) and Vlissides *et al.* (1996).

Two further patterns books are Buschmann *et al.* (1996) (which represents the progression and evolution of the pattern approach into a system capable of describing and documenting large scale applications) and Fowler (1997), which considers how patterns can be used for analysis to help build reusable object models.

In addition to the papers mentioned earlier in this chapter, there is also a Web page dedicated to the patterns movement (which includes many of the papers referenced as well as tutorials and example patterns). The URL for the Web page is: `http://st-www.cs.uiuc.edu/users/patterns/patterns/`.

12.9 References

Alexander, C., Ishikawa, S. and Silverstein, M. (with M. Jacobson, I. Fiksdahl-King and S. Angel) (1977). *A Pattern Language*. Oxford University Press, Oxford.

Alexander, C. (1979). *The Timeless Way of Building*. Oxford University Press, Oxford.

Beck, K. and Johnson, R. (1994). Patterns generate architectures, *Proc. ECOOP'94*, pp. 139–149. Springer-Verlag, Berlin.

Birrer, A. and Eggenschwiler, T. (1993) Frameworks in the financial engineering domain: an experience report, *Proc. ECOOP'93*, pp. 21–35. Springer-Verlag, Berlin.

Budinsky, F.J., Finnie, M.A., Vlissides, J.M. and Yu, P.S. (1996). Automatic code generation from design patterns, *IBM Systems Journal*, 35(2).

Buschmann, F., Meunier, R., Rohnert, H., Sommerlad, P. and Stal, M. (1996). *Pattern-Oriented Software Architecture – A System of Patterns*. John Wiley & Sons, New York.

Coplien, J.O. and Schmidt, D.C. (eds) (1995). *Pattern Languages of Program Design*. Addison-Wesley, Reading, MA.

Gamma, E., Helm, R., Johnson, R. and Vlissades, J. (1993). Design patterns: abstraction and reuse of object-oriented design, *Proc. ECOOP'93*, pp. 406–431, Springer-Verlag, Berlin.

Gamma, E., Helm, R., Johnson, R. and Vlissades, J. (1995). *Design Patterns: Elements of Reusable Object-Oriented Software*. Addison-Wesley, Reading, MA.

Fowler, M. (1997). *Analysis Patterns: Reusable Object Models*. Addison-Wesley, Reading, MA.

Johnson, R.E. (1992). Documenting frameworks with patterns, *Proc. OOPSLA'92, SIGPLAN Notices* 27(10), 63–76.

Krasner, G.E. and Pope, S.T. (1988). A cookbook for using the model–view–controller user interface paradigm in Smalltalk-80, *JOOP* 1(3), 26–49, 1988.

Vlissides, J.M., Coplien, J.O. and Kerth, N.L. (1996). *Pattern Languages of Program Design 2*, Addison-Wesley, Reading, MA.

Patterns Catalogs

13.1 Introduction

There are a growing number of patterns catalogs available, including the Gang of Four patterns (from the original Patterns book), the J2EE patterns from Sun, various anti-patterns and Java-based patterns (Grand, 2002). In this chapter we will focus on the patterns that formed the seminal patterns book (Gamma *et al.*, 1995). The patterns in this book are often referred to as GoF (for Gang of Four) patterns to distinguish them from other patterns.

The GoF book is a weighty tome in its own right (over 370 pages) and the *Patterns in Java* book is over 450 pages. In this chapter, therefore, I will not try to reproduce every pattern in the GoF book (let alone any additional patterns, of which there are now plenty) due to the constraints of space. In addition, these patterns are already documented in these books. Instead, this chapter will try to give you a flavour of each of the GoF patterns so that you will at least have some familiarity with them when you come to look at other books or talk about patterns with your colleagues.

13.2 GoF Patterns

There are 23 GoF patterns, divided into three categories: "Creational Patterns", "Structural Patterns" and "Behavioural Patterns", described below.

- *Creational Patterns*. These patterns provide guidance on the creation of objects. They help hide the details of the object instantiation from the code that uses those objects. That is, they make a system independent of how its objects are created, composed and represented. This leads to high cohesion between the objects and their users, but to a low coupling between the users and the way the objects are created. For example, if I have a Java interface that is implemented by three different classes, then by using a Factory pattern I might instantiate one of the three classes, depending on the current situation. All the users of the object returned need to know is what interface they all implement. The actual implementation may change each time the factory is used, but this detail is hidden.

- *Structural Patterns*. Such patterns describe the organization of objects; that is, how classes and objects are composed to form larger structures. For example, a large department store near where I live appears from the outside to be a single entity with a very grand frontage. However, behind this frontage is a completely new shop containing various independent stores. This means that as a customer I see from the outside a single and quite grand whole. But from the inside there are multiple smaller shops and brands all working together. This is the essence of the Façade pattern.

- *Behavioural Patterns*. Behavioural patterns are concerned with organizing, managing and assigning responsibilities to objects during execution; that is, the focus on the patterns of communication between the objects involved during some task. Typically, these patterns characterize complex control flows that are difficult to follow at run time. They therefore help to shift the emphasis away from the low-level flow of control to the higher level object interactions.

We will look at each category in more detail in the remainder of this chapter. We will also explore some of the more commonly used patterns in a little more detail.

13.3 Creational Patterns

There are five different patterns within the creational patterns category: Factory Method, Abstract Factory, Builder, Prototype and Singleton. These patterns are presented below.

13.3.1 Factory Method

This provides a pattern that describes the use of a factory class for constructing objects. The methods on the factory return objects that implement a given interface. The user of the factory only knows about the interface. Thus different objects can be created depending on the current situation (as long as they implement the interface).

For example, the following code snippet presents a factory method for instantiating appropriate document types. The current type information is loaded from a properties file (not shown) and is independent of the client. In turn, the client has no knowledge of the type of document created, only that it is a document (note that we are assuming that document is an interface and that WordDocument and StarOfficeDocument implement that interface; see Figure 13.1):

```
public class DocumentFactory {
  // type is a value loaded from a properties file
  ...
  public static Document getDocument() {
    Document doc = null;
    if (DocumentType.WORD == type) {
```

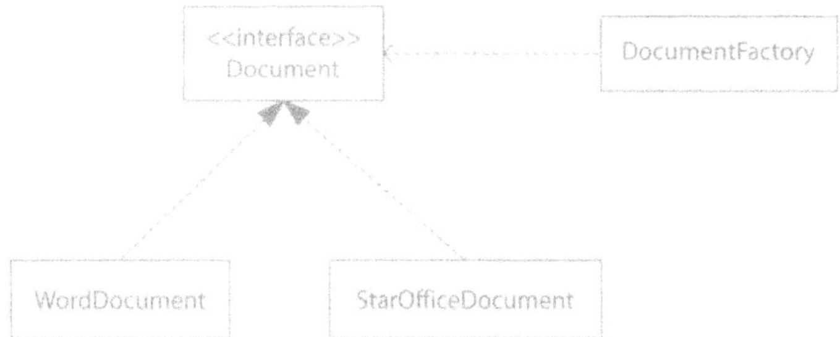

Figure 13.1 Relationships between the elements in the factory method example.

```java
      doc = new WordDocument();
    } else if (DocumentType.STAROFFICE == type) {
      doc = new StarOfficeDocument();
    }
    return doc;
  }
}
```

13.3.2 Abstract Factory

This describes a pattern for creating families of related or dependent objects.

13.3.3 Builder

This pattern separates out the construction of a complex object from its use. Thus the client can specify what type of object is required and what its content might be, but never need to know about how that object is constructed and initialized.

13.3.4 Prototype

This pattern allows a user object to create a customized object based on a prototype of what is required. That is, the pattern describes how a new object can be created based on a customization of an existing object.

13.3.5 Singleton

The singleton pattern describes a class that can only have one object constructed for it. That is, unlike other objects it should not be possible to obtain more than one instance within the same virtual machine. Thus the singleton pattern ensures that only one instance of a class is created. All objects that use an instance of that class use the same instance.

The motivation behind this pattern is that some classes, typically those that involve the central management of a resource, should have exactly one instance. For example, an object that manages the reuse of database connections (i.e. a connection pool) could be a singleton.

The singleton pattern can be used where:

- there must be exactly one instance of a class and it must be accessible to clients from a well-known access point
- the sole instance should be extensible by subclassing and clients should be able to use an extended instance without modifying their code (in which case the constructor should be protected)

The question thus arises "how do you ensure a single instance of an object?". One way to do this in Java is to have a static variable (called instance, say) that holds the reference to the single instance that can be created. This static variable can be private. The instance can then be accessed via a static accessor method (such as getInstance()). This method can then return the instance of the singleton class. If the constructor (or constructors) for this class is made private then you can be guaranteed that only the class will be able to create the single instance. Note that in Java, if no constructor is defined the compiler will provide a public default constructor automatically, thus allowing instances of your singleton to be created outside the class!

As an example, consider the following code. A factory class is being used to provide access to a single instance of the DataAccessManager object. The DataAccessManager constructor only has package visibility and cannot therefore be accessed outside of the DataAccessManager package. As the DataAccessManagerFactory class holds a single static instance of the DataAccessManager everything outside the package will have to access this single instance via the factory.

```java
public class DataAccessManagerFactory {
  /**one and only DataAccessManager **/
  private static DataAccessManager DAMInstance = null ;

  /**Private constructor prevents direct instantiation**/
  private DataAccessManagerFactory() {}
  /**
   * Returns the one and only instance of DataAccessManager
   */
  public DataAccessManager getDataAccessManager(){
    if (DAMInstance == null) {
      synchronized(this) {
        if (DAMInstance == null) {
          DAMInstance = new DataAccessManager();
        }
      }
    }
    return DAMInstance;
  }
}
```

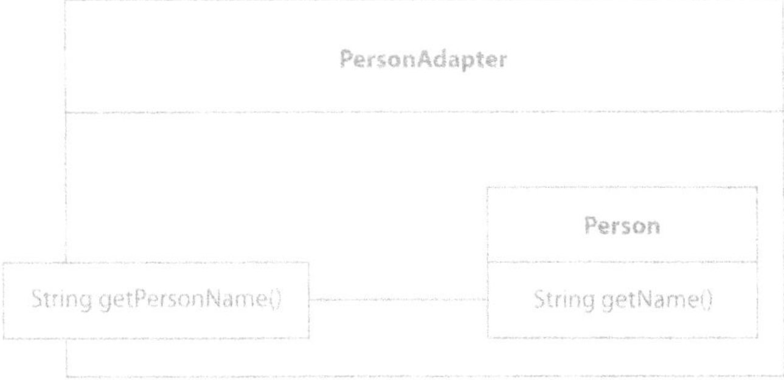

Figure 13.2 An implementation of the adapter pattern.

13.4 Structural Patterns

The structural category has seven patterns. These patterns are Adapter, Bridge, Composite, Decorator, Façade, Flyweight and Proxy. Each is discussed briefly below.

13.4.1 Adapter

The adapter pattern is used to convert the public interface of one class into the interface of another class. For example, let us assume that we have one piece of code that requires a method with the signature `String getPersonName()` and a class `Person` that has a method with the signature `String getName()`. We could wrap an adapter around the person object that maps the `getPersonName()` method to `getPerson()` (see Figure 13.2).

13.4.2 Bridge

This pattern provides an intermediary object between an abstraction and its implementation. This is particularly useful when there is a hierarchy of abstractions and another (corresponding) hierarchy of implementations. Rather than combine the two into many distinct classes, the bridge pattern implements the abstractions and implementations as independent classes that can be combined dynamically.

For example, in Figure 13.3 the abstraction hierarchy is `MotorCar` and `SportsCar`. However, there are various implementations of these abstractions that could be used (for both `MotorCar` and `SportsCar`). One way of dealing with this is to have a bridge interface between the abstract concept of a `MotorCar` and the concrete concept of a Golf or Jaguar XJ8. The bridge interface provides all the methods that the concrete implementations must implement (in this case the method `drive`). The method in the abstract concepts can then call the `drive` method on the classes that implement the bridge interface. In this cases there are two concrete implementations of the `MotorCarImplementation` interface, these are Jaguar XJ8 and Golf. In turn, the more specialized concept of a `SportsCar` has its own bridge interface and two concrete classes that implement that interface (namely Jaguar XK8 and Golf GTI). Note that the concrete classes also have a hierarchy in which the Golf GTI is a

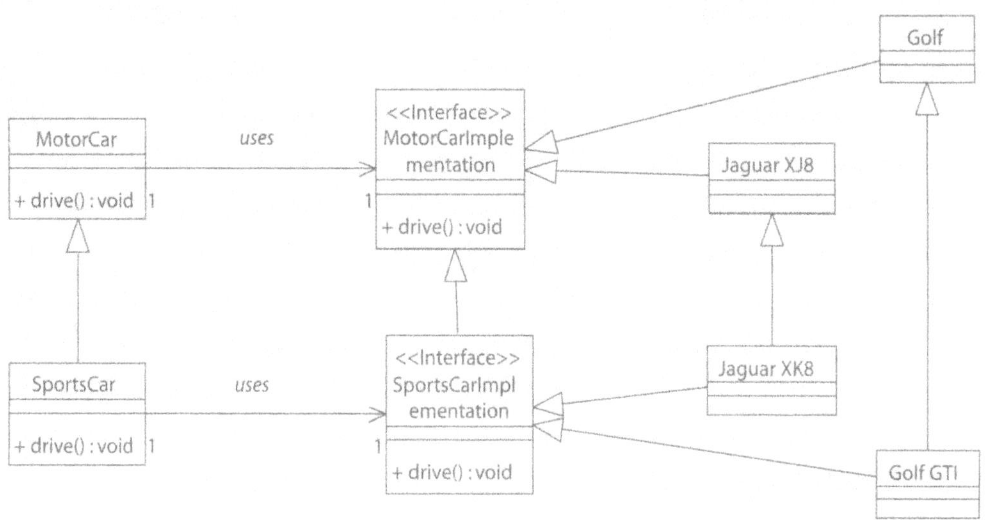

Figure 13.3 The bridge pattern.

specialization of the standard Golf and the Jaguar XK8 coupe is a specialization of a standard Jaguar XJ8.

13.4.3 Composite

The composite pattern allows multiple objects to be treated as a single object or as an individual in the same way.

13.4.4 Decorator

This is used to wrap around an object to extend its functionality. The resulting wrapped object should be indistinguishable from the original to clients. For example, imagine an object that generates comma-delimited tables. We could wrap different objects around this to post-process the output into HTML, XML etc. If the interface presented to the client is the same as the original object then clients need not know that there is a decorator wrapped around the original. A good example of this pattern is the use of filters in the J2EE. A filter is an object that can be wrapped around a servlet and has the chance to pre- and post-process the requests and responses being sent to and from the servlet (or JSP).

13.4.5 Façade

This pattern allows a (simplifying) object to unify a (potentially more complex) interface to a set of objects. The façade can often be viewed as an interface to a subsystem. It has the effect of simplifying the interface between the clients and the subsystem objects. This is illustrated in

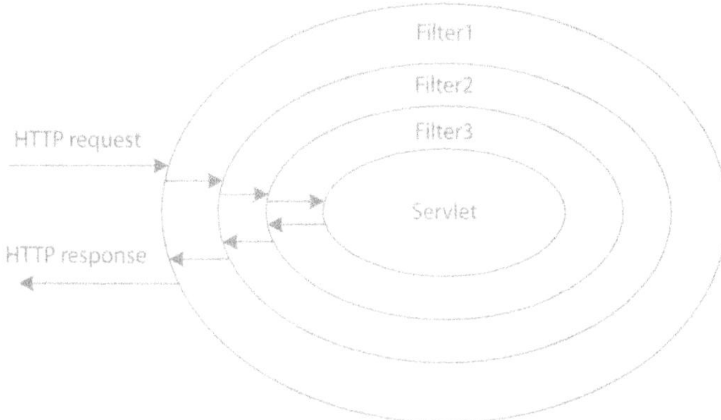

Figure 13.4 A filter chain wrapped around a servlet.

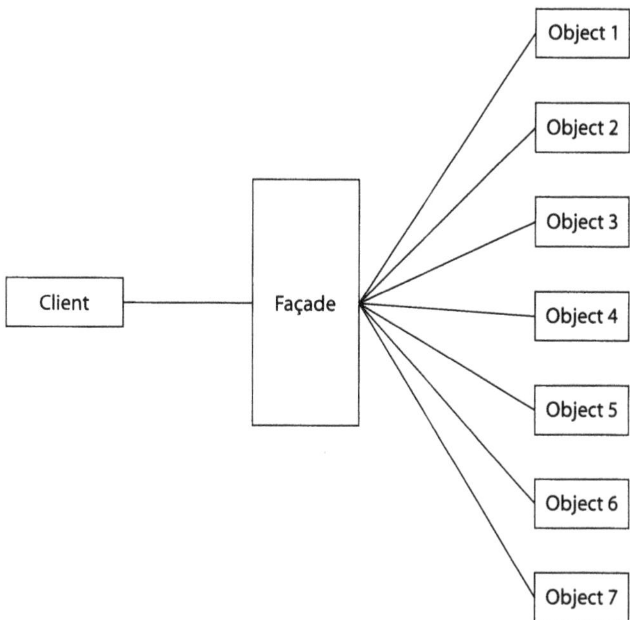

Figure 13.5 The façade pattern.

Figure 13.5, where a client only has to deal with a single façade object. The façade object then deals with the interactions with multiple subsystem objects.

13.4.6 Flyweight

This pattern allows a single instance (or a few instances) to represent many instances, all of which share the same data. This means that the application can avoid some of the expense of multiple instances that all contain the same information by sharing just one (or a few).

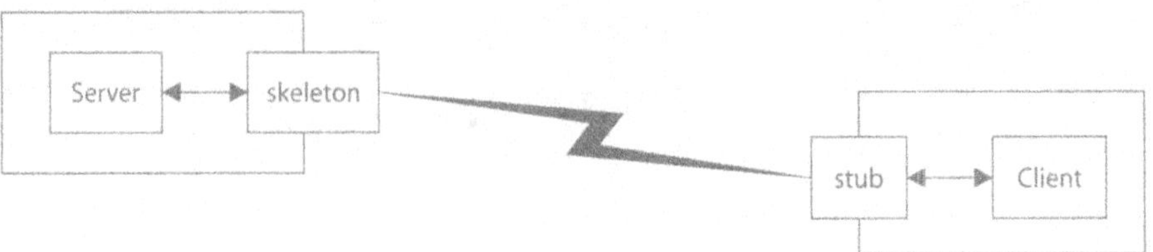

Figure 13.6 Using the skeleton and stub proxy classes in RMI.

13.4.7 Proxy

The proxy pattern provides a buffer between a client and the object that will actually service method requests. This buffer is a surrogate or placeholder for the actual object. It can be used to control access to the actual object, to determine which object should actually receive the call, to handle network communication etc. A good example of the use of proxies is Remote Method Invocation (or RMI) in Java. In RMI, local proxies are u sed to mimic remote objects and to handle all network communication; see Figure 13.6.

13.5 Behavioural Patterns

There are 11 patterns in the behavioural patterns category of the GoF patterns. These are discussed briefly below.

13.5.1 Chain of Responsibility

This patterns allows a request for an action to be sent from a client object to a set of objects. Each object receives the rest sequentially and is given a chance to process that request and then to pass the request on to the next object in the sequence. This is illustrated in Figure 13.7, where a client sends a method request to Object 1. This is then sent on to Object 2. Object 2 in turn sends the request on to Object 3 and so on. Each object can itself process the request, if it so wishes, before it sends the request on.

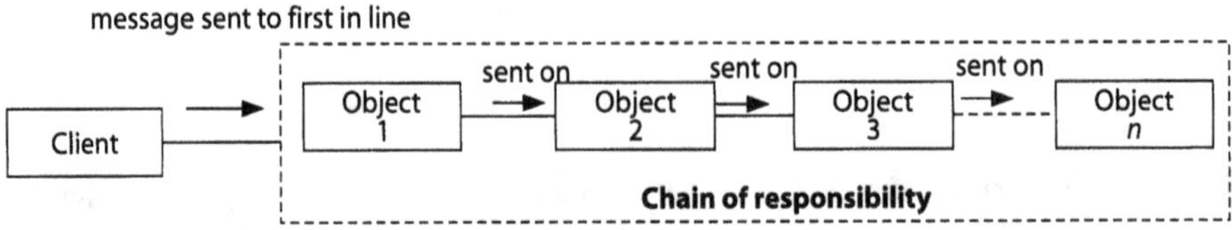

Figure 13.7 Chain of responsibility pattern.

13.5.2 Command

This pattern is used to represent a request to perform some operation on an object without hard coding that request. Instead, a command object is instantiated and configured to indicate the operation to perform and any parameters to pass. This also allows the command objects to be manipulated, stored, queued sequenced and (in some cases) undone.

13.5.3 Interpreter

This pattern describes the definition of a (usually simple) programming language and an interpreter that will execute the commands in the language. This might be appropriate if you find that you need to solve the same set of problems repeatedly and that a small set of operations can be used to describe the solution to that problem.

13.5.4 Iterator

The iterator pattern describes a way in which it is possible to access the elements of some larger data structure sequentially. This pattern is exemplified by the `java.util Iterator` concept. This is illustrated in the following code:

```java
List list = f.getList();
Iterator it = list.iterator();
while (it.hasNext()) {
  System.out.println(it.next());
}
```

13.5.5 Mediator

The mediator pattern is one that promotes the loose coupling of a set of communicating objects. This pattern was discussed in the last chapter. The aim of the mediator is to define an object that encapsulates how a set of objects interact. The mediator pattern promotes loose coupling by keeping objects from referring to each other explicitly.

The motivation behind this is that object-oriented design encourages the distribution of behaviour among objects. However, this can lead to a multiplicity of links between objects. In the worst case every object needs to know about/link to every other object. This can be a problem for maintenance and for the reusability of the individual classes. This is illustrated in Figure 13.8. In this example, there are five objects that all need to communicate with each other. This results in 10 bidirectional links (in Java terms, 20 references). If a sixth object wished to be added to this communications network we would end up with 15 bidirectional links (or 30 Java references) and potential changes to five existing classes. This has major implications for maintainability as well as stability.

These problems can be overcome by using a mediator object. In this scheme other objects are connected together via a central mediator object in a star-like structure. The mediator is then responsible for controlling and coordinating the interactions of the group of objects.

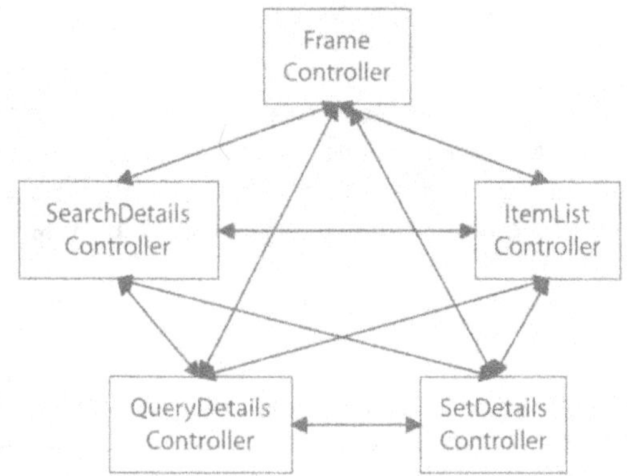

Figure 13.8 Communicating objects.

The example illustrated in Figure 13.8 could be reconfigured using the mediator pattern, as illustrated in Figure 13.9. In this case there are only five bidirectional links, and if we add a sixth object there would be only six bidirectional links.

The mediator handles communication between colleague objects. In turn, each colleague knows its mediator object. It communicates with this mediator object in order to communicate with other colleagues. Thus the mediator object receives messages from its colleagues and relays them to other colleagues as appropriate. Exactly what form these messages take and how the mediator passes them on to its colleagues are not part of the design pattern – it is the responsibility of those applying the pattern to decide on these details. Examples of the form that messages can take include strings, objects, serializable objects and ints. In turn, how the mediator sends this information on to the colleagues is implementation-dependent – it could be implemented as a simple iteration through a list, via some form of IP broadcast mechanism or via some messaging system (for example via the JMS API).

The mediator pattern can be used in a wide range of situations, including:

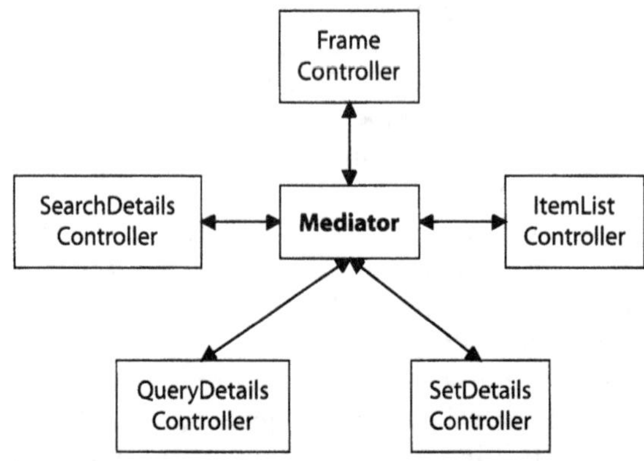

Figure 13.9 Objects communicating via a mediator.

- A set of objects communicate in well-defined but complex ways. The resulting interdependencies are unstructured and difficult to understand.
- Reusing an object is difficult because it refers to, and uses, many other objects.
- A particular behaviour is distributed among a number of classes and we wish to customize that behaviour with the minimum of subclassing.

13.5.6 Memento

This pattern is used to obtain a snapshot of the state of an object without violating its encapsulation. The memento object can be passed around from object to object capturing state information that can then be used to determine system activity.

13.5.7 Observer

This pattern defines a one-to-many dependency between objects so that when one object changes state, all its dependents are notified of the change and can take appropriate action. The Observer/Observable mechanism in Java is an example of an implementation of the observer pattern. This is illustrated in Figure 13.10. In this figure, the Observable object must send itself the setChanged() method followed by the notifyObservers() method. This then causes an update message to be sent to all the objects currently registered with the Observable object. These Observer objects can then update themselves as required.

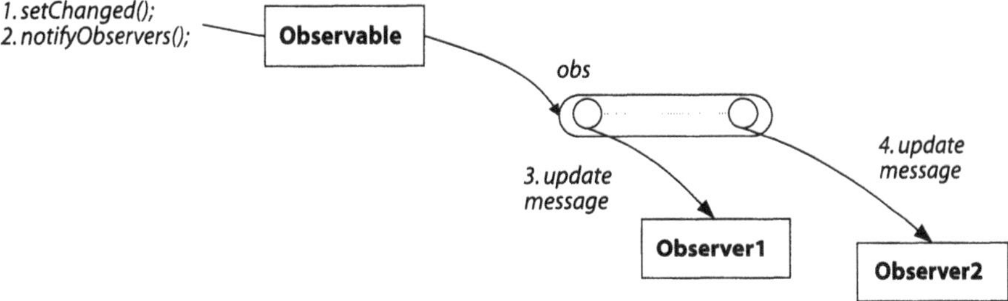

Figure 13.10 The Observer/Observable pattern implemented in Java.

13.5.8 State

This pattern describes a state-based set of operations. That is, when an object's state changes, so does its behaviour.

13.5.9 Strategy

This pattern describes a set of structures that define an abstract parent class method that can be implemented with different algorithms in different subclasses. Thus a different solution strategy can be adopted by selecting a different subclass. If the client works with variables of the superclass but actually has subclasses supplied (possibly by a factory method), then the client does not need to know about the changes in strategy.

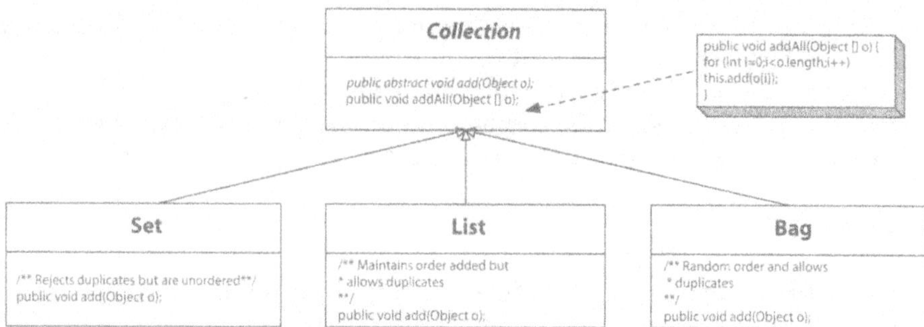

Figure 13.11 The template method pattern.

13.5.10 Template Method

This pattern is used to describe how a skeleton algorithm that calls methods that are abstract in
the current class can be implemented in the subclass. This is illustrated in Figure 13.11. In this
figure an abstract superclass Collection defines two methods. One, the addAll(Object [] o)
method takes an array of objects and loops through the array calling the method add on each
object. The method add, however, is abstract in the Collection class. This is not a problem
because it is not possible to make an instance of an abstract class. Any concrete subclasses will
have to implement the add method, and thus any concrete subclasses will be able to execute the
addAll method. Each subclass in this example then implements the add method in a different
way. For example, the Set class does not worry about maintaining the order in which objects were
added, but does ensure that there are no duplicates. The List class in contrast allows duplicates,
but maintains the order in which the objects were added. The Bag class allows duplicates but does
not maintain the order in which objects are added. Thus each of the subclasses will provide a
different version of the template method defined in Collection.

13.5.11 Visitor

This pattern allows logic that will be common to a variety of classes to be defined in a visitor
object. This visitor object is then passed to each object in turn and is used to perform the opera-
tion. The Comparator interface in the java.util package could be considered to be an example
of the visitor pattern. This pattern is described in more detail in Chapter 16.

13.6 Summary

In this chapter we have reviewed the GoF patterns. Although these patterns were written some
time ago, they are still as relevant today as they were when the GoF book was written. Indeed, I
find myself using many of these patterns regularly and returning to this book to refresh my
memory on the patterns available. I do not, of course, limit myself only to these patterns (for

example Grand (2002) has many additional patterns which are also very useful), but they are certainly an excellent starting point.

13.7 References

Gamma, E., Helm, R., Johnson, R. and Vlissades, J. (1995). *Design Patterns: Elements of Reusable Object-Oriented Software.* Addison-Wesley, Reading, MA.
Grand, M. (2002) *Patterns in Java: A Catalog of Reusable Design Patterns Illustrated with UML,* 2nd edn, Vol. 1. John Wiley & Sons, New York.

Applying the Model–View–Controller Pattern

14.1 Introduction

Anyone who has ever tried to construct modular object-oriented user interfaces using Java and Swing knows how hard it can be. The result can easily end up being difficult to debug, complex to understand and maintain, and certainly not reusable (except by cutting and pasting!). However, huge benefits can be obtained by separating out the user interface (i.e. GUI components) from the application logic/code. This has been acknowledged for a long time, and a number of approaches have been proposed over the years for separating the presentational aspect of an application from the logic of that application. In the case of client Java applications used in multi-tier environments this is still true. In this chapter and the next, we will explore the use of the model–view–controller architecture/pattern (or just as the MVC for short). The MVC originated in Smalltalk, but the concept has been used in many places. This chapter considers what the MVC is, why it is a good approach to GUI client construction and what features in Java support it.

14.2 What Is the Model–View–Controller Architecture?

With the advent of JDK 1.1 a new event model was introduced into Java. This event model is much cleaner than the previous approach and can result in simpler, clearer and more maintainable code. The introduction of this event model, along with existing Java facilities, allows the construction of modular user interfaces. In particular, it allows the separation of the display of information from the control or the user input to that display, as well as from the application. This separation is not a new idea and allows the construction of GUI applications that mirror the model–view–controller architecture. The intention of the MVC architecture is the separation of the user display from the control of user input and the underlying information model, as illustrated in Figure 14.1 (Krasner and Pope, 1988). There are a number of reasons why this is useful:

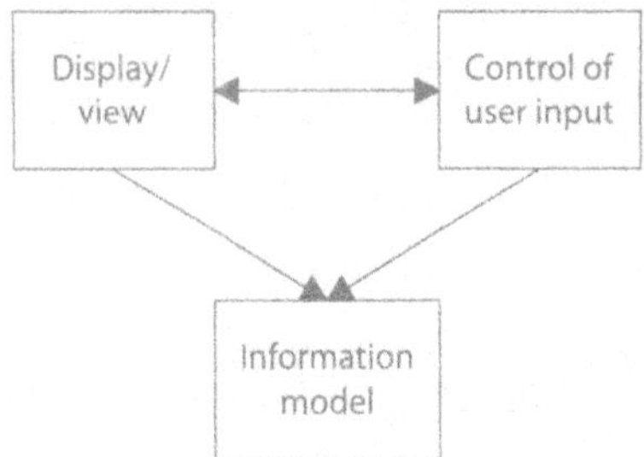

Figure 14.1 The model–view–controller architecture.

- reusability of application and/or user interface components
- ability to develop the application and user interface separately
- ability to inherit from different parts of the class hierarchy
- ability to define control style classes which provide common features separately from how these features may be displayed

This means that different interfaces can be used with the same application, without the application knowing about it. It also means that any part of the system can be changed without affecting the operation of the other. For example, the way that the graphical interface (the look) displays the information could be changed without modifying the actual application or how input is handled (the feel). Indeed, the application need not know what type of interface is currently connected to it at all.

14.3 What Java Facilities Support the MVC

Java provides two facilities that together can allow the separation of the application, interface and control elements. These are:

- The observer/observable model. This allows application programs and user interfaces to be loosely coupled.
- The delegation event model. This provides listeners which act as controllers handling various events that may occur.

The use of the observer/observable mechanism is very powerful and has been used to create MVC-style clients. However, in this chapter we will focus on the use of the delegation event model. Why? Essentially because more developers are familiar with the delegation event model and it can be used as successfully as the observer–observable model to allow models to notify their views of the need to perform a redisplay-style operation.

14.3.1 The Delegation Event Model

The Java delegation event model introduced the concept of listeners (Sevareid, 1997). Listeners are effectively objects that "listen" for a particular event to occur. When it does they react to it. For example, the event associated with the button might be that it has been "pressed". The listener would then be notified that the button had been pressed and would decide what action to take. This approach involves delegation because the responsibility for handling an event, generated by one object, may belong to another object.

The delegation model changed the way in which users created GUIs back in JDK 1.1. Using this model they defined the graphic objects to be displayed, added them to the display and associated them with a listener object. The listener object then handled the events that were generated for that object.

For example, if we wish to create a button which will be displayed on an interface and allow the user to exit without using the border frame buttons, then we would need to create a button and a listener for the action on the button:

```
exitButtonController = new ExitButtonController();
exitButton = new Button(" Exit ");
exitButton.addActionListener(exitButtonController);
```

This code creates a new user-defined listener object, ExitButtonController, then creates a new button (with a label "Exit"). It then adds the exitButtonController as the action listener for the button. That is, it is the object which will *listen* for action events (such as the button being pressed). The ExitButtonController class (presented below) provides a single instance method actionPerformed() which will initiate the System.exit(0) method.

The resulting class and instance structures are illustrated in Figure 14.2. As you can see from this diagram, the separation of interface and control is conceptually very clean.

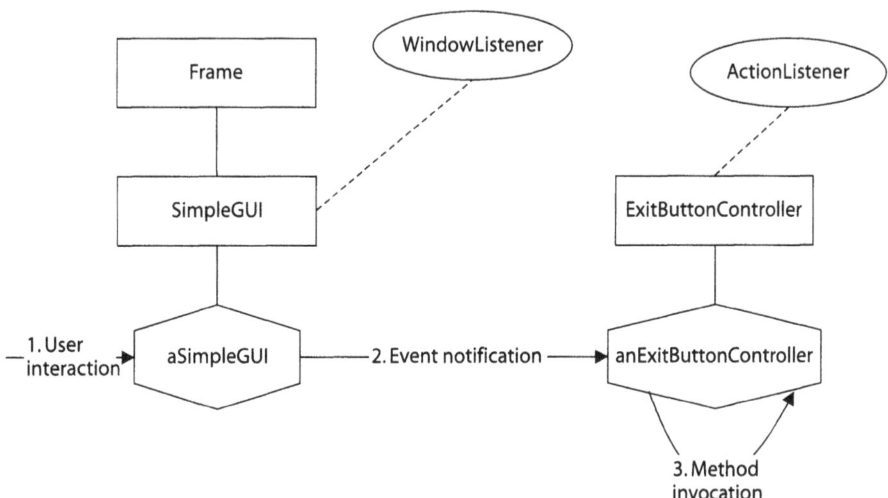

Figure 14.2 The class and object diagram using the delegation event model.

The `ExitButtonController` class definition is presented below. There is of course no reason why you should call such a class a Controller; you could equally have called it an `ExitButtonEventListener`. However, the Listeners are the interface definitions. By choosing a different type of name, we make it clear that we are talking about the classes intended to provide the execution control.

```java
class ExitButtonController implements ActionListener {
  public void actionPerformed(ActionEvent event) {
    System.exit(0);
  }
}
```

14.4 The MVC in Java

To provide a framework for the MVC within Java we can adopt a number of techniques; however, the approach adopted here is illustrated by Figure 14.3. This diagram shows three interfaces (namely Controller, View and Model) that act as markers for the core concepts or entities in the MVC framework. Note that the Controller and View interfaces define accessor methods for obtaining the model and either the view or controller respectively.

In Figure 14.3 the interface of most note is the Model interface. This interface contains just one method: the `notifyChanged(ModelEvent event)` method. This method will be used by all implementations of models to notify any interested objects of changes in the state of the Model. At this point all we know is that such a method will be provided and that the parameter to this method is `ModelEvent`.

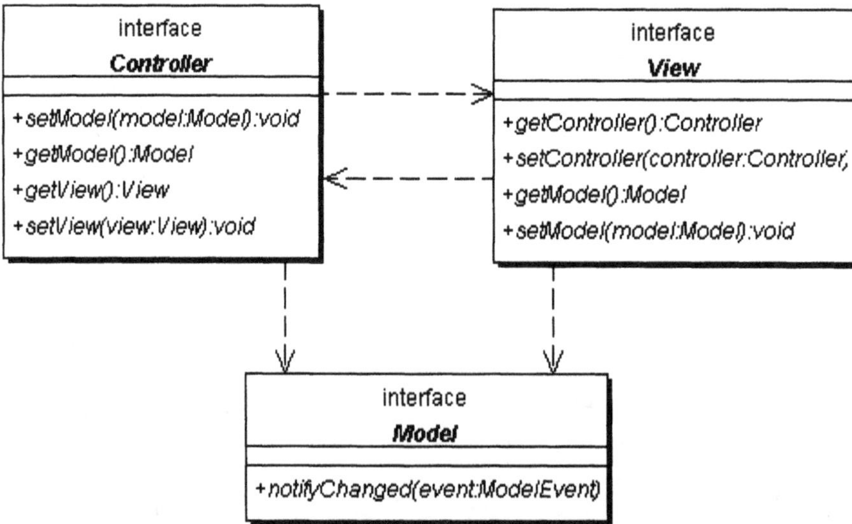

Figure 14.3 The interfaces defining the MVC entities.

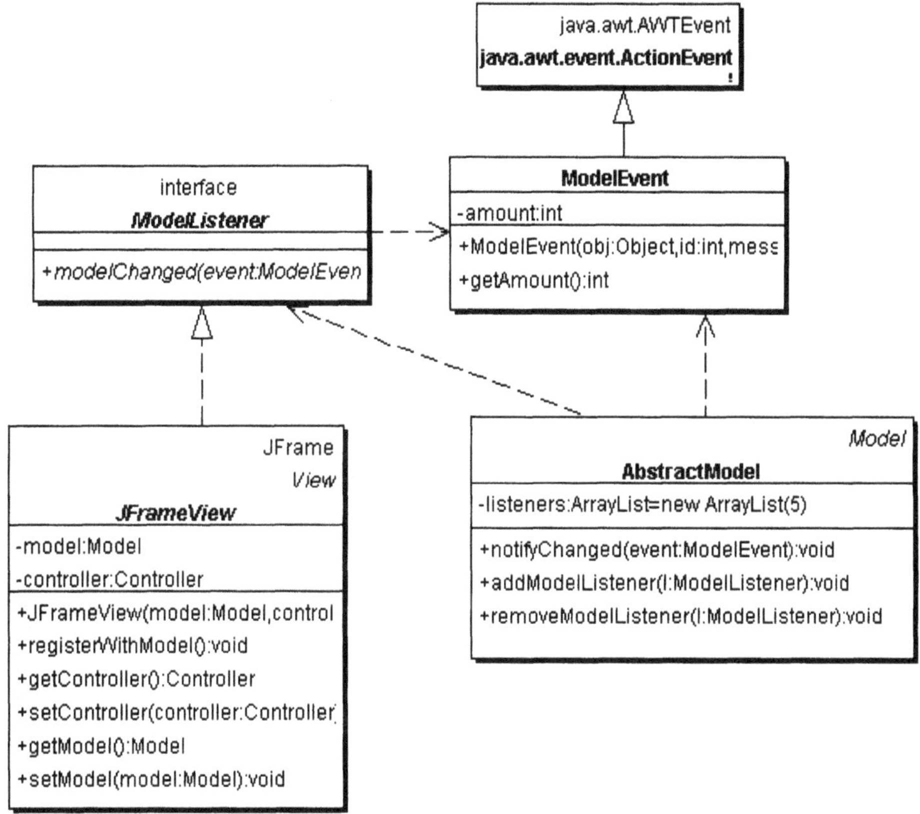

Figure 14.4 The event notification aspects of the framework.

This leads on nicely to Figure 14.4. This is the heart of the notification mechanism used within this implementation of the MVC. When a model wishes to notify interested objects of a change in its state it must create a ModelEvent object (just as JButton creates an ActionEvent to notify a handler that a user has clicked on it). In this case the ModelEvent object has been made a subclass of ActionEvent; however, it does not need to subclass this class – it could subclass any Event object as identified by a designer. The ModelEvent class adds an additional property to those inherited, which allows a ModelEvent to hold an amount value (this is really tying too closely to the calculator application – see the next section – but keeps things simpler later on).

As we are defining our own event class, we also need to define a listener interface for objects that wish to be notified of ModelEvent. The ModelListener interface does this. Note that the JFrameView class (the root of all windows that wish to act as the view element of an MVC framework) implements the ModelListener interface. Thus all JFrameViews (and its subclasses) can be notified of ModelEvents.

Finally, the AbstractModel class provides an implementation for notifyChanged that takes a ModelEvent and sends that event in turn to each of the listeners registered with the

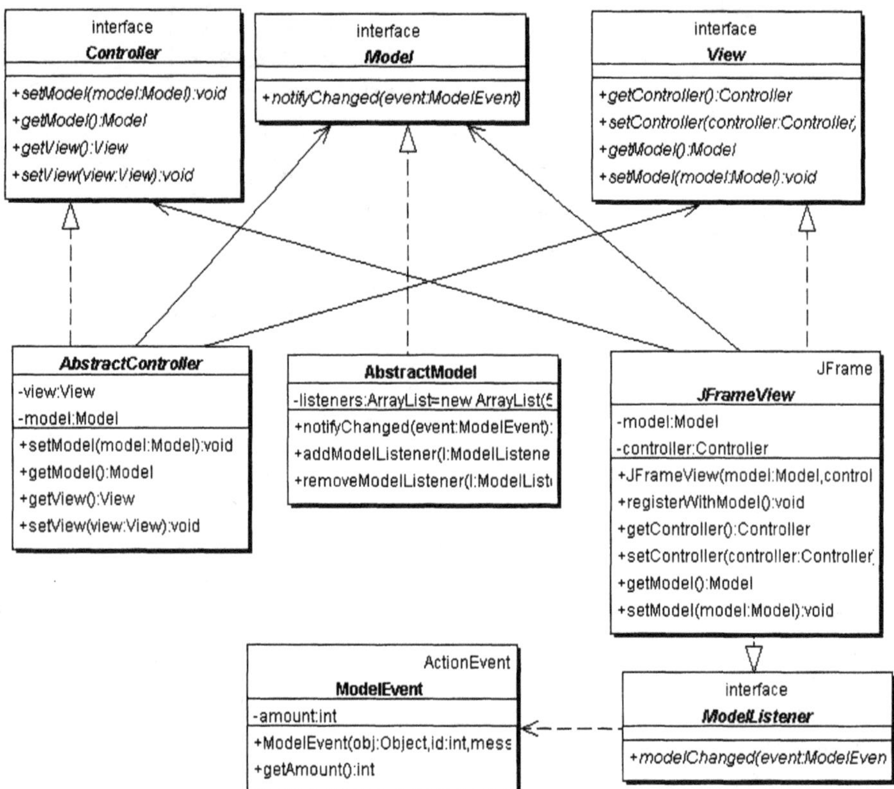

Figure 14.5 The whole generic MVC framework.

model. Views (and any other listener objects) can register with any subclasses of
`AbstractModel` via the `addModelListener` method, which takes an object whose class
implements the `ModelListener` interface as a parameter. Objects can remove themselves
from listener to the models events via the `removeModelListener` method.

Figure 14.5 illustrates the final generic MVC framework as implemented in this chapter.
Note that each of the root classes (`AbstractController`, `AbstractModel` and
`JFrameView`) reference the associated interfaces rather than the classes. This helps main-
tain the generic nature of the framework.

14.5 A Simple Calculator Application

To illustrate how this framework may be used in a simple application we shall construct a very
simple calculator application, as illustrated in Figure 14.6. This application only allows integer
addition or subtract for values in the range 0 to 9. It is not possible to enter the value 10 – this is to
keep the application *very* simple.

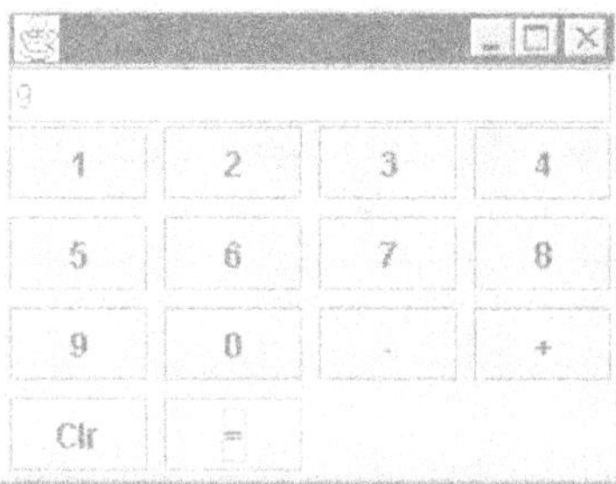

Figure 14.6 The GUI for the calculator application.

The overall structure of the application is that illustrated in Figure 14.7. Note that the view object and the controller objects have inherited links that allow them to communicate. However, although the interface and the controller objects have links to the application model (CalculatorModel); the application model knows nothing directly about the view or the controllers. This means that the application logic in the calculator is independent of the view and its controllers and may actually have various different GUI interfaces associated with it. One of the advantages of this approach is that any one of the three elements can be modified without the need to change the others.

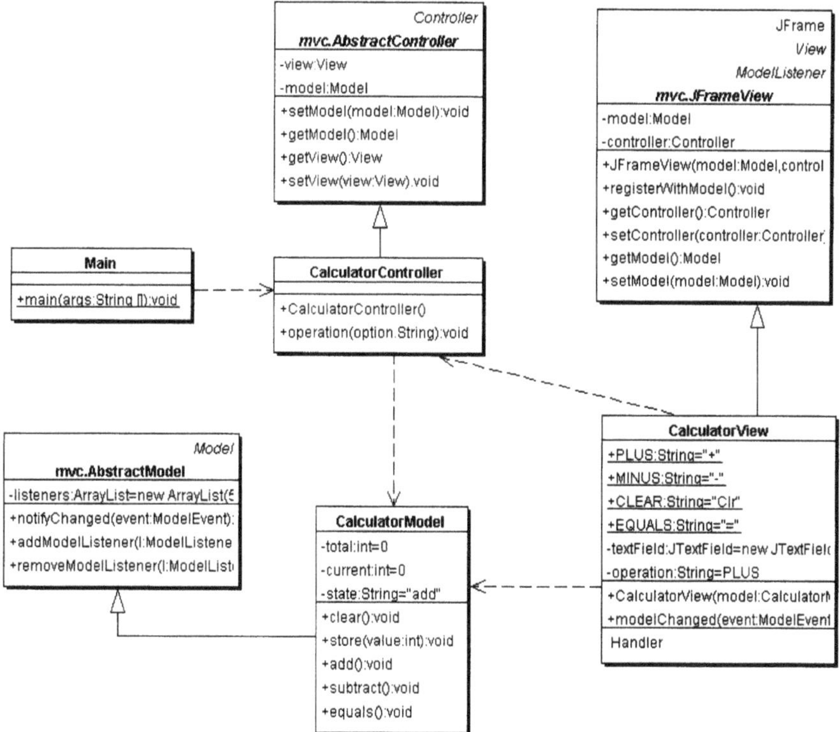

Figure 14.7 The MVC architecture as implemented by the calculator application.

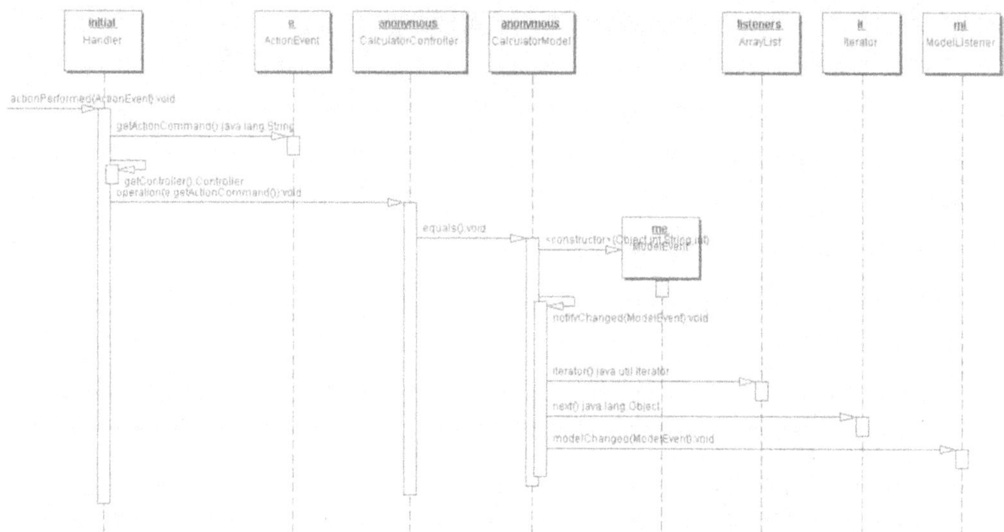

Figure 14.8 Interaction in the MVC.

The system interaction is illustrated in Figure 14.8. This figure illustrates the various messages sent once a user clicks on the deposit button. There are a number of points you should note about this example:

- Neither the display nor the controller holds onto the balance. It is obtained from the account whenever it is needed.
- The controller relies on the delegation event model to determine that it should do something.
- When the controller asks the model to change it doesn't tell the display – the display finds out about the change through the observer/observable mechanism.
- The account is unaware that the message deposit(amount); came from the controller. Thus any object could send a deposit message and the account would still inform its dependents about the change.

14.5.1 Swing Component Event Handling

In the approach being described in this chapter the event-handling code resides within the View classes (as it is essentially a Swing-related operation, and all Swing-related functionality should sit within the View). This means that an event handler (for example an inner class) implements the actionPerformed method, but then calls a method on the controller that will determine what should happen next.

The controller in turn receives the information provided by the actionPerformed method of the event handler and now determines what action should happen next. In this particular application it determines whether the model should be notified of an operation such as addition, subtraction, clear or equals, or that the model should be passed the integer entered by the user. However, it does no more than this.

In turn, the application model (the `CalculatorModel`) handles what the behaviour of each of the add, subtract, clear and equals methods should be. Once it has done this, it creates a `ModelEvent` and calls `notifyChanged`, passing the `ModelEvent` in. This method, inherited from the parent class, then notifies the view that it must update itself via the `modelChanged` method. In our case the view obtains the new value to display from the event and displays it within the `JTextField` at the top of the `CalculatorView`.

14.5.2 Frames, Panels and Layout Managers

The interface object is, of course, made up of a number of objects, such as a frame, a number of panels, and graphic components such as buttons and text fields. In turn, layout managers are used to control the way in which these objects are arranged within the window frame. An interesting point to note is that the exit button controller is used without any modification from previous examples. In addition, the abstract `buttonController` class (from which the `buttonPanelController` class inherits) is a reusable class for any object acting as a controller within an MVC-style architecture.

14.5.3 The Application Code

The source code for this application (see the end of the chapter) builds upon the generic MVC framework defined earlier. This involves more work the first time this framework is followed, but the overhead is reduced for future applications.

14.6 Discussion

In this chapter I have tried to describe a way of constructing graphical user interface applications (and of course applets) that is robust, principled and reusable. It allows the various classes to inherit from different parts of the class hierarchy, to implement different interfaces and to provide clearly defined functionality, all of which lead to clearer, more comprehensible code. It can be seen that such an approach allows the GUI to be structured in an object-oriented manner. It would, of course, be possible to place all of the application within a single class. This class would hold the application code, the window definition and the event-handling code. However, we would have lost the following advantages:

- reusability of parts of the system
- the ability to inherit from different parts of the class hierarchy
- modularity of system code
- resilience to change
- encapsulation of the application

Although these issues might not be a problem for an application as simple as that presented here, for real-world systems they would certainly be significant. You should now be aware of the benefits of adopting the MVC architecture and should try to adopt this approach in your own systems.

In the next chapter we will consider a modified version of the MVC framework, referred to as the Hierarchical MVC, that allows more complex and realistic applications to be constructed.

14.7 References

Krasner, G. E. and Pope, S. T. (1998). A cookbook for using the model–view–controller user interface paradigm in Smalltalk-80. *JOOP* 1(3), 26–49.
Sevareid, J. (1997). The JDK 1.1's new delegation event model. *Java Report*, pp. 59–79.

14.8 Listings

Listing 14.1 The Model interface.

```java
package mvc;

/**
 * This interface must be implemented by all classes that wish to play the
 * Model role within the MVC framework.
 * <p>
 * The only method specified by the interface is the <code>notifyChanged()
 * </code> method. */
public interface Model {
  void notifyChanged(ModelEvent event);
}
```

Listing 14.2 The Controller interface.

```java
package mvc;
/**
 * The Controller interface is the interface which must be implemented by
 * all classes which wish to take the role of a Controller.
 * All controllers must be able to reference a model and a view object.
 * <p>
 * The primary role of a Controller within the MVC is to determine what
 * should happen in response to user input.
 */
public interface Controller {
  void setModel(Model model);
  Model getModel();
  View getView();
  void setView(View view);
}
```

Listing 14.3 The View interface.

```java
package mvc;
/**
 * This interface must be implemented by all classes that wish to take the
 * role of the View within the MVC framework.
 * The role of a View is the display of information and the capture of
 * data entered.
 */
public interface View {
  Controller getController();
  void setController(Controller controller);
  Model getModel();
  void setModel(Model model);
}
```

Listing 14.4 The AbstractModel class.

```java
package mvc;
import java.util.ArrayList;
import java.util.Iterator;

/**
 * Abstract root class of Model hierarchy - provides basic
 * notification behaviour
 */
public abstract class AbstractModel implements Model {
  private ArrayList listeners = new ArrayList(5);
  /**
   * Method that is called by subclasses of AbstractModel when they want
   * to notify other classes of changes to themselves.
   */
  public void notifyChanged( ModelEvent event ){
    ArrayList list = (ArrayList)listeners.clone();
    Iterator it = list.iterator();
    while (it.hasNext()) {
      ModelListener ml = (ModelListener)it.next();
      ml.modelChanged(event);
    }
  }

  /**
   * Add a ModelListener to the list of objects interested in ModelEvents.
   */
  public void addModelListener(ModelListener l) {
    listeners.add(l);
  }
```

```
  /**
   * Remove a ModelListener from the list of objects interested in
   * ModelEvents
   */
  public void removeModelListener(ModelListener l) {
    listeners.remove(l);
  }
}
```

Listing 14.5 The AbstractController class.

```
package mvc;
/**
 * The root of the Controller class hierarchy is the AbstractController
 * class.
 * This class defines all the basic facilities required to implement a
 * controller. That is, it allows a view and model to be linked to the
 * controller.
 * <p>
 * It also provides a set of constructors and set and get methods for
 * views and models
 */
public abstract class AbstractController implements Controller {
  private View view;
  private Model model;

  public void setModel(Model model) {
    this.model = model;
  }

  public Model getModel() {
    return model;
  }

  public View getView() {
    return view;
  }

  public void setView(View view) {
    this.view = view;
  }
}
```

Listing 14.6 The JFrameView class.

```java
package mvc;
import javax.swing.*;
/**
 * The JFrameView class is the root class of the view class hierarchy for
 * top level (swing) frames. It allows a controller and a model to be
 * registered and can register itself with a model as an observer of that
 * model.
 * <p>
 * It this extends the JFrame class.
 * <p>
 * It requires the implementation of the <code>modelChanged(ModelEvent
 * event);</code> method in order that it can work with the notification
 * mechanism in Java.
 */
abstract public class JFrameView extends JFrame implements View, ModelListener{
  private Model model;
  private Controller controller;
  public JFrameView (Model model, Controller controller) {
    setModel(model);
    setController(controller);
  }

  public void registerWithModel() {
    ((AbstractModel)model).addModelListener(this);
  }

  public Controller getController() {
    return controller;
  }

  public void setController(Controller controller) {
    this.controller = controller;
  }

  public Model getModel() {
    return model;
  }

  public void setModel(Model model) {
    this.model = model;
    registerWithModel();
  }
}
```

Listing 14.7 The ModelEvent class.

```java
package mvc;
import java.awt.event.ActionEvent;

/**
 * Used to notify interested objects of changes in the
 * state of a model
 */
public class ModelEvent extends ActionEvent {
private int amount;
  public ModelEvent( Object obj, int id, String message, int amount){
    super( obj, id, message ) ;
    this.amount = amount;
  }
  public int getAmount() {
    return amount;
  }
}
```

Listing 14.8 The ModelListener class.

```java
package mvc;
public interface ModelListener {
  public void modelChanged(ModelEvent event);
}
```

Listing 14.9 The Main class.

```java
package calculator;
public class Main {
  public static void main(String [] args) {
    new CalculatorController();
  }
}
```

Listing 14.10 The CalculatorController class.

```java
package calculator;
import mvc.*;
public class CalculatorController extends AbstractController {
  public CalculatorController() {
    setModel(new CalculatorModel());
    setView(new CalculatorView((CalculatorModel)getModel(), this));
    ((JFrameView)getView()).setVisible(true);
  }
  public void operation(String option) {
```

```java
      if (option.equals(CalculatorView.MINUS)) {
        ((CalculatorModel)getModel()).subtract();
      } else if (option.equals(CalculatorView.PLUS)) {
        ((CalculatorModel)getModel()).add();
      } else if (option.equals(CalculatorView.CLEAR)) {
        ((CalculatorModel)getModel()).clear();
      } else if (option.equals(CalculatorView.EQUALS)) {
        ((CalculatorModel)getModel()).equals();
      } else {
        ((CalculatorModel)getModel()).store(Integer.parseInt(option));
      }
    }
  }
```

Listing 14.11 The `CalculatorModel` class.

```java
package calculator;
import mvc.*;

public class CalculatorModel extends AbstractModel {
  private int total = 0;
  private int current = 0;
  private String state = "add";
  public void clear() {
    total = 0;
    store(0);
  }

  public void store(int value) {
    current = value;
    ModelEvent me = new ModelEvent(this, 1, "", current);
    notifyChanged(me);
  }

  public void add() {
    state = "add";
    total = current;
  }

  public void subtract() {
    state = "subtract";
    total = current;
  }

  public void equals() {
    if (state=="add") {
```

```
      total += current;
    } else {
      total -= current;
    }
    current = total;
      // now notify any interested parties in the new total
      ModelEvent me = new ModelEvent(this, 1, "", total);
      notifyChanged(me);
    }
}
```

Listing 14.12 The CalculatorView class.

```java
package calculator;
import javax.swing.*;
import java.awt.*;
import java.awt.event.*;
import mvc.*;

public class CalculatorView extends JFrameView {
  public static final String PLUS = "+";
  public static final String MINUS = "-";
  public static final String CLEAR = "Clr";
  public static final String EQUALS = "=";
  private JTextField textField = new JTextField();
  private String operation = PLUS;

  public CalculatorView(CalculatorModel model, CalculatorController
                         controller) {
    super(model, controller);
    textField.setText("0");
    this.getContentPane().add(textField, BorderLayout.NORTH);
    JPanel buttonPanel = new JPanel();
    Handler handler = new Handler();
    JButton jButton1 = new JButton("1");
    jButton1.addActionListener(handler);
    JButton jButton2 = new JButton("2");
    jButton2.addActionListener(handler);
    JButton jButton3 = new JButton("3");
    jButton3.addActionListener(handler);
    JButton jButton4 = new JButton("4");
    jButton4.addActionListener(handler);
    JButton jButton5 = new JButton("5");
    jButton5.addActionListener(handler);
    JButton jButton6 = new JButton("6");
    jButton6.addActionListener(handler);
```

```java
    JButton jButton7 = new JButton("7");
    jButton7.addActionListener(handler);
    JButton jButton8 = new JButton("8");
    jButton8.addActionListener(handler);
    JButton jButton9 = new JButton("9");
    jButton9.addActionListener(handler);
    JButton jButton0 = new JButton("0");
    jButton0.addActionListener(handler);
    JButton minusButton = new JButton(MINUS);
    minusButton.addActionListener(handler);
    JButton plusButton = new JButton(PLUS);
    plusButton.addActionListener(handler);
    JButton clearButton = new JButton(CLEAR);
    clearButton.addActionListener(handler);
    JButton equalsButton = new JButton(EQUALS);
    equalsButton.addActionListener(handler);

    buttonPanel.setLayout(new GridLayout(4, 4, 5, 5));
    this.getContentPane().add(buttonPanel, BorderLayout.CENTER);
    buttonPanel.add(jButton1, null);
    buttonPanel.add(jButton2, null);
    buttonPanel.add(jButton3, null);
    buttonPanel.add(jButton4, null);
    buttonPanel.add(jButton5, null);
    buttonPanel.add(jButton6, null);
    buttonPanel.add(jButton7, null);
    buttonPanel.add(jButton8, null);
    buttonPanel.add(jButton9, null);
    buttonPanel.add(jButton0, null);
    buttonPanel.add(minusButton, null);
    buttonPanel.add(plusButton, null);
    buttonPanel.add(clearButton, null);
    buttonPanel.add(equalsButton, null);
    pack();
}

// Now implement the necessary event handling code
public void modelChanged(ModelEvent event) {
  String msg = event.getAmount() + "";
  textField.setText(msg);
}

// Inner classes for Event Handling
class Handler implements ActionListener {
  // Event handling is handled locally
  public void actionPerformed(ActionEvent e) {
```

```
        ((CalculatorController)getController()).operation(e.getActionCommand());
      }
    }
  }
```

15

The Hierarchical MVC

15.1 Introduction

In the last chapter we examined the use of the model–view–controller framework as a way of architecting graphical applications in Java. In this chapter we will extend on that framework to present a more realistic approach to building real-world graphical Java applications (whether as part of a multi-tier system or as a standalone program).

An important distinction to note at this point is that we are talking about the MVC (and later the hierarchical version of the MVC) in an architectural context and not at the low level used by Java's Swing set of classes. Although the two approaches are related at the abstract level, they differ greatly in their implementation.

15.2 Why Isn't This Enough?

The MVC is an excellent basis on which to build a graphical application. However, as it stands it is not a complete solution. The basic problem is that, in general, if you tried to use just one Controller, one Model and one View for your whole application, the result would be unmanageable. For example, let us imagine that we were trying to build an email tool. With one single model we might be trying to represent:

- read, unread, deleted and pending emails
- address books
- emails under construction
- the POP or SMTP configurations
- the sender's profile (name, return email etc.)
- attachments, signatures etc.

The resulting model, even if it referenced other objects, would be unmanageable.

What is required is the ability to break the application down into its constituent elements. One way in which we could do this would be to have separate parts of the architecture deal with the address book, the sender element, reading mail, creating mail etc. This is where the hierarchical MVC comes in.

15.3 The h-MVC

The hierarchical MVC framework (referred to in this chapter as h-MVC) is a modification of the basic MVC framework that encourages the decomposition of an application, or client, in an n-tier architecture. It is of course not the only way in which such a GUI-oriented application (or client) can be decomposed, but some of the benefits of this approach include:

- Building on a well-established existing framework (the MVC).
- Standardizing structures and interactions between different aspects of the application, leading to greater understanding between developers.
- Simplifying code maintenance, as each aspect can be developed, modified or updated separately.

15.4 The h-MVC Details

The h-MVC breaks down the client part of an application (whether a standalone application or part of an n-tier system) into separate MVC triads. Each MVC is then responsible for one aspect of the client.

Between the MVCs, well-defined interfaces exist to allow information and behaviour-oriented requests to flow. These interfaces are supported by links between the controllers. The rationale behind this is that the controllers are responsible for determining the flow of control within an MVC triad.

Therefore, if one MVC triad needs to communicate with another MVC triad, then it is the controllers that should be responsible for this. This in turn means that the links between one MVC triad and another will necessarily be maintained by the controllers.

In this view we are applying OO principles to the design and implementation of the client. That is, each MVC triad has:

- a particular responsibility
- clearly defined interfaces to other MVCs

15.5 Layered Application

The following (simple) example application (Figure 15.1) will be used to illustrate the ideas behind the h-MVC. This application allows a user to input some simple search criteria in the

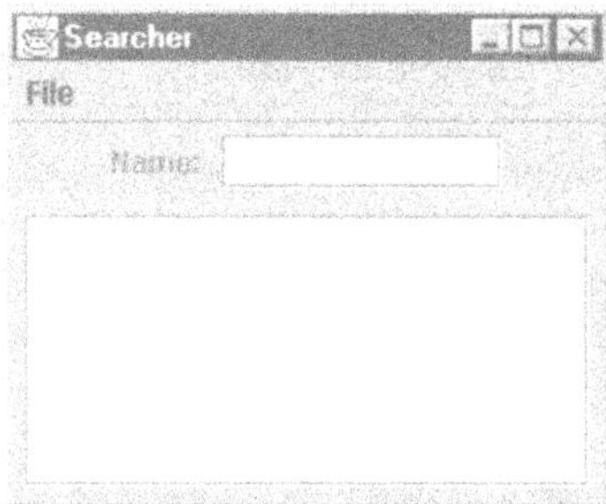

Figure 15.1 The search application.

name, age and sex fields. These can then run the search, the results of which are presented in the search results view. See Figure 15.2 for an example of the application's GUI.

The application is actually constructed using three MVC triads. The first triad represents the overall frame, the second deals with the search criteria, and the third deals with presenting the results of the search. This is illustrated in Figure 15.3.

The hierarchy represented by the links between the controllers in the three MVC triads is illustrated in Figure 15.4. Note that in this figure it is the controllers that are linked; there are no direct links from one view to another, nor are there direct links from one model to another.

The interface object is, of course, made up of a number of objects such as a frame, a number of panels, and graphical components such as buttons and text fields. In turn, layout managers are used to control the way in which these objects are arranged within the window frame. These aspects of the view are outside the scope of the h-MVC. However, some practical implications of this should be noted. The most important of these is that although, from an MVC perspective, one view has no reference to another view, from a Swing perspective, the inner views must be added to the outer views in order to be displayed. Indeed, at the topmost level, the sub-views must be added to the frame's content pane – thus it is necessary for a controller to be able to supply a reference to its view in order that the parent controller can obtain this view and pass it to its view for adding (in a Swing sense) to that view.

This hierarchical MVC framework builds directly upon the MVC framework presented in the previous chapter. Indeed, as far as the basic MVC architecture is concerned, we need not

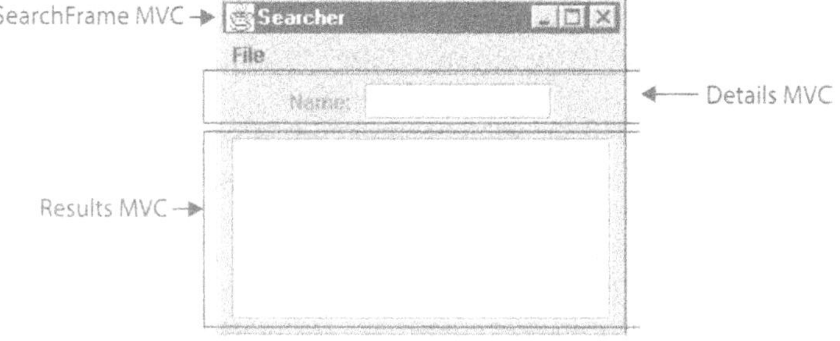

Figure 15.2 The MVC structure of the search application.

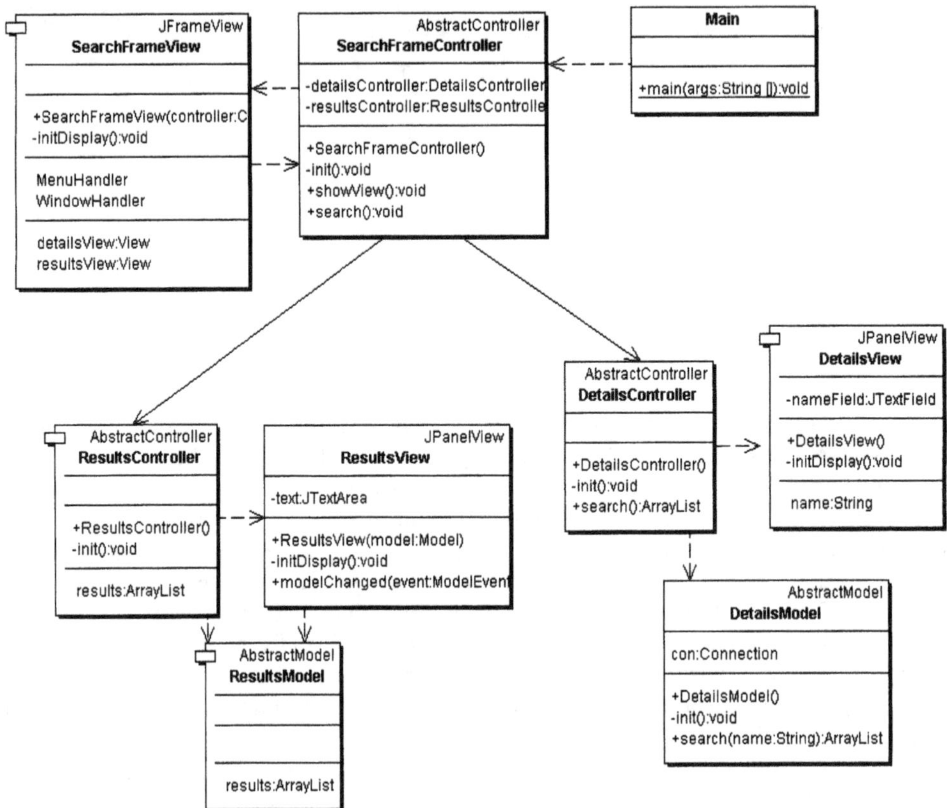

Figure 15.3 The classes in the search application.

make any changes to that framework. That framework provided *super* classes for various types of view, such as `JFrameView` for top-level views, `JPanelView` for inner views and `JDialog` views for dialog-based MVCs. In turn, the frame provides a root class for all models and a root class for all controllers. The structure of the framework is presented in Figure 15.5.

The search application uses the MVC framework to build a hierarchical MVC-based system. That is, the controllers, models and views in the search application extend appropriate classes in the MVC. These classes thus inherit all the behaviour provided by the MVC framework classes as well as defining the details specific to the search program. This is illustrated in Figure 15.6.

Note that one controller can reference another controller via an instance variable reference. That is, an instance variable in the `SearchFrameController` can maintain a reference to the `DetailsController`. Similarly, a second instance variable in the `SearchFrame-Controller` can maintain a reference to the `ResultsController`. The type of these instance variables can be the type of the subcontroller being referenced or of an interface that hides the details of the sub-MVC classes (in such cases the actual implementation can be obtained from a factory class).

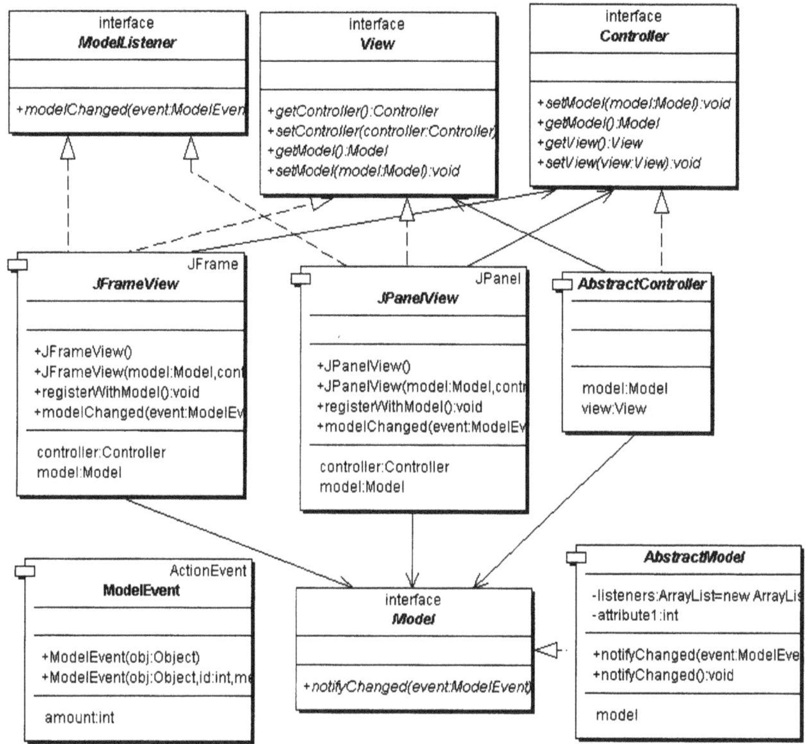

Figure 15.4 The MVC framework.

15.6 Initialization

The pseudocode diagram presented in Listing 15.1 illustrates the process of instantiating and initializing the simple search application.

Listing 15.1 The initialization of the search application.

```
Instantiate the SearchFrameController
  Instantiate the SearchFrameView passing in the SearchFrameController as
      a reference
  Set the view in the controller
  Instantiate the DetailsController
    Create the DetailsModel
    Create the DetailsView and initialize the display
  Instantiate the ResultsController
    Create the ResultsModel
    Create the ResultsView and initialize the display
  Set the details view on the SearchFrameView
```

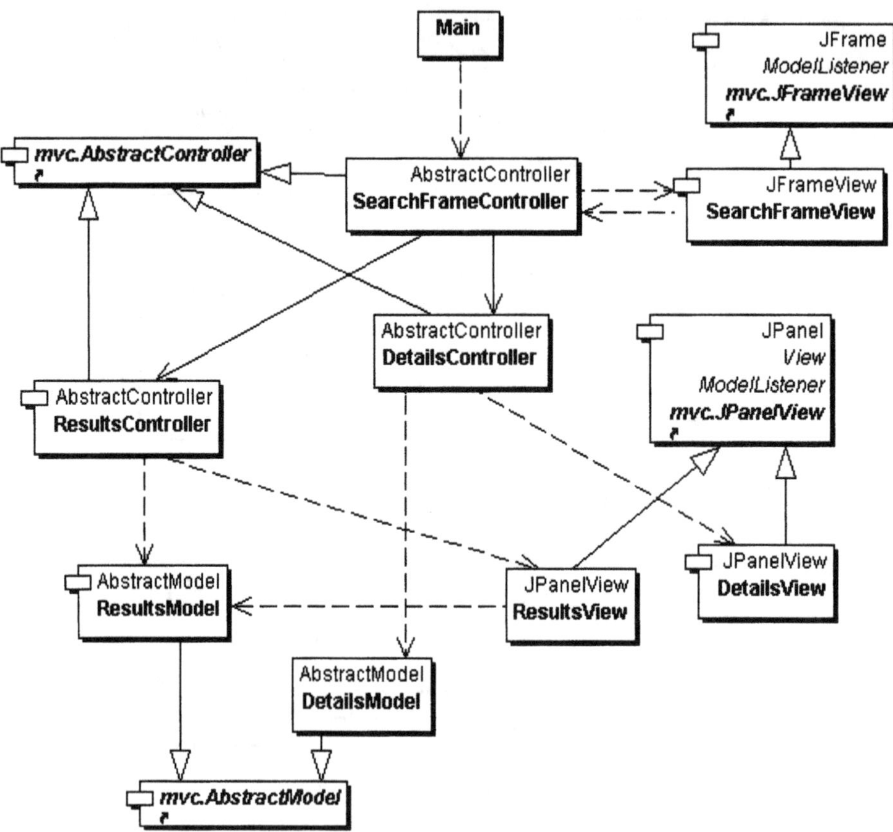

Figure 15.5 The relationships between the search application classes and the MVC framework classes.

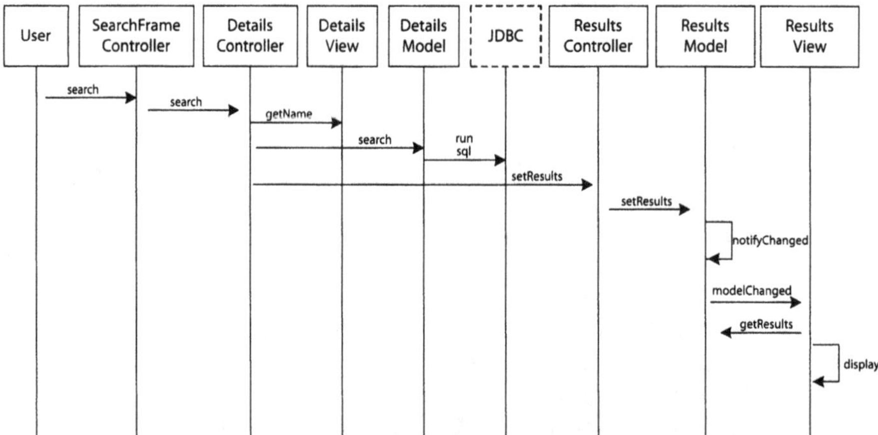

Figure 15.6 The search menu behaviour.

```
Set the results view on the SearchFrameView
Size the SearchFrameView
Display the SearchFrameView by asking the SearchFrameController to display
    its view
```

There are a number of points to note about these steps. Firstly, the main class in the main package instantiates the top-level controller. The constructor that executes in response to the request to instantiate the SearchFrameController then calls the private init() method to initialize the controller. The init() method takes the following steps:

1. Creates the associated model (if one is required).
2. Sets the model reference in the controller.
3. Creates the associated view, putting in a reference to itself and the model.
4. Instantiates the subcontroller (in this case the DetailsController).
5. Obtains the view associated with the subcontroller and registers it appropriately with the SearchFrameView.
6. Sets up the SearchFrameView size.

These six steps are typical of a controller's initialization method (and typically may instantiate more than one subcontroller). Once the init() method terminates, control returns to the main method, which requests that the controller displays its view. This causes the controller to call show() on the SearchFrameView and display the application GUI.

15.7 Hierarchical Behaviour

The search menu option is defined on the top-level SearchFrameView. The sequence diagram for the behaviour initiated by this menu is presented in Figure 15.6.

This sequence diagram is typical of the flow of control within an h-MVC application. Initially the top-level controller is passed the request to run search by the event handler in the view (represented by the user in the sequence diagram). This controller must then pass the request on to the DetailsController. The DetailsController then interrogates the Details View for the current input values to be used in the search, as represented by the values in the input field. Having extracted these values it then passes the search details information (that is the name to search on) to the Details Model. The model in an MVC framework represents the business logic aspect of the client. In this case it generates a simple SQL string and uses JDBC to query a simple database containing names and addresses. This returns JDBC ResultSet. The ResultSet reference can then be passed back to the controller, which can pass it on to SearchFrameController. The SearchFrameController can then pass it on to the relevant subcontroller, in this case the ResultsController.

The Results MVC is responsible for displaying the results of the search in a simple text area. The ResultsController therefore passes the JDBC ResultSet on to the ResultsModel. The model then extracts the date to be displayed from the ResultSet. The

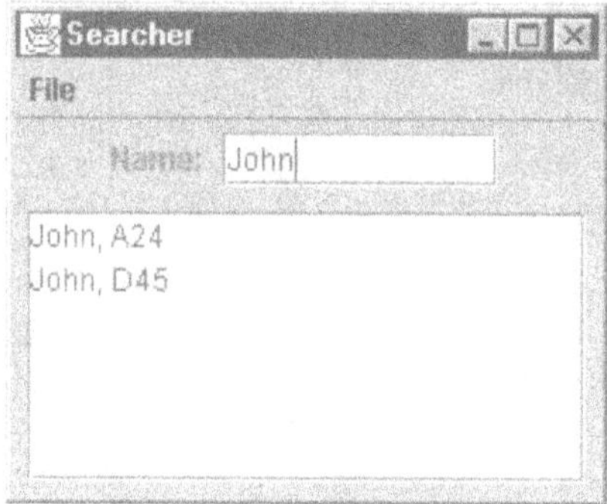

Figure 15.7 Displaying the results of a search.

ResultsModel then uses the update method inherited from the Model class in the basic MVC framework to notify any interested objects that it has changed. In this particular case, the only object registered as being interested in the model is the ResultsView. The ResultsView therefore receives notification of the model's changed state and can query the model for the current information it provides. This information can then be displayed by the ResultsView in the text area held within it. The final result is presented in Figure 15.7.

15.8 The Advantages of the h-MVC

The h-MVC can break down potentially complex GUI-based applications into simpler units. It can also reduce the dependencies between the various elements in this client. It can encourage reuse, as a commonly used MVC triad can be applied in multiple situations. This has major benefits in maintainability, management of development resources and comprehensibility.

15.9 The Disadvantages of the h-MVC

The biggest disadvantage of the h-MVC is the additional complexity imposed (on top of the complexity of the MVC) to support not only the separation of the presentation (the view) from the flow of control (the controllers) and the business logic (the model), but also the hierarchical aspects. That is, to follow the basic execution of the system involves not only up to three classes in one MVC, but multiple hierarchical MVC triads! However, this cost is mitigated by the benefits in terms of maintenance and extensibility (once a developer is familiar with the h-MVC).

A second disadvantage is that it is hard for the top-level MVC triad to communicate with a low-level MVC triad (and vice versa). In many cases this is not necessary, but in some cases it is. Without additional support this can mean that high-level controllers and models need to reference low-level controllers and models directly. At best this is undesirable, and at worst it results in a complex, un-maintainable, easily broken "bird's nest" of an application. However, this issue can be resolved by using additional frameworks such as an ActionMapper and an EventManager (both based on standard patterns).

An ActionMapper is merely a simple singleton object that maps Java actions to keys. This allows one view to create an action (say a low-level inner view) that can be retrieved by another view (say the top-level frame) so that the same action may be used for a button inside a subview and a menu on the top-level frames menu bar. This works very well in practice and is a very lightweight object.

An EventManager is more complex and deals with the need to notify different objects of events that have occurred. For example, a low-level MVC may perform some action that means that the top-level MVC should disable some functions. The low-level inner MVC triad can send an event to the EventManager. The EventManager can then forward this event to interested parties. The EventManager is a type of mediator object and as such implements the Mediator pattern.

The third major disadvantage of the approach is that there is currently no tool support available for the MVC, let alone the h-MVC. Therefore the developer must manually engineer applications based on the h-MVC from first principles.

15.10 Summary

The h-MVC framework provides a scalable and robust architecture upon which to build complex graphical applications, whether as part of a standalone application or as an n-tier system. The ability to break the application down into its constituent parts simplifies project management, development and maintenance. In turn, this can significantly reduce development time and the potential risks involved.

The Visitor Framework

This chapter presents the use of the visitor pattern to allow separate parts of an application to obtain state information about other parts of an application without having direct access (or knowledge of those parts). This is particularly useful in producing highly modular applications that are resilient to change but have high cohesion. The examples presented follow on from the previous chapters on building the client element of an *n*-tier architecture.

16.1 Background

The visitor pattern can be implemented in many different ways and for many different purposes, and as with any pattern it is necessary to apply the pattern to your own design situation before implementing it. This is an important point to note: patterns are not concrete designs for particular systems. This is because a pattern must be instantiated in a particular domain to be used. This involves evaluating various trade-offs or constraints as well as detailed consideration of the consequences. It also does not mean that creativity or human judgment has been removed, as it is still necessary to make the design and implementation decisions required. Having done that, the developer must then implement the pattern and combine the implementation with other code (which may or may not have been derived from a pattern).

Patterns are also not frameworks (although they do seem to be exceptionally well suited for documenting frameworks). This is because frameworks present an instance of a design for solving a family of problems in a specific domain (and often for a particular language). In terms of languages such as Smalltalk and Java, a framework is a set of abstract cooperating classes. To apply such a framework to a particular problem it is often necessary to customize it by providing user-defined subclasses and to compose objects in the appropriate manner (e.g. the Smalltalk MVC framework). That is, a framework is a semi-complete application. As a result, any given framework may contain one or more instances of multiple patterns, and in turn a pattern can be used in many different frameworks.

16.2 The Visitor Pattern

The visitor pattern is one of the so-called "Gang of Four" patterns produced by Erich Gamma, Richard Helm, John Vlissides and Ralph Johnson. It is one of the Behavioural Patterns, meaning that this pattern is concerned with the ways in which classes or objects interact and distribute responsibility. There are in fact two other types of pattern described in the Gang of Four book: Creational Patterns and Structural Patterns. Creational patterns are concerned with the creation of objects. Structural patterns are concerned the describing the composition of objects and classes.

The précis of the visitor pattern presented in Gamma *et al.* (1995) states that:

> Visitor: Represents an operation to be performed on the elements of an object structure. Visitor lets you define a new operation without changing the classes of the elements on which it operates.

That is, the visitor pattern represents a way of placing logic that would need to be distributed across a set of classes into one place. The visitor object is then passed among objects of these classes and the visitor can then perform operations or extract data as it goes. This has the advantage of simplifying the participating classes, reducing the distribution of the logic among these classes as well as reducing the cross-references that would otherwise be necessary.

As this chapter builds on the previous chapters, our usage of the visitor pattern will be for a particular purpose. In the previous chapter we presented the hierarchical MVC (referred to as h-MVC). The h-MVC framework is a modification of the basic MVC framework that encourages the decomposition of an application, or client, in an *n*-tier architecture. Some of the benefits of this approach include:

- building on a well-established existing framework (the MVC)
- standardizing structures and interactions between different aspects of the application – leading to greater understanding between developers
- simplifying code maintenance code as each aspect can be developed modified or updated separately

The h-MVC breaks the client part of an application (whether a standalone application or part of an *n*-tier system) down into separate MVC triads. Each MVC is then responsible for one aspect of the client.

Between the MVCs, well-defined interfaces exist to allow information and behaviour-oriented requests to flow. These interfaces are supported by links between the controllers. The rationale behind this is that the controllers are responsible for determining the flow of control within an MVC triad.

Therefore, if one MVC triad needs to communicate with another MVC triad, then it is the controllers that should be responsible for this. This in turn means that the controllers will necessarily maintain the links between one MVC triad and another.

Figure 16.1 illustrates the structure of an application built with the h-MVC. This application contains three MVC triads: one for the top-level frame (actually this MVC triad does without the model as there is no application data to hold at this level, but we still use the term "triad" for consistency), one for the details part of the display and one for the results part of the display. This relates to the actual running program, as illustrated in Figure 16.2.

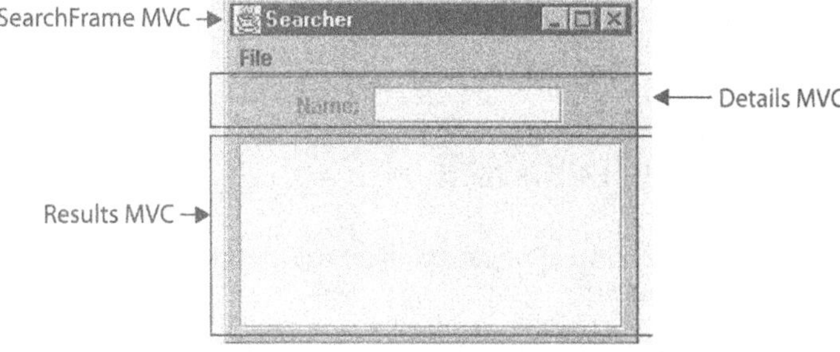

Figure 16.1 The structure of an application based on the h-MVC.

A disadvantage of the h-MVC is that it is hard for top-level MVC triads to communicate with a low-level MVC triad (and vice versa). In many cases this is not necessary, but in some cases it is. Without additional support this can mean that high-level controllers and models need to directly reference low level controllers and models. At best this is undesirable and

Figure 16.2 The MVC structure of the search application.

at worst it results in a complex, un-maintainable, easily broken "bird's nest" of an application.

For example, consider the situation where the top-level MVC triad in the search application presented in Figure 16.2 needs to determine whether anything is currently displayed in the results window. It might need to do this to determine whether to enable or disable menu options etc. However, the Results MVC could be complex and made up of any number of lower level MVC triads. To determine the state of this (and any lower level MVCs) we would need to write code that allowed an MVC to be queried for its state and to return some state-based information. As different MVCs might be able to offer different types and amounts of state information this could lead to a large amount of code needing to be written – all of which would be very specific to the MVC triad. It might also mean that the top-level MVC triad would have to have links to all lower level triads and knowledge of their state-based information.

One way to get around this would be to provide a class based on the visitor pattern that could "visit" various MVC triads collecting whatever state-based information is available. The top-level MVC triad could then interrogate the visitor object to find out whatever information it needed. Thus the top-level MVC triad is decoupled from lower level MVC triads. All that needs to be shared is an awareness of what type of information can be supplied to the visitor. A framework based on this approach is presented in the next section.

16.3 The Visitor Framework

The visitor architecture (illustrated in Figure 16.3) is actually very simple. It comprises two classes and an interface. The interface defines the method that all objects that wish to receive a Visitor object must implement. In turn, the Visitor class provides facilities for creating one or more state descriptions. A state description is an object, typically used to represent the state of an object or group of closely related objects. Thus a Visitor may have several state descriptions associated with it to allow it to describe the state of various unrelated objects (or groups of objects).

In this framework the state description is implemented as a StateMap, keyed on the map name. In terms of implementation this association can be implemented as a HashMap or similar.

To use this architecture, one object must create the Visitor object and pass the object to the visitable objects. These objects can then fill out the state information in the state map (for an example, see the simple application in Section 16.5).

16.4 Using the Visitor Framework

To use the visitor framework in an application there are a number of things you will need to do. These are presented below:

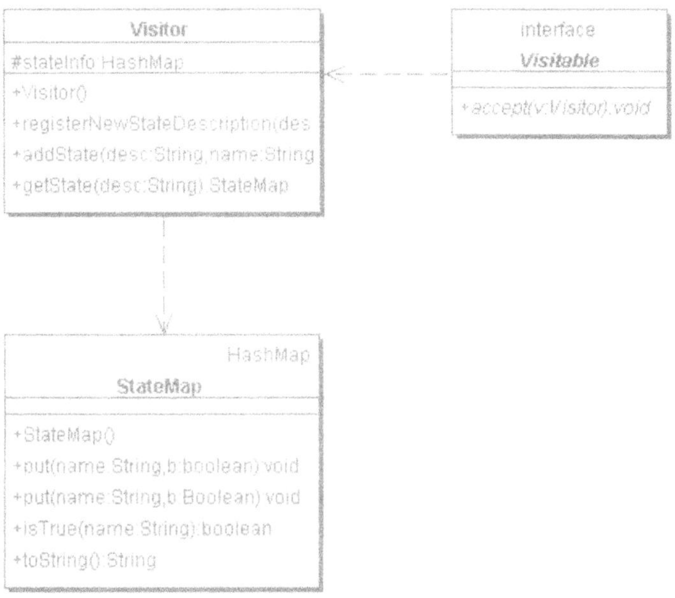

Figure 16.3 The Visitor package.

1. Define 1 or more sets of state constants. These states will be used to populate the state map. In general there should be one set of state constants per state map. This can be (and should be) done using appropriate interfaces to define sets of constants. For example:

```java
public interface ParserStateConstants {
    public static final String FILE_SELECTED = "File Selected";
    public static final String FILE_LOADED = "File Loaded";
    public static final String FILE_PARSED = "File Parsed";
    public static final String FILE_SAVED = "File Saved";
}
```

2. For each state map required in the application, identify a key to use for that state map. For example:

```java
public interface VisitorConstants {
    public static final String PARSER_MODEL = "Parser Model";
    public static final String TOOL_FRAME_MODEL = "Tool Frame Model";
}
```

3. Identify situations in which you need to determine the state of objects that may be distributed around the application (and in general not directly accessible from the current object). In these cases, create a Visitor object, issue it to the appropriate object(s) and then use the resulting populated Visitor object to determine what you should do next. Note that the objects receiving the Visitor object should all have implemented the Visitable interface.

For example, in a view you might need to determine whether an option is enabled or not:

```java
public void browseFileStatus() {
  Visitor v = new Visitor();
  ((Visitable)controller).accept(v);
  StateMap sm = v.getState(VisitorConstants.PARSER_MODEL);
  boolean fileLoadedState = sm.isTrue(ParserStateConstants.FILE_LOADED);
  if (fileLoadedState) {
    ...
  } ...
}
```

4. Identify the objects that need to be Visitable in order that the state of the system can be captured. The classes of the objects must implement the Visitable interface and must therefore implement the public void accept(Visitor) method.

5. Next decide what the accept method does in each case. In general, controllers will pass the Visitor object on to their models and to other controllers as appropriate. For example:

```java
public class BrowserController .... {
  ...
  public void accept(Visitor v) {
    ((Visitable)getModel).accept(v);
    ((Visitable)parserController).accept(v);
  }
  ...
}
```

As it is application models that hold the persistent data in the system, then these objects are the most natural (but not the only) places in which the state of the system should be found. It is thus within models that in general the state information is set. To do this, the following steps must be followed:

*   Register a new state description with the Visitor object.
*   Add some state information for the state description.

For example

```java
public void accept(Visitor v) {
  v.registerNewStateDescription(VisitorConstants.PARSER_MODEL);
  v.addState(VisitorConstants.PARSER_MODEL,
    ParserStateConstants.FILE_LOADED,
    true);
  ...
}
```

6. Test your behaviour

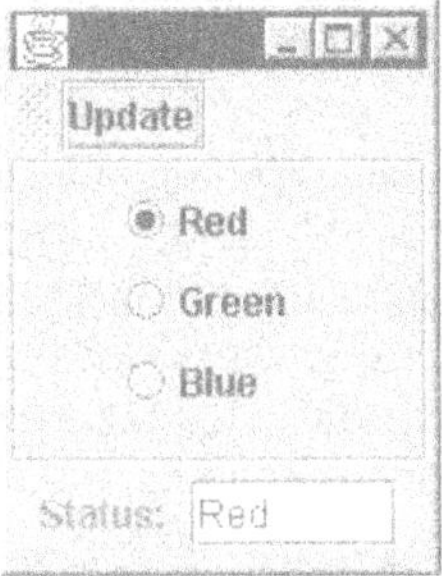

Figure 16.4 The simple application.

16.5 A Simple Application

The simple application described here consists of a simple GUI that allows a user to select one of a set of radio buttons for Red, Green and Blue. The user can then use the Update button to get the system to generate a Visitor object that is sent around the application picking up the state information (essentially which option is currently displayed). The resulting Visitor object is used to determine what the output presented in the text field in the main display should be. The GUI of the application is presented in Figure 16.4.

To keep things simple no application models have been used in this example. This is allowed within the MVC as a model is optional and only necessary if there is application behaviour/logic or data that should be maintained. In this case, to simplify the implementation and highlight the use of the visitor pattern we are only using Controllers and Views. The structure of the application is illustrated in Figure 16.5.

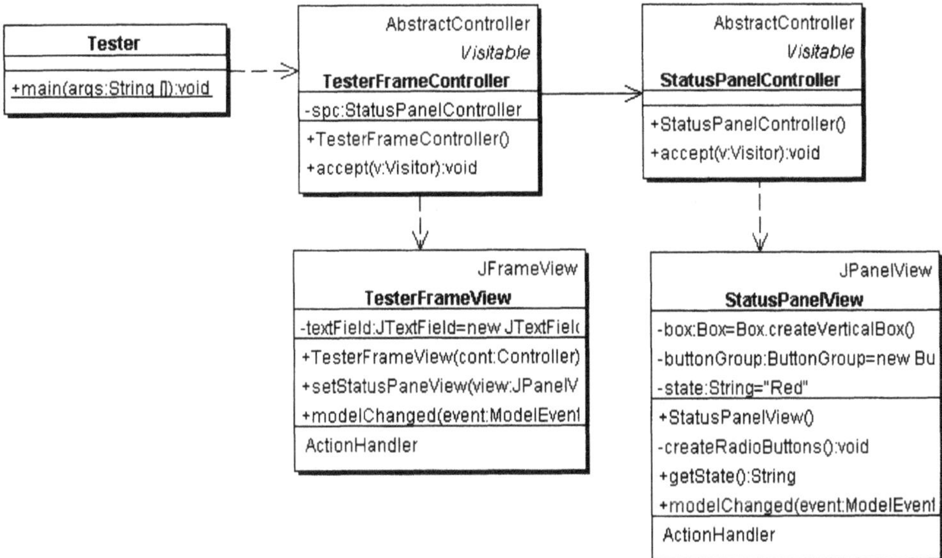

Figure 16.5 The tester application structure.

The Tester class acts as the root of the application and contains the Main method. This method creates an instance of the TesterFrameController and nothing more. The TesterFrameController class is then responsible for constructing the other classes in the application. It creates the TesterFrameView, and initiates the construction of the Status-PanelController. Having done that it requests the view from the StatusPanel-Controller and adds that view to the TesterFrameView. The TestFrameView creates the toolbar at the top of the display and the labelled text field at the bottom of the display. It also provides an inner class called ActionHandler to deal with the action event raised when the user selects the Update button. At this point the view can be packed and then displayed to the user.

The StatusPanelController is responsible for creating the StatusPanelView. The StatusPanelView creates the main bordered box display containing the buttons in a button group. This is done inside the createRadioButtons method. It also defines an inner class, called ActionHandler, that stores the result of the user selecting different radio buttons so that it can provide the selected colour on demand (via the getState() method).

The visitor framework is employed within this application as illustrated in Figure 16.6.

Both the controllers implement the Visitable interface and are thus dependent upon the Visitor class. That is, they are passed a Visitor object when their accept method is called.

The accept method in the TesterFrameController delegates the responsibility for filling out the Visitor object to the StatusPanelController. The StatusPanel-Controller interrogates the StatusPanelView to determine the state of the display. It then sets up a State Description to hold the state information. Once it has done that it terminates.

The accept method is initiated by the ActionHandler inner class of the TesterFrame-View, which needs to determine what value to place into the text field it is displaying (this would more normally be placed within the application model). For example:

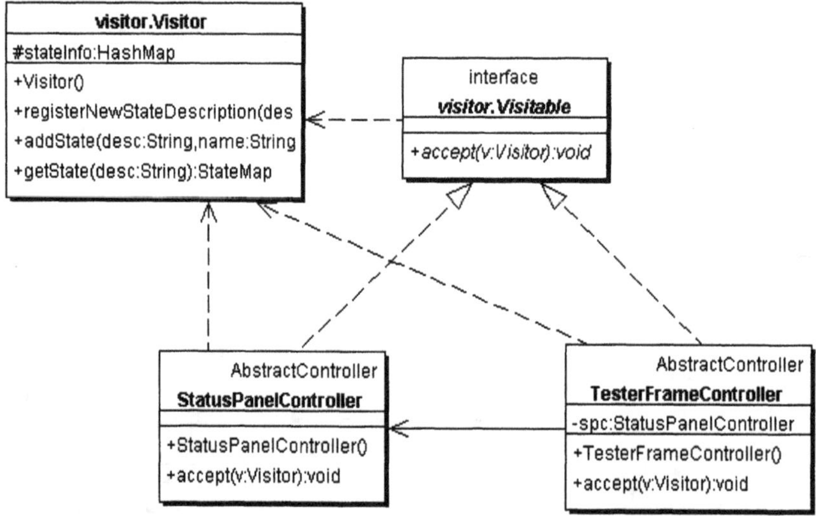

Figure 16.6 Using the visitor framework within the tester application.

```java
class ActionHandler implements ActionListener {
  public void actionPerformed(ActionEvent e) {
    Visitor v = new Visitor();
    ((Visitable)getController()).accept(v);
    StateMap sm = v.getState("Colour status");
    if (sm.isTrue("red")) {
      textField.setText("Red");
    } else if (sm.isTrue("green")) {
      textField.setText("Green");
    } else {
      textField.setText("Blue");
    }
  }
}
```

16.6 Summary

An important point to note is how the framework presented in this chapter is an application of the generic visitor pattern rather than an exact implementation of that pattern. This is natural, as patterns are design knowledge rather than specific designs. That is, they express a concept that needs to be applied within the context of an application. This is exactly what we have done here.

The use of the Visitor framework allows the decoupling of elements of a GUI application that would otherwise require close coupling to allow state-based information to be retrieved.

In the next chapter we will examine an EventManager (based on standard patterns).

An EventManager is more complex and deals with the need to notify different objects of events that have occurred. For example, a low-level MVC may perform some action that means that the top-level MVC should disable some functions. The low-level inner MVC triad can send an event to the EventManager. The EventManager can then forward this event to interested parties. The EventManager is a type of mediator object and as such implements the mediator pattern

16.7 References

Alexander, C., Ishikawa, S. and Silverstein, M. with Jacobson, M., Fiksdahl-King, I. and Angel, S. (1977). *A Pattern Language*. Oxford University Press, Oxford.

Alexander, C. (1979). *The Timeless Way of Building*. Oxford University Press, Oxford.

Johnson, R. E. (1992). Documenting frameworks with patterns. *Proc. OOPSLA'92, SIGPLAN Notices* 27(10), 63–76.

Birrer, A. and Eggenschwiler, T. (1993). Frameworks in the financial engineering domain: an experience report. *ECOOP'93*, pp. 21–35.

Gamma, E., Helm, R., Johnson, R. and Vlissides, J. (1995). *Design Patterns: Elements of Reusable Object-Oriented Software.* Addison-Wesley, Reading, MA.

Grand, M. (2002) *Patterns in Java: A Catalog of Reusable Design Patterns Illustrated with UML,* 2nd edn, Vol. 1. John Wiley & Sons, New York.

16.8 Listings

Listing 16.1 The `Visitable` interface.

```java
package Visitor;

/**
 * All objects that should be involved in receiving a Visitor
 * object should implement this interface. It indicates that the
 * implementing class expects to be handed a Visitor object that it will
 * add its data to.
 */
public interface Visitable {

/**
 * This method receives a Visitor object. Implementing classes
 * are expected to implement this method such that it creates (if
 * appropriate) a new state description and then adds state behaviour to
 * this @param v The Visitor object
 */
public void accept( Visitor v ) ;
}
```

Listing 16.2 The `Visitor` class.

```java
package Visitor;

import java.util.HashMap;
import java.util.ArrayList;
import java.util.Iterator;

/**
 * This class represents an object that can be instantiated and
 * passed to Visitable objects. These objects will add their
 * own state descriptions to the Visitor object and state
 * data to those description. For example
 * <pre>
 * v.registerNewStateDescription("FileState");
 * v.addState("FileState", "Loaded", true);
```

```
 * </pre>
 * Note that the add state method takes a string to indicate the state
 * descritpion followed by the state and then the boolean value
 */
public class Visitor{

  /** Holds the StateMap objects
   * defining the various state descriptions **/
  protected HashMap stateInfo;

  /**
   * Creates an empty Visitor object
   */
  public Visitor(){
    stateInfo = new HashMap();
  }

  /**
   * Register a new State description - create an ArrayList and
   * place it in the HashMap of state info, with the value of the String
   * parameter as the key to the map.
   * @param desc the description of the state
   */
  public void registerNewStateDescription(String desc){
    StateMap info = new StateMap();
    stateInfo.put( desc, info );
  }

  /**
   * Add the state of an object to the state info collection which is
   * identified by desc.
   * @param desc the state map description
   * @param name the state
   * @param the value of the state in the state map
   */
  public void addState(String desc, String name, boolean value) {
    StateMap map = (StateMap)stateInfo.get(desc);
    map.put(name,value);
  }

  /**
   * Returns a state map object for the geiven state description
   * @param desc the state descritpion
   * @return the state map
   */
  public StateMap getState( String desc ){
```

```
    return (StateMap)stateInfo.get(desc);
  }
}
```

Listing 16.3 The StateMap class.

```java
package Visitor;

import java.util.HashMap;
import java.util.Iterator;

/**
 * Class which is used to store state information.
 * Used in association with the
 * Visitor class to allow multiple state maps to be defined.
 * Currently stores Boolean
 * values only, for properties defined by String used as
 * key into the HashMap.
 */
public class StateMap extends HashMap{

  /**
   * Creates a new empty state map object
   */
  public StateMap() {
  }

  /**
   * Take a property name, and a boolean value, and add entry to the
   * table, with the boolean value converted to a Boolean. This is a
   * convienience method for put(String, Boolean)
   * @name the name of the state to set
   * @b the boolean value (i.e. true or false)
   */
  public void put( String name, boolean b ){
    super.put( name, new Boolean(b) );
  }

  /**
   * Add a new entry to the table, with a Boolean value for a given
   * name.
   * @param name the state to set
   * @param b the boolean value for this state
   */
  public void put( String name, Boolean b ){
    put( name, b );
```

```java
  }

  /**
   * Return the value held for the given key, as a boolean.
   * @param name the state to test
   * @return boolean indicating the value of the state
   */
  public boolean isTrue( String name ){
    return ((Boolean)super.get(name)).booleanValue();
  }

  /**
   * Converts the state map into a printable form
   * @return the string representing this statemap
   */
  public String toString(){
    StringBuffer buffer = new StringBuffer() ;
    Iterator iterator = this.keySet().iterator() ;
    buffer.append("StateMap contains " + this.size() + " entries\n");
    while( iterator.hasNext() ){
      String key = (String) iterator.next() ;
      buffer.append( key + ": " + this.get( key ) + "\n" );
    }
    return buffer.toString() ;
  }
}
```

Listing 16.4 The Tester class.

```java
package test;
public class Tester {

  public static void main(String [] args) {
    new TesterFrameController();
  }
  /** @link dependency */
  /*#TesterFrameController lnkTesterFrameController;*/
}
```

Listing 16.5 The TesterFrameController class.

```java
package test;

import mvc.*;
import Visitor.*;
```

```java
public class TesterFrameController extends AbstractController implements
      Visitable {
  private StatusPanelController spc;

  /** @link dependency */
  /*#TesterFrameView lnkTesterFrameView;*/

  public TesterFrameController() {
    setView(new TesterFrameView(this));
    spc = new StatusPanelController();
    ((TesterFrameView)getView()).setStatusPaneView((JPanelView)spc.getView());
    ((JFrameView)getView()).pack();
    ((JFrameView)getView()).setVisible(true);
  }

  public void accept(Visitor v) {
    ((Visitable)spc).accept(v);
  }
}
```

Listing 16.6 The `TesterFrameView` class.

```java
package test;

import javax.swing.*;
import java.awt.*;
import java.awt.event.*;

import mvc.*;
import Visitor.*;

public class TesterFrameView extends JFrameView {
  private JTextField textField = new JTextField(6);

  public TesterFrameView(Controller cont) {
    setController(cont);
    textField.setText("");

    // Now use a toolbar for the update button
    JToolBar toolbar = new JToolBar();
    // VERY IMPORTANT: Now add the panel to the content pane
    getContentPane().add(toolbar, BorderLayout.NORTH);

    ActionHandler handler = new ActionHandler();

    JButton b = new JButton("Update");
```

```
    b.addActionListener(handler);
    toolbar.add(b);

      JPanel panel = new JPanel();
      panel.add(new JLabel("Status: "));
      panel.add(textField);
      getContentPane().add(panel, BorderLayout.SOUTH);
    }

    public void setStatusPaneView(JPanelView view) {
      getContentPane().add(view, BorderLayout.CENTER);
    }

  public void modelChanged(ModelEvent event){}

    class ActionHandler implements ActionListener {
      public void actionPerformed(ActionEvent e) {
        Visitor v = new Visitor();
        ((Visitable)getController()).accept(v);
        StateMap sm = v.getState("Colour status");
        if (sm.isTrue("red")) {
          textField.setText("Red");
        } else if (sm.isTrue("green")) {
          textField.setText("Green");
        } else {
          textField.setText("Blue");
        }
      }
    }
  }
}
```

Listing 16.7 The StatusPanelController class.

```
package test;

import mvc.*;
import Visitor.*;

public class StatusPanelController extends AbstractController implements
    Visitable {
  public StatusPanelController() {
    StatusPanelView view = new StatusPanelView();
    setView(view);
  }

public void accept(Visitor v) {
```

```java
      String colour = ((StatusPanelView)getView()).getState();

      v.registerNewStateDescription("Colour status");
      v.addState("Colour status", "red", (colour == "Red"));
      v.addState("Colour status", "green", (colour == "Green"));
      v.addState("Colour status", "blue", (colour == "Blue"));
   }
}
```

Listing 16.8 The StatusPanelView class.

```java
package test;

import javax.swing.*;
import java.awt.*;
import java.awt.event.*;

import mvc.*;
import Visitor.*;

public class StatusPanelView extends JPanelView {
  private Box box = Box.createVerticalBox() ;
  private ButtonGroup buttonGroup = new ButtonGroup() ;
  private String state = "Red";
  public StatusPanelView() {
    this.add(box) ;
    this.setBorder(BorderFactory.createEtchedBorder( ) ) ;
    createRadioButtons();
  }

  private void createRadioButtons() {
    ActionListener listener = new ActionHandler();
    //create the JRadioButton
    JRadioButton button = new JRadioButton("Red") ;
    //set whether or not the button is selected
    button.setSelected( true ) ;
    //Add the actionListener to the button
    button.addActionListener( listener ) ;
    //Add the button to the box
    box.add( button ) ;
    //Add the button to the ButtonGroup
    // this enforces single selection only
    buttonGroup.add( button );

    button = new JRadioButton("Green") ;
    button.setSelected( false ) ;
```

```java
      button.addActionListener( listener ) ;
      box.add( button ) ;
      buttonGroup.add( button );

      button = new JRadioButton("Blue") ;
      button.setSelected( false ) ;
      button.addActionListener( listener ) ;
      box.add( button ) ;
      buttonGroup.add( button );
    }

    public String getState() {
      return state;
    }

    public void modelChanged(ModelEvent event){}

    class ActionHandler implements ActionListener {
      public void actionPerformed(ActionEvent event) {
        String cmd = event.getActionCommand();
        state = cmd;
      }
    }
  }
```

The EventManager

17.1 Introduction

One of the problems that can occur in a complex application (for example within a GUI client in an *n*-tier application) is how different parts of the client should communicate. For example, consider the application presented in Figure 17.1.

In this graphical application there a number of distinct areas that could be implemented by separate model–view–controller triads. One of the aims of the MVC is to separate out a graphical application into distinct functional areas, thus increasing modularity of code but maintaining a high level of cohesion. One problem introduced with this is how inner MVC triads should communicate with higher level MVC triads. For example, in the graphical client presented in Figure 17.1, how should changes to the Local field in the bottom MVC be transmitted to the top-level MVC for the whole application? Below we will consider the use of an EventManager to support such communication.

17.2 The Use of Patterns

The EventManager employs two design patterns: the singleton pattern and the mediator pattern. As such it is an excellent example of the difference between the abstract nature of a design pattern and the concrete nature of an implementation. The two patterns involved do not directly work with each other; however, they have been applied to the design of the EventManager to achieve the overall goals of the EventManager – in particular those of high cohesion but low coupling between diverse objects and global accessibility:

- High cohesion but low coupling: the need to allow different parts of an application to communicate in a coherent and maintainable manner without the overhead of many cross-references.

Figure 17.1 A sample GUI client.

- Global accessibility: the EventManager must be accessible in many places, throughout the application. As such a diverse set of objects need to reference the EventManager, there must therefore be a way of accessing the EventManager throughout the application.

The two patterns used within the EventManager are described below, following which discussions of how they are used and the design of the EventManager are presented.

17.3 The Mediator Pattern

This pattern is based on that presented in Gamma *et al.* (1995) on pages 273–282 and has been discussed a number of times in this book. However, we shall consider come of its strengths and weaknesses. In particular, the mediator pattern has the following benefits and drawbacks:

- It limits subclassing to the mediator (e.g. by changing the routing algorithm in mediator you can change the system's behaviour).
- It de-couples colleagues.
- It simplifies object protocols from many-to-many down to one-to-many.
- It abstracts how objects cooperate.
- It centralizes control.

17.4 The Singleton Pattern

The second pattern employed by the EventManager is the singleton pattern. Again this has been discussed earlier in this book.

As with the mediator pattern there are several consequences to using the singleton pattern:

- Controlled access to sole instance. Because the singleton class encapsulates its sole instance, it can have strict control client access to that instance.
- Reduced name space. The singleton object is not a global object; rather, it is an object that can be accessed through its singleton class global. Thus the class may impose restrictions on the access to that singleton object.
- Permits subclassing. A singleton class does not inherently stop a developer from subclassing that object and either making the subclass a singleton or allowing as many instance of the class as necessary.
- It is quite straightforward to modify a singleton to become a limited number object (rather than limiting the instances to 1 you could limit the instances to 2, 3 or 4, for example).

17.5 The Design of the EventManager

There are two aspects to the design of the EventManager, the first is that it is a singleton object accessed through the static method `getInstance()`. The second is that it acts like a mediator. One object sends a message to the EventManager telling it to notify other objects that an event has occurred (such as a data file being loaded). The class structure of the three classes that comprise the EventManager framework are presented in Figure 17.2.

The two classes in the framework are the `EventManager` itself and the `ManagerEvent`, while a single interface completes the framework: the `EventManagerListener`. To use the framework a class must implement the `EventManagerListener` interface (in order to receive events). In Figure 17.2 a test harness package (`event.test`) has been defined with

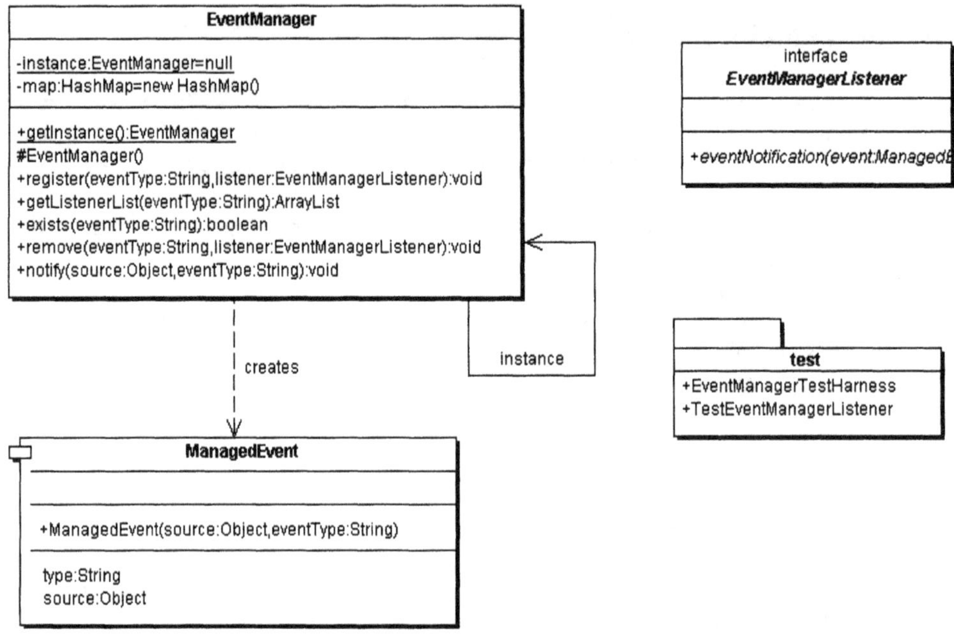

Figure 17.2 The classes in the EventManager framework.

two classes: one that implements the `EventManagerListener`, the `TestEventManager-Listener` and one that will register instances of the `TestEventManagerListener` class with the `EventManager` and initiate the notification of events to the `EventManager`. However, before we look at these test classes in detail we will consider the core framework classes and interface.

17.5.1 The EventManager

The EventManager supports the singleton pattern via the private static variables instance and the public static method `getInstance()`. Thus client code that needs to obtain a reference to the EventManager must obtain that reference via the `getInstance()` method thus:

```
EventManager em = EventManager.getInstance();
```

Note that the `getInstance()` method uses "lazy initialization" to obtain a reference to a new instance of the EventManager the first time it is called. Thus if the EventManager is never used an instance of it is never created. Also, if you examine the listing for the EventManager note that the `getInstance()` method has been made thread safe.

The EventManager itself holds a HashMap, map, of event listeners keyed on the type of event. That is, all the listeners interested in being notified about a specific event are held in an `ArrayList` associated with the type of event. This is illustrated in Figure 17.3.

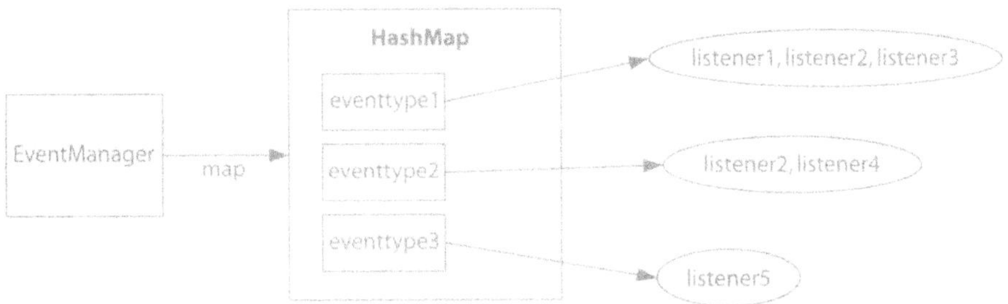

Figure 17.3 The structure of the listener lists.

Thus when an event is sent to the `EventManager` it can easily and quickly obtain a list of listeners interested in that event.

`EventManagerListeners` may be added to and removed from the lists by registering and removing for a given event type. This is done using the `register( String eventType, EventManagerListener listener)` method, for example:

```
em.register("event1",testListener0);
```

This would register the `testListener0` object with the `EventManager`. It is also possible to remove listeners from receiving notification of events in a similar manner.

To cause an event to be sent to one or more listener the `EventManager` provides the `notify` method (`public void notify(Object source, String eventType)`). This method dynamically creates an event object for each type of listener that is registered for the `eventType` specified.

The notification method for each listener must be sent a single `ManagedEvent` object that specifies the source and the event type. Each listener will be guaranteed to have such a method as they will have implemented the `EventManagerListener` interface (which specifies the `eventNotification(ManagedEvent)` method). The `ManagedEvent` class and the `EventManagerListener` are described below.

17.5.2 The `ManagedEvent` Class

The `ManagedEvent` class is a simple class (see the listings at the end of the chapter) that maintains the type and the source of the event and provides a constructor and accessor methods for this information. It could be easily extended to create more sophisticated event classes if required. Note that we have not extended any of the Java-provided events for simplicity's sake, although this would be another option.

17.5.3 The `EventManagerListener` Interface

This interface must by implemented by any class that wishes to be a listener of `ManagedEvents` via the `EventManager`. It is a simple interface containing a single method, the `eventNotification(EventManagerEvent)`.

Any class implementing this interface may register with the `EventManager`, using the `EventManager.register()` method.

The `eventNotification(EventManagerEvent)` method will be called whenever `EventManager.notify()` is called with an event type that the listener has registered for.

17.6 Using the EventManager

To use the EventManager is relatively straightforward. The object that wishes to receive notification of some event must implement the `EventManagerListener`. In turn, it must then be registered with the `EventManager`. Once this is completed an object can then call the notification method on the `EventManager` specifying the event type that the listener is registered for. This is illustrated in the `TestEventManagerListener` (which implements the `EventManagerListener` interface) and the `EventManagerTestHarness` which sets up the `EventManager` and calls the appropriate methods. The result of running this test harness is presented in the listings.

17.7 The EventManager in a Graphical Client

The EventManager described above could now be used within a GUI client to allow different elements of the client to communicate. For example, if we are using model–view–controller (MVC) triads (as described in previous chapters) then an MVC triad representing a low-level screen such as that in Figure 17.1 could now communicate with the top-level MVC via the EventManager.

17.8 Reference

Gamma, E., Helm, R., Johnson, R. and Vlissides, J. (1995). *Design Patterns: Elements of Reusable Object-Oriented Software*. Addison-Wesley, Reading, MA.

17.9 Listings

Listing 17.1 The `EventManager`.

```
package event;

import java.util.*;

public class EventManager {
```

```java
//------------------------------------------------------------------------
// Class/Static variables
//------------------------------------------------------------------------

// Contains the one and only instance of the EventManager
private static EventManager instance = null;


//------------------------------------------------------------------------
// Instance variables
//------------------------------------------------------------------------
private HashMap map = new HashMap();

/**
 * Returns the singleton instance of the EventManager.
 **/
public static EventManager getInstance() {
  //Double check to avoid two instances being created in case of thread
  //race condition
  if (instance == null) {
    synchronized(EventManager.class) {
      if (instance == null) {
        instance = new EventManager();
      }
    }
  }
  return instance;
}

/**
 * Protected default constructor. Prevents the EventManager being
 * directly constructed.
 **/
protected EventManager() {
}

public void register( String eventType, EventManagerListener listener ) {
  System.out.println(eventType + " registering: " + listener);
  this.getListenerList(eventType).add(listener);
}

protected ArrayList getListenerList(String eventType) {
  ArrayList list = (ArrayList)map.get(eventType);
  if (list == null){
    list = new ArrayList();
    map.put(eventType,list);
  }
```

```java
    return list;
  }

  protected boolean exists(String eventType) {
    return (map.get(eventType) != null);
  }

  public void remove(String eventType, EventManagerListener listener) {
    // Make sure a ListenerList exists in the map, if one does not exist
    // this unregister is considered redundant
    if (this.exists(eventType)) {

      // removeListener will return false if the listener was not
      // registered in the first place, if this is so the unregister
      // is considered redundant
      this.getListenerList(eventType).remove(listener);
    }
  }

  public void notify(Object source, String eventType) {
    System.out.println("Notifying listeners of event type " + eventType);

    // Make sure a list exists in the map, if one does
    // not exist this notification is considered redundant
    if (this.exists(eventType)){

      ArrayList list = this.getListenerList(eventType);
      // If there are any listeners in the list notify them
      if (list.size() > 0){
        ManagedEvent me = new ManagedEvent(source, eventType);
        Iterator it = list.iterator();
        while (it.hasNext()) {
          EventManagerListener eml = (EventManagerListener)it.next();
          eml.eventNotification(me);
        }
      }
    }
  }
}
```

Listing 17.2 The ManagedEvent class.

```java
package event;

public class ManagedEvent {
  private Object source;
```

```
  private String type;
  public ManagedEvent(Object source,String eventType) {
    this.source = source;
    type = eventType;
  }

  public String getType() {
    return type;
  }

  public Object getSource() {
    return source;
  }
}
```

Listing 17.3 The EventManagerListener interface.

```
package event;

public interface EventManagerListener {

  /**
   * Called by the EventManager when an event (of a type that the
   * implementing class is registered for) occurs.
   * <p>
   * @param event The EventManagerEvent that is being broadcast
   **/
  public void eventNotification(ManagedEvent event);
}
```

Listing 17.4 The TestEventManagerListener class.

```
package event.test;

import event.*;

public class TestEventManagerListener implements EventManagerListener{

  private String name = null;
  public TestEventManagerListener(String name) {
    this.name = name;
  }

  public void eventNotification(ManagedEvent e) {
    System.out.println("-------------------------------------------------");
    System.out.println("I am a TestEventManagerListener my name is " + name);
```

```
    System.out.println("      My eventNotification(EventManagerEvent) method
                              has been called");
    System.out.println("      The source of the event was "+e.getSource());
    System.out.println("      The event's type was " + e.getType());
  }
  public String toString() {
    return name;
  }
}
```

Listing 17.5 The EventManagerTestHarness.

```
package event.test;

import event.*;

public class EventManagerTestHarness {

  private EventManager em = EventManager.getInstance();

  private void test() {

    EventManager em = EventManager.getInstance();

    TestEventManagerListener testListener1 =
        new TestEventManagerListener("Test Listener 1");
    TestEventManagerListener testListener2 =
        new TestEventManagerListener("Test Listener 2");

    em.register("event1",testListener1);
    em.register("event1",testListener2);
    em.register("event2", testListener1);

    em.notify(this,"event1");
    em.notify(this,"event2");
  }

  public static void main(String[] args)  {
    EventManagerTestHarness h = new EventManagerTestHarness();
    h.test();
  }
}
```

Listing 17.6 Running the event manager test harness.

```
event1 registering: Test Listener 1
event1 registering: Test Listener 2
event2 registering: Test Listener 1
Notifying listeners of event type event1
--------------------------------------------------
I am a TestEventManagerListener my name is Test Listener 1
    My eventNotification(EventManagerEvent) method has been called
    The source of the event was event.test.EventManagerTestHarness@71610299
    The event's type was event1
--------------------------------------------------
I am a TestEventManagerListener my name is Test Listener 2
    My eventNotification(EventManagerEvent) method has been called
    The source of the event was event.test.EventManagerTestHarness@71610299
    The event's type was event1
Notifying listeners of event type event2
--------------------------------------------------
I am a TestEventManagerListener my name is Test Listener 1
    My eventNotification(EventManagerEvent) method has been called
    The source of the event was event.test.EventManagerTestHarness@71610299
    The event's type was event2
```

J2EE Patterns

18.1 Introduction

In previous chapters we have discussed the use of design patterns for applications in general and for graphical client-based applications in particular. However, design patterns are just as relevant for server-side applications as they are for client-side ones. In this chapter we will look at the patterns developed (primarily by Sun) for use with the Java 2 Enterprise Edition (J2EE). These patterns focus on developing server-side applications and Web applications in particular.

18.2 What Are J2EE Design Patterns?

So far we have discussed design patterns in general. We will now, therefore, consider J2EE design patterns. In particular, this raises a question: "What are J2EE design patterns?". They are essentially "J2EE technology-based solutions to common problems". By common problems, we are not referring to common "business" or "application"-specific problems. Rather, we are referring to recurring issues relating to how to structure, maintain and manage applications built using J2EE technologies. For example, how should a large business-critical J2EE Web application be structured? How should the servlets and JSPs be organized? Where and when should EJBs be used? etc.

At present, the definitive reference for Sun's J2EE patterns is the book by Alur *et al.* (2001). This book describes J2EE patterns as being architecture-oriented patterns and categorizes them into three logical tiers:

- *Presentation tier.* This tier focuses on the objects and behaviour that are required to service requests from the client tier (where the client tier may be a Web page within a Web browser, a Java application or applet, a mobile device such as a PDA or phone, etc.). The primary J2EE technologies that are part of the presentation tier are JSPs and servlets.

- *Business tier.* This tier focuses on the J2EE technologies that support the business logic initiated from the presentation tier (or in some cases directly from the client tier). The J2EE technologies that focus on this tier are Enterprise JavaBeans.
- *Integration tier.* This tier focuses on the J2EE technologies that support communication with external resources. These technologies include JMS, JDBC and J2EE connector technology.

Alur *et al.* note that the J2EE patterns catalog is constantly evolving, so that these categories might require refinement in time. However, at the time of writing the aim is to keep things simple and not over-complicate the issue.

Each logical tier encapsulates a set of patterns that deal with an aspect of a J2EE-based application (although the focus is on Web-based applications that may or may not use other J2EE technologies such as EJBs, JMS and JNDI).

18.3 A Catalog of J2EE Patterns

The J2EE Pattern catalog has evolved over a number of years since 1999 (internally to Sun)/2000 (externally from Sun). Each pattern has be revised several times based on feedback from within the J2EE community worldwide. This is an ongoing process, and one that is likely to result in additional patterns as well as modifications to existing patterns. At the time of writing there are 15 J2EE patterns in the Sun J2EE catalog, divided between the three logical tiers:

The presentation tier patterns are:

- **Decorating Filter.** Facilitates pre- and post-processing of a request.
- **Front Controller.** Provides a centralized controller for managing the handling of a request.
- **View Helper.** Encapsulates logic that is not related to presentation formatting into Helper components.
- **Composite View.** Creates an aggregate View from atomic sub-components.
- **Service To Worker.** Combines a `Dispatcher` component in coordination with the `FrontController` and View Helper Patterns.
- **Dispatcher View.** Combines a `Dispatcher` component in coordination with the `FrontController` and View Helper Patterns, deferring many activities to View processing.

The business tier patterns are:

- **Business Delegate.** Decouples presentation and service tiers, and provides a façade and proxy interface to the services.
- **Value Object.** Exchanges data between tiers.
- **Session Facade.** Hides business object complexity, centralizes workflow handling.
- **Aggregate Entity.** Represents a best practice for designing coarse-grained entity beans.
- **Value Object Assembler.** Builds composite value object from multiple data sources.
- **Value List Handler.** Manages query execution, results caching and result processing.
- **Service Locator.** Hides complexity of business service lookup and creation; locates business service factories.

The integration tier patterns are:

- **Data Access Object.** Abstracts data sources, provides transparent access to data.
- **Service Activator.** Facilitates asynchronous processing for EJB components.

Of course you are not limited to using only these patterns, as you may identify your own J2EE patterns. These patterns may be specific to your own business areas or they may be additional "generic" patterns that suit your way of operating. For example, back in 1999 at JayDee Technology we started to develop our own patterns for J2EE technologies before we were aware of Sun's catalog. This means that we have developed a number of our own J2EE patterns that are used in-house and have explicit support within our own software libraries.

We do not have the space here to present in detail all of the J2EE Patterns from the Sun catalog, let alone the patterns we and others have also adopted. Instead we direct you to Sun's J2EE Web site (`http://developer.java.sun.com/developer/technicalArticles/J2EE/patterns/`) and to Alur *et al.* (2001).

In the remainder of this chapter we will briefly present the FrontController J2EE Pattern as an example of a pattern from the J2EE Pattern catalog and the Request–Event–Dispatcher pattern from our own J2EE Pattern catalog.

18.4 The FrontController Pattern

In this section we will present (in outline) the FrontController. For a complete description see the J2EE Pattern Catalog Web site. This section presents much the same information but provides (due to space limitations) a cut-down version of the *Strategies* section.

18.4.1 Context

This operates within the context of handling HTTP requests for a Web applications.

18.4.2 Problem

Within Web applications each JSP or servlet could be a unique point of entry to the Web application. This approach has a number of problems, including:

- Each view is required to provide its own system services, often resulting in duplicate code.
- View navigation is left to the views that may result in intertwined view content and view navigation.
- Security may be harder to enforce due to multiple entry points.
- Maintenance may be harder due to many different paths through the system.

18.4.3 Forces

- Common system services processing completes per request. For example, the security service completes authentication and authorization checks.

- Logic that is best handled in one central location is instead replicated within numerous Views.
- Decision points exist with respect to the retrieval and manipulation of data.
- Multiple views are used to respond to similar business requests.
- A centralized point of contact for handling a request may be useful, for example to control and log a user's progress through the site.
- System services and view management logic are relatively sophisticated.

18.4.4 Solution

Use a Controller as the initial point of contact for handling a request. The Controller manages the handling of the request, including invoking security services such as authentication and authorization, delegating business processing, managing the choice of an appropriate view, handling errors, and managing the selection of content creation strategies.

The Controller provides a centralized entry point that controls and manages Web request handling. By centralizing decision points and controls, the Controller also helps reduce the amount of Java code, called scriptlets, embedded in the JSP.

Centralizing control in the Controller and reducing business logic in the view promotes code reuse across requests. It is a preferable approach to the alternative – embedding code in multiple views – because that approach may lead to a more error-prone, reuse-by-copy-and-paste environment.

Typically, a Controller works in coordination with a Dispatcher component. A Dispatcher is responsible for view management and navigation. Thus, a Dispatcher manages choosing the next View to present to the user and provides the mechanism for vectoring control to this resource. A Dispatcher can be encapsulated within a Controller or can be a separate component (see the ServiceToWorker pattern). In J2EE the servlet dispatcher can play this role.

The FrontController pattern suggests centralizing handling of requests, but does not limit the number of handlers in the system. There may very well be multiple FrontControllers in a system, with each mapping to a set of distinct services.

Structure

The class diagram presented in Figure 18.1 illustrates the basic structure of a FrontController hierarchy (it also illustrates that a Front Controller could be implemented using a servlet or a JSP).

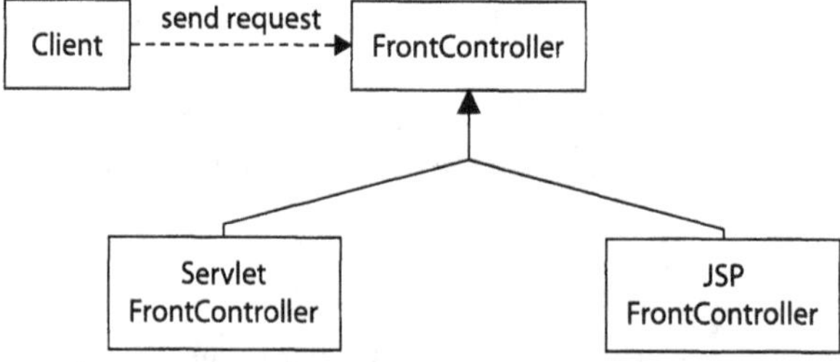

Figure 18.1 The FrontController class hierarchy.

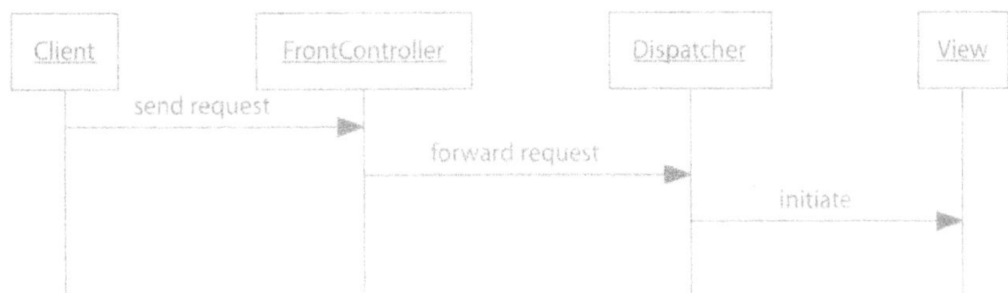

Figure 18.2 Using a FrontController to handle a request.

Participants and Responsibilities

The sequence of events that occur when a FrontController (typically implemented as a Servlet) receives a request from a client is illustrated in Figure 18.2. It shows the FrontController receiving (the typically HTTP) request. It then determines to which View the request should be forwarded. A view is implemented as a servlet or a JSP. To initiate the receiving a view a dispatcher object is used: for example, the J2EE RequestDispatcher class.

18.4.5 Strategies

There are several strategies relating to Controller implementation. We shall briefly mention one strategy (which has been hinted at above). For other strategies see the patterns Web site.

The implementation strategy we shall examine is known as the ServletFront Strategy. This strategy suggests implementing the FrontController as a servlet. Though semantically equivalent, it is preferred to the "JSP FrontController Strategy". The FrontController handles request processing, managing and controlling aspects of this processing. Since these responsibilities are related to, but logically independent of, display formatting, they are more appropriately included in a servlet instead of a JSP.

18.4.6 Consequences

- **Centralized control**
  This patterns defines a central point of control. This can be very good for logging application access and usage, for security and for centralizing business logic. However, it is possible to introduce a single point of failure.
- **Improved reusability**
  Allows common code to be positioned within the front controller.
- **Validation and error handling**
  The controller can also manage validation and error handling, because these operations are often done per request.

18.4.7 Related Patterns

- **View Helper pattern**
  In the View Helper pattern, the helper contains business logic that is accessed by the view. In some cases some of this business logic may be better placed within the FrontController.

- **Service to Worker**
  The Service to Worker pattern is the result of combining the View Helper pattern with a Dispatcher, in coordination with the FrontController pattern.
- **Dispatcher View**
  The Dispatcher View pattern is the result of combining the View Helper pattern with a Dispatcher, in coordination with the Front Controller pattern.

18.5 The Request–Event–Dispatcher Pattern

This pattern was developed by us to deal with a number of maintenance and management issues within an evolving Web application. Some of these were practical, related to the need to integrate work from different developers. Others related to the need to be able to adapt to changing user requirements. Actually this pattern is only one of the patterns identified to do this, another being a Web application version of the traditional Model–View–Controller architecture.

18.5.1 Context

This operates within the context of determining how to deal HTTP requests within a Web application.

18.5.2 Problem

Given a single point of entry to a Web application, we need to coordinate the delegation of these requests to appropriate parts of the application. If this is "directly" encoded into the FrontController, then to "integrate" a new feature into the Web application, the FrontController will need modification (for each and every features). Similarly, each development team would need their own separate FrontController during development. but these would need to be integrated at system build time (with any conflicts being addressed).

18.5.3 Forces

- Separation of FrontController from the implementation of various system features.
- Separate different areas of the Web application from each other.
- Ensure a standard and clean interface between the FrontController and "event" handlers.
- Ensures event handlers are not directly dependent on the FrontController.
- Ensures a standard framework for receiving and processing "request events".

18.5.4 Solution

Use a servlet to determine where to send the request, based on the event groups that handlers have registered for.

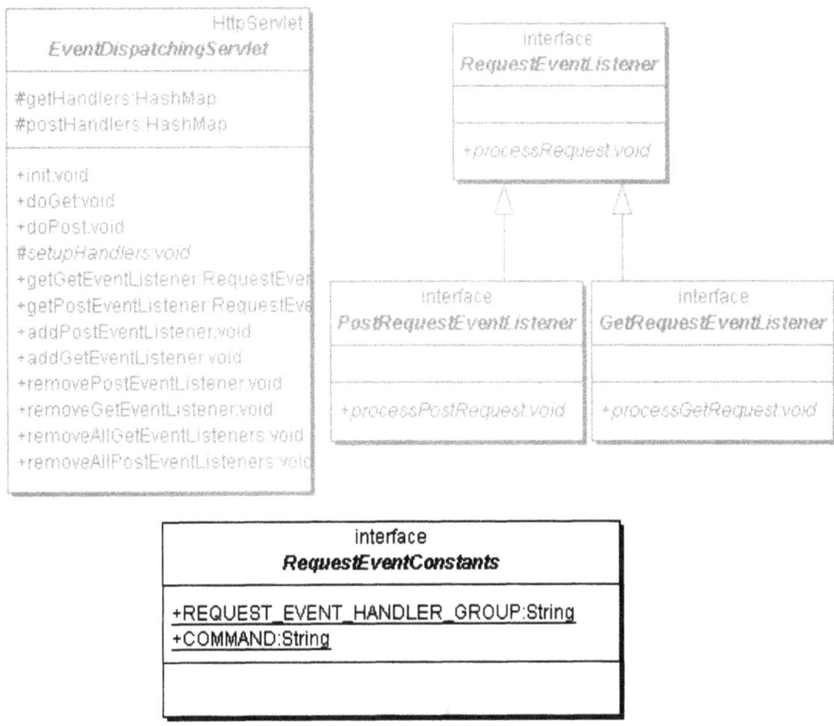

Figure 18.3 The Request Event Dispatch class diagram.

Structure

The class diagram presented in Figure 18.3 represents the interfaces and class involved in the Request Event Dispatcher pattern. Note that to use this pattern you must supply a subclass for the EventDispatchingServlet that implements the setupHandler method. A "request event" is an abstraction of an HTTP request arrival event that must be handled by a RequestEventListener object.

Participants and Responsibilities

Figure 18.4 shows the sequence diagram representing the Request Event Dispatching pattern. It depicts how the controller handles a request.

- **EventDispatchingServlet**
  This servlet is responsible for delegating the "request event" on to the appropriate handler. It has methods for the addition and removal of RequestEventListener objects.
- **RequestEventListener**
  This interface defines the method that the "handler" object must implement in order to receive "request events".

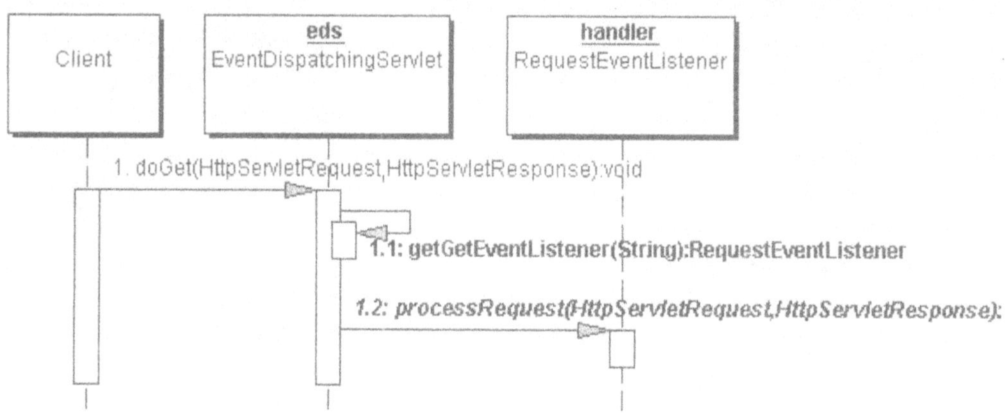

Figure 18.4 Request Event Dispatching sequence diagram.

18.5.5 Strategies

The Request–Event–Dispatcher pattern describes a framework by which a FrontController servlet can delegate request events onto other parts of a Web application in a similar manner to the Swing Event Delegation model.

Before any processing can start, the "event handler" object must be registered with the servlet. This is done using one of the two add<Type>EventListener methods.

The objects initially registered to handle request events are defined in the setupHandler method. This is an abstract method that must be implemented by subclasses that will be used as an EventDispatchingServlet.

During further processing additional handlers may be registered and existing handlers may be removed.

To be a handler, an object must implement the RequestEventListener interface or one of its sub-interfaces.

In the Request–Event–Dispatcher pattern, an EventDispatchingServlet receives an "event", where an "event" is a HTTP request that contains a REQUEST_EVENT_HANDLER_ GROUP parameter. This is used to identify the "group" of handlers to receive the "request event".

The EventDispatchingServlet decides which RequestEventHandler to delegate the HTTP request to, based on the value of the REQUEST_EVENT_HANDLER parameter.

The EventDispatchingServlet looks up in a map the appropriate handlers to receive the named event. It then passes the request to this handler (by calling the processRequest method defined by the RequestEventListener interface).

The RequestEventListener interface is presented below:

```java
public interface RequestEventListener {
  public void processRequest(HttpServletRequest req,
                             HttpServletResponse res)
    throws ServletException, IOException;
}
```

The EventDispatchingServlet class is presented below:

```java
public abstract class EventDispatchingServlet extends HttpServlet {
  /** Holds list of get handler objects **/
  protected HashMap getHandlers = new HashMap();
  /** Holds list of post handler objects **/
  protected HashMap postHandlers = new HashMap();

/**
  * Need to set up handlers in init method
  **/
  public void init(ServletConfig config) throws ServletException {
    super.init();
    setupHandlers();
  }

/**
  * Handle get requests
  **/
  public void doGet(HttpServletRequest req,
                    HttpServletResponse res)
    throws ServletException, IOException {
    System.out.println("EventDispatchingServlet.doGet()");
    String panel =
      req.getParameter(RequestEventConstants.REQUEST_EVENT_HANDLER_GROUP);
    RequestEventListener rl = getGetEventListener(panel);
    rl.processRequest(req, res);
  }

/**
  * Handle the post requests
  **/
  public void doPost(HttpServletRequest req,
                     HttpServletResponse res)
    throws ServletException, IOException {
    System.out.println("EventDispatchingServlet.doPost()");
    doGet(req,res);
  }

protected abstract void setupHandlers();

  public RequestEventListener getGetEventListener(String name) {
    return (RequestEventListener)getHandlers.get(name);
  }

public RequestEventListener getPostEventListener(String name) {
```

```java
    return (RequestEventListener)postHandlers.get(name);
  }

  public void addPostEventListener(String name, RequestEventListener rl) {
    postHandlers.put(name, rl);
  }

  public void addGetEventListener(String name, RequestEventListener rl) {
    getHandlers.put(name, rl);
  }

  public void removePostEventListener(String name) {
    postHandlers.remove(name);
  }

  public void removeGetEventListener(String name) {
    getHandlers.remove(name);
  }

  public void removeAllGetEventListeners() {
    getHandlers.clear();
  }

  public void removeAllPostEventListeners() {
    postHandlers.clear();
  }
}
```

18.5.6 Consequences

- **Improves pluggablity of new features**
  It is straightforward to plug new features into a Web application in a managed and controlled manner.
- **Need to determine event group**
  Each request that is sent to the `EventDispatchingServlet` needs to include a parameter indicating the event group to use. This can be implemented as a hidden parameter in for example, a form. If this is forgotten the "request event" will not be routed appropriately.
- **Improves reusability**
  As a particular service or function of the Web application is not directly tied into other parts of the Web application, there is greater potential for reuse.

18.5.7 Related Patterns

It can be seem as another strategy for implementing a FrontController, although that is not its primary role. It can also be viewed as an implementation strategy for a Dispatcher – again, that is not its primary function.

18.6 J2EE-based Model–View–Controller

The difficulties of constructing modular, object-oriented presentation layer elements, using servlets and JSPs is well known to anyone who has ever tried to build a servlet- or JSP-based application of any size. The result can easily end up being difficult to debug, complex to understand and maintain, and certainly not reusable (except by cutting and pasting!). However, huge benefits can be obtained by separating out the user interface (i.e. HTML rendering components) from the application logic/code. This has been acknowledged for a long time and a number of approaches have been proposed over the years for separating the presentational aspect of an application from the logic of that application. In the case of J2EE Java applications used in multi-tier environments this is still true. In this section, we will explore the use of the model–view–controller architecture/ pattern (or just as the MVC for short). The MVC originated in Smalltalk but the concept has been used in many places. It has been used extensively in Java Swing-based clients, but is also relevant to Web-based applications (and is the basis of the concepts in the Struts Apache project; see `http://jakarta.apache.org/struts/index.html`).

18.6.1 Context

Deals with structuring the presentation layer (servlets and JSPs) of a J2EE application.

18.6.2 Problem

It is all too easy to construct JSPs that have huge areas of Java embedded within scriptlets, making them very difficult to understand and hard to maintain, and destroying the many benefits of JSPs. It can also be hard to decide when to use a JSP and when to use a servlet.

18.6.3 Forces

- Reusability of application and/or user interface components.
- Ability to develop the application and user interface separately.
- Ability to inherit from different parts of the class hierarchy.
- Ability to define control-style classes which provide common features separately from how these features may be displayed.

18.6.4 Solution

The intention of the MVC architecture is the separation of the user display (the view), from the control of user input (mouse clicks, text entered etc.), from the underlying information/application model as illustrated in Figure 18.5 (Krasner and Pope, 1988). Note that in the figure the View and the Controller both "know" about each other, but the model knows nothing about how it is being displayed nor about how user input is being handled. This makes the model reusable with different displays.

This means that different views (interfaces) can be used with the same application, without the application knowing about it. It also means that any part of the system can be changed without affecting the operation of the other. For example, the way that the client

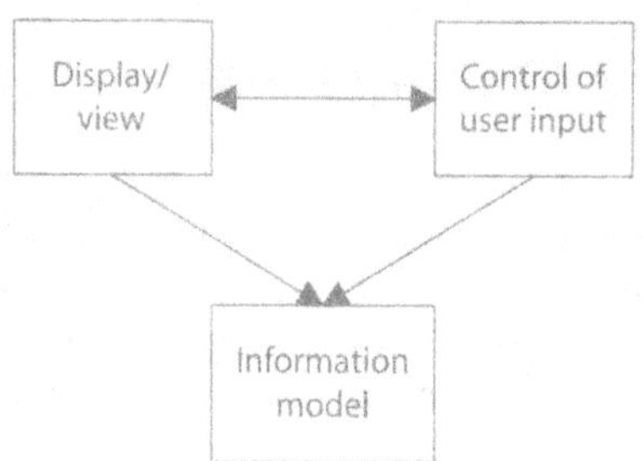

Figure 18.5 The model–view–controller architecture.

(the look) displays the information could be changed without modifying the actual application or how input is handled (the feel). Indeed, the application need not know what type of interface is currently connected to it at all.

Structure

However the MVC is implemented, there will always be a Model element, a Controller element and a View element. In the case of a J2EE technology, implementation of the MVC the View may be either a servlet View or a JSP View. In general, it is most common to find that the view is implemented as a JSP as JSPs are geared towards generating the HTML that will be sent to the client tier. This is ideal in the MVC as the controller and the model should already have performed any processing and application logic before the JSP is required to generate a response back to the client. The definition of three marker interfaces for the Model, View and the Controller, along with the differing view implementations is presented in Figure 18.6.

Participants and Responsibilities

The three participants in the MVC are the Model, View and Controller. Their responsibilities are as follows:

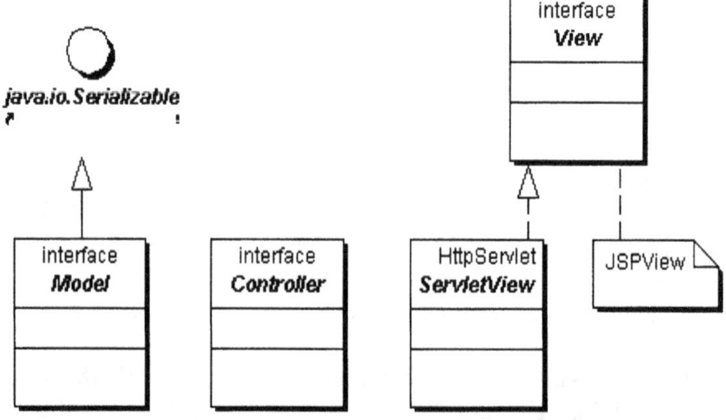

Figure 18.6 The elements of the MVC pattern.

- **Controller**
  This element is responsible for receiving the initial request for any particular operation. It must determine what should happen when this request is received. This may involve creating or accessing the model element. In a J2EE-based implementation the model may be stored for later retrieval within the HTTPSession object associated with the user's request. Once whatever operation is required is completed, the controller is then responsible for initiating the view. In a J2EE MVC implementation, this initiation will be performed by dispatching an appropriate JSP or HTML file (or possibly a servlet).

- **Model**
  The model represents the application logic. In a J2EE technology implementation of the MVC this may involve accessing EJBs, remote objects, databases via JDBC or any other server side components. It is really a buffer (possibly a façade) between the presentation layer and any business or application logic being invoked.

- **View**
  The view generates the response sent back to the client tier for the J2EE application. This may involve extracting information from the model (accessed via the session object) and wrapping it up within HTML etc.

18.6.5 Strategies

There are a number of strategies that can be used to implement the MVC pattern for a J2EE application. For example, if you use the Struts framework from Apache you will base the whole implementation around the use of Tags etc.

An example of a `createCRF` method from a controller based on the J2EE MVC model (taken from the Fault Tracker case study described in more detail in the next chapter) is presented below. This method is called in response to a user selecting an option on a Web page. The request is received by a handler and the `createCRF` method is called on the controlled (CRF stands for "Change Request Form"). It illustrates how the controller obtains a model from the session (or places one in the session if one is not available). It also illustrates how the model is used to initiate some business behaviour (in this case the creation of a CRF) and then how the view is generated by dispatching the request.

```java
public void createCRF(HttpServletRequest request,
                      HttpServletResponse response)
  throws ServletException, IOException {
  try {
    // extract model from session
    HttpSession session=request.getSession(true);
    CrfEditingModel model= (CrfEditingModel)session.getAttribute(
        SessionConstants.CRF_EDITING_MODEL);

// check if need to create a model
    if (model==null) {
      model=new CrfEditingModel();
      session.setAttribute(SessionConstants.CRF_EDITING_MODEL,model);
    }
```

```
        model.createCRF();

    // dispatch request onto crf editor view ("mapping registered in
        // web.xml file)
        dispatcher.dispatch("crfEditorView",request,response);
    } catch (Exception e) {
        // dispatch request onto crf operation failure view
        dispatcher.dispatch("crfOperationFailureView",request,response);
    }
}
```

18.6.6 Consequences

The consequences of using this design pattern include:

- Reusability of parts of the presentation layer.
- The ability to inherit from different parts of the class hierarchy.
- Modularity of presentation layer code.
- Resilience to change.
- Identification of the roles of servlets and JSPs.
- Encapsulation of the presentation aspects of the application.
- Additional complexity/greater abstraction in the presentation layer.
- Increased difficulty in tracing interactions within the presentation layer (some form of logging is essential).

18.6.7 Related Patterns

Patterns related to this pattern include:

- **The Request Event Dispatching pattern.** The Handlers defined within this pattern may call methods on the controllers of the MVC pattern.
- **FrontController.** The Controller of the MVC could be implemented as or treated as a FrontController.
- **View Helper.** The model could be treated as a view helper.
- **Service to Worker.** The model may exploit an implementation of this pattern to initiate business logic.
- **Dispatcher View.** This pattern is used by the controller to initiate the JSP or Servlet associated with the controller.
- **Business Delegate.** The model may be treated as a business delegate or may use a business delegate to access business logic.
- **Value Object.** The model may use Value Objects to access information on the business tier.
- **Service Locator.** The model may use Service Locator objects to access EJBs etc.
- **Data Access Object.** The model may use a Data Access Object to obtain data from a database or back end business object.

18.7 Summary

In this chapter we have introduced the concept of Design Patterns and in particular J2EE Patterns. We have also described Sun's J2EE Pattern catalog. We have also briefly presented one of these design patterns providing an example of how you can identify your own patterns and document these. In the next chapter we will examine a larger application that makes extensive use of J2EE patterns.

18.8 Further Reading

A number of books and a great many papers have been written about patterns in recent years, the most influential of which is Gamma *et al.* (1994) by the so-called "Gang of Four": Erich Gamma, Richard Helm, Ralph Johnson and John Vlissides. There are also a series of conferences on Patterns referred to as PLoP (for Pattern Language of Program design). Two proceedings are available: Coplien and Schmidt (1995) and Vlissides *et al.* (1996).

Two further patterns books are Buschmann *et al.* (1996) (which represents the progression and evolution of the pattern approach into a system capable of describing and documenting large scale applications) and Fowler (1997) which considers how patterns can be used for analysis to help build reusable object models.

There is also a Web page dedicated to the patterns movement (which includes many of the papers referenced as well as tutorials and example patterns). The URL for the Web page is `http://st-www.cs.uiuc.edu/users/patterns/`. In addition, there is a Sun Web site dedicated to J2EE patterns: `http://developer.java.sun.com/developer/technicalArticles/J2EE/patterns/`. This is also an interest group that you can subscribe to (and participate in): see `http://archives.java.sun.com/archives/j2eepatterns-interest.html`.

18.9 References

Alexander, C. (1979). *The Timeless Way of Building.* Oxford University Press, Oxford.

Alexander, C., Ishikawa, S. and Silverstein, M. with Jacobson, M., Fiksdahl-King, I. and Angel, S. (1977). *A Pattern Language.* Oxford University Press, Oxford.

Alur, D., Crupi, J. and Malks, D. (2001). *Core J2EE Patterns: Best Practices and Design Strategies.* Prentice Hall, Upper Saddle River, NJ.

Beck, K. and Johnson, R. (1994). Patterns generate architectures, in *Proc. ECOOP'94.* Springer-Verlag, New York, pp. 139–149.

Birrer, A. and Eggenschwiler, T. (1993). Frameworks in the financial engineering domain: an experience report. In *Proc. ECOOP'93.* Springer-Verlag, New York, pp. 21–35.

Budinsky, F. J., Finnie, M. A., Vlissides, J. M. and Yu, P. S. (1996). Automatic code generation from design patterns. *IBM Systems Journal,* 35(2).

Buschmann, F., Meunier, R., Rohnert, H., Sommerlad, P. and Stal, M. (1996). *Pattern-Oriented Software Architecture – A System of Patterns*. Wiley & Sons, Chichester.

Coplien, J. O. and Schmidt, D. C. (eds.) (1995). *Pattern Languages of Program Design*. Addison-Wesley, Reading, MA.

Fowler, M. (1997). *Analysis Patterns: Reusable Object Models*. Addison-Wesley, Reading, MA.

Gamma, E., Helm, R., Johnson, R. and Vlissades, J. (1993). Design patterns: abstraction and reuse of object-oriented design. In *Proc. ECOOP'93*. Springer-Verlag, New York, pp. 406–431.

Gamma, E., Helm, R., Johnson, R. and Vlissades, J. (1995). *Design Patterns: Elements of Reusable Object-Oriented Software*. Addison-Wesley, Reading, MA.

Hunt, J. (2002). *Java and Object Orientation: An Introduction*, 2nd edn. Springer-Verlag, London.

Johnson, R. E. (1992). Documenting frameworks with patterns. In *Proc. OOPSLA'92, SIGPLAN Notices* **27**(10), 63–76.

Krasner, G. E. and Pope, S. T. (1988). A cookbook for using the Model–View–Controller user interface paradigm in Smalltalk-80. *JOOP* **1**(3), 26–49.

Vlissides, J. M., Coplien, J. O. and Kerth, N. L. (1996). *Pattern Languages of Program Design 2*. Addison-Wesley, Reading, MA.

19

The Fault Tracker J2EE Case Study

19.1 Introduction

In this chapter we will look at some aspects of a much larger J2EE technology application. Due to space limitations we will only be able to dip into this application. However, it should illustrate the use of some of the design patterns mentioned in the last chapter, as well as indicate the use of some of the J2EE technologies discussed in this book, including servlets, JSPs, EJBs, security restrictions etc.

19.2 The Fault Tracker Application

The Fault Tracker application is a J2EE technology application designed to support the formal problem reporting procedures and change in requirements procedures often applied to bespoke software development projects.

A Request for Change (or RFC) relates to a change by a client or customer in the agreed requirements or to a change required to the software system in response to a "bug" identified by a Problem Report Form. Monitoring, maintaining and tracing such changes are extremely important to any software engineering organization, as they have an impact not only on the end result but also on costs, testing, sign off etc.

A Problem Report (or PRF for Problem Report Form) relates to a "bug" which may be resident in any (or all) of the aspects of a software engineering project. This includes the requirements, design, UML model, code, tests or associated documentation. Monitoring, managing and tracing the progress of these "bugs" is also very important as this will affect the quality of the end product.

The Fault Tracker application manages and maintains records of all RFC and PRFs for a particular project. It is accessible via the Web using a Web browser and exploits the full J2EE multi-tier architecture. That is, it uses a Web browser to host the client aspects of the tool, servlets and JSPs for the presentation aspects of the tool, EJBs for the business logic and a relational database for the long-term storage of data.

Given that such a system can be quiet complex, it also exploits design patterns from both Sun's J2EE Pattern catalog and some additional design patterns (as described in the last chapter).

In the remainder of this chapter we will look at the domain that the Fault Tracker is applied to (i.e. managing and tracking problem reports and requests for change). We will then step through part of the Fault Tracker application. Having done this we will consider the design patterns used and examine the implementation of these patterns with the tool.

19.2.1 Requests for Change

Care should be taken when "bugs" are reported by clients that the "bug" in question is not actually a change in requirements. If a change in requirements is identified this often has implications for charging and costing, and thus must be handled in a different manner.

A change in requirements should be reported by a Request for Change (RFC) form. This form should state what it is believed that the change in requirements is (and will often need to refer to the original requirements document and additional minutes etc.).

Once generated the RFC should be handed to the Project Manager, who will confirm whether it is an RFC or a PRF. If the Project Manager accepts it as a CRF then the CRF should be entered into the Request for Change Log.

If a paper-based system is being used then completed forms are to be kept secured in a ring binder or similar. With the Fault Tracker software these forms are electronically maintained in the same format.

The use of the Fault Tracker system for recording "requests for change" is described in the following problem reporting and corrective action procedure:

1. When a Request for Change is identified (often from the bug log system), an RFC form should be completed and allocated a status of **Open.**
2. The RFC must then be given to the Project Manager, who will assign a unique RFC number to the form and who will then investigate the requirement (possibly with the aid of other team members as appropriate) and confirm that it is an RFC and determine what effort is involved in meeting this change.
3. The PRF will be updated with the results of the investigation.
4. The client must then be contacted to discuss the impact of the RFC. The status of the RFC should now be **With Client.**
5. If the RFC is accepted by the client and agreement is reached about the implications of this, the RFC should then be allocated to appropriate team members for requirements modification, design and implementation. The changes should be subject to the same control procedure as any other development, although additional care needs to be taken to ensure all affected items are included (such as user manuals etc.). The RFC should now be in **Accepted** status.

If the client rejects the RFC, either because they decide they do not need that requirement or because they do not believe that it is an RFC, then the RFC is allocated the status **Rejected.** If the latter case is true then the Project Manager and others must discuss with the client the appropriate action to take.

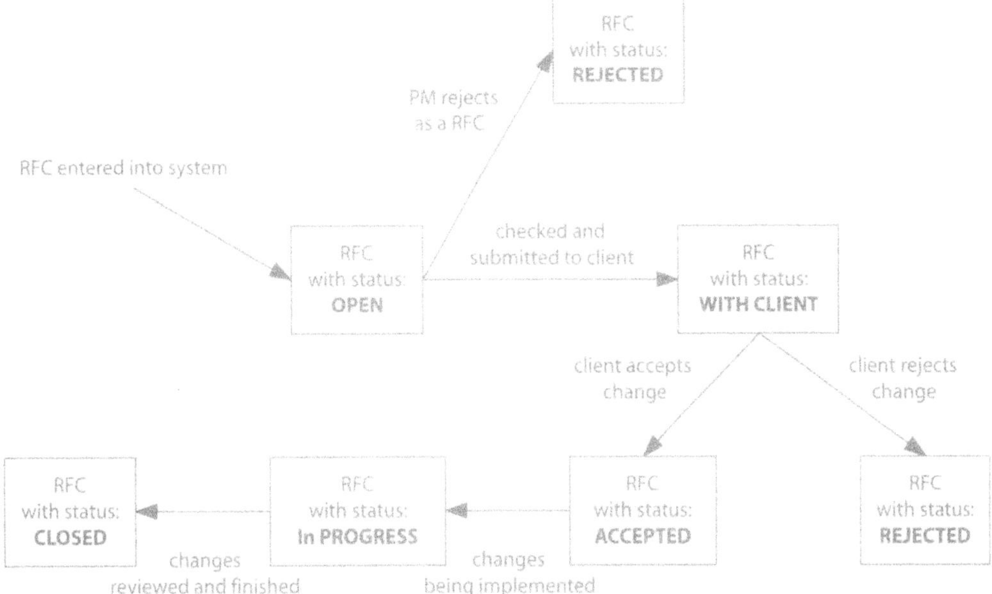

Figure 19.1 The life cycle of the RFC form.

6. Once the person or persons involved in implementing the change have completed the task (including the re-reviewing of the change and allocation of **Released** status to the items involved), the Project Manager will test the changed software to ensure that the update works. If this is the case, the RFC will be changed to **Closed** status and the binder information updated accordingly.

7. If the correction was not successful, the Project Manager will advise on further action and if necessary complete a new PRF. New forms should only be completed if a new change is identified or if the original change introduced additional problems.

The life cycle of an RFC form is presented in Figure 19.1.

19.2.2 Problem Reporting

Problems relating to configuration items, including specifications, design diagrams/models/ notes, and code must go through a formal problem reporting procedure once they have reached **Release** status. In many organizations the Problem Report Form (PRF) is the basis of this process.

Completed forms are to be kept secured in a ring binder or similar, as well as online within a Problem Reporting System.

The binder should contain dividers with the following headings:

- Summary of current status (this should contain a table of the current outstanding PRFs and a table of the closed PRFs – and who they were allocated to)
- Open problems

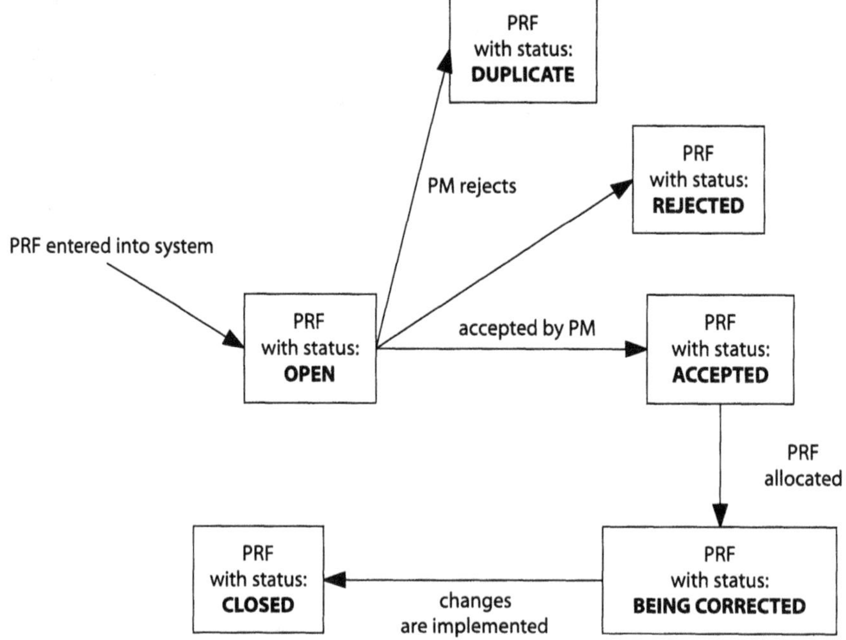

Figure 19.2 The life cycle of a PRF.

- Closed problems
- Rejected and duplicate problems

The use of the Fault Tracker system for handling "Problem Report Forms" is described in the following problem reporting and corrective action procedure:

1. On discovery of a problem in a configuration item that has been allocated a Release status, the details of the problem should be noted on a Problem Report Form (PRF). In some cases this will happen in-house; in other cases a bug report will be filed by a client. Details of the bug must be taken from the client's report and entered into our own system. The PRF is then assigned a status of **Open.**
2. The PRF must then be given to the Project Manager, who will assign a unique PRF number to the form and who will then investigate the problem (possibly with the aid of other team members as appropriate) and identify what items need to be changed (if any). The PRF now enters an **Accepted** status.

    If the Project Manager identifies that this PRF duplicates one that already exists, the status of the PRF is made Duplicate and a link is made to the actual PRF form. No further action is taken regarding this PRF.

    If the Project Manager rejects the PRF (for example because it is not an error but the way the system works or because it is an operating system feature), then the status of the PRF is changed to Rejected.

3. The PRF will be updated with the results of the investigation. If the problem is to be fixed by another team member they will be noted as the person who will implement the fix. The PRF can now be assigned a status of **Being Corrected**. Any necessary redesign, reimplementation etc. should be subject to the same controls as the initial design and implementation. If the problem is identified as a *Request for Change*, then it should be handed over to the Change Request system.
4. Once those involved in correcting the problem have completed the task (including the re-reviewing of the change and allocation of **Released** status to the items involved), the Project Manager will test the corrected software to ensure that the correction works. If this is the case, the PRF will be changed to **Closed** status and the binder information updated accordingly.
5. If the correction was not successful, the Project Manager will advise on further action and if necessary complete a new PRF. New forms should only be completed if a new problem is identified or if the original change introduced additional problems.

The life cycle of the PRF form is illustrated in Figure 19.2.

19.3 Using the Fault Tracker

Fault Tracker is a J2EE technology-based application. This means that it is comprised of Web pages on the client tier (displayed within a Web browser such as IE), servlets and JSPs on the presentation tier, EJBs on the business tier and a relational database at the back. As such it is typical of many J2EE applications.

To access the Fault Tracker application a user must enter the appropriate URL in a Web browser. In this example we are running the Fault Tracker on JBoss with Tomcat on the localhost. The application is accessed using the URL `http://localhost:8080/ft`, where `ft` is the application root specified in the `application.xml` file in the EAR. The `web.xml` file in the WAR contained within the EAR specifies that the welcome page is `index.html`. This front page is presented in Figure 19.3. Note that this is the only page of the whole Fault Tracker Web application that is outside of the security control.

To use the Fault Tracker a user must be registered with the Fault Tracker. All users of the Fault Tracker system must have the security role `ftUsers`. This can be administered using the internal memory security realm or, as is the case with Fault Tracker, using an external service such as LDAP. Some users also have the role `ftAdmin`. If they are Fault Tracker administrators then various administration options are presented to them within Fault Tracker. If a user is not an administrator these options are not presented.

To access the application the user must click on the "login and select a project" link on the front page. This link takes the user into the security controlled area of the application. This causes the login screen presented in Figure 19.4 to be displayed. Note that this application is using the "BASIC" login form (i.e. no custom login page has been defined).

Once users have logged in they are presented with the "Select a Project" Web page. All "bug" or "change requests" in the Fault Tracker are associated with a particular project.

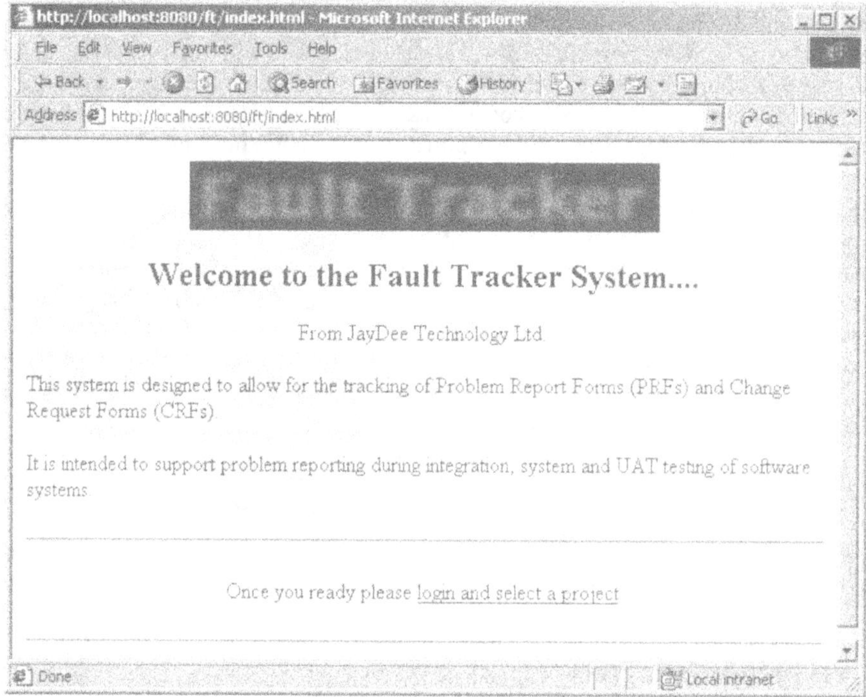

Figure 19.3 The Fault Tracker front page.

Therefore the first thing users must do is to select the project they wish to work with. Note that administrators are also presented with the option to carry out some administration functions at this point (non-administrators do not see this option). This is illustrated in Figure 19.5.

Figure 19.4 Logging into the Fault Tracker.

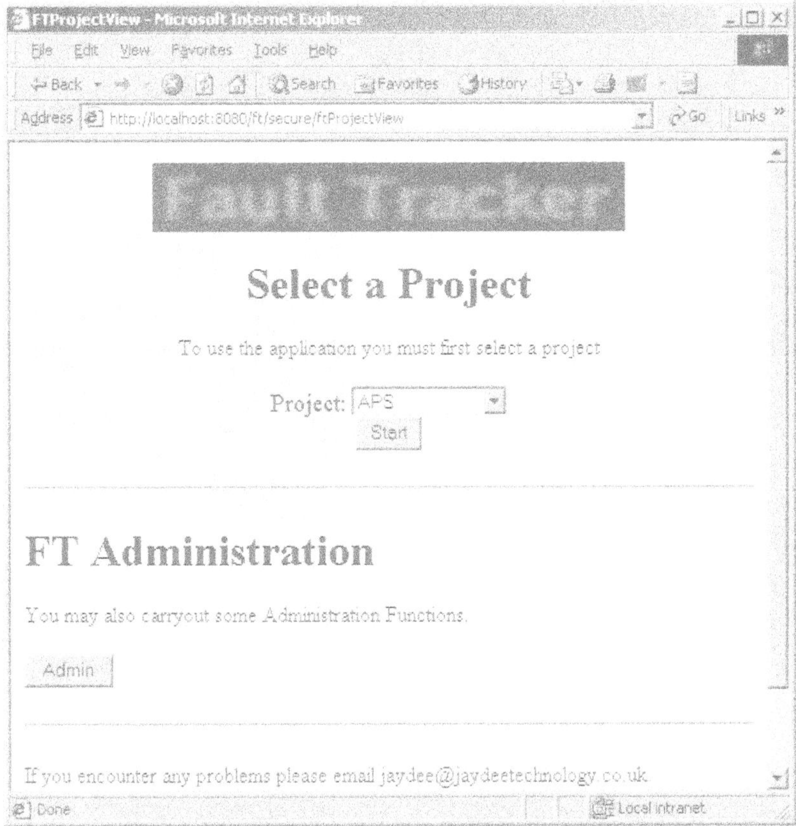

Figure 19.5 The Project Selection/Administration selection page.

When users select the project they wish to work with, the Fault Tracker displays the main Fault Tracker working environment. This display is broken up into four regions. There is a header and footer which frame with main display. On the left is the main menu options allowing PRFs and CRFs (which stands for Change Request Forms) to be created, edited, searched for and reports generated etc. The centre area of the display is used to display the results of any operation (such as creating a new CRF etc.). This working environment is presented in Figure 19.6.

Users can now select an option from the left-hand menu. For example, if they choose to create a new CRF (Change Request Form), then the central area displays a form with various sections to be filled in (for example see Figure 19.7).

In Figure 19.7 a user is describing a "Change Request" supplied by the end client. Once all the relevant data has been entered the user can commit the creation of the CRF (note that the CRF Number is automatically generated).

The user could then create additional forms, edit existing forms, search for forms or generate reports on different categories of form etc.

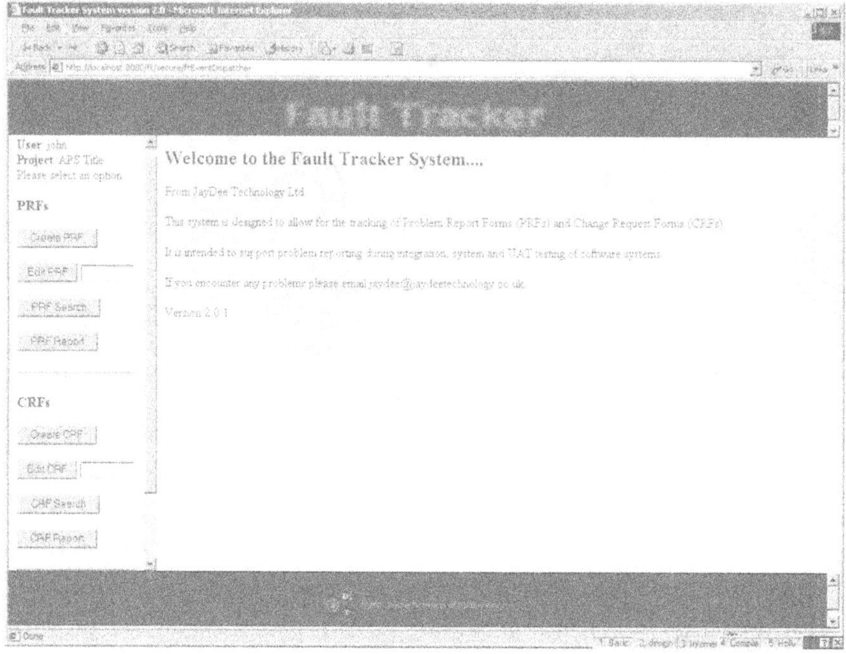

Figure 19.6 The main Fault Tracker working environment.

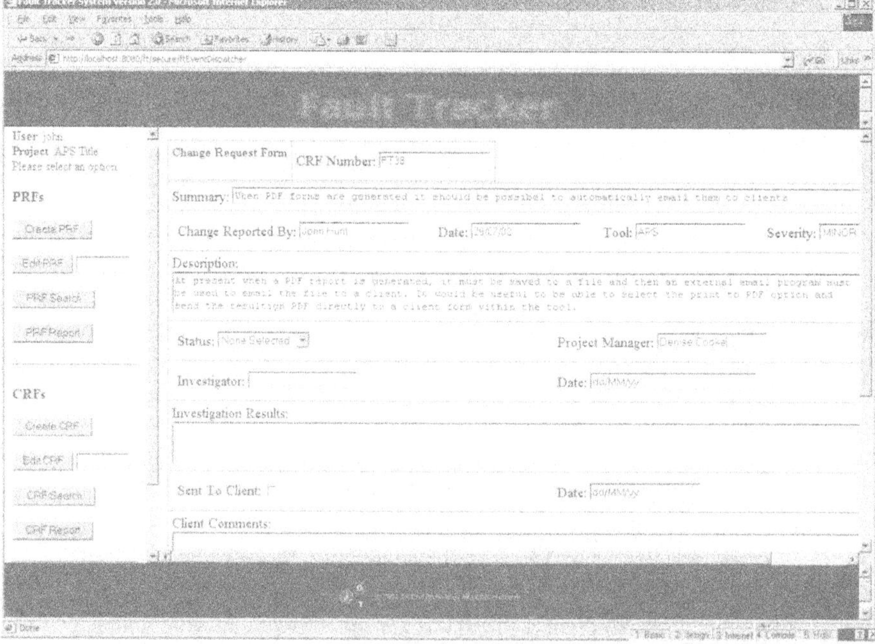

Figure 19.7 Creating a CRF.

19.4 The Design of the Fault Tracker

The design of the Fault Tracker is based on the specification of an underlying architecture that encompasses a number of the design patterns described in the last chapter. The patterns used are:

- Request Event Dispatching pattern. Used to dispatcher "request events" to the appropriate MVC structures.
- Model–View–Controller pattern. Used to manage each "view" in the application.
- Dispatcher View pattern. Used to dispatch JSP views for the MVC structure.
- Business Delegate. Used to act as a buffer between the models in the MVC presentation tier and the EJBs in the business tier.
- Service Locator. Used to allow the business delegates to locate the EJBs.

19.4.1 What Is the Architecture?

A software architecture encompasses:

- **The *overall* plan for the structure of the system.** That is, it is the blueprint for the system. It should be possible to read the architecture and gain an appreciation for how the system was structured (without needing to know detail of the structural elements).
- **The key structural elements and their interfaces.** That is, what elements make up the system, their interfaces and how they are plugged together.
- **How those elements interact (at the top level).** That is, when the various elements of the architecture interface, what they do, and why they do it.
- **How these elements form subsystems and systems.** This is a very important aspect of the architecture. Early identification of the core subsystem of the design not only helps organize future design (and implementation) work, it helps promote reuse and the comprehensibility of the system.
- **The architectural style** that guides this organization.

The intent is that within this architecture, designers are then free to work in the "spaces" left for them by the architecture. However, this is not the end of the story, as the software architecture also involves:

- How the system will be used.
- What the functionality of the final system is expected to be.
- Any performance issues that need to be addressed (these may involve more detailed development of the software architecture's implementation to assess performance constraints).
- Resilience to further development.
- Economic and technology constraints and trade-offs. The architecture can consider different solutions to the same problem, allowing different technological solutions to be aired and the most appropriate adopted (for example, CGI scripts versus Java servlets on a Web server).

The overall package structure of the Fault Tracker application is presented in Figure 19.8.

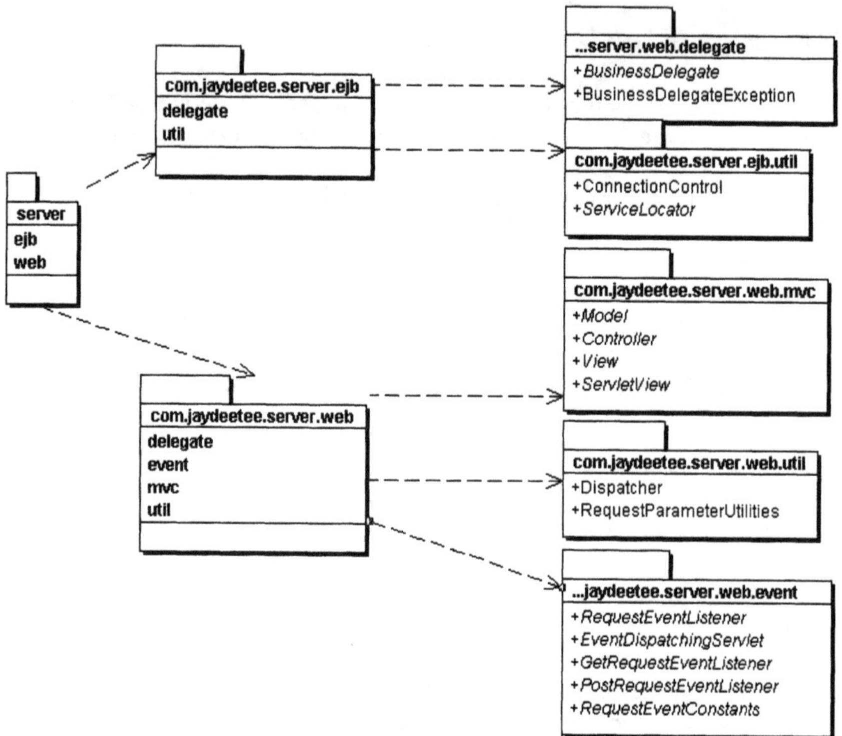

Figure 19.8 The generic frameworks used in the Fault Tracker.

As indicated by the package names, the generic frameworks used within the Fault Tracker have been divided into classes related to the EJB (or business logic) tier and classes related to the Web (or presentation) tier.

Within each package hierarchy the lowest level packages provide the classes and interfaces that support a particular framework (or pattern). For example:

- `com.jaydeetee.server.ejb.util`: this package defines the `ServiceLocator` pattern and its implementation `ConnectionControl`.
- `com.jaydeetee.server.ejb.delegate`: this package implements the `BusinessDelegate` pattern.
- `com.jaydeetee.server.web.mvc`: this package implements the infrastructure required by the J2EE implementation of the MVC.
- `com.jaydeetee.server.web.util`: this package implements the `Dispatcher` view pattern and a utilities class.
- `com.jaydeetee.server.web.event`: this package implements the `RequestEventDispatcher` pattern.

The application-specific packages are all under the `com.jaydeetee.ft` root package (see Figure 19.9). These are broken up into the EJB-oriented packages and the presentation-oriented packages. The EJB-oriented packages are:

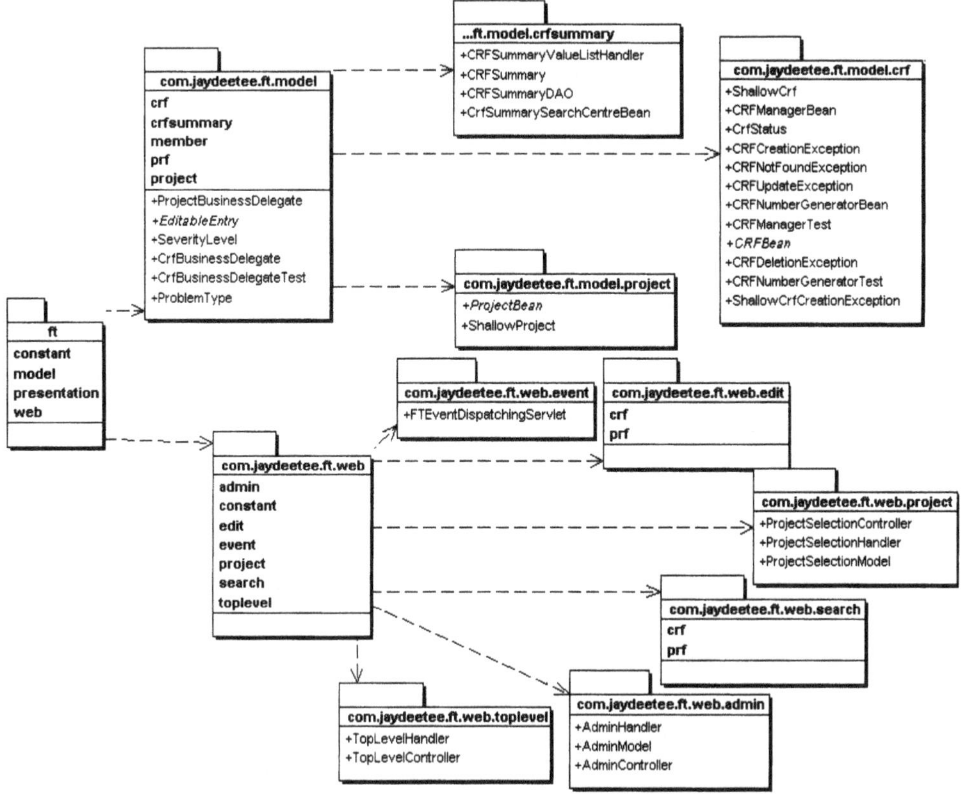

Figure 19.9 The application-specific packages in Fault Tracker.

- `com.jaydeetee.ft.model`: this package is the root of the packages that define the EJBs in the application. It also defines the business delegates and additional support classes.
- `com.jaydeetee.ft.model.crfsummary`: this package defines the EJBs that return CRF summary information used with the search operations.
- `com.jaydeetee.ft.model.crf`: this package defines the CRF entity EJBs and the CRFManager session beans that access the entity beans.
- `com.jaydeetee.ft.model.project`: this package defines the project entity bean and the representation of a project entity bean.

The presentation-oriented packages are:

- `com.jaydeetee.ft.web`: this package is the root of all the presentation tier packages.
- `com.jaydeetee.ft.web.event`: this package defines the `FTEventDispatchingServlet`.
- `com.jaydeetee.ft.web.edit`: this package contains two sub-packages one for CRFs and one for PRFs that handle editing these forms. The packages contain the presentation-oriented classes and servlets.
- `com.jaydeetee.ft.web.project`: this package defines the servlets and supporting classes that support the selection of a project.

- `com.jaydeetee.ft.web.search`: this package includes two sub-packages, one for CRFs and PRFs that support the search operations within Fault Tracker.
- `com.jaydeetee.ft.web.admin`: this package supports the presentation of the various administration functions within the Fault Tracker.
- `com.jaydeetee.ft.web.toplevel`: this package handles requests generated from the main menu options.

We will examine the implementation of the Request Event Dispatching pattern in more detail. This pattern requires a front controller style `EventDispatchingServlet` linked to `Handler` objects that receive the HTTP request and then initiate some server behaviour.

In the Fault Tracker the `FTEventDispatchingServlet` subclasses the `EventDispatchingServlet` class. Figure 19.10 illustrates the relationship between the `FTEventDispatchingServlet` and five of the handlers defined in the Fault Tracker system. The dependency line (dashed line) between the `FTEventDispatchingServlet` and the handlers is labelled with the event (or command) that causes the request to be sent to that handler. Note that a command is a parameter sent with the HTTP request from the "view" element.

For example, the act of selecting an option causes an HTTP request to be sent to the `FTEventDispatchingServlet` with a hidden parameter indicating the handler to initiate. The `FTEventDispatchingServlet` then delegates the request to the appropriate handler. For example, if you select to edit a CRF, then the request is forwarded to the `CrfEditingHandler` and subsequently to the `CrfEditing` MVC structure. This is illustrated in Figures 19.11 and Figure 19.12.

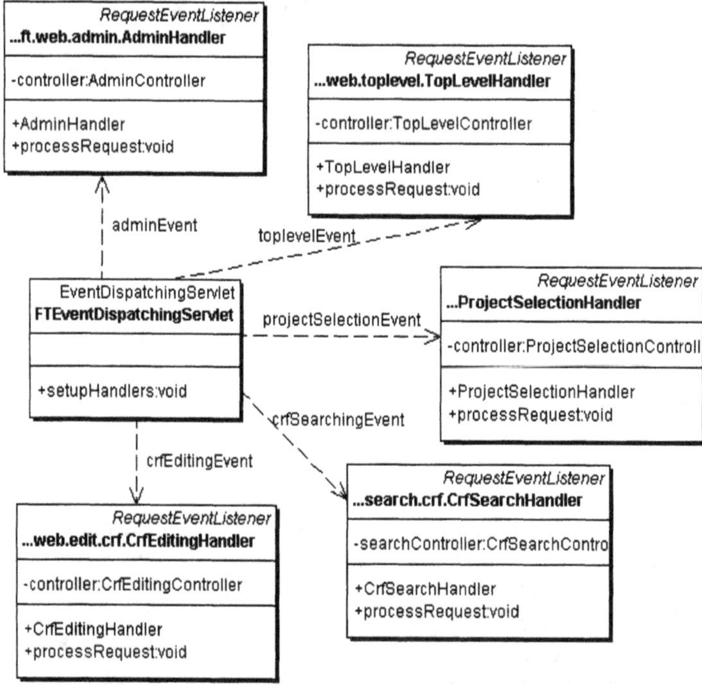

Figure 19.10 Implementing the Request Event Dispatching design pattern.

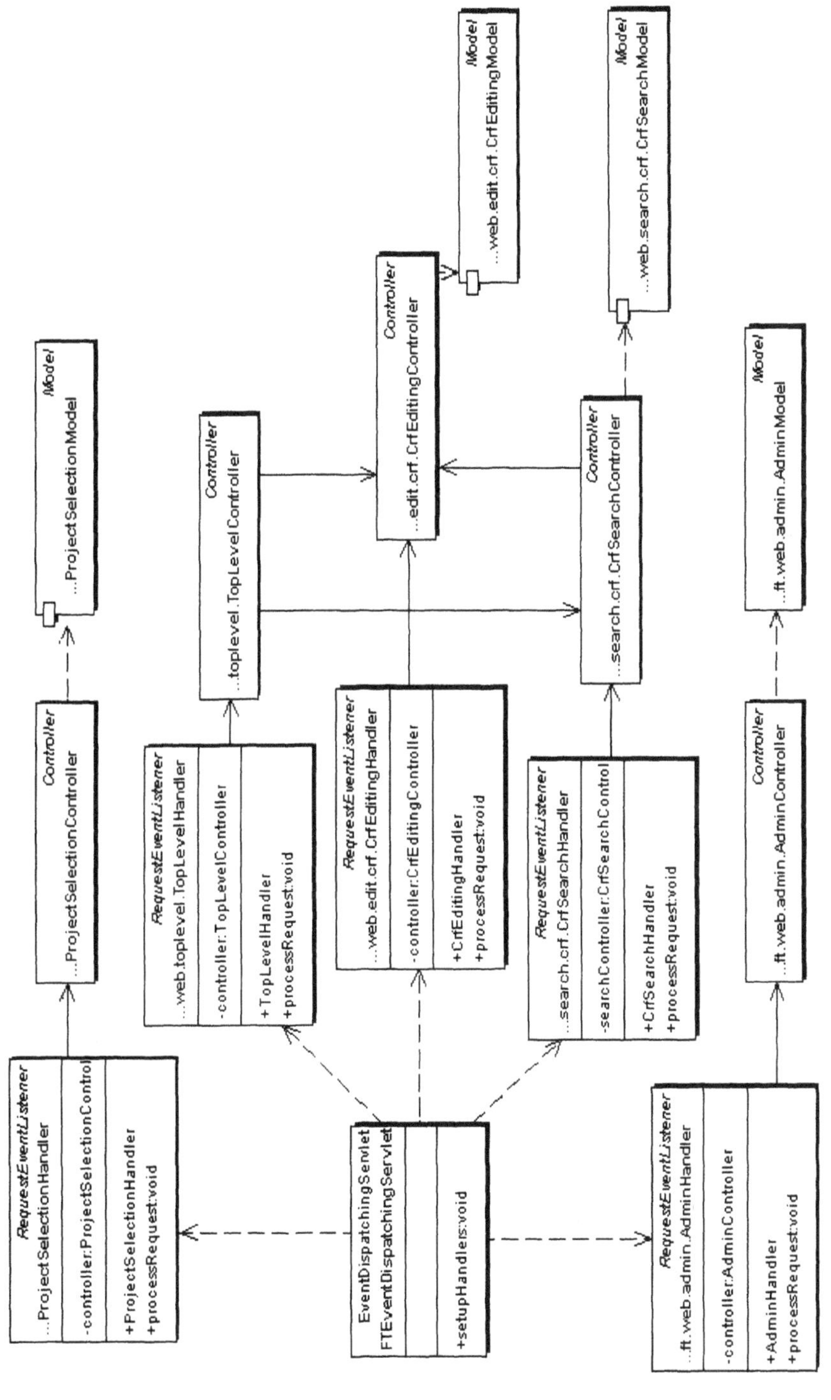

Figure 19.11 Relating the Request Event Dispatching design pattern and the Model–View–Controller pattern.

Note that in Figures 19.11 and 19.12 the dashed arrow from the controllers to the models indicates the indirect dependency between these two objects implemented by storing the model within the HttpSession.

Also note that in Figure 19.12 the controller maintains a reference to the Dispatcher object that will cause the JSP to generate a response back to the client. As a JSP is not a standard Java class it is represented in this figure by the note headed CrfEditingView.

The complete set of steps performed by the CrfEditing MVC classes in dealing with a request to edit a CRF is presented in Figure 19.13. The illustrates the following series of steps:

1.   Handler receives request from FTEventDispatchingServlet.
2.   Handler extracts the COMMAND from the HttpServletRequest object to determine what operation is required (in this case it is CrfEditing).
3.   The editCrf method is called on the CrfEditingController.
4.   The controller obtains a reference to the HttpSession from the HttpServletRequest.
5.   Next the controller attempts to extract the CrfEditingModel from the HttpSession. If no model exists then one is created and added to the HttpSession.
6.   The controller now calls the editCrf method on the CrfEditingModel.
7.   The model then uses the CrfBusinessDelegate to access the business tier (not illustrated in this sequence diagram) to obtain the information for the CRF editing view. Note that this returns a "shallow" copy of the CRF entity beans data for use in the presentation tier.

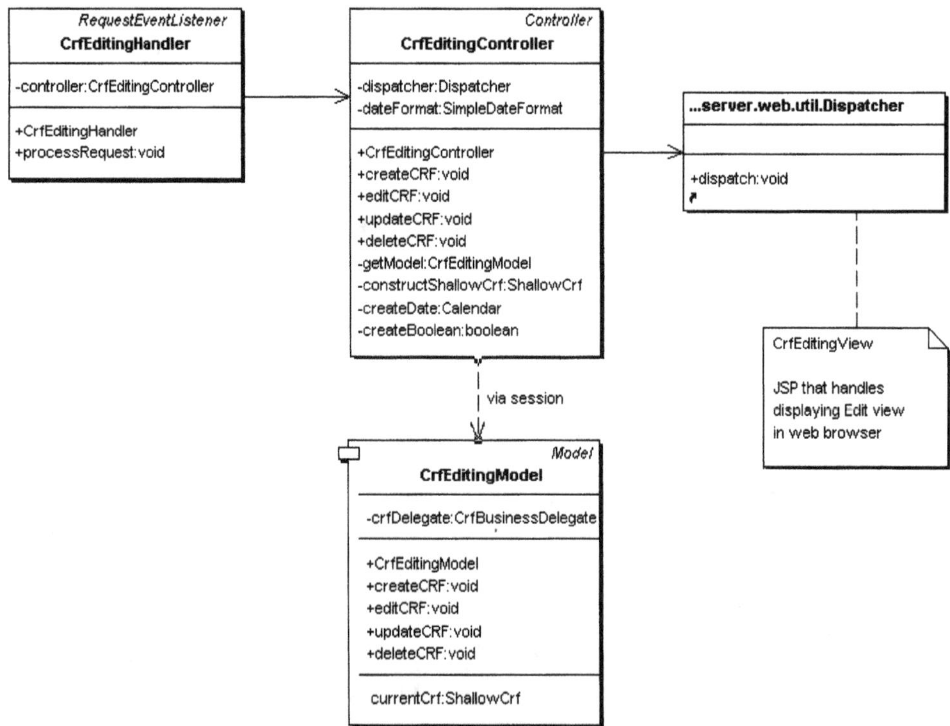

Figure 19.12 Realizing the MVC design pattern in Fault Tracker.

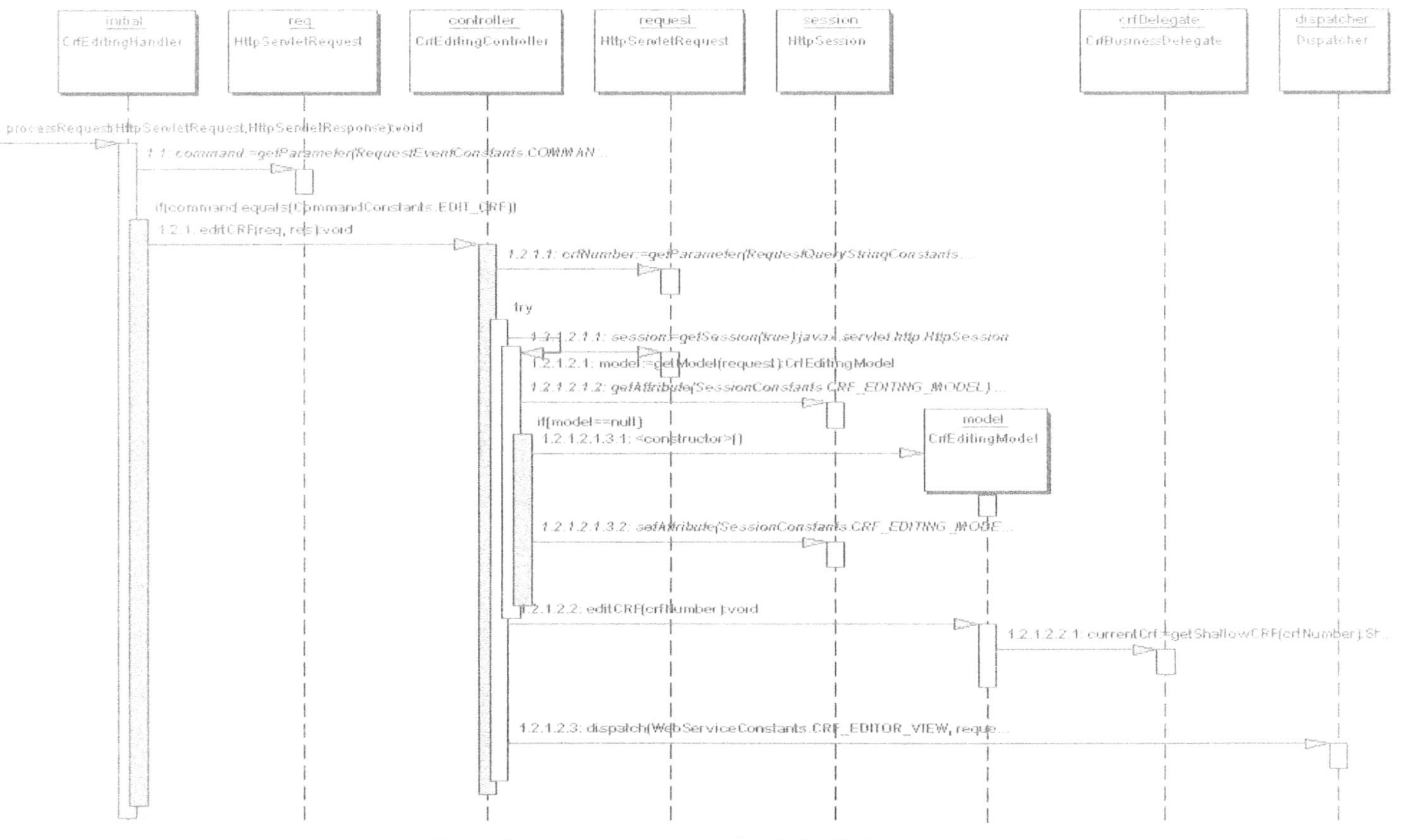

Figure 19.13 Handling a request within the MVC structure.

8.　The controller then uses the Dispatcher to cause the `CrfEditingView` JSP to be displayed to allow the CRF to be edited.

9.　The `CrfEditingView` JSP extracts the information to display from the `CrfEditingModel` held in the `HttpSession` object.

10.　A response is then sent back to the client browser from the JSP.

The only aspect of the application this does not cover is the relationship between the model, the `CrfBusinessDelegate` and the EJB tier. This is illustrated in Figure 19.14. This diagram shows how the `CrfBusinessDelegate` object uses the `ConnectionControl` (which implements the `ServiceLocator` pattern) to access the EJB tier. The `ServiceLocator` pattern hides the API lookup (naming) services, EJB access complexities etc. from the Business Delegate. It hides, for example, the issues associated with accessing the home interface via a JNDI lookup, narrowing the resulting object and using the home interface to create the EJB object etc. It is also a generic class and can be used with any EJB.

Figure 16: Accessing the EJB tier from the web tier in Fault Tracker

Note that in Figure 19.14 the `ConnectionControl` accesses a `Session` bean (the `CRFManager` EJB). This acts as the buffer between the presentation layer and the entity EJBs used. In the figure, only the `CRFBean` itself is presented, although additional entity beans are also used (for example to generate a unique id for the CRF bean).

This is where the `ShallowCRF` class comes in. This class is used to extract the relevant information from the `CRFBean` without needing to make the entity bean visible to the presentation layer.

19.5 Summary and Conclusions

In this chapter we have examined some of the design patterns and structures used within a larger J2EE technology application (the Fault Tracker). What has been presented here is only part of this application, and indeed the full application has many more elements to it (including integrated email, messaging etc.). However, it should illustrate both the size and complexity of such applications. It should also illustrate how these issues can be controlled by the judicious use of well-established, as well as domain-specific, design patterns.

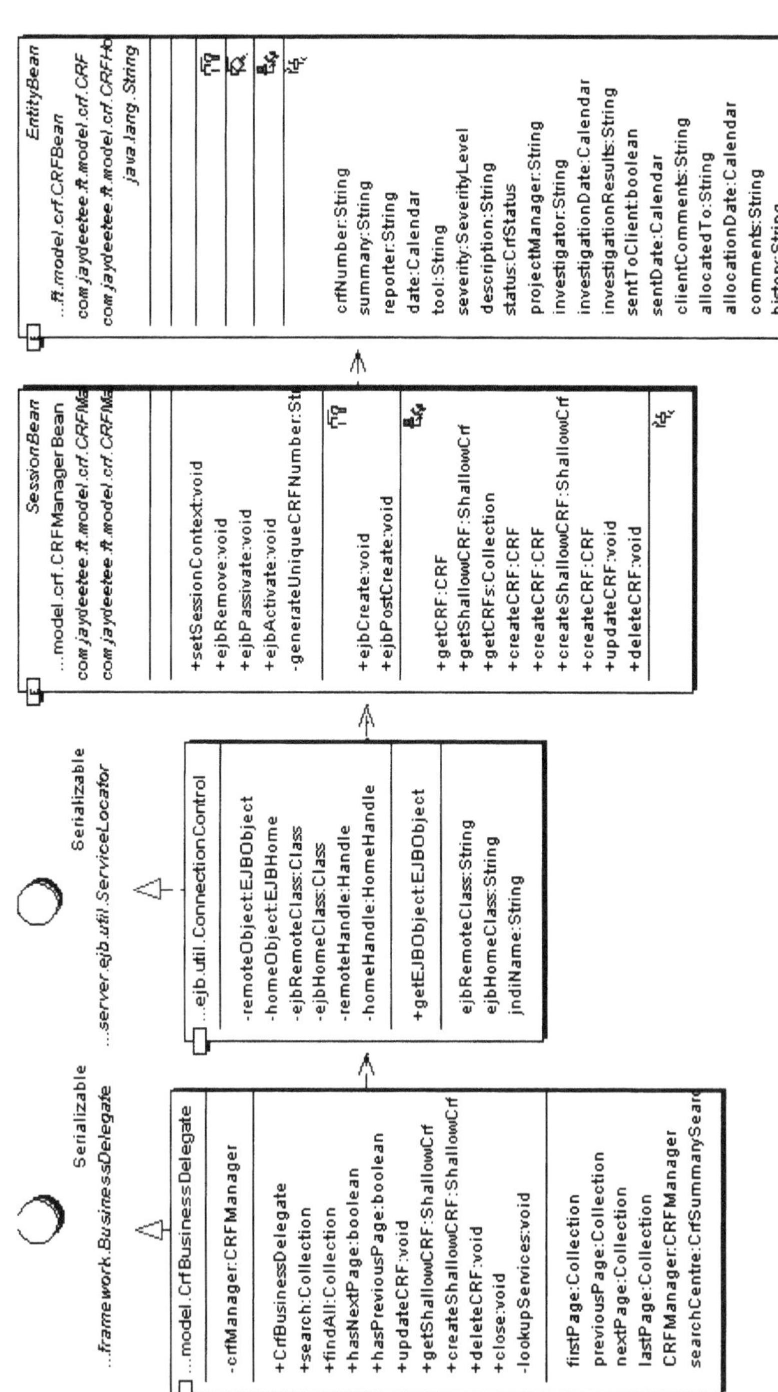

Figure 19.14 Accessing the EJB tier from the Web tier in Fault Tracker.

Part 3

The Unified Process in the Real World

Are UML Designs Language-Independent?

20.1 Introduction

This chapter aims to consider whether your use of the UML is language-independent or not. To do this it will consider the facilities provided by the UML when modelling a system versus the facilities provided by the Java platform. Of course, if we were considering a different implementation language/environment we would need to consider the unique features of that language or platform. However, as this book focuses on Java we will only discuss Java. We will consider how Java maps to a variety of UML constructs, such as packages, interfaces, classes, templates and associations.

20.2 OOD Is Language-Independent – Right?

For a long time it was suggested that an object-oriented design is language-independent and that any language can be used to implement such a design (but that an object-oriented language will make it easier). Indeed, in the early 1990s I would have subscribed to this view; it was the perceived wisdom of the time. However, my experience has been that it makes life a great deal easier if you take into account the target language (or languages) for which you are designing. Indeed, this has been brought home to me on numerous occasions, to such an extent that I now say that in practice you need to consider target "platform" issues and that if you don't do so in your design you may well develop a design which is unimplementable (without a great deal of modification). That is, UML diagrams don't mean a thing unless you can implement them! For example, the concept of a parameterized class is supported in UML; however, to Java such classes are meaningless! While it is not impossible to map such classes into Java you would need to invent this mapping yourself. As such a mapping would at best be non-standard this could be confusing for maintaining, updating or modifying your design/code.

In turn there are certain *idioms* that recur within object-oriented programming languages, and each language has its own idioms. Java is certainly no exception to this, and such idioms should be acknowledged and where appropriate exploited within a design. By idioms I mean essentially certain ways of doing things or using standard classes in combinations. Design patterns are an example of generic idioms; however, Java has its own idioms which can be exploited. Some of these idioms have been made more formal than others and you can view Enterprise JavaBeans as the ultimate example. They specify a very particular way of developing (and deploying) Java code that needs to be taken into account when designing a Java system (which employs Enterprise JavaBeans).

Finally, let us consider the various Java technologies that exist and which may affect a design. These include (but are not limited to) various interprocess communications mechanisms such as RMI, JavaIDL, TCP/IP socket programming and IP Multicast sockets, as well as Java streams, the Swing architecture (based on the model–view–controller pattern) and others (to be considered later in this chapter). All of these may affect how you wish to structure your design.

20.3 Making UML Work for You

UML is a large notation designed to describe a wide variety of software systems: for example, MIS systems, real-time systems (at least to some extent), interactive systems and batch-oriented processing. However, in general you as a software engineer are not trying to produce all these systems in one go. Indeed, many organizations (or at least departments within large organizations) specialize in particular types of system, such as interactive client-side applications. Such a software system will not need (and is not best described) using every available aspect of the UML notation. It is much more appropriate (and actually much better for a project team) to identify an appropriate core notation set that will be used. This means that everyone can get familiar with this core set and can ignore the aspects of UML that they do not use.

It is also useful to accept that UML does not cover every eventuality that you might want to represent or describe. In such cases do not try to force UML to fit what you want. Either use a different notational format (for example by borrowing some notation from data modeling) or by inventing your own project notation (without of course trying to reinvent UML!). Also do not get too hung up on "UML notational details"; if what you have drawn is understood by those that need to understand it, then it is sufficient!

Also remember that a diagram can say a thousand words, but that putting that diagram in context can make the thousand words comprehensible to the reader. Therefore use notes to explain what is being presented and any design decisions or trade-offs. If these notes are simple enough you can place them as notes on the diagram. If they are more detailed and require it, link a Word (or Star Office) document to your model.

Finally, remember that UML is not a method, the end goal or indeed the project documentation on its own. Rather, it should be an aid to the main aim of this whole process – the production of working software systems!

20.4 Questions to Consider

The UML allows many characteristics of a system to be modelled, but there are a number of questions you should consider when applying the UML to any language, and Java in particular. These questions include:

1. Does the language support all of the features provided by the UML. Let us take one classic example: the UML supports the concept of multiple inheritance. However, languages such as Smalltalk and Java do not, although C++ does. Thus for a Java project multiple inheritance should not be used.
2. What types does a language support? The UML allows anything, within reason, to be used as a type. You should limit your types (particularly within the design phase) to those types supported by the target language. For example, you should only use Java types for compatible declarations. This may mean that you should leave specifying the type to be used until you know the implementation language. This is not necessarily a problem, as early in the design phase (and the analysis phase) you may wish to use abstract domain-specific concepts rather than Java types (e.g. currency versus double).
3. Designs must be limited to the features of language used. If the language being used inherently supports concurrency (as Java does) then your designs can make explicit use of this feature. If they don't then avoid this or consider how it might be provided in the target language.

20.5 The Java Platform

At this point we will digress and consider what features a Java-specific design might focus on. That is, what the architectural elements in Java, the implementation features and the technologies that might be of interest are. These are listed below.

- *Packages.* Packages in Java are collections of classes and interfaces which exist within the same directory and which have a shared (package) visibility.
- *Interfaces and classes.* Classes are the basic building blocks in Java, while interfaces act as specifications allowing a high degree of pluggability (or component-based reuse as opposed to inheritance-based reuse). Classes can inherit from one other class and implement zero or more interfaces. In turn, interfaces can inherit from interfaces (but not classes).
- *Fields.* In Java there are both instance variables and class variables, which are collectively known as fields or attributes in the UML. The difference between instance and class (or static) variables is very significant, but may be lost in UML diagrams (where a small symbol is used to highlight the differences).
- *Methods.* In Java there are both instance and class methods. These both map onto operations in the UML and again the difference for Java is very significant, with a number of very important implications associated with using static methods. However the UML only indicates the difference with a small symbol!

- *Constructors.* In Java constructors are a very important concept; however, the UML does not really have a concept of a constructor and thus does not distinguish them from other operations. Care must therefore be taken with the design and documentation of constructors.
- *JavaBeans/Enterprise JavaBeans.* Java has two specific component-oriented models: one for client-side applications (JavaBeans) and one for server-side applications (Enterprise JavaBeans or EJB). These can have a significant impact on a design. However, unsurprisingly the UML does not provide explicit support for the framework within which an EJB exists.
- Java also provides a number of good software engineering features, including reusable APIs which can be exploited to avoid reimplementing the wheel, synchronization for multithreaded applications and explicit exception handling. While a number of these should not affect a high-level design, they may affect the lower levels of a design and should therefore be catered for.

20.6 Classes in the UML

Mapping UML classes to Java is straightforward: there is a direct one-to-one relationship between UML classes and Java classes. One of the nice features of UML classes is that you can use optional compartments so that you can also document the events handled by, and the responsibilities of, a class. This is particularly useful in Java, as the delegation event model can not only be used for graphical user interfaces but also for connecting JavaBeans and other objects together. You may wish to highlight constructors, as the UML does not have a specific constructor concept (see later) and you need to be careful of inheritance, as Java only supports single inheritance.

20.7 Fields in the UML

UML fields map directly to instance or class (static) variables in Java. Of course the difference between an instance or class variable is very significant in Java, and care needs to be taken to ensure that they are used in the correct manner.

To ensure that the resulting design maps to Java it is also important to following the guidelines:

- *Use Java access control types* (such as public, private, protected and default or package visibility) and no others.
- *Use valid Java names (and styles).* Do not start variable names (or class and interface names) with a numeric character – they must start with a Unicode character. Also, in Java classes and interfaces always start with a capital letter and methods and variables with a lower-case letter. Subsequent words in both cases are highlighted using capital letters rather than underscores or other separators. It helps everyone involved if the designers adopt this standard as well as the implementers. Note that if your organization adopts a different standard then that should be adopted by both designers and implementers.

- *Use valid Java or user-defined types.* Only use valid Java types (particularly as the design nears the implementation stages), including user-defined types. However, if you start adopting this style early on you will not have to change the types at a later stage. Of course, early on you may wish to defer the decision regarding the exact type until a later stage, and that is quite normal.
- *Specify valid Java initial values.* Assume the standard default values for Java instance variables (such as false for boolean, 0 for int, 0.0 for double and null for reference types). This will make your designs less cluttered. When you need to specify a non-standard default value, make sure you use a valid Java value.

20.8 Operations in the UML

Operations are implemented as Java methods. The mapping from UML to Java is the same as for fields, with the same set of guidelines plus a few additional considerations. These are:

- *Parameter list as valid Java parameters.* Parameters for an operation should follow the Java conventions and should specify valid Java types (these may include user-defined types). This is particularly true as the design nears the implementation stage. However, if you start adopting this style early on you will not have to change the types at a later stage. Of course, early on you may wish to defer the decision regarding the exact type until a later stage, and that is quite normal.
- *Return type as valid Java type.* The same is true for the operation's return type. In Java all methods have a return type. This type is either void if nothing is returned or a valid Java type, such as `int`, `double`, `boolean` or any class currently in scope.

20.9 Constructors

Constructors have a special meaning in Java. They act as initializers (so the name is a little unfortunate), allowing the newly created object to be initialized before being released for general use. There are some very specific rules governing constructors in Java, including:

- Constructors are not called via the dot notation and can only be *called* in a very limited way. This can either be done when the object is created using the new keyword or as the first line of another constructor.
- Constructors are not inherited by subclasses. However, at least one constructor is always called for every parent class, right back up the inheritance hierarchy.
- Constructors must have the same name as the class they are defined within.
- Constructors must not have a return type, if they are given a return type they become a method in the class that just happens to have the same name as the class.
- If a programmer does not define a constructor explicitly, the Java compiler provides a null parameter constructor that does nothing. If, however, one or more constructors are defined, then the automatically generated one is not provided.

The UML does not distinguish between operations and constructors, but the distinction between them in Java is very important. You therefore need to be very careful regarding the way in which you define and document what will become constructors in Java. It is not a good idea just to ignore them in your design, as they are fundamental to the operation of Java and are very important in configuring objects before they are used.

20.10 Packages in the UML

UML packages map directly to Java packages. However, this mapping is not as straightforward as it may at first seem. In Java packages are encapsulated units which can possess classes and interfaces. Packages are extremely useful:

- They allow you to associate related classes and interfaces.
- They resolve naming problems that would otherwise cause confusion.
- They allow some privacy for classes, methods and variables that should not be visible outside the package. You can provide a level of encapsulation such that only those elements that are intended to be public can be accessed from outside the package.

However, a Java package is essentially nothing more than a collection of classes and interfaces stored in the same directory (with some special scoping rules applied). UML packages are somewhat more than this.

In the UML packages have similarities to aggregation. If a package owns its content it is *composed aggregation*, but if it refers to its contents (i.e. imports elements from other packages) it is *shared aggregation*. Don't be confused here with Java imports, which merely make classes or interfaces in other packages *visible* to the current package – there is no aggregation happening with Java. This is the first major difference between Java packages and UML packages.

The second major difference is associated with visibility. In the UML, packages, just like classes, can have the visibility applied to them modified, showing how other packages can access their contents. The UML defines four different levels for package visibility. These are:

- private
- protected
- public
- implementation

The first three may appear familiar to Java developers (as Java has private, protected and public visibility modifiers as well). Firstly, the default visibility for the contents of a package is public (in Java it is the package visibility or the unnamed visibility). Secondly, packages themselves don't have a concept of visibility associated with them! This may not be a major difference; however, if we consider what each of them means in the UML we find very significant differences. The meanings of the different visibility modifiers are:

- *Public* means that other elements in other packages can see and use the contents of the package.

- *Private* means that only the package that owns an element or the package that imports that element can use it. This is very different from Java, where private means private to an object (top-level classes cannot be private).
- *Protected* means that only the package that owns or imports the element can use it; however, packages which inherit from this package will also be able to access the elements of the package (note the inheritance of packages!).
- *Implementation* is similar to private visibility, with the additional idea that elements which have a dependency on a package cannot use the elements inside that package if it has implementation visibility.

In addition to visibility, UML packages can also have interfaces and can be *specializations* of other packages. In Java only classes can implement interfaces, and thus only classes can publish or present an interface. Packages in Java cannot inherit from other packages.

You should therefore avoid using package inheritance as it has no direct mapping to Java. Although it is quite an elegant way to describe how the model's packages are related, it will only complicate the process of translating the design into Java. Secondly, you should avoid using package visibility modifiers, as again they really have no equivalent in Java, and indeed some aspects of package visibility can be quite confusing for the Java developer (not least because the same names are used for different concepts).

Interestingly, however, it is quite possible (and actually good style) to use package interfaces in Java. This is because an interface associated with a package can be a very good way of decoupling the classes used inside the package from the classes which wish to use the class. For example, let us consider Figure 20.1.

The package diagram illustrates that the package `vehicles` publishes an interface `drives` (which classes in other packages may depend upon). What does this mean to Java, where packages cannot have interfaces, although we have said that this is a good approach to adopt within Java? The following Java code illustrates how a `factory` class may be used to provide the implementation of the interface and how a public interface can be treated as a package's interface:

```java
package vehicles;

public interface Drives {
  public boolean drive(String dest);
}
```

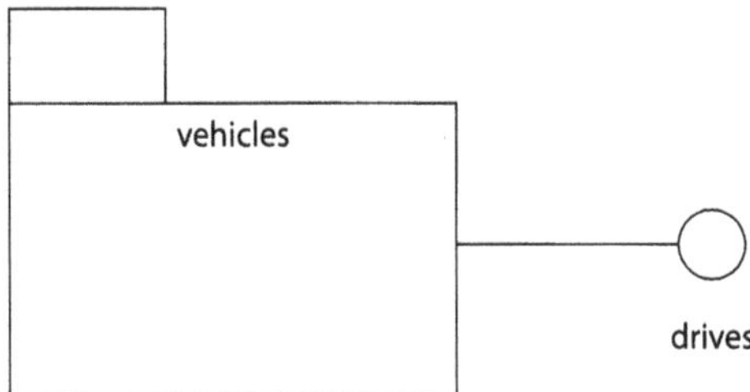

Figure 20.1 A package with an interface.

```java
public class VehicleFactory {

public static Drives getVehicle() {
   return new Car();
 }
}

public class Car implements Drives {
  public boolean drive(String dest) {
    ...
  }
}
```

The above code defines two classes and an interface for the package vehicles (note that as each of the elements is public they should all be in their own files with a package declaration at the beginning). The interface is the public face of the package and specifies what methods will be available to users of the classes defined within the package. The VehicleFactory class is used as a way of obtaining an object, and implements the interface without needing to reference that class. The VehicleFactory class is just that: a factory of different types of vehicle. It is not itself an actual vehicle object, whereas Car is. The big advantage of this approach is that if we create further classes VehicleFactory can return different objects depending on the circumstances, but the users of this package need never know about any of the different classes used! This has become a standard idiom in Java and can be used safely even though there is no direct package interface concept in Java!

20.11 UML Interfaces

UML interfaces map directly to Java interfaces. However, Java interfaces have both a method specification and public static final constants. Thus an interface can be given these concepts if the target language is Java.

20.12 Templates

The UML supports the concept of parameterized classes as templates. Such concepts are directly supported by languages such as C++. However, Java does not support templates. It is possible to map parameterized classes into Java using interfaces and component-based reuse, for example. However, it is not necessarily a direct or obvious mapping. Indeed, almost everyone who has tried to implement such a mapping has come up with a slightly different way of doing so! This of course means that the resulting mapping could lead to confusion and be a source of potential problems in the future. It is therefore best to avoid using parameterized classes when designing for Java.

20.13 Associations

There are many possible ways of mapping the different types of association in UML into Java. The simplest and most obvious approach is to use an instance variable in one object to reference another object. However, this has a number of limitations and is often too simplistic. The primary problem with this approach is that it is impossible to directly use the instant variable approach for anything other than a single unidirectional link. In most cases you require either a bidirectional link or multiple objects referenced by the link (possibly with some ordering or sorting), and you may even require a key to determine which link to follow. Associations may also have attributes of their own. Each of these scenarios requires greater flexibility (and behaviour) than a single instance variable reference can provide.

Another option is to use a specific association class (or classes). These classes represent the association. They sit between the two objects being associated (see Figure 20.2). In the case of Figure 20.2 the link class represents an association between a Developer class and a Project class. The link may be unidirectional or bidirectional, depending upon the application. Of course the references between the developer object, the link object and the project object are held in instance variables. However, the association itself is not represented by a reference but by the link object. Thus the link object can have attributes and operations just like any other object. This is therefore a much more powerful alternative than merely using a reference.

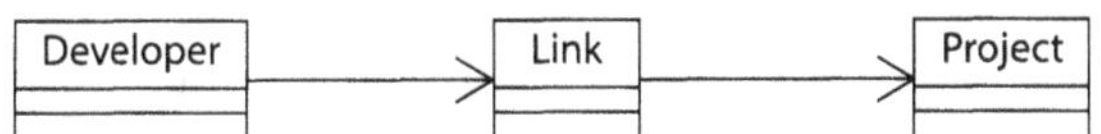

Figure 20.2 A link class representing an association.

To illustrate this idea, simple source code is provided below for the three classes in Figure 20.2. Note that we are only highlighting how the association may be implemented, and are not focusing on the attributes or operations which may be supported by each class.

```java
public class Developer {
  private Link link;
  public void addLink(Link l) {
    link = l;
  }
}

public class Project {
  private Link link;
  public void addLink(Link l) {
    link = l;
  }
}

public class Link {
  private Project project;
```

```
private Developer developer;

public Link(Project project, Developer developer) {
    addToLink(project, developer);
}

addToLink(Project project, Developer developer) {
    this.project = project;
    project.addLink(this);
    this.developer = developer;
    developer.addLink(this);
  }
}
```

In some cases it is necessary to have a link object, for example when we are dealing with ternary associations (as illustrated in Figure 20.3).

In some cases there will only ever be a single instance of a class within the system. Such objects are often referred to as singleton objects (and indeed the singleton pattern has become well documented). A singleton object may be referenced by many different objects throughout the system, and therefore there needs to be an easy way to implement such associations. One way in which singletons can be implemented is as purely class-side attributes and operations (such as the class Math in the Java platform). However, such an implementation, while certainly feasible, may have limitations for the future. Class-side information is never inherited in Java; thus, if you used only class-side attributes and operations there would be no potential for subclassing this class to create a different type of singleton object. Of course the advantage of this approach is that it is easy to access the class. As long as it can be imported, any public class-side operations or attributes can be directly accessed.

Another approach is to use instance-side operations and attributes and only ever create one instance of that class. This removes problems associated with inheritance (assuming that you have implemented the class appropriately). However, it does raise the issue of how other objects access this instance. One way is to pass a reference to the instance to other objects. However, if many objects need to access the singleton this can become messy. Another option is to create an instance of the object as soon as the class is loaded (using a static initializer for example). This instance can then be maintained within a class-side public final attribute. This attribute can then be accessed wherever the class is imported, but it is an instance that is then obtained. For example:

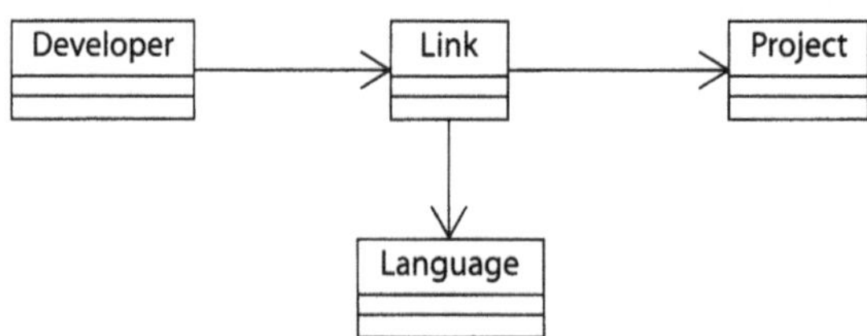

Figure 20.3 Representing a ternary association.

```
public class Single {
  public static Single s1;
  static {
    s1 = new Single();
  }
}
```

20.14 Multiplicity in the UML

In the UML it is possible to specify a range of different attributes of an association. These can indicate the number of associations (e.g. 1 or 2) and they can also be used to indicate ranges of number (e.g. 1–3) as well as any ordering and sorting of the associations. However, such information has no direct mapping into Java. Unless you implement code to support ranges, for example, Java will not impose any such constraints.

There are some classes now available in the latest release of Java (Java 2) which provide better support for ordering and sorting collections of objects (see the java.util package). However, these classes are not explicitly intended for use with associations. Instead, a developer needs to decide how to use such classes to implement the constraints on an association.

The end result is that an association may need to be implemented in Java as an instance variable maintaining a reference, as a link object (as described above) or as a collection of references (or link objects).

Such decisions will affect not only the potential performance of the system but also the comprehensibility of the design versus the implementation. You should therefore produce guidelines which are adopted throughout a project and adhere to them. Where the guidelines are broken, explicit reasons should be given to ensure that those enhancing or maintaining the design and implementation understand what they are being presented with.

20.15 Aggregation and Composition

As well as standard associations, the UML supports the concepts of aggregation and composition. An aggregation is a specialized form of association in which a whole is related to its part(s). It is a *part-of* relationship (whereas an association is a *works-with* or *uses* relationship). In turn, composition is a variation on an aggregation that indicates that the sub-part cannot exist on its own. For example, a human heart is something that is an aggregate of a human body which does not function outside of the body (thus it is a compositional relationship). In turn, a car engine might or might not be a compositional part of a car. For example, in a warehouse of parts, an engine may well be an object in its own right that can exist outside the scope of the car.

Aggregation is a concept that is only supported by the UML; there is nothing special in Java which supports the general concept of aggregation. However, Java does have a concept referred to as an inner class. An inner class is a class which defines an object which can only exist with reference to the outer class. That is, you cannot make an instance of an inner class without referring to an instance of the outer class. This can be very useful and might at first appear to support compositional aggregation.

Inner classes, however, may limit the reusability of a design. An inner class cannot be created as a standalone object. Thus if we created a class Gearbox as an inner class of a Car, then we could only ever use the class Gearbox with reference to instance of the class Car. This would mean that we could not use the class Gearbox with a Lorry, a Tractor, a Motorcycle or similar. However, from the point of view of our design, each possesses an object called a gearbox which is an aggregate part of the main object. We have therefore imposed unnecessary restrictions on the design due to an implementation design we have made.

Care must be taken with using inner classes to represent aggregation (and particularly composition), as this may be an oversimplification.

20.16 Singleton Objects

As was stated earlier, singleton classes can be defined in Java. However, there is nothing inherent to Java that will ensure that only a single instance of a class will be created. Even the listing provided earlier for a singleton class did not stop any other code from creating another instance of the class Single. Therefore if you wish to ensure that only a single instance of a class will ever be created you must code this by using facilities provided in the Java language itself. This can be done using a class-side attribute (such as count) and a test in any (or all) constructors for that class. For example, the following class guarantees that only a single instance can be created.

```java
public class Example {
  private static int count =0;
  public Example() {
    if (count != 0) {
      // raise exception
    } else {
      count++;
    }
}}
```

20.17 Synchronous and Asynchronous Messages

The UML supports a number of different message types, including simple, synchronous and asynchronous types (see Figure 20.4). Simple messages indicate the direction of the flow of control, but no details about that flow of control.

A synchronous message is one in which the message being sent does not return until the operation initiated by the message is completed. This is the approach adopted by message calls in Java. When a message is sent to an object, that message causes a method to execute.

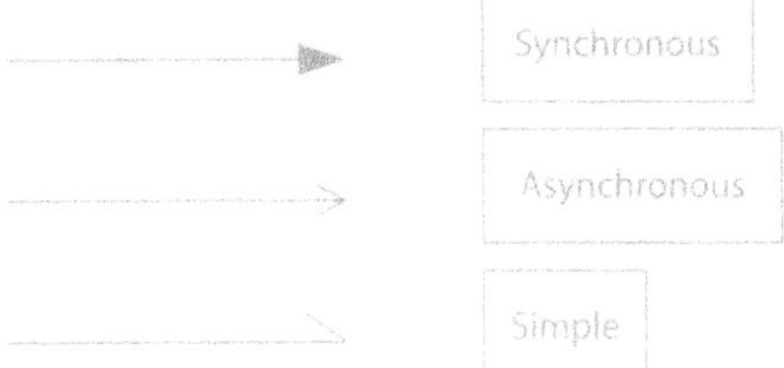

Figure 20.4 UML message types.

The flow of control remains with this method until it has completed all its tasks before returning to the calling method.

Asynchronous messages are messages in which the caller is not blocked when the method is called. This message type is typically used in real-time systems where objects execute concurrently. Java does not have direct support for asynchronous messages. Instead they must be coded for. One way of doing this is to use Java threads. These are lightweight concurrent processes that execute concurrently. In such a situation, when a message indicates that a method should be called asynchronously a new thread should be initiated to handle the method, allowing the flow of control in the original thread to return to the caller.

If such an implementation is not clearly documented, it may be difficult for developers to see the relationship between the UML diagram and the Java code (note that the difference between the two arrows used to indicate the different types of message is not great).

20.18 From Code to the UML

It is possible to generate UML diagrams directly from Java code. Obviously the Java code can only represent some of the information in a UML diagram; however, it can be extremely useful as an aid to understanding an implementation in Java. It may be necessary to do this if there is no design documentation available (a position I have found myself in before now), or to compare the actual implementation with the original design or to synchronize the design with the implementation. It can also be an effective tool for aiding in the walkthrough process of a quality assurance procedure.

Some systems which generate UML diagrams from code refer to this as re-engineering. In the main it is a one-step process which takes the current state of the software and generates a set of (typically) class diagrams from that code. Some systems can dynamically update either the design or the code (depending on which is being modified). This ensures that the design and the software are always synchronized. Of course, this does not mean that this is an acceptable way to do design, but it can be very useful. An example of such a tool is Together/J from TogetherSoft (see Figure 20.5). A freeware edition of this software system (referred to as the whiteboard edition) can be downloaded from `http://www.togethersoft.com/`.

In my case I first design a system using an appropriate UML design tool (such as Rational Rose or indeed Together/J). This is done without attempting to implement the design, but following the discussions presented in this book (i.e. care is taken to design something implementable). Then once I move to the implementation phase, I use Together/J and my Java development tool (such as Forté Developer for Java) as complementary tools.

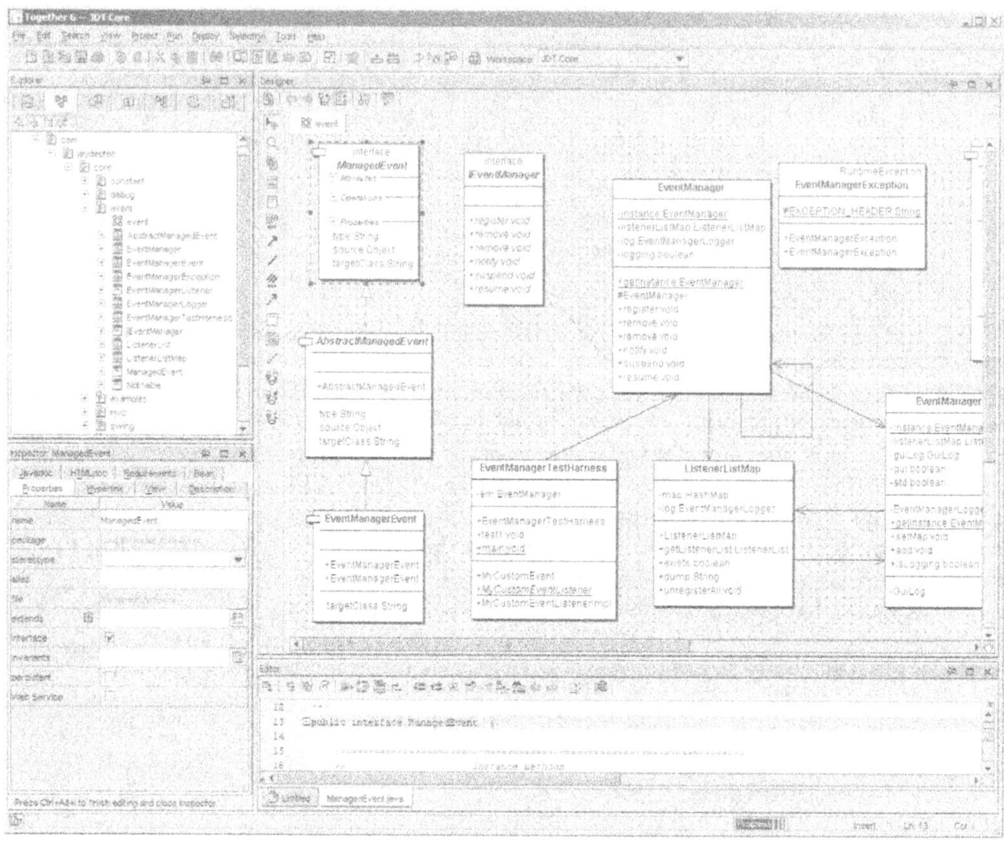

Figure 20.5 UML diagrams generated from Java code by Together.

Together/J is used for implementing, reviewing and modifying the structural elements of the system (such as classes, associations, inheritance and attributes), while my Java IDE is used for the functional parts such as operations and constructors.

20.19 Conclusions

The overall conclusion of this chapter is therefore that you do indeed need to take into account the target language when you are generating a UML design! This is true whether you are using OMT, Booch or the Unified Process itself. Indeed, I believe that this is actually true for any object-oriented design method with any type of notation (whether UML or not)!

21

Customizing the Unified Process for Short Time-Scale Projects

21.1 Introduction

The Unified Process (UP for short) is primarily aimed at large, long-lived projects: those projects which involve a large number of developers, possibly in different locations, and which will need to be developed and maintained over many years. However, not all software development fits such a profile; many projects are much shorter and involve far fewer people.

This chapter considers how the Unified Process can be modified for smaller, short-term projects. To do this it takes an particular (imaginary) project as the basis for considering what modifications to make to the Unified Process. It is necessary to consider the requirements of one particular project rather than making generalized comments, because every software development is different. As such, other than making high-level generalizations it would be hard to be specific about how the Unified Process could be customized. By taking a concrete example, we are able to show, in one particular instance, how the Unified Process can be customized.

The remainder of this chapter is structured in the following manner. Section 21.2 considers the particular problems of the Unified Process for small projects. Section 21.3 returns to the Unified Process and considers its nature as a framework rather than a prescriptive method. In particular, it considers the effects that the following will have on the Unified Process:

- experience with the application domain
- experience with the technology being used
- understanding of the requirements of a particular system
- the nature of the task being attempted

343

- the size of development task
- time, budget and resources
- how much management buy-in exists

Section 21.4 then considers how our sample project might adapt the Unified Process. Section 21.5 presents the modified Unified Process.

21.2 Particular Problems of Small Projects

We should start off by clarifying what is meant by a small project. We are not necessarily referring to the physical size of the project team or the number of lines of code being developed or the complexity of the functionality. What we are referring to is that the project is *smaller* in some sense than a project with a large number of developers which may last for several years. Examples of large development projects might be the ill-fated London Ambulance system or the UK DSS benefits system.

Instead, a *small* project may range from a two-person development project lasting for six months and implementing a simple account management system to a project with half a dozen developers producing a design analysis system for the automotive industry involving a twelve-month development cycle. In other words, *small* isn't really the best way of describing these projects (and possibly *not-large* might be better), but is the simple placeholder we are using.

So what problems do *small* projects face when trying to apply the Unified Process? Well, to begin with there is the problem of knowing where to start with the Unified Process. This is particularly true if the developers are trying to wade through some of the fairly heavy-weight documents produced by the "Three amigos" themselves (for example *The Unified Software Development Process*; Jacobson *et al.*, 1999).

The problem of wading through these heavyweight texts is partly due to the assumption that the project being considered is a *large* project (and that developers can selectively decide which parts to leave out if they are not appropriate). One problem with this is that you need to understand the Unified Process well enough to be able to decide which parts to leave out, and you can't do that if you are trying to learn how to use the Unified Process at the same time!

When it comes down to it, the Unified Process makes a number of assumptions which are not necessarily valid for smaller projects. These all affect how you might wish to modify the unified process itself. These assumptions include:

- *Control of the whole life cycle.* It is assumed that the *team* has full control over the whole of the life cycle of the product, from inception through to long-term maintenance. This is often not the case, as the business case and (often) the requirements are laid down long before the development team ever comes near the project. This also tends to mean long before the project comes into contact with anyone who is familiar with the UML and the Unified Process!
- *A large piece of software.* The Unified Process assumes that a large piece of software is being developed (either as a single standalone system or as part of some distributed system using

a client–server or similar architecture). For many small Internet-based projects, this is not the case. The software itself is not going to be that large, and although it may well be used in some form of distributed architecture (over a network) it is not really a thin client/fat server architecture. That is, the server may not be particularly fat itself!

- *A large (possibly distributed) development team.* For many development teams you can fit all the members of the team into a single room and let them thrash things out (or ignore each other!). However, there are not that many people involved (personal anecdotal evidence suggests that typical numbers are often between four and six developers on many Java-based Internet-related projects – of course there are also much larger developments, but we are not considering those here).
- *A long time period (for maintenance and releases).* The Unified Process assumes that the software being developed will be in use for a long extended period of time and will probably be subject to maintenance and future releases. While for many small projects this is also true, it is not necessarily the case. For example, many Internet projects have a very short lifespan before they are removed and replaced with new systems!
- *Assumes that risks relate to parts of the project.* The Unified Process suggests identifying those areas of a project which are the high-risk areas and gearing your development around those. However, in a small project the high-risk areas may be the whole system, or due to smaller functionality it may not be possible to separate the areas of risk from the remainder of the system, as both are needed to do anything. Of course, it is still possible to address the areas of risk first to ensure that the whole project is feasible.
- *Assumes potential for incremental and iterative development.* The Unified Process is based on the idea of being able to develop a system in an incremental and iterative manner. However, if a project is small and will only last for three months there is limited scope for iteration and incremental development (i.e. the whole project may be the equivalent of an increment in a large development!).
- *Potential for alpha and beta releases.* The Unified Process considers how you can release alpha and beta releases of software to help the deployment process. However, if your time-scale is three months and the software itself is relatively small, it is unlikely that you will have time for alpha and beta releases. Indeed, at best you might be able to test your system at a number of beta test sites for a short period of time.
- *Planning for the above.*

It is important to understand that none of the above is intended as a criticism of the Unified Process *per se*. If the Unified Process did not cover the issues related to the above, it could only be applied to smaller projects. What we are considering in this chapter is how to modify the Unified Process to ensure that it is most suitable for smaller projects (this is a much easier task than deciding how to extend a method in order to deal with larger projects!).

21.3 The Unified Process as a Framework

As was stated in earlier in this book, the Unified Process is a framework to be adopted as required. As each project will have its own requirements and thus might lead to a different configuration of the Unified Process, the issues to consider here are:

- Knowledge and experience of the application domain.
- Knowledge and experience with the technology being used (in this case Java as well as the UML and the Unified Process itself).
- Understanding of the requirements of the system.
- Size of the task.
- Nature of the application, for example whether it is short-lived or not.
- The time-scales available.
- Budgetary considerations.
- Resources available such as tools and people.
- How much support you are receiving from management.

Each of these issues is considered in more detail below.

21.3.1 Experience of Application Domain

By experience of the application domain we mean "knowledge and experience of the domain and similar systems in that domain". Such experience will affect the inception phase of the Unified Process. This is because it is the inception phase which defines the scope of the project and develops the business case. It may also establish the feasibility of the project.

Such situations occur where a new version of a product is being re-engineered in Java (or some other object-oriented language). This may mean that:

- A business case already exists, both for the system and for the technology being employed.
- The scope of the system is already well understood, minimizing the need to carry out a detailed analysis of this. Of course it may well be necessary to consider the details of the scope of the system, particularly as there may be a limited (and possibly short) time period involved.
- The feasibility should be known (at least related to achieving the functionality in some software), although lack of experience in the chosen development language may affect the feasibility and may require some feasibility analysis to be carried out.

The end result is that the requirements analysis process should be considerably shorter than if this was a first development in a new application domain.

21.3.2 Experience with Technology

This includes experience with the design techniques being applied, the implementation platforms and languages being used, and any technology with which you need to integrate or communicate. In particular, it means familiarity with Java, third-party products and legacy systems (and the interfaces used to access these legacy systems with a C API or a CORBA-compliant ORB such as ORBIX). This is a significant issue, as it is rare that all these are known for a particular project. Usually one or more areas are new or unknown (in time this may change within an organization, but as you are reading this book it is likely that at least the Unified Process is new to you!).

Varying levels of experience with the technology involved affect a number of aspects of the Unified Process, in particular:

- The development of the requirements, and the use case analysis in particular, if less is known up front. It may mean that is it necessary to carry out additional prototyping or design and implementation phase work in order to be sure of what can and can't be done.
- The analysis phase may be particularly affected, as the greater the understanding regarding the elements involved in the project, the less need for prototyping (and vice versa).
- The design phase may also benefit from the potential for reuse of design elements if the organization has design information available in an appropriate format. This may be particularly useful, as the designs are known and their validity is known. Of course, such design reuse is not trivial, and work may need to be done to integrate the reusable design elements into the evolving design (the work of the patterns movement is a good example of design reuse).
- The implementation phase may be particularly affected, as the greater the knowledge of the technologies used the easier this phase should be, and the less that is known about the technologies the greater is the potential for problems to arise in this phase. Ideally such risks should be identified up front and dealt with early on.

One advantage of assessing the project team's (and organization's) knowledge of the technologies early on is that it may also make it easier to identify risks earlier. If this is done it may be possible to exploit that within the remainder of the planning for the project.

21.3.3 Understanding of Requirements

Another factor affecting the customization of the unified process is the level of knowledge that a project has regarding the requirements of the system. This will be affected by a number of factors, such as the background knowledge of the domain versus the application. If, for example, you have worked extensively within the automotive engineering field, it is likely that you have extensive domain knowledge, which may make it easier to determine the requirements for a new system in the same domain (although of course it may not). Equally, if you have extensive knowledge of a particular type of application in one domain, it may well help you determine the requirements for that type of application in a different domain. For example, a design analysis system in the automotive domain may well be similar to a design analysis system in the marine or aerospace domains (although there are likely to be important and telling differences between them).

Of course, if what you are undertaking is a reimplementation of an existing system which your organization previously developed in a procedural language, then it is very likely that the detailed requirements of the application will be very well known indeed. Of course, new requirements are always slipped in to such reimplementations, and it is important to understand the implications of such additional requirements.

However, the greater the knowledge of the domain and the application the easier the use case analysis should be (as less is unknown). However, one temptation in such situations is to get carried away with the use case analysis (UCA), which can be as much a problem as not doing sufficient use case analysis. If the use case analysis is so detailed that the readers can't see the wood for the trees, then the analysis is of no use!

21.3.4 The Size of the Task

Essentially, the larger the task, the greater the need for Unified Process support, while the smaller the task, the greater the number of activities which become overkill! For example, the analysis discipline may become too simple to be of use to anyone and may actually act as a distraction rather than as a focus. The deployment model may be a waste as it may convey so little information as to be worthless (and a single sentence would do just as well). For example, if the application is a single standalone system running on a single processor then the deployment model is of little use.

You should also consider how the dynamic behaviour of the system should be represented. One problem for *small* projects with limited time-scales is that it is easy to focus on the static structure of the classes and interfaces and forget about the dynamic behaviour of the system. Yet without the dynamic behaviour of the system, not much is going to be accomplished. However, statecharts may not give much added value and may be time-consuming to produce. If the system to be built has limited state-based behaviour then they may be unnecessary. In addition, sequence and collaboration diagrams both provide a view of essentially the same information (with slightly different emphasis). It may thus be overkill to develop both types of diagram (and many tools such as Rational Rose allow you to automatically generate one from the other).

Finally, although component diagrams can be very useful for associating source code with class files and jar files in Java, they don't provide much in the way of additional information for small projects. They may well be deemed unnecessary (although at least some of the information they represent will still need to be recorded somewhere).

Remember that the Unified Process should be an aid not a burden, a support and not a hindrance in what you are trying to accomplish. If the Unified Process itself is forcing you to apply techniques which seem wholly inappropriate for the size of the task at hand, then they may well not be suitable – it's for you to decide.

21.3.5 The Nature of the Task

The Unified Process assumes that the development task is large and that the project is likely to be long-lived. Thus the nature of the task at hand is that it is a large, long-lived thing. However, what about a project with a three month development time frame and a three month life? Should you just abandon the Unified Process completely? If this system is business critical in some sense than NO! However, there are some issues that should be taken into account, for example:

- Maintenance may not be an issue: as soon as the three months is up the software will be scrapped (although in reality such software tends to end up running for longer periods of time and may well incur maintenance releases etc.).
- Future development may not be an issue, as the project is to be scrapped at the end of the period. However, how many such projects have gone on to become much larger and longer lived? It is not uncommon to find that some software which was only intended as a short-term stopgap has become a company standard!
- Meeting requirements will still be an issue. Whenever a piece of software is developed there are some requirements (explicit or implicit) on what that software needs to do. This is just as true of the programs written by single developers for their own requirements as of the large business-

critical corporate system developed over a number of years. Thus it is still critically important that the software actually do what is required. The use of use cases as the driving force behind the Unified Process certainly helps to keep this in focus throughout a development (whether small or large).

Of course, some aspects of the Unified Process may not be appropriate. For example, for small projects it may not be possible to identify the core architecture separately from the whole system. That is, the whole system may well be the architecture. It is still useful to consider the architecture, as this may be useful in helping others to further develop the system at a later date; however, it is not necessarily useful to separate out an explicit architectural development stage.

For any project, however small or large, it is still likely that the following will be needed:

- A (possibly) quicker use case analysis, but be careful not to miss out essential functionality.
- A design phase which may focus on developing the architecture of the system, but that architecture will be the system in its entirety. That is, the key elements of the system are identified and developed, but hooks should be left in for future development (as this almost always happens in one form or another).
- The implementation and testing phases will still exist and are as important as ever. Just because the project being developed is not a large corporate-wide application does not mean that less time (relatively) should be devoted to testing the system or indeed to implementing it.

However, it is not uncommon to find that the analysis phase is dropped. This is, at least in part, because the application is smaller and the design can be readily developed and understood without the need for an explicit analysis phase.

The end result is likely to be less iterative and incremental than the Unified Process suggests, but then the systems are smaller in themselves. It is still true, however, that identifying the risks in the development is still a key aspect, as is the use case-driven nature of the process.

21.3.6 Time/Budget/Resources

Most development projects (whether in the software industry or not) involve a certain amount of trade-off between these the time available, the budget available and the resources available. It is often the case that either one or more are constrained and may be less than is felt necessary. For example:

- *Time.* The more time you have the greater the flexibility to apply more engineering methods.
- *Budget.* The smaller the budget, the less tools, support, designers, etc. involved.
- *Resources.* The resources available to a project are often affected by the budget; however, they may be a factor in their own right.

Too little of any one of these and you will find that the pressure to "cut corners" increases. You will then need to select these corners carefully!

21.3.7 Management Support/Buy-in

Let's face it: you need it! Without managerial support it is difficult to apply techniques such as the Unified Process. This is at least in part because you need to have the weight of management behind you to *encourage* reluctant colleagues/team members to adopt it. But it is also because a software development following the Unified Process is likely to be very different from a development project following more traditional methods (such as a method adopting the waterfall model). This means that the way that the development is monitored and resourced should be different. If management tries to adopt a traditional approach to monitoring your project it will find that the requirements have not been completed when they expected, etc. This can cause a great deal of conflict and extra pressure on the development team (and the team leader in particular).

Secondly, it is very important to have at least one manager (preferably a senior manager) to champion the Unified Process and help the development team carry it through. This is because the manager needs to deal with the internal politics and act as a buffer between other management and the development team. The team leader should be concentrating on the development task in hand and should not be worrying about constantly justifying the approach selected to higher management. Indeed, having a manager to champion your cause may well be one of the critical factors in the success of the first Unified Process project in an organization which has previously used more traditional techniques.

You also need management support in order to get additional support in the form of expert mentoring. Such support may come from external sources (such as specialist training and consulting organizations) or it may come from within the organization if it is available there. However, it has been found essential to help guide the ongoing development process in many organizations. This is because there are many problem areas and pitfalls to your first object-oriented development, let alone one using Java, the UML and the Unified Process for the first time! However, it is not uncommon to hear management saying things such as "why should we have someone from outside come and tell our people how to develop software" or "well if you need such support you are obviously not very good!". In either case they are being foolish and short-sighted, as a short-term investment in such mentoring can save a great deal in the long term. It is also an indication that the development team has acknowledged what it doesn't know; as the saying goes, "the idiot is the man who thinks he knows everything, the wise man is the one who knows that he doesn't".

It is also worth acknowledging that one week's training in the Unified Process, UML or Java does not make an expert in any of these subjects. It is also unfair to compare five, ten or twenty years experience in technologies such as COBOL, SSADM or similar to one week's worth of training. Thus unless management appreciates this, a great deal of conflict can arise when it considers that its developers with ten years experience of COBOL (but a week of Java and Unified Process) should be able to design from scratch the first business-critical object-oriented system developed by the organization!

The final point made above is also important from the aspect that management should be careful that it is not asking too much of its designers and developers. For example, in the above situation a software house may be expecting its developers to take on:

- their first Java development project
- migration to a new database and a new operating system (this may not necessarily be the case, but is common)
- familiarization with the Unified Process and the UML!

Any one of these could make a development project difficult; all three may well be a bit much to expect unless additional support is provided!

21.4 Adapting the Unified Process for a Small Project

21.4.1 A Typical Short-Term Project

To put the following discussion into context we will describe a theoretical software project which is not that dissimilar to others that I have been involved with. This project is to be used over an intranet. It is to provide access to a personnel system so that employees can find out who works in which offices, their names, emails and contact numbers. The system must be live within three months and is currently expected to have a lifespan of three to six months before the whole thing may be replaced.

The systems requirements are based around:

- a database that already exists and is managed by a personnel system
- a set of forms to allow users to enter queries regarding people or departments
- the need retrieve information from the database and display that information on the users' machines

As this project is not expected to be maintained or further enhanced the requirements are quite closed and relatively straightforward.

21.4.2 Short Time-Scale Project Approach

So how should we modify the Unified Process? The key issues to focus on are described below.

Get the right requirements right! This means that the core of what you are going to do will still be driven by the use case analysis. However, you need to make sure that you use "use case analysis" as a tool and do not make it a burden. The use cases will then help you to drive the design of the architecture as well as to ensure that the architecture provides the necessary functionality. They will also help to test the architecture and to document it.

The next major issue is to ensure that you get the architecture right (even though the whole system may be the architecture, it is certainly a good place to start). Designing and developing an architecture helps you to create a coherent and consistent skeleton for your system. In this case we have a skinny system, and as such there may not be much meat on the bones, but that's fine. By developing the architecture it means that you will explicitly try to identify key classes, their roles and the associations they are involved in.

Another thing to consider explicitly is that you need to manage risk just as much (if not more) in a small project as in a larger project. This means that you should determine areas of risk up front and attack them first. This may involve prototyping where appropriate to test out technology and further assess risk. (Given the time-scales involved such prototypes may have to become part of the architecture, but if this happens you need to be careful to ensure that the prototype was developed in an appropriate manner!)

Finally, you should try to use Java interfaces as much as possible to make the architecture pluggable. Although at present the system is not expected to exist for very long, this situation may change, and you may need to enhance, maintain or further develop it in some way. Even if you don't, the architecture you have developed (or at least parts of it) may be reusable in other situations. Interfaces may well help to promote this.

Another important feature of large and small projects is that you should try to get tool support for your design and development. Examples of tools which might be appropriate include Rational Rose and Select as well as tools such as Togethersoft's Together/J. All of these allow you to develop UML-oriented designs and support code generation from such designs. These can make the process of working with the UML and the Unified Process much faster and much less obstructive.

The overriding issue for any project, however, is to manage risks – and this is possibly even more important for a short time-scale project, as you are going to be faced with the consequences of not managing risks much sooner and have less leeway to deal with it.

21.5 The Modified Unified Process

The result is a modified Unified Process in which those aspects that are inappropriate for a small development project are dropped but the core of the Unified Process is retained. This core is really what makes the Unified Process special and what provides the most benefit. The other aspects are required in larger projects to make the core work.

The core elements of the Unified Process are the use case analysis, its emphasis on an architecture and the explicit management of risk. Thus the core elements which are to be retained relate to these aspects of the Unified Process. There therefore need to be at least the requirements, design, implementation and test disciplines. However, these disciplines may well be modified in light of the nature of the project. Thus, for example, it may not be appropriate to prioritize the use cases in the requirements discipline as there may be so few use cases. Equally, as the size of the system is that much smaller, the architecture designed in the design discipline may reflect the entirety of the system; thus the design of the architecture equates to the design of the system, and there will therefore be less additional design required. It may also be that subsystems are not required etc. In turn, the implementation will focus on the architectural implementation, as that is the main emphasis of the whole system. Finally, the testing phases will contain the same activities but will be focused solely on the architecture. The resulting disciplines and activities are illustrated in Figure 21.1.

The products of this modified Unified Process will primarily be:

- use case analysis
- object model/class diagrams/packages
- dynamic model, including sequence diagrams
- test results

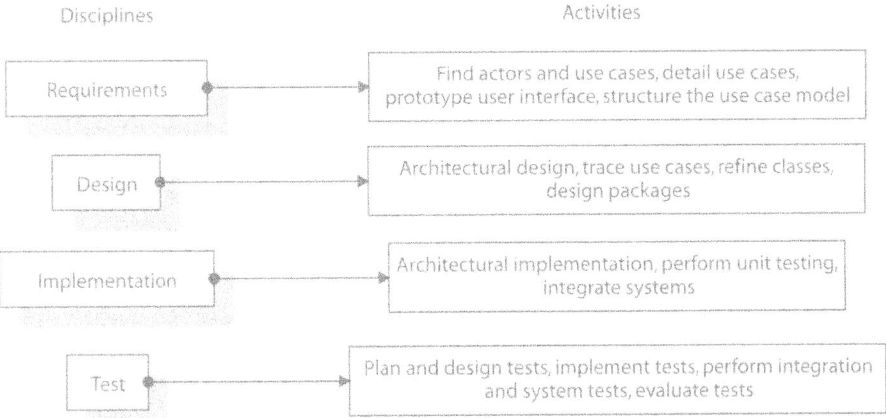

Figure 21.1 The modified activities.

Of course, one of the key factors of this version of the Unified Process is that there is no separate architectural phase; thus the disciplines do not have this element at the start, but instead this is the whole discipline. The result is that the way we might present the relationships between the various disciplines is as presented in Figure 21.2 rather than that presented earlier in this book.

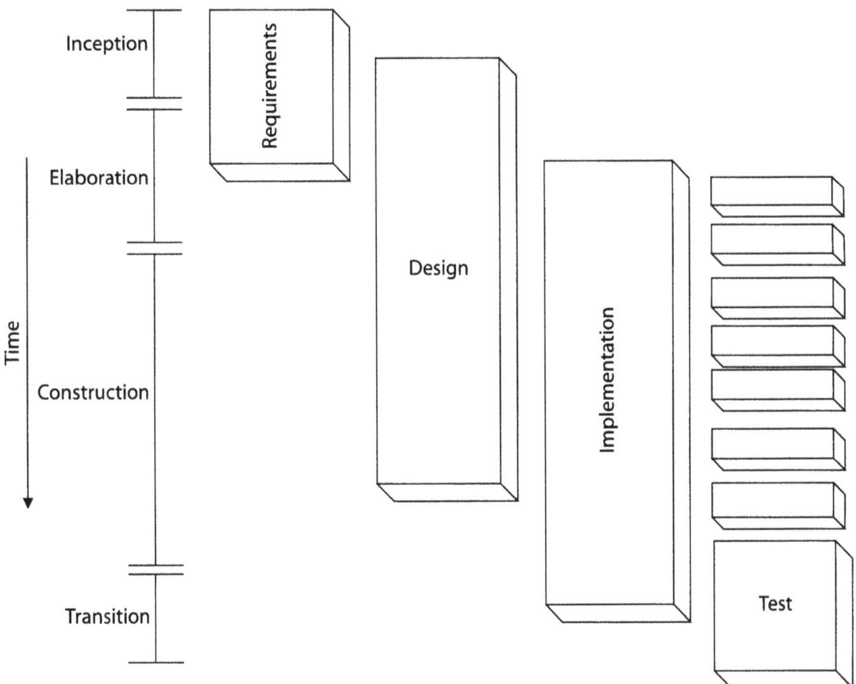

Figure 21.2 The modified Unified Process.

21.6 Summary

The Unified Process can be, and indeed should be, modified to suit your particular project. In this chapter we have highlighted a number of the issues that you should consider. These are a starting point – you should not blindly follow any particular formula. You therefore need to use your own judgement to decide how to apply the Unified Process. Once you have done this, you should not be inflexible. If it appears that some activity really is not providing any added value, then it may well be that it is not useful (however, you should not drop an activity merely because it is a lot of work – it could also be very valuable work!). In turn, if, as you are developing your design, you find that some previously dropped activity might well address current concerns or problems, than include this activity. No two projects are the same (not least because different people bring different skills and experience and the combinations involved in turn all affect the project), so there is no right or wrong answer. However, merely blindly following the Unified Process in its entirety just for the sake of it is also not the right answer!

21.7 Reference

Jacobson, I., Booch, G. and Rumbaugh, J. (1999). *The Unified Software Development Process*. Reading, MA: Addison-Wesley.

Augmenting the Unified Process with Additional Techniques

22.1 Introduction

The last chapter discussed how the Unified Process could be modified for *smaller* scale projects. This chapter will consider how the Unified Process can be augmented with additional techniques from the wide range of techniques now available within the object-oriented community. This is important, as the Unified Process is a framework rather than a complete methodology, and thus it is intended for such augmentation (and indeed such augmentation is necessary for many real world projects).

The remainder of this chapter is structured in the following manner. Section 22.2 will consider the role of the Unified Process as a framework. It will also assess the aim behind making it a framework rather than a single solution. Section 22.3 will highlight one of the weak areas of the Unified Process. Section 22.4 considers how the Unified Process can be augmenting with an additional technique to address this weakness. Section 22.5 then illustrates the Unified Process structure with the augmenting activity.

22.2 The Unified Process as a Framework

Let us first quote from Jacobson's (1999) book on the Unified Process:

> The Unified Process... is a generic process framework that can be specialized for a very large class of software systems, for different application areas, different types of organizations, different competence levels and different project sizes...

That is, the Unified Process is not intended to be complete. Indeed, it is intended as a generic framework which can be customized and augmented as required. In the last chapter we customized the Unified Process for smaller projects; in this chapter we are augmenting it.

355

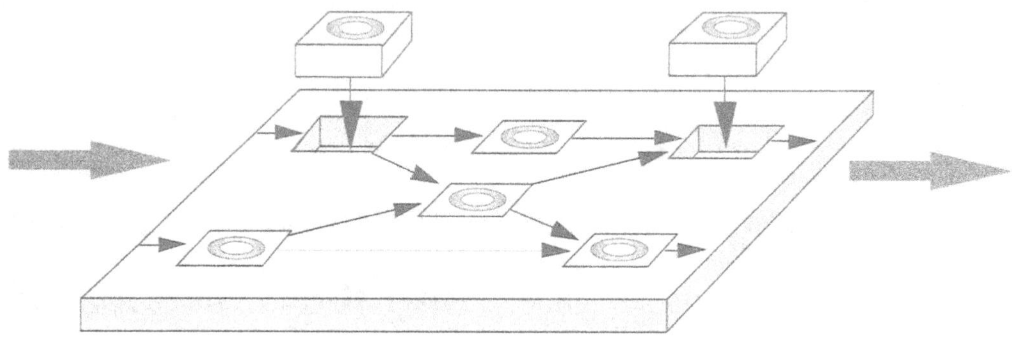

Figure 22.1 The Unified Process as a framework.

As Figure 22.1 illustrates, the intention is that it should be possible to use different techniques, either from those suggested in the core Unified Process or to exploit additional techniques as required. How information flows between these different activities is controlled by the Unified Process framework, but exactly what the activity is that either consumes or produces the various products within the Unified Process is left open.

The whole aim of this is that you choose the techniques you use as appropriate for your requirements (with regard to the current project development) and your background. If you have people in your team who are experienced with a particular technique it makes sense to exploit that experience rather than to try and force them to use a different technique, both of which have the same end result!

It is worthwhile considering the goals of the Unified Process and thus why a framework approach was adopted. These goals are presented below:

The Unified Process was designed for flexibility, extensibility and modifiability. It thus describes a series of disciplines (note the original name for a discipline – workflow – this implies that the Unified Process describes how information and products flow through the system and are produced, modified, changed and updated). These workflows/disciplines then produce artefacts that are the products passed between the disciplines (and within disciplines). To complete the picture, each workflow/discipline of course comprises a number of activities. It is actually these activities which produce the artefacts.

We can thus say that the Unified Process is engineered (Figure 22.2) in that it specifies who carries out the activities, what the products of the activities are (i.e. the artefacts) and how the artefacts pass between activities and disciplines. If you like, it describes a production line.

This means that it is possible to pull out an activity and/or plug in a new one. As long as the new activity can deal with the same input and produces the same artefact, then that activity is compatible with the Unified Process. That is, the Unified Process framework supports a plug-and-play approach to new or modified activities. Herein lies part of its power and its appeal: the designers of the Unified Process have not tried to prescribe a complete solution for every possible scenario. The intention is that you may need to modify it to match your specific requirements – requirements which the originally designers could not have predicted.

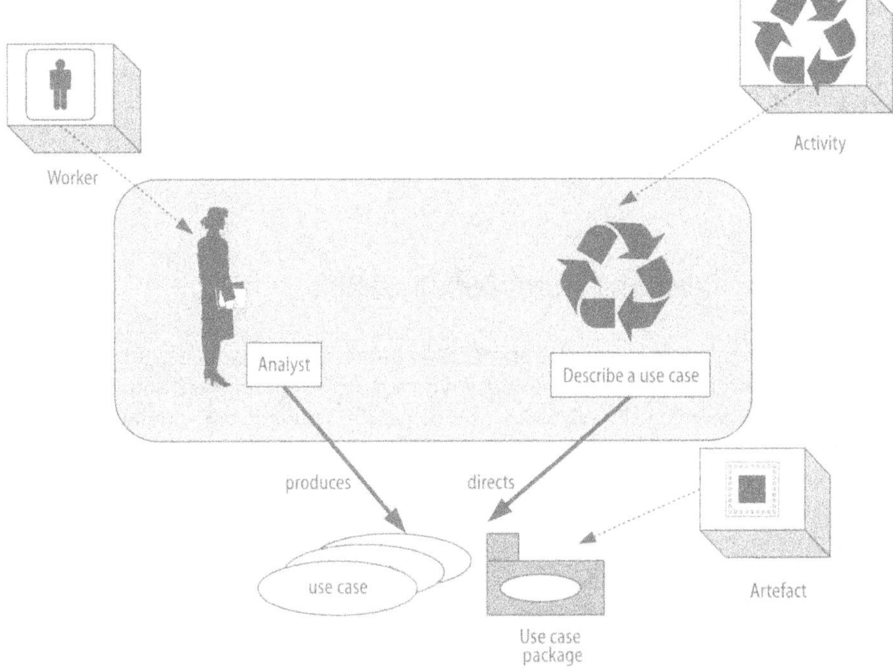

Figure 22.2 The engineered nature of the Unified Process.

22.3 Class Identification

To illustrate the idea of augmenting the Unified Process by plugging in a new activity, let us consider the process of identifying an initial candidate set of classes. This activity is of course crucial to any object-oriented system. However, this is a notoriously difficult task. The Unified Process does try to provide some support for it in both the analysis and design disciplines. However, the analysis discipline focuses on three stereotypical classes: the entity, control and boundary classes.

This simplifies the process of class identification for the analysis discipline, but can be both misleading and over-simplistic. It can be misleading, because these three classes tend to allow designers to produce very procedural analysis designs, with the boundary class representing the user interface, the entity class representing some long-lived data and the control class representing all the behaviour. This can be difficult to translate into the more object-oriented world of the design discipline. It is also simplistic, in that it leaves out a great deal of detail (which is of course the intention of the analysis discipline). However, this in itself can be misleading, as designers gain a false sense of security that they have the core classes identified.

Once they approach the design discipline, they are then encouraged to consider a much wider range of classes. The analysis classes may well be a starting place, but a great deal of detective work is still required (and of course the analysis discipline may not have been carried out if the project is small or time constraints do not permit it).

The problem then becomes one of where you look for classes, how you find them, and what the process is by which you can explore the possible set of candidate classes. The Unified Process really provides very little support for this. The class-finding activity could do with some help! Enter the CRC or class–responsibility–collaboration technique. This technique is presented in the next section.

22.4 CRC: Class–Responsibility–Collaboration

CRC, or the class–responsibility–collaboration technique, is an early technique from the field of object-oriented design. Originally it was put forward as a design method, and indeed forms the basis of the method described by Wirfs-Brock *et al.* (1990). This is an early method which is a very good method for teaching object orientation, but is not complete enough to base a real-world development on. However, it does provide an excellent example of how to use CRC, with plenty of illustrations and detailed discussion.

The reason for our interest in CRC is that it is an ideal method to be used as an exploratory class identification technique. It helps designers to explore the domain in which they are working and it encourages them to identify candidate classes, to determine their role in the system and to find those classes with which they need to collaborate in order to achieve their role.

Although the actual technique is not described within the Unified Process, the artefacts that it produces, i.e. the candidate classes, their roles, responsibilities and their collaborations, fit with the Unified Process. Thus CRC can be plugged into the Unified Process as illustrated in Figure 22.3.

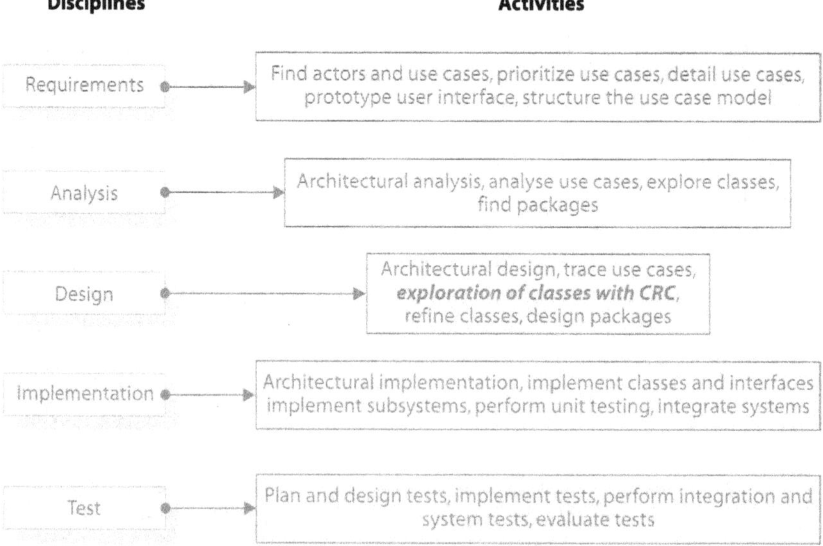

Figure 22.3 The augmented Unified Process.

22.5 What Is CRC?

It would be possible to leave the description of the CRC at this point. However, to illustrate how useful it is (particularly for those less experienced in object orientation) a description of CRC will now be provided. It is probably a good idea to include a process similar to this early on in the design (explicit or not), as it really is a very good way of exploring what classes are in your domain.

22.5.1 The Basic Idea

The basic idea behind CRC is that it helps to find candidate classes. Once you have a set of classes it is much easier to identify redundant ones, duplicates and missing classes, and generally to refine the classes you have. It's getting those first candidate classes which can be most difficult. CRC highlights where to start look for classes and how to represent and review these first tentative classes. Wirfs-Brock suggests that you document the classes you identify on cards (Figure 22.4; the sort of cards you get in the old-fashioned paper Rolodex devices). It is suggested that these are big enough for you to write some useful information on, but small enough that you can lay them out on a table and review where you are. You should use whatever medium suits you best: a large whiteboard can be just as useful as cards etc. You should use whatever works for you. Note that there are some shareware and freeware products available that provide electronic cards that you might like to try.

Class: Question	
Superclass: JDObject	
Subclasses: GraphicQuestions, TextQuestion, CodeQuestion	
Responsibilities: Hold question options Know the correct answer Maintain an explanation of the answer	**Collaborations** Answer Explanation

Figure 22.4 A Wirfs-Brock card.

The key steps in CRC are:

- Consider what classes there might be. This involves considering the elements in the domain as well as the way in which the domain is described.
- Identify responsibilities of classes including what questions to ask. Responsibilities may become attributes or operations later in other activities within the Unified Process, for the moment they are merely responsibilities on the class.
- Determine collaborations between classes. This begins the identification of the structure of the system.

The whole of the CRC fits well with the class-finding activities of the Unified Process. Indeed, much of what we have added already to the standard Unified Process in terms of additional guidance on finding, identifying and refining classes, attributes and operations can be traced back to CRC and Wirfs-Brock (among others). The various steps of the CRC are discussed briefly below.

22.5.2 Identifying Classes

This actually begins in CRC by trying to find objects, and from objects finding classes (groups of related objects). Wirfs-Brock provides a great deal of guidance on this, and although the primary assumption is that there is either a problem specification available or you have the ability to describe your application and its functionality, it is a useful starting point. Many of the questions it raises (which have been incorporated into earlier chapters of this book) are very useful and still relevant today. As you find classes, they can be documented with a brief description of their role, plus their name. As subclasses become known (and superclasses identified) this information can also be provided. Figure 22.4 illustrates these aspects of a class as well as the responsibilities and collaborations of a class.

22.5.3 Identifying Responsibilities

In CRC, once you have made a first pass at identifying the required objects/classes, you can determine what each object/class will do. If you have objects which may be instances of a particular class, this should become clearer as they will have similar (if not the same) responsibilities. The responsibilities are basically identified by asking two questions (Wirfs-Brock *et al.* elaborate on this, but we are keeping things simple here). These questions are:

- What does each object/class of objects have to know in order to accomplish its part in the overall goals of the system (for *goals* you can read *use cases*)?
- What steps towards accomplishing each goal (use case) is it responsible for?

Responsibilities are thus a way in which you can apportion the functionality of the system among the objects and classes of objects being identified. This means that if some aspect of this functionality is missing it must either be allocated as a responsibility to an existing class (or object) or a new class (or object) must be identified.

Note that these questions do not consider how the responsibility is to be implemented, only that the class must provide that functionality. The *how* will be part of later activities in the Unified Process. However, we will know *what* functionality will be required and *which* objects (or classes of object) will provide that functionality.

22.5.4 Determining Collaborations

In general, within an object-oriented system, an object which does not collaborate with any other object is going to be of very little use. Typically, the behaviour of the system is distributed among the various objects which comprise the system, and thus the overall operation of the system is achieved by the interactions (or collaborations) which occur between the objects. Thus collaboration between objects is vital to any object-oriented system. CRC makes this explicit, and one of the basic elements of the whole technique. Once your candidate classes are being identified and their responsibilities determined, it will be necessary to find the interactions between the objects. Thus for any particular object it is necessary either to identify those classes which require its services or those classes which provide a service it requires.

22.6 Summary

Additional techniques can, and indeed should, be used within the Unified Process. The Unified Process is not perfect for all applications of all sizes for all project teams (and indeed it was never intended to be). In fact, the Unified Process is not even complete (and again it was never intended to be). As gaps in what it provides (for you) are identified then it is possible to identify additional appropriate techniques and to plug them into the Unified Process, as we have done in this chapter.

22.7 References

Jacobson, I., Booch, G. and Rumbaugh, J. (1999). *The Unified Software Development Process*. Addison-Wesley, Reading, MA.
Wirfs-Brock, R., Wilkerson, B. and Wiener, W. (1990). *Designing Object-Oriented Software*. Prentice Hall, Englewood Cliffs, NJ.

23

Inheritance Considered Harmful!

23.1 Introduction

The full title of this chapter is really *Inheritance Considered Harmful: When to Use Inheritance and When to Use Composition.* This indicates that really this chapter takes the view that there are times when inheritance is useful, but equally there are times when component-based reuse is better. It is important to acknowledge this, as many (older) books on object orientation assume that inheritance is the only way for reuse to be achieved within a design or implementation.

It is not uncommon to hear the cry that "we used an object-oriented programming approach and still had problems". Such problems are, of course, due to a variety of mistakes made by project leaders, designers and developers. In some cases they can be attributed to lack of training, lack of experience or poor methods. However, one major claimed benefit of object orientation often fails to materialize even when appropriate training has been provided and suitable design methods applied: reuse.

Another cry that can be heard is that "all object orientation provides is a more suitable framework for software development". This may well be true, but inheritance is supposed to allow increased levels of reuse, providing improved quality and speed of development. However, many project managers will state that they have achieved very low levels of reuse through inheritance. Why is this? In turn, many non-object-oriented languages (such as Ada83 and Modula 2) place a great deal of emphasis on compositional reuse.

The lack of reference to compositional reuse (Rumbaugh *et al.*, 1991; Hunt, 1997) is possibly indicative of the emphasis placed on inheritance within the object-oriented community rather than the potential contribution of the two approaches. One exception to this is Szyperski (1998), whose book focuses on component-based reuse but who devotes a whole chapter to the issue of inheritance and how to provide a disciplined approach to inheritance.

This chapter explores what impact inheritance actually has on issues such as code reuse in practice rather than in theory. This is based partly on the extensive experience of the author in developing object-oriented systems. Given this exploration, an analysis is performed of why inheritance can, in some situations, be detrimental to reuse. From this, guidance can be

363

provided to ensure that developers are able to maximize the benefits of inheritance while minimizing the drawbacks that can occur.

The remainder of this chapter is structured in the following manner. Section 23.2 considers what inheritance is and what the aims and benefits of inheritance are. Section 23.3 considers some of the potential drawbacks of inheritance if care is not taken with its application. Section 23.4 considers the balancing act that must be performed between inheritance, reuse and code dependency. Section 23.5 discusses compositional reuse (as opposed to reuse via inheritance) and how that is performed. It also considers its strengths and weaknesses. Section 23.6 considers approaches to promoting reuse within object-oriented systems. It does this by indicating that developers should try to minimize code dependency where appropriate by using compositional reuse, but should not try to duplicate code unnecessarily and should use inheritance instead. Section 23.7 suggests that sophisticated tool support is required to maximize the use of inheritance and components in object-oriented systems.

23.2 Inheritance

23.2.1 What Is Inheritance?

The *Dictionary of Object Technology* (Firesmith and Eykholt, 1995) defines inheritance as:

> The definition of a derived class in terms of one or more base classes

That is, by using inheritance it is possible to define one class as being like another class but with certain differences (e.g. extensions). For example, objects may have similar (but not identical) properties. One way of managing (classifying) such properties, is to have a hierarchy of classes. A class inherits from its immediate parent class(es) and from classes above the parent. The inheritance mechanism permits common characteristics of an object to be defined once but used in many places. Any change is thus localized.

If we define a concept *animal* and a concept *dog*, we do not have to specify all the things that a dog has in common with other animals. Instead, we inherit them by saying that dog is a **subclass** of animal. This feature is unique to object-oriented languages; it promotes (and it is claimed achieves) huge amounts of reuse. As Coleman *et al.* (1994) state, it is "...widely viewed as the fundamental technique supporting reuse". This is backed up by Cox (1986), who says that "few programmers realize just how natural it can be to program using inheritance". However, there is very little concrete evidence to support this, and what evidence there is appears to be anecdotal.

However, in contrast Cox (1986) has also stated that "Inheritance is not a necessary feature of an object-oriented language, but it is certainly an extremely desirable one". This is an interesting statement, as inheritance is often taken as the defining characteristic of object-oriented systems. If we consider the four elements often presented as comprising object-oriented languages (namely encapsulation, polymorphism, abstraction and inheritance), various procedural programming languages can be seen to provide them all except inheritance. It is the unique element of object-oriented systems. It could be argued that without inheritance a programming language is at best object-based (e.g. Ada83) and not object-oriented.

23.2.2 Aims and Benefits of Inheritance

Inheritance in object-oriented programming languages supports reuse of existing code within new applications. It does this by allowing a developer to define new code in terms of existing code and new extensions. This is a different kind of code reuse from that found in non-object-oriented languages. For example, in Ada83 a programmer can reuse the TextIO package for input and output, but cannot extend any elements of the TextIO package directly in order to provide a new type of input–output operator. In contrast, the Java IO package provides a variety of classes designed for input and output (such as FileReader, FileWriter, InputStream and OutputStream). If a developer wishes to create an InputStream which only reads numbers then a new subclass of InputStream can be created with the appropriate read() methods defined. The remainder of the InputStream class's code would then be reused (without the need to copy any source code).

One significant benefit of this is the increased productivity such reuse can provide. A developer need only define the ways in which a new class differs from an existing class to have a fully functioning class. In addition, if a bug is found in the code inherited from the parent class, then it need only be corrected in the parent class. All of the parent class's subclasses receive the corrected version of the code automatically. This therefore reduces the maintenance effort required.

In Java inheritance also provides for the implementation of, and typing for, polymorphism. This is a significant aspect of any object-oriented language. Polymorphism is a powerful concept that can greatly enhance the productivity of a developer by increasing the reusability of the code produced.

It can also be argued that inheritance can improve the reliability of code. This is because code that has been implemented and tested in a superclass has a greater chance of remaining valid in its subclasses than code that has effectively been cut and pasted from one source file to another.

In languages such as Java, inheritance also allows for "enrichment of type". That is, given the type Component a developer can subclass Component and provide classes that are still of type Component but which provide additional functionality. Indeed, this is the way in which user interfaces are developed within Java relying on the fact that the add() methods expect a type of graphic Component to be provided. In some cases a component such as a Button may be presented, while in others a whole Panel might be provided.

It is important to note that this form of reuse is internal to the encapsulation wall normally present around an object[1]. This means that a subclass has access to the internals of a parent class in a way that objects are never allowed. This ability to break the encapsulation "bubble" can be useful, as it provides for more flexible reuse than would otherwise be

---

1 In Java it is possible to introduce encapsulation to inheritance. For example, any variable or method, whether static or not, can be specified as private. This means that not only can no object outside the class access these variables or methods, but also that access to these variables and methods is denied to subclasses.

possible. For example, in a component-oriented reuse model, a developer only gets access to the whole component, while via inheritance the developer can pick and choose which parts of the parent class are reused and which parts are rewritten.

23.2.3 The Role of Inheritance

The role of a subclass is presented in Hunt (1997) as being to modify the behaviour of its parents. In particular, this modification should refine the class in one or more of the following ways:

- *Changes to the external protocol*, the set of messages to which the instances of the class respond.
- *Changes in the implementation of the methods*, the way in which the calls are handled.
- *Additional behaviour* that references inherited behaviour.

If a subclass does not provide one or more of the above then it is not an appropriate subclass of the parent class. The exceptions to these rules are the subclasses of the class Object. This is because Object is the root class of all classes in Java. As you must create a new class by subclassing it from an existing class, you can subclass from Object when there is no other appropriate class.

23.3 Drawbacks of Inheritance

Inheritance is not without its own set of drawbacks. If inheritance is applied without due consideration problems can arise. In some situations it can:

- reduce the comprehensibility of code
- make maintenance harder
- make further development harder
- reduce reliability of code
- reduce overall reuse!

In addition, if access modifiers, such as those in Java, can affect the visibility of data and methods in subclasses, then they can affect the potential for reuse.

It is useful to consider what can cause these drawbacks. There are in fact a number of factors that come into play. In the following subsections we will consider each of the issues raised above and what factors contribute to their existence.

23.3.1 Reduces Comprehensibility of Code

The Yo-Yo Problem

Inheritance can pose a problem for a programmer trying to follow the execution of a system by tracing methods and method execution. This problem is known as the *yo-yo* problem (see Figure 23.1) because, every time the system encounters a message which is sent to "this" (the current

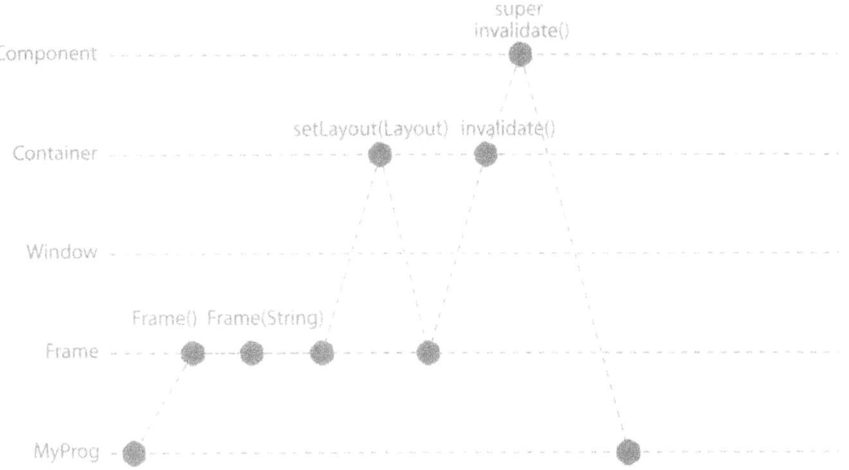

Figure 23.1 The yo-yo problem.

object), it must start searching from the current class. This may result in a developer jumping up and down the class hierarchy while trying to trace the system's execution path.

The problem occurs because the developer knows that the execution search starts in the current instance's class, even if the method that sends the message is defined in a superclass of the current class. For example, consider the very simple Java program in Listing 23.1. This program does nothing more than create an instance of a frame (it does not even make it visible). However, if a developer wished to trace the methods which are executed then the steps illustrated in Figure 23.1 would have to be followed.

Listing 23.1 `MyCLass.java`

```java
public class MyClass {
  public static void main(String args []) {
    new Frame();
  }
}
```

In Figure 23.1, the programmer starts the search for the Frame constructor in Frame, but finds that the constructor calls another constructor Frame(String). The programmer must therefore look in this second constructor (again in the class Frame). This second constructor calls the setLayout(Layout) method. To find the definition for this method, the programmer must first look in the class Frame; however, this class does not define this method. The programmer must then look for the superclass of Frame (which is Window). However, Window also does not define setLayout(Layout). The search must therefore move to the parent of Window (which is the class Container). Here in this class a definition for setLayout(Layout) is found. However, this method calls invalidate on "this", which means that the programmer must restart the search in Frame. The method definition is again (eventually) found in the class `Container`. However, this method calls `super.invalidate()`. It therefore necessary to continue searching back up the class hierarchy to find the inherited version of `invalidate` (in this case defined in the class `Component`, although the search could have gone back to the class `Object` – the root class of all classes in Java). Even with the browsing tools provided in some environments, this can still be a tedious and confusing process (particularly for those new to object orientation).

Code Dependency

Inheritance can potentially increase the dependencies between the code in the parent class and the code in all subclasses. For example, consider the Undo framework in Swing. This comprises of a central `UndoManager` and a number of `UndoableEdit`s that represent each edit that can be undone (or redone). The idea is that you subclass `AbstractUndoableEdit` to create suitable edits for your application.

From the point of view of inheritance, the problem is that the `UndoManager` has two methods, `canUndo()` and `canRedo()`, which determine whether there are edits available to undo or redo respectively. The `canUndo()` method works correctly on its own. The `canRedo()` method, however, when used on its own, only allows a single redo, after which it declares that there are no more "redos" available on the stack (even when there are). However, if an application ignores `canRedo()` and tries to redo regardless then it is successful.

The problem here is that there is a (subtle) dependency between the methods called by subclasses of `AbstractUndoableEdit` and the `canUndo()` and `canRedo()` methods in the parent class. Such subclasses are required to call the superclass's `undo()` and `redo()` methods. This is not obvious. The one-line Javadoc description of `undo()` and `redo()` does not mention this (only the full text does). This problem is compounded, as a developer would expect `undo()` and `redo()` to do nothing in an abstract class.

This means that in order to evaluate a potential change to some class X it is necessary to consider the impact of this change on multiple subclasses. If care is not taken then it can be a simple matter to damage the operation of apparently unrelated parts of the system while fixing an apparently simple "bug" in another part of the system.

This situation is exacerbated as it may also be necessary to understand the implementation of the superclass when implementing a subclass. This can be because the implementation of the superclass:

- assumes a particular behaviour from one method or combination of methods
- assumes that subclasses will provide a specific behaviour in one or more methods
- relies on the state of one or more variables which become critical to the operation of the class
- contains an overly complex structure in order to allow for inheritance

The emergence of an overly complex structure can arise when a developer has tried to force the potential for reuse among a set of classes. This commonly occurs when a developer has implemented a number of classes, has then noticed that they have some common features and has tried to create a suitable parent class to represent the commonalities. In these situations the developer is familiar with the structure of the subclasses and can design around them. A parent class can therefore be developed that is flexible enough to allow each subclass to provide the specialization required. However, for any other developer examining this parent class at a later date, it may be far from obvious what the purpose of the class is or why the class is structured in the way that it is.

The result is that in order to extend the parent class the developer must gain a detailed understanding of the structure of any subclass (this may be because instance variables are referenced, internal methods executed or internal states relied upon).

From analyzing many class hierarchies in which this has occurred, it is possible to identify the programming cliches which most often given rise to inappropriate dependencies between subclasses and parent classes. These can be described as:

- Subclasses which override methods used by other inherited methods (which are thus reliant on the behaviour and results of the overridden methods).
- Extension of inherited methods using super. In this way other inherited methods rely on the extended method. In addition, the subclass must ensure that its use of the super method as well as its extensions are appropriate.
- Subclassed behaviour relies on or changes the state of key instance variables.

23.3.2 Makes Maintenance Harder

One of the aims presented above for inheritance was the minimization of the maintenance task. However, in reality, if care is not taken, inheritance can make the maintenance task harder. This is due to a number of contributory factors. Firstly, it may be necessary to examine two or more classes (in the class hierarchy) in order to determine the behaviour of a single class (for example to understand how text is manipulated in the TextArea class in Java, a developer must examine both the TextArea and (its superclass) the TextComponent classes). This situation is made worse by the need to examine multiple classes for any objects passed to, or created by, the class under consideration. This is because this issue applies to each of these objects. In part this is because subclasses can break the encapsulation "bubble". It is therefore not sufficient merely to consider the published protocol of a class as being what it provides to another class. Within the encapsulation bubble the subclass may have made any number of changes. This problem is also referred to as the "semantic fragile base class problem" Szyperski (1998).

The maintenance issue is also affected by the yo-yo problem and the code dependency issue already discussed. Thus the maintenance issues can be summarized as:

- The need to analyze two or more classes to determine the behaviour of an object.
- The need to understand the implementation of descendant classes before maintenance of a superclass.
- The need to analyze any superclass(es) before modification of a subclass.

23.3.3 Makes Further Development Harder

In many situations it is necessary to understand how a parent class was intended to be extended before it is possible to define a subclass (for example, the controller class in the Smalltalk model–view–controller framework). However, as the implementation of one class is now reliant on

an understanding of the implementation of a parent class the resultant code may be opaque, leading
to inherent maintenance and possible reliability problems. In addition, methods which may be available
to the subclass may reference variables which are hidden from that subclass (for example private
instance variables in Java). If a subclass attempts to define an instance variable with the same name as
the hidden variable, the behaviour of the resulting subclass may be erroneous.

For example, consider the two classes presented in Listing 23.2. The Parent class is the
superclass. This class defines two public methods setName(String) and getName() which
are used to access the private instance variable name (note that the method
setName(String) also prints the value of the instance variable name to the standard
output). The subclass, Child, defines its own instance variable name (which is public).
Finally, the Child class defines a constructor which takes a string and uses the inherited
method setName(String) to set the instance variable name. The Test class defines the
main method from which an application can be executed. This method creates a new
instance of the Test class using the string "Phoebe". It then prints out the value of the
inherited (public) instance variable name.

Listing 23.2 The Parent and Child classes

```
public class Parent {            public class Child extends       public class Test extends
  private String name;             Parent {                          Child {
  public void setName(String       public String name;             public Test(String s) {
      aname) {                     public Child(String s) {            super(s);
    name = aname;                    setName(s);                    }
    System.out.println(name);     }                                public static void main(
  }                              }                                     String args []) {
  public String getName() {                                        Test t = new
    return name;                                                       Test("Phoebe");
  }                                                                 System.out.println(t.name);
}                                                                   }
                                                                  }
```

The result of executing the Test application is that the two values are printed to the standard output (the string "Phoebe" and the value null):

```
c:> java Test
Phoebe
null
```

Thus the method setName(String) prints the value of the instance variable name as Phoebe, but
the method main prints it as the value null – why is this? It is because the methods
setName(String) and getName() execute within the scope of the Parent class, which has a private
instance variable name, while the method main executes within the scope of the class Test.
The class Child has defined its own public instance variable name, which is inherited by the class
Test. The two instance variables name are not the same. However, it is not difficult to introduce
exactly this situation into an actual program. The problem here is that a developer may be unaware
that an intermediate class has introduced a new public instance variable which was not the
variable referenced by setName(String) and getName() (this is easily done if a developer does
not read all the documentation for every class in the hierarchy very carefully – but who does!).

Therefore the same object may possess code accessing variables with the same name but apparently different values (because they are in fact different variables). This can have a detrimental effect on comprehensibility, maintenance, reliability etc.

23.3.4 Reduces Reliability of Code

Identifying appropriate tests for a subclass can be problematic. However, for a long time there was a feeling that object-oriented systems required less testing than systems constructed with traditional procedural languages (for example see Rumbaugh *et al.* (1991)). This was because there was the impression that if a superclass has been thoroughly tested then anything inherited from that superclass by a subclass did not need testing. However, this is misleading because in defining a new subclass a user has changed the context within which the inherited methods will execute. For example, inherited methods may call a method that has been overridden. This means that the correct operation of the inherited methods can no longer be assumed. This is illustrated in the (contrived) example in Listing 23.3.

Listing 23.3 The First and Second classes

```
public class First {                      public class Second extends First {
  protected boolean flag = true;            public boolean isFlagSet() {
  public boolean isFlagSet() {                return !flag;
    return flag;                            }
  }                                         public static void main (
  public void printResult() {                 String args []) {
  if (isFlagSet())                            Second s = new Second();
    System.out.println("Result");             s.printResult();
  }                                         }
}                                         }
```

The class First defines an instance variable flag. This instance variable is set to true. The method printResult() uses the result returned by isFlagSet() to determine whether to print out the string "Result" or not. In the class First the result will be printed. However, the class Second inherits from the class First but overrides the isFlagSet() method. It does this by redefining the result returned as being the negation of the value of flag. Thus when the inherited method printResult() is called it executes the new definition of isFlagSet(), resulting in no string being printed.

Even if the inherited methods do not reference any methods defined in the subclass, the subclass may modify a variable inherited from the superclass. The inherited methods may then be found to be dependent on the state of this variable. Again their correct operation cannot be assumed.

The problem is that each existing class's features may not require any re-testing (in the subclass) and may very well function acceptably, but a developer is relying on a continuing hypothesis. Of course this hypothesis may have held many times before, but there is no guarantee that it will hold in the future. Interestingly, the same problem also occurs with Ada generics. In this case each instantiation of the generic package may work as intended, but equally they may fail.

In the worst possible case the whole of the subclass (the inherited methods and those defined in the subclass) needs to be tested. However, in most systems this would not be acceptable, as the full set of methods may run into the hundreds (and the developer may not have the knowledge or experience to be able to identify an appropriate set of tests for all methods). In practice only a small percentage of the inherited methods actually need to be tested. The provision of regression tests with a class can be used to simplify the task of testing these methods. Of course the identification of the appropriate methods is still fraught with difficulty. For a discussion of the effects of inheritance on object-oriented testing see Perry and Kaiser (1990).

23.3.5 May Reduce Reuse

Due to reduced comprehensibility and increased code dependency, resulting in increased difficulty of maintenance, developers may be led away from reusing existing classes. This can result in developers:

- reimplementing the wheel
- cutting and pasting required code
- failing to analyze superclass(es) sufficiently

This is a particularly important problem facing inheritance, as it negates one of the prime motivations for having inheritance in the first place.

23.3.6 The Semantically Fragile Base Class Problem

In some languages (such as C++) when a base (or root) class is modified it is necessary to recompile (dependent) clients and any subclasses. If this is not done then code that previously executed without any problems may now generate runtime errors. This compatibility problem relates to binary compatibility between super- and subclasses. The problem is that some languages assume that a subclass does not need to be recompiled just because a parent class has been recompiled (if the changes are purely syntactic); that is, new methods have been added or methods have moved up or down the hierarchy above a subclass. This issue is addressed by IBM's System Object Model (SOM) architecture (IBM, 1994). Interestingly, Szyperski (1998) points out that although SOM claims to deal with the "fragile base class problem", it only really deals with the syntactic "fragile base class problem" and does not address the semantic "fragile base class problem".

23.3.7 Access Modifier Effects on Reuse

Java provides the developer with the ability to finely specify what is available outside a class and to whom it is available. Thus a developer can hide almost everything within the encapsulation bubble (something must be available to other classes, otherwise the class is useless) or make everything available. In-between, the developer can specify at the level of variables or methods how much access is allowed. Table 23.1 indicates the access modifiers available in Java.

As this table shows, attempting to control the access that other objects have to an object's methods or data can also affect the access that subclasses can have to the parent's methods or data. For example, if a developer specifies an instance variable as being private, then subclasses of that class cannot access that instance variable either. Indeed, deciding to use

Table 23.1 Access modifiers and their effects in Java.

Class	public	Available in all packages
	default	Available only in the current package
	final	Cannot subclass this class
Variables and methods	public	Available in all packages
	default	Visible only in current package
	protected	Visible in current package and in subclasses in other packages
	private	Visible only in current class
Variables	final	Once set the value cannot be changed
Methods	final	Cannot be overridden in subclasses

the default access modifier for methods and variables has the subtle effect of allowing subclasses in the same package access but not subclasses in another package. Having such a fine level of control can be a two-edged sword. If it is used appropriately, parent classes can make sure that subclasses only have access to the appropriate aspects of the parent class. However, as some books on Java recommend that any implementation that uses more than the public and private modifiers is either very good or very bad, some developers may be put off using the most appropriate access modifiers.

A further subtlety is that if any methods are defined as final they cannot be overridden. This may initially seem a very good thing, as a subclass cannot harm the inherited functionality (at least in theory – see later in this chapter). However, it is very difficult to envisage all the ways within which a class may be used. For example, if we wished to create a specialized version of the class Vector in order to improve the performance of the basic class (for example by removing the use of the synchronized keyword) we would need to be able to override a number of the default methods. However, these methods are specified as final. This means that it is not possible to subclass Vector sensibly. We must therefore define a completely different class and start from scratch. Not only does this result in a great deal of extra effort, it also means that our code will have to be written either for our own version of the Vector class or for the default version, but not for both (unless we rely on using parameters of type Object which are then cast to the appropriate class when we need to apply any operators).

We have therefore generated the following guidelines. These guidelines are intended to promote the greatest chance of reuse while maximizing the encapsulation of the executing objects.

1. Use protected as your default access modifier – this leaves the way open for future extension within subclasses without letting all and sundry have access to the class.
2. If you make an instance variable private, provide accessor methods that have protected access. This will allow subclasses to read and write the data without accessing the data item directly. This is actually a good technique to use in general, as it also buffers your code from changes to the way you are holding your data.
3. Only use private when a method really is private to the current class. That is, there is no possible situation in which you can possibly envisage anyone ever needing to access the method.
4. Never merely use the default access modifier. Not only does it mean that anything within the current package can access the current element, but no subclass can (a dubious state

of affairs). It also suggests that you haven't thought about what access requirements there are.

5. Think carefully before making a variable, method or class final. You never know when you might want to define a subclass that needs to override the method's definition. Instead, use Javadoc documentation to make it clear that you did not expect anyone to override this method – at least then they know what you were thinking and can ignore you if they wish. If you do make a variable, method or class final make sure that you know the reason why (i.e. in order to promote performance) and document it.

6. Use `final` to set critical variables so that subclasses can't change them. However, think carefully before you do this in order that you clearly understand why no subclass must ever change the variables value.

23.4 Balancing Inheritance and Reuse

The discussion in Section 23.3 can be seen as quite damning for inheritance. However, this is not the end of the story, as it is important to consider what conclusions can be drawn from the results of this discussion. There are at least four possible conclusions, summarized below:

- Inheritance *is* extremely useful (consider classes such as `Frame` and `Panel` in Java).
- Reuse *promises* higher levels of productivity, maintainability and reliability.
- Inappropriate reuse by extension (inheritance) can have detrimental effects on productivity, maintenance and reliability.
- Inheritance is not the only form of reuse.

Below we consider how classes are modified through inheritance, and the associated dangers. From this we propose the use of composition to promote reuse in some situations.

23.4.1 Categories of Extension

When inheritance is used, an existing class (the superclass) is extended to create a new class (the subclass). The way in which it is extended can be categorized as modifying the external protocol of the superclass or changes to the behaviour (implementation) of methods. These two categories are considered in more detail below.

Changes to the External Protocol

When a subclass adds new methods which are available outside the class, it changes the external protocol of the superclass. This happens in a number of different situations, considered below.

1. The subclass adds entirely new methods. This is generally a safe use of inheritance, except that the subclass should try to use the superclass's methods rather than access the instance variable directly – this gives the superclass control over how its state is changed.

2.	The subclass provides convenience wrappers for existing methods. For example, a subclass might provide a `setPoint(Point)` method that subclasses its superclass's `setPoint(int, int)` method. This use of inheritance is generally safe, except that it introduces a hidden dependency between the methods. The subclass itself might be extended and it would not be obvious which of the methods should be overridden to modify its behaviour. To minimize this problem, wrapper methods should be declared final.

3.	The subclass restricts methods provided by the superclass. This may include removing methods or changing method parameters to more restrictive types. Currently in Java there is no way to restrict the methods inherited from a class – if this is necessary to maintain the integrity of the subclass, reuse should be achieved through composition rather than inheritance. An alternative approach is to override the offending methods so that they throw an exception, but this can be confusing and makes the class harder to extend and use.

Changes in the Implementation of the Methods

If a subclass overrides a superclass's methods, then it modifies the behaviour of the superclass. Again there are a number of different situations within which this can happen, considered below.

1.	The subclass provides a service for the superclass by overriding a method (structural inheritance). Again, this is generally a safe use of inheritance, providing that the purpose of the method is well defined. Excessive complexity can be a problem here – if there are complex interactions between a set of methods to be overridden, or if there are a large number of these methods, it is better practice to "plug in" an external class that encapsulates the required behaviour.

2.	The subclass needs to perform additional actions when a method is called (functional inheritance). Used sparingly, this use of inheritance does not obscure the code too much. However, if too much code is added there is a danger that the original purpose of the method will be changed, which can make the class harder to understand. A better approach is for the superclass to allow listeners to be notified when a value changes or when an action is performed. This can lead to a clearer structure in the code.

3.	The subclass needs to replace the behaviour in a particular method (functional inheritance). Inheritance needs to be used cautiously here. By overriding the behaviour of a method, you are likely to be creating complex dependencies between methods that can lead to obscure code. A better approach is to support plug-in classes that encapsulate the required behaviour. As well as leading to clearer code, this may also make the code easier to test and more flexible.

23.4.2　Implications for Inheritance

From this is it clear that inheritance has an important part to play in the development of complex software systems. However, it is also clear that it needs to be used with greater caution than is often the case. In particular, object-oriented systems developers need to pay greater attention to the other primary form of reuse – compositional reuse. One way to distinguish between inheritance-based reuse and compositional reuse is that inheritance-based reuse is primarily developer-oriented reuse (*developer* here refers to those developing the functionality of the elements which might comprise a component) while compositional reuse is user-oriented reuse (that is, no further development of the component takes place). The next section discusses compositional reuse in more detail. In particular, it selects the JavaBeans component model as an example of a compositional approach.

23.5 Compositional Reuse

Compositional reuse relates to the "combination of independent components into larger units". These components can be combined in different ways as long as their interfaces are compatible (in a similar manner to a jigsaw puzzle). In general, no further development for the components themselves takes place. Instead, a user of a component is allowed to customize the behaviour of a component via predefined properties or methods. JavaBeans exemplifies this approach.

JavaBeans is an architecture for the definition and reuse of software components (Englander, 1997; Hunt and McManus, 1998). The goal of JavaBeans is to define a *software component model* for Java. Examples of beans might be spreadsheets, database interfaces, word processors, graphic components such as buttons, business graphs etc. It would then be possible to add such beans to your application without the need to refine the bean. It is intended that most beans should be reusable software components that can be manipulated visually in some sort of builder tool. Thus in the case of the word processor bean we might select it from a menu and drop it onto an application, positioning its visual representation (i.e. the text writing area) as required. The key issue here is that you should be able to use a bean without ever having to examine its implementation, subclass it, or otherwise modify its code. That is not to say that you cannot change it in some way. However, it is expected that the user of a bean does so via its published interface (by changing property values, sending it events or by directly calling methods).

23.5.1 Strengths of Compositional Reuse

Software components designed for compositional reuse have great potential. They can greatly improve a developer's productivity and the reliability of software. For example, in Java, Buttons, TextAreas and Labels are all beans. They can therefore be used within a Panel or a Frame without further development. In addition, a Panel or Frame is a component that works with a second object (a layout manager) to determine how components are displayed. Thus a graphical user interface can be developed without the need to subclass any existing classes. Instead, all that a developer must do is to write the code which will glue all these elements together. If a tool builder such as the BeanBox (DeSoto, 1997) is used, even this task can be simplified.

An important question to ask is how is this achieved? Why is it that compositional reuse can be so effective? Part of the answer to this is "low software dependency". That is, when a developer uses a software component the only dependency between the developer's code and the component is the component's interface. The developer cannot get inside the encapsulation bubble. There is therefore no dependency between the developer's code and the internals of the component (i.e. its structure or internal state). This is very significant. It means that as long as the interface to the component remains the same the user will experience no problems with the component even if its internals are completely altered.

23.5.2 Weaknesses of Compositional Reuse

If compositional reuse is so good, what is the point in having or using inheritance? Here lies the problem – compositional reuse allows the developer to use a component. However, it is a take it or leave it approach. That is, you get what you see and are not allowed to change the internals of the component. By contrast, inheritance allows for far greater flexibility (and of course it is this very flexibility which can be a problem). Without inheritance but with compositional reuse a developer would end up with a great deal of duplication of code in situations where they require similar (but slightly different) behaviour to that which already exists. Of course, by duplicating code they would be introducing "implicit" dependency between the duplicated code. That is, if a bug was found in one piece of code that had been duplicated, it would be necessary to find all the duplicated pieces of code and to correct that bug individually in each. Not only is this a tedious task, it is also prone to error. For example, one of the duplicates might be missed, or a mistake might be made in one of the duplicates, which introduces a completely different bug into that duplicate. Of course these were specifically the issues which originally led to the introduction of inheritance. It is therefore clear that what is required is a combination of both inheritance-oriented and compositional reuse. However, as was indicated in the introduction, compositional reuse is paid scant attention in much of the object-oriented community (although this may well be changing due to initiatives such as JavaBeans and ActiveX).

Another issue associated with compositional reuse is how to integrate a component into existing software. The JavaBeans model relies heavily on the delegation event model. This model delegates events to handlers which must respond to the events in the appropriate way. This is the common alternative to method calling in object composition architectures. However, in situations where straight method calling is used it is simpler to trace the execution of a system than in using the delegation event model. This is because the delegation event model obscures what is actually happening within software, as it is implicit in the way the software is configured and how the delegation mechanism works. The result is that event delegation is in general more flexible (and more powerful) than direct method calling, at the expense of producing opaque systems. Thus mechanisms such as event delegation should be used with care.

The next section considers the implications of the results of this and the last section.

23.6 Promoting Reuse in Object-Oriented Systems

There is a (natural) tension between code minimization and code dependency. Developers tend to want to minimize the amount of code being written and the dependency between elements of that code. The less code that has to be written the greater the productivity (at least theoretically). In turn, the lower the dependency the easier it will be to maintain, test and reuse. It is important to note that implicit dependency exists even when a "cut and paste" approach has been used to code reuse (and that such an approach certainly does not lead to code minimization).

From Section 23.5 it is clear that an approach based purely on compositional reuse is insufficient. Equally, it is clear that problems can arise with inheritance due to misuse. It is therefore proposed that the judicious use of composition and inheritance has the potential to provide the greatest benefit. That is, the strengths of the two approaches should be combined to minimize the weaknesses.

In order to achieve the above aim guidance needs to be provided on when to use which approach. Some very general guidelines are relatively easy to identify which embody the main philosophy:

- Use composition and inheritance to promote reuse. Do not focus on one approach while ignoring the other.
- Attempt to minimize dependency between subclass and superclass (don't access variables etc.). Use inheritance via a specified interface. That is, force more encapsulation during inheritance. For example, make key instance variables only accessible by accessor methods (i.e. by using the `private` modifier in Java).
- Use the following guidelines for creating a potential subclass:

  1. As well as considering the interface presented to a user of the class, consider the interface presented to a potential subclass. Kiczales and Lamping (1992) describe the interface between a superclass and a subclass as the *specialization interface*. Distinguishing between the client and specialization interfaces is important, as they are presenting different aspects of the same class to different entities for different purposes.

  2. Control access to the internals of the class by providing protected methods. Only make instance variables directly visible to a subclass if:

      (a) a subclass can change the value of the variable to anything without violating the integrity of the superclass.

      (b) there is no requirement that the superclass knows when the variable is changed.

  This is effectively "typing the specialization interface" (Szyperski, 1998), so that the legal modifications which can be made by a subclasses code are specified.

  3. When overloaded methods are simply wrappers around other methods, make them final so that a subclass can only override the method that does the work.

  4. Support listener classes that can be notified of significant events in the class.

  5. In complex classes, try to encapsulate sub-behaviours in external classes. This supports "plug-in" extensions (see also Stata and Guttag, 1995).

  6. Make clear what you expect a subclass to do. Depending upon the language this can be done in a number of ways. For example, in Java the `javadoc` comments can be used to automatically generate online documentation, and in Borland's Delphi (née Object Pascal) a developer can use the keyword `virtual` to indicate that a method can be overridden, while in turn a subclass must use the keyword `override` to indicate that it is aware it is overriding the parent method. This is in effect specifying the expected behavioural changes of the subclass.

- Use the following guidelines for subclassing (note these assume that the guidelines for a potential superclass have been followed for the superclass):

  1. If methods that are inherited from the superclass can violate the integrity of the subclass, use composition rather than inheritance.

2. When overriding methods, don't change their original purpose.

3. Remember that the subclass itself can be extended, and consider the interface that it presents to its potential subclasses (from both itself and its parent).

- Look for situations which are appropriate for "Design for *pluggable* extension" rather than "method" extension as exemplified by Frame and Panel in Java. The way in which they lay out the graphic components that they display is dependent on the behaviour of a layout manager. This is an object that is plugged into the frame or panel. It alters the way that they operate without the need to subclass.

- Attempt to provide structural classes in which the function can be provided by subclasses (or plug in objects) when creating a root superclass. Complete structural, but non-functional, classes are ideal for inheritance (e.g. Applet, Canvas and Object). These are classes that provide the entire infrastructure required for a specific type of behaviour. Users then specify their own extensions which fit into (but do not alter) that infrastructure. For example, the Applet class provides a powerful, and complex to implement, framework within which developers can implement their own functionality (e.g. the methods init(), start(), stop() and suspend()) without ever needing to know how that framework operates (or how to modify it). The Canvas class is similar: cf. the paint() method.

- Identify situations in which you can provide classes which implement a complete functional object. These complete functional classes are ideal for composition (e.g. Button, ObjectOutputStream). These are classes that require no extension in order to provide a fully functional object. For example, to obtain a labelled button in Java requires only the instantiation of the Button object with the appropriate string passed to its constructor as a parameter. In terms of JavaBeans these classes are beans.

- Provide structural classes with gaps for functional classes (e.g. the class Thread with Runnables in Java). This approach orients the design process around the creation of structural classes (which are intended for inheritance) that may be customized by functional classes (which are presented to them as objects with which they cooperate). This reduces dependency and is intended to increase reuse.

23.7 Tool Support

The guidelines presented in the previous section can be followed more easily given appropriate tool support. These tools need to be fully aware of the language syntax and semantics, and should provide support specifically to deal with the problems encountered when using class hierarchies. Some editors are available which do take into account some of the issues associated with inheritance (for example, the Full Browser used with some Smalltalk systems; Goldberg, 1984). However, many systems separate out the compositional aspect of development from the inheritance aspect. Indeed, many of them consider composition only for the graphical user interface and ignore its use for more general software development.

Integrated development environments need to go much further than at present in providing support for using class hierarchies. We are not aware of a system that simulates the effects of limited visibility to the developer, for example taking into account the use of private, protected, default or public views in Java. The lack of such support makes it difficult for the developer to see what interface is presented to a subclass, or to examine how a super-class is expected to be viewed.

In order to provide proper support for inheritance and composition, visualization tools should be included which enable the developer to trace paths of interaction within the class hierarchy. These tools should highlight name clashes and make it obvious to the developer when methods and instance variables are being overridden or hidden. As a simple example, suppose a developer intends to override a method called "finalize", but instead defines a completely new method called "finalize". A good tool should make this immediately apparent to the developer. Such tools would simplify the process of tracking method execution and variable access in object-oriented programs (Stasko *et al.*, 1998).

The tool support for object-oriented development must also deal with version and configuration management, especially when the language provides support for these concepts. In particular, the tool should not allow, or at least should warn the developer if an attempt is made, a system to be built using out-of-date components.

Modern object-oriented programming languages offer sophisticated facilities which can be very powerful. However, we have not yet seen an integrated development environment that enables developers to exploit this power fully and safely.

23.8 Conclusions

In this chapter we have considered the benefits and drawbacks of inheritance within an object-oriented programming language. We have challenged the general perception that inheritance is by its very nature always good and have considered when it should and should not be used. We have reassessed compositional reuse and made the case that it is as important, in an object-oriented language, as inheritance in order to achieve the maximum possible reuse. We can therefore provide a summary of our findings that can be used as a set of guiding principles for object-oriented development:

- Avoid code dependency except on published protocol.
- For structural inheritance direct extension is fine.
- For functional inheritance compositional extension is to be encouraged.
- Avoid inheritance if it is going to damage code cohesion.

Thus the final conclusion of this chapter is that inheritance can be harmful to a development project's long-term chances of success if inheritance is misused. However, in general it is essential for the power it provides to object-oriented systems.

23.9 References

Bitman, W.R. (1997). Balancing software composition and inheritance to improve reusability, cost and error rate. *Johns Hopkins APL Technical Digest*, 18(4), 485–500.

Coleman, D., Arnold, P., Bodoff, S., Dollin, C., Gilchrist, H., Hayes, F. and Jeremes, P. (1994) *Object-Oriented Development: The Fusion Method*. Prentice Hall, Englewood Cliffs, NJ.

Cox, B.J. (1986). *Object-Oriented Programming: An Evolutionary Approach*. Addison-Wesley, Reading, MA.

Cox, B.J. (1990). There *is* a silver bullet. *BYTE*, October, pp. 209–218.

DeSoto, A. (1997). *Using the Beans Development Kit 1.0: A Tutorial*, JavaSoft. `http://splash.javasoft.com/beans/`.

Englander, R. *Developing JavaBeans*. O'Reilly and Associates.

Firesmith, D.G. and Eykholt, E.M. (1995). *Dictionary of Object Technology*. SIGS Books.

Goldberg, A. (1984). *Smalltalk-80: The Interactive Programming Environment*. Addison-Wesley, Reading, MA.

Hunt, J.E. (1997). *Smalltalk and Object Orientation: An Introduction*. Springer-Verlag, London.

Hunt, J.E. and McManus, A. (1998). *Key Java: Tips and Techniques*. Springer-Verlag, London.

IBM (1994). *The System Object Model (SOM) and the Component Object Model (COM): a Comparison of Technologies From a Developer's Perspective*. White Paper, IBM Corporation, Object Technology Products Group, Austin, TX.

Kiczales, G. and Lamping, J. (1992). Issues in the design and specification of class libraries. *Proc. OOPSLA92, ACM SIGPLAN Notices*, 27(10), 435–451.

Perry, D.E. and Kaiser, G.E. (1990). Adequate testing and object-oriented programming. *Journal of Object-oriented Programming*, 2(5), 13–19.

Rumbaugh, J., Blaha, M., Permerlani, W., Eddi, F. and Lorensen, W. (1991). *Object-Oriented Modeling and Design*. Prentice Hall, Englewood Cliffs, NJ.

Ryant, I. (1997). Why inheritance means extra trouble. *Communications of the ACM*, 40(10), 118–119.

Stasko, J.T., Domingue, J.B., Brown, M.H. and Price, B.A. (eds.) (1998). *Software Visualization*. MIT Press, Cambridge, MA.

Stata, R. and Guttag, J. (1995). Modular reasoning in the presence of subclassing. *Proc. OOPSLA95, ACM SIGPLAN Notices*, 30(10), 200–214.

Szyperski, C. (1998). *Component Software: Beyond Object-Oriented Programming*. Addison-Wesley, Reading, MA/ACM Press, New York.

Incremental Software

24.1 The Incremental Software Development Process

In this book we have concerned ourselves with the Unified Process (Jacobson *et al.*, 1999), and we have also looked at how the Unified Process can be adapted for different situations. However, what we have yet to do is to discuss how to really manage the Unified Process or an instantiation of this such as the Rational Unified Process (sometimes known as RUP) (Kruchten, 2000) when it is the iterative and incremental aspects that are emphasized. Such a process is iterative and incremental and is adaptive because in many situations it is necessary to be responsive to changes in business or user requirements as well as to feedback from users.

The Unified Process, although a sound basis upon which to base the development process, is a framework which explicitly recommends modification where appropriate. One area in which we have found it beneficial to amend the Unified Process is to make it also feature-centric (Coad *et al.*, 1999; Carmichael and Swainston-Rainford, 2000; Carmichael and Haywood, 2002). Feature-centric means that each iteration centres on the identification and realization of system features. A feature is a schedulable requirement associated with the activity used to realize it. These requirements may be user-related requirements, application behaviour requirements or internal requirements. The features can then be grouped into work packages which can act as the basis of the planning required to monitor and manage the software development process.

In this chapter we first consider the incremental software development process as a whole and contrast it with the more traditional waterfall model. We then explain the need for a feature-centric approach in order to control the planning and management processes within an iterative approach (this is necessary, as such an approach can increase the complexity of the management process). Following this, we explain the benefit in defining a timebox for each iteration so that the duration of each is known (even if the content is not). The chapter is completed by a discussion on planning an iterative project and planning each iteration.

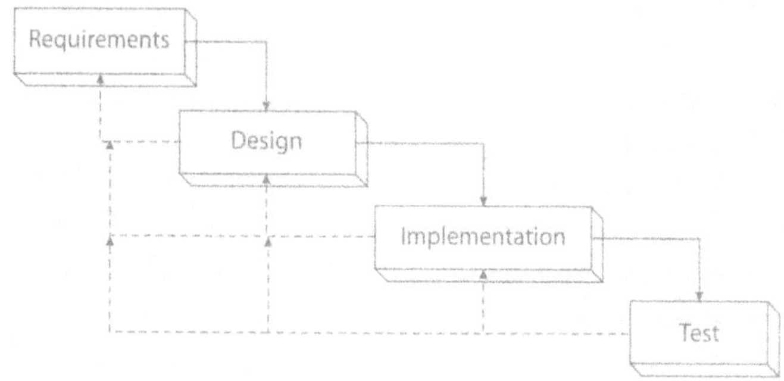

Figure 24.1 The waterfall model.

24.2 Incremental Software Development

24.2.1 Iterative Versus Waterfall

The Unified Process is iterative and incremental, as it does not try to complete the whole design task in one go. One of the features of the waterfall model of software engineering used by many design methods (see Figure 24.1) is that it primarily assumes that you will complete the requirements analysis before you start the design phase. In turn, you will complete the design phase before you start the implementation phase, and so on. It does accept that there may be some feedback of information from one phase to any preceding phases and that this feedback may impact upon the products of the preceding phases. However, this is a secondary issue and the assumption is that you will be able to complete the vast majority of one phase before ever considering the next phase. This may be true if this is the fifth or sixth system you have built in the same domain for the same type of application. It is unlikely to be the case with your first application in a new domain (such as your first e-commerce project!).

In contrast to the waterfall model, the Unified Process has an iterative and incremental model. That is, the design process is based on iterations that either address different aspects of the design process or move the design forward in some way (this is the incremental aspect of the model). This does not mean that the Unified Process is a process based on rapid prototyping. Any prototypes that are developed in the Unified Process are used to explore some aspect of the design. This could be to verify some architectural issue, design options or similar. Indeed, the use of an iterative and incremental approach in the Unified Process requires more planning (rather than less planning) as compared to approaches such as those based on the waterfall model.

24.2.2 A Spiral Development Process

Essentially the following holds with the iterative approach in the Unified Process:

- You plan a little.
- You specify, design and implement a little.

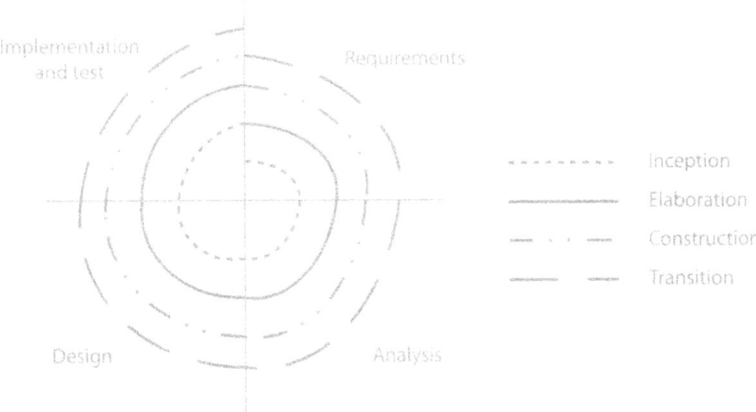

Figure 24.2 The spiral model of software development.

- You integrate, test and run.
- You obtain feedback before the next iteration.

This approach is illustrated in Figure 24.2. This figure depicts the spiral nature of this approach to software development. Note that in effect each iteration around the spiral is a mini-software development project.

The end result is that you incrementally produce the system being designed. While you do this you explicitly identify the risks to your design/system up front and deal with them early on. Note that this does not mean that you are hacking the system together; nor are you carrying out some form of rapid prototyping. However, it does mean that a great deal of planning is required, both up front and as the design develops.

24.2.3 Architecture-Centric

One problem with an iterative and incremental approach is that if no order or structure was defined for the application it would grow more and more unwieldy and more and more disorganized as each iteration progressed. To ensure that all the various parts fit together there needs to be something. That something is the architecture. The architecture is the skeleton on which the muscles (functionality) and skin (the user interface) of the system will be hung. A good architecture will be resilient to change and to the evolving design and implementation. The Unified Process explicitly acknowledges the need for this architecture by being architecture-centric. It describes how you identify what should be part of the architecture and how you go about designing and implementing the architecture. The remainder of the Unified Process then refers back to that architecture.

Obviously the generation of this architecture is both critical and difficult. Therefore the Unified Process prescribes the successive refinement of the executable architecture during each iteration, thereby attempting to ensure that the architecture remains relevant.

24.2.4 Getting Control

An important aspect to address at this point is the potential explosion in planning effort that may be required to deal with the iterative life cycle model that is being described here. It is certainly more complex than a linear waterfall life cycle to plan and manage. However, given that our goal is to simplify the life cycle in order that we can deal with the risks and complexities as well as uncertainties of the development process, we need to regain some control of the planning and management aspects of such a project. A key strategy for this is feature-centric planning. This is discussed in the next section. Feature-centricity is not the only aspect of regaining control of an iterative project; another is that of timeboxing each iteration. The final aspect is being adaptive.

Thus to regain control of an iterative project the guidelines are:

- The process should be *feature-centric*. This means that the units of requirements (e.g. use cases) should be unified with the units of planning (e.g. workpackages and tasks).
- Project planning should be based around *timeboxes* (rather than phases) so that the length of each iteration is known.
- The project plan should be *adaptive*; that is, responsive to the changing risks and benefits of the system and business environment.

Each of these concepts is discussed in the following sections.

24.3 Feature-Centric Development

The term "feature-centric" is used to refer to development processes that combine the expression of requirements with the units of activity for planning purposes. A feature in such a process can be viewed as a unit of "plannable functionality". Feature Driven Development (FDD) uses features in this way. Note that features are closely related to use cases and to the realization of use cases in the standard Unified Process.

A *feature* is a schedulable piece of functionality, something that delivers value to the user. Note the emphasis on schedulable. That is, a feature is derived from a planning perspective rather than from the user perspective or the requirements perspective. This is an important distinction and why features differ from requirements or use cases (even if they are derived from them).

To aid in planning, features go further. They must also be associated with:

- a priority (so that they can be ordered)
- a cost (so that they can be accounted for)
- resources (so that they can be scheduled)

Costs and resources can be determined by examining the number of person days taken to accomplish the feature. Priority can be harder to determine, but should take into account:

- the architectural importance of the feature
- the utility to the user

- the risk involved
- the requirements of the system/use cases

Consideration should given to each in determining the priority.

24.4 Timeboxing Iterations

The emphasis in most formal development processes is on the *phases* that a project goes through and then on the steps within the phases that may or may not be carried out iteratively. This is true of modern processes such as the standard Unified Process as much as of more traditional processes such as the waterfall process. However, with iterative processes, although the details of the current iteration may be known, details of the next or subsequent iterations are less clear. Indeed, as the aim of each iteration is to allow that iteration to be planned at the start of the iteration, the time taken for an iteration may only become clear at the start of the iteration. This is not very good for budget planning, for release planning or indeed for management of the project. It certainly has issues with fixed release dates.

There is therefore a conflict between the flexible and responsive nature of an iterative approach and the constraints of budgets and time-scales.

This is where timeboxing comes in. Rather than defining each iteration by the features it will implement, it is possible to define an iteration in terms of the time period it will take and the ordered list of features that will be attempted during the time period. Features that are lower down the priority list will only be attempted if time allows; otherwise they will be relegated to a later iteration.

Timeboxing iterations has a number of benefits, including the ability to:

- schedule and plan for incremental releases of the software
- schedule and implement features
- manage budgets
- monitor progress within fixed time constraints

all within a flexible and responsive process.

What this also means is that regular reviews (typically on a weekly basis) are required to consider how workpackages and tasks are progressing, which (if any) are behind schedule and why and how to consider the impact on the project both from a technical and a business point of view. This may then lead to modification of the workpackages and features to be included in the current iteration.

24.5 Being Adaptive but Managed

What is required is a management process that is flexible enough to deal with the changing requirements of the business and users and to deal with the emerging uncertainties. It also needs to be one in which we can still monitor progress, determine resources, ensure quality and guarantee delivery. Most traditional management styles set out what will be done when and for how long right at the start of a project and well before detailed design and implementation has begun. The project is then measured against these estimates, with little or no room for change. However, an iterative project explicitly acknowledges the need for change and the need for management.

To this end an iterative project is effectively planned and replanned at each stage of the spiral presented back in Figure 24.2. There is an overall planning activity before the whole process starts and then there are planning activities at the start of each iteration. In addition, regular (weekly) reviews may also affect the current plan for an iteration.

In terms of management monitoring of project activity, person days for tasks should be monitored (on a weekly basis) and fed into the project plan to determine how the project is progressing relative to the planned effort. However, due to issues such as holidays and sick leave it is also necessary to compare the current progress in elapsed time with the project plan.

In the rest of this section we consider the planning activities that take place initially at the start of a set of iterations (such as for "Civil Compliance and Cost Assessment Audits") and the plans for an actual iteration.

24.5.1 Planning an Iterative Project

Before any project embarks on an iteration development process there are a number of steps that should be followed. These steps are:

1. Identify and prioritize features (the feature list should be continually revised throughout the project).
2. Group into workpackages.
3. Allocate tasks to resources (that is, allocate tasks to project members).
4. Identify iterations and allocate features.
5. Timebox iterations/calculate costs.
6. Plan iterations (which should be continually revised during the lifetime of the project).

The key here is that iterations are based on "timeboxes" so that their length is known and can be managed. Iterations are also based on workpackages, constructed around features, so that they can be responsive to user feedback and to changing business requirements.

24.5.2 Planning an Iteration

Each iteration will comprise a similar set of steps. These steps are presented graphically in Figure 24.3.

The key steps in any iteration are:

1. Iteration initiation meeting. The length of the iteration should already have been determined, but may be revised at this point. The features to be addressed in this iteration should be revised and confirmed along with the resources to be applied etc. This meeting should involve all stakeholders in the project.

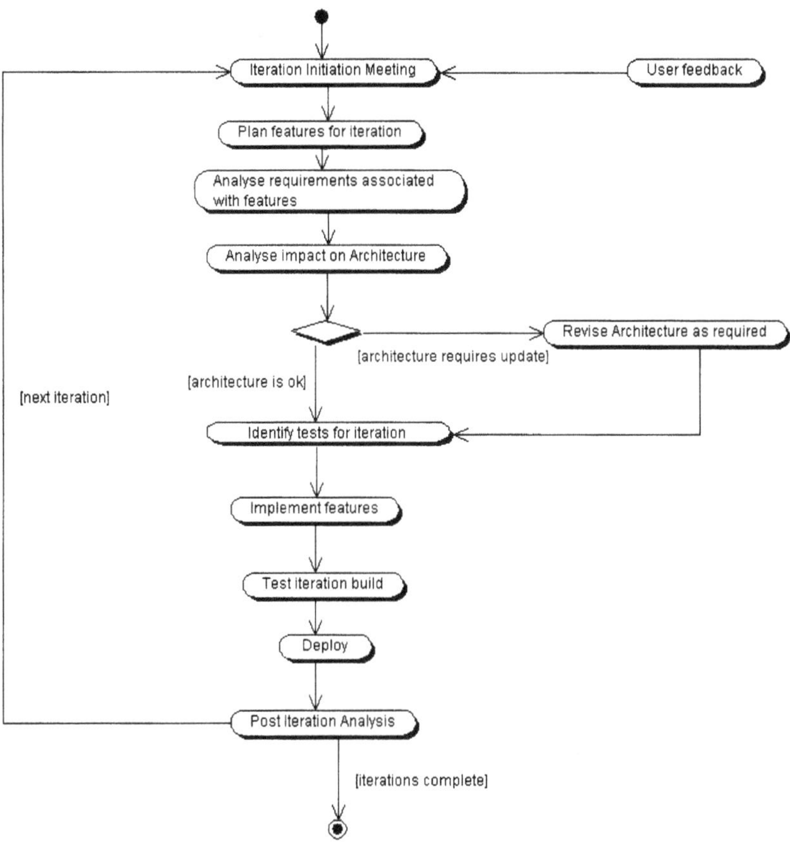

Figure 24.3 The steps within an iteration.

2. Plan features for iteration. Having agreed the features to be addressed, a detailed plan should be produced, mapping features to workpackages and workpackages to tasks. The tasks in turn should be allocated to actual resources etc. This plan must be accepted by the key stakeholders (including the clients).

3. Analyze the requirements associated with the features. This may involve writing a use case document, designing new GUI displays, determining the user interaction sequence etc. The acceptance criteria for this iteration should also be identified and agreed.

4. Analyze the impact on the architecture. The architecture is the backbone upon which the iterative process operates; therefore the next step to perform is to examine the impact that any new features are likely to have on the architecture. It may also involve identifying new architecturally significant entities that feed into the next step.

5. (Optionally) Revise architecture as required. This step involves revisiting and amending the application architecture in response to the features required by this implementation. Note that this may mean that some of the design and analysis work associated with core features may be performed at this stage to determine their architectural impact.

6.   Next, a new test plan and specification should be written for this iteration. Note that this document may not include all tests, as some features may only be implemented if time allows. The specification of the tests for these features should be considered to be a task within the workpackage that will address that feature.

7.   The next step involves implementing the features. The features are actually implemented via tasks that should be monitored as normal (although reference should be made to the timebox of the iteration).

8.   Once the features are implemented, the new system should be tested (this includes the generation of a test report).

9.   The new application should then be deployed to the client, who should perform any agreed system acceptance tests. This may lead to the revision of the deployed systems if and when deficiencies are identified. Following system testing the client may perform UAT testing, which may lead to further revision of the deployed application.

10.   A post-iteration meeting should review the progress made during the iteration and any issues that arose, and reprioritize any features that were not addressed. Again this should involve all project stakeholders.

11.   At this point a decision should also be made regarding the validity of the next iteration and whether any further iterations are required.

One outstanding issue for this iterative approach is what comprises the acceptance tests at the end of an iteration. This cannot be carved in stone up front, as the iteration may have changed once started (as features may have been moved due to changing business or user requirements). This is an area that requires careful management and understanding between the various stakeholders in the project. Typically it means that the "features" implemented must be tested and that the acceptance tests must be based on these features. However, as the features may change, the acceptance tests need to be flexible enough to take this into account.

24.6 Architecture-Centric

Feature Driven Development (FDD) or Feature-Centric Development (FCD) are only feasible (and successful) if there is a solid architecture on which each iteration can build.

24.6.1 Why Have an Architecture?

Let us review the argument being made about why an architecture is a critical element of the object-oriented design process. We need an architecture to:

- *Understand the system.* Software systems can be large and complex, and must meet conflicting requirements. An architecture provides a convenient blueprint or model of the system to be produced. It abstracts out much of the implementation detail, but "positions" the elements that must meet the various functional requirements.
- *Organize development.* It helps organize "plumbers" and "electricians". That is, it helps firstly to separate out different concerns, so that those involved in the "plumbing" of the sys-

tem only need to worry about plumbing issues. However, it also identifies how they are related, so that the points at which different concerns intersect are well documented and clearly specified (for example in the central heating boiler).

- *Promote reuse.* The problem with writing reusable code is that you need to identify that what you are producing is reusable. I have personally been in situations where two people on one project are reproducing the same solution but from different aspects. In at least one case they were sitting opposite each other. It is certainly easier to produce reusable code the second, third or even fourth time you are designing and implementing a system than the first. Indeed, in many systems, the only form of reuse that occurs is at the class level (i.e. at a very detailed level), and is identified by the coder during implementation. However, an architecture can help at a much higher level by identifying critical systems and subsystems early on. Common subsystems can then be made reusable.

- *Promote continued development.* Few systems of any size or consequence are produced and never altered. Instead, it is much more common for a system to evolve over time, with new requirements being identified and new functionality added or existing functionality modified. The original architecture can be essential in helping to control the evolution of the system over time (both within a single release and between releases of a system). Indeed, a good architecture need change little over the life cycle of a system, but can be instrumental to the success of future releases. This is because it provides the overall structure into which the new additions or modifications must be fitted. Often the actual design of the system is too detailed to allow an overview to be gained, and thus future designers and implementers may misinterpret part of a design or (worse) ignore it. The architecture can help to minimize such problems.

24.6.2 Plan Incremental Building of Software

Once you have put an architecture in place you are in a position to plan an incremental, feature-centric approach to further implementation and extension. The development of the architecture should have helped to identify the appropriate subsystems, active classes, interfaces etc. which can be used as the starting point for further iterations of a development process.

The approach advocated by the Unified Process is to build your system in iterations. Each iteration adds some of the functionality required by the system, but not all of it. The end result should be that all the required functionality is included. This is a very good approach, as you always have a version to fall back on and you can involve users at an early stage in the development process by giving them (limited functionality) alpha releases to explore. It also helps to detect any other defects or unidentified problem areas at intermediate stages rather than at the end of the project.

The key to doing this successfully is to ensure that each iteration represents a manageable build within the time-scales set, and that each build incorporates an appropriate subset of the functionality required by the system. This may need careful analysis of the use cases to identify appropriate functionality for each iteration.

This is not to say that an incremental and iterative approach to software development is either "hacking" or indeed "rapid prototyping". It is in fact a highly planned and coordinated approach to software engineering. It acknowledges and absorbs the risks inherent in all software development and particularly in "green field" first-time developments.

It should also be noted that the architecture does not try to be all-encompassing, incorporating hooks for all possible required features. Rather, it should represent the core features and provide all those hooks for architecturally significant features or those features that are mostly likely to be incorporated.

24.7 Performance Measurements and Reporting

One issue that may be of concern to many project managers at this point is "how do I manage such a project". Some may even say that it is not possible to manage such a project. In fact such a project can, and indeed must, be managed. My personal opinion is that such a project requires more rather than less planning and management, but that this is to the benefit of the project and is not therefore an onerous task. In the remainder of this chapter I summarize the basics of this approach to monitoring, managing and planning such a project – this is based on our actual experiences within JayDee Technology Ltd (a company that has used the UP and the approaches laid out in this chapter since early 2000).

24.7.1 Weekly Progress Meetings

The significant management team members (such as the Chief Technical Architect, the Project Manager and the Project Leader) should meet weekly with all current project team members to assess progress and discuss the activities performed in the previous week. The minutes of this meeting should include details of the work performed and the work to be carried out during the following week. The meeting will also compare the progress to the project plan and consider potential schedule slippage, adjust plans associated with later development in light of the current trend (note that an individual week's slippage may not be significant), and discuss any additional project issues.

24.7.2 Monthly Meetings

At the end of each month an end-of-month review meeting should take place with the client. Prior to this meeting the end of month report should have been produced. This report should contain the following elements:

- end of month (management) overview of progress
- a detailed description of the month's progress
- any impact on the plan and the modified plan
- the activities for the forthcoming month

It is at this meeting that any proposed revisions to the Project Plan should be made. These revisions will not be made final without the agreement of the client. Detailed discussions about how to deal with any significant slippage should occur.

After the monthly meeting, the end of month report should be sent to the client.

24.7.3 Progress Reporting

All team members must keep a timesheet (or similar) on which they note the amount of time they spend on each task per project (some project members may be involved in more than one task at any one time). Time spent in project-related meetings should be included on this timesheet. Note that both the reviewer's and reviewee's time should also be included, as each task includes time for both the reviewer and the preparation made by the reviewee.

In addition, project members should maintain a project diary (held electronically on the central server and not locally on their own machine). This should record how much time they spend and on what during the week. This diary could be as simple as a text document.

The information contained in these diaries should be provided at the weekly progress meeting.

For time and materials-based projects, at the end of each week the timesheets should be given to the Project Manager for inclusion in the project finances.

The information provided by the team members during the weekly progress meeting should be entered into the project progress document for each task.

The project progress document is an Excel spreadsheet that should show:

- the name of the task
- the number of days allocated to the task
- the person allocated to the task
- the estimate for each aspect of the task
- the actual time spent on that aspect so far
- the Estimated Time to Complete (ETC) for that aspect
- the variance for the task

This spreadsheet will be sent on a weekly basis to the client with the minutes of the weekly meeting.

24.7.4 Process for Managing Change

The clients will be able to provide feedback to the weekly communication from you in the form of the minutes of the weekly meeting and associated spreadsheets. They should reply as soon as possible after the receipt of this email to indicate either of the following:

- acceptance of the planned schedule of work for the following week
- suggested amendments to the planned schedule of work for the following week
- indication of any feature changes that affect the future planned activities

The Project Leader will consider the reply from the client and convene a meeting with the Chief Technical Architect to discuss the implication of any amendments if the planned schedule is not accepted. If there are any queries, they will contact the client for clarification. If there are major resource implications, they will discuss these with the client before proceeding. When agreement has been reached with the client about how to proceed, the Project Leader will meet the project staff to reassign tasks where necessary.

24.7.5 Sample Timesheets

The following are sample time sheets. The first illustrates a timesheet for the Project Manager and the second illustrates a time sheet for a Project Software Engineer.

Name: Denise Cooke		Project: APS2 Iteration 1	
Week Commencing:	**Monday 9th September**		
Task	**Comments**		**Hours**
OT2	Weekly project meeting		2.0
OT1	Project management		8.00
		Total Hours:	10.0

Name: Steve Mabbort		Project: APS2 Iteration 1	
Week Commencing:	**Monday 9th September**		
Task	**Comments**		**Hours**
OT2	Weekly project meeting		2.0
DT02	Analysis and Design for new audit type		12.00
DT03	Analysis and design of file review summary classes		26.00
		Total Hours:	40.0

24.8 References

Carmichael, A. and Haywood, D. (2002). *Better Software Faster.* Prentice Hall, Upper Saddle River, NJ.

Carmichael, A. and Swainston-Rainford, M. (2000). The features game. *OT2000 Conference*, Oxford, 27–29 March.

Coad, P., Lefebvre, E. and De Luca, J. (1999). *Java Modeling In Color With UML: Enterprise Components and Process.* Prentice Hall, Upper Saddle River, NJ.

Jacobson, I., Booch, G. and Rumbaugh, J. (1999). *The Unified Software Development Process.* Addison-Wesley, Reading, MA.

Kruchten, P. (2000). *The Rational Unified Process: an Introduction*, 2nd edn. Addison Wesley Longman, Reading, MA.

Agile Modeling

25.1 Introduction

The last chapter discussed one way in which it is possible to manage incremental projects based on the Unified Process. However, a question you may have been asking yourself while reading this was "What happens to the models?". Feature Driven Design (FDD) as a philosophy only promotes so much design and modelling up front (just enough, in fact, to support what will be required by the features). The rest is left as part of the "realization" of a feature. That is, a particular feature, for example "load a file", may involve multiple tasks such as "design the load a file classes", "implement the load a file classes" and "test the load a file classes". Surely this implies that the model-centric approach of the UP must be dropped? That is, in the UP a great deal of time and effort is spent on creating requirements, analysis and design models before any coding starts. With a feature-based approach you no longer create the whole design (including the models) up front. So what are we to do?

One solution to the problem described above is Agile Modeling. The essence of Agile Modeling is that you do just enough design and modelling for what is needed at the time and expect to come back and change, review, refactor and add more detail, later on, to appropriate areas of the model. Agile Modeling is one example of a group of techniques that are generally know as "Agile". These include eXtreme Programming (or XP). Interestingly, FDD can also be characterized as agile.

In this chapter we will *briefly* examine the concept of Agile Modeling, as a whole book could (and indeed has been) devoted to this subject. For more details on Agile Modeling see the references at the end of this chapter. We will focus on how Agile Modeling applies to the Unified Process. I will also endeavour to add my own thoughts on this subject, as this chapter and its predecessor reflect how my organisation (JayDee Technology Ltd) currently carries out software development. Why do I mention this? Because we have been using an approach based on the Unified Process which has been evolving since 2000. Our approach was referred to internally as a modified Unified Process until we first came across Feature Driven Design and Agile Modeling. We then realized that independently we had evolved essentially these techniques and integrated them with a simplified version of the Unified

Process. This had not been done in isolation, but with the consent (and often input) of our clients as well as through discussions with academics working in the field. Of course, the critical question is does it work? The answer to that is that it does for us. We have delivered a variety of systems over the last three years on time, within budget and to the general satisfaction of our clients.

The chapter is organized in the following manner:

- Section 25.2 discusses modelling misconceptions.
- Section 25.3 presents the manifesto for Agile Modeling.
- Section 25.4 describes Agile Modeling itself.
- Section 25.5 considers the relationship between the Unified Process and Agile Modeling.
- Section 25.6 discuses documentation and Agile Modeling.
- Section 25.7 discusses the use of CASE tools and Agile Modeling.

25.2 Modelling Misconceptions

Before discussing Agile Modeling it is worth reconsidering some modelling myths and misconceptions that need to be clarified. These have a bearing on Agile Modeling, as a modelling misconception can lead to a denial of the benefits that can be accrued from Agile Modeling.

1. *Models equal documentation*
Nothing could be further from the truth. A model is *part* of the documentation, but is by no means sufficient as documentation. That is, a model, as good as it may be, cannot adequately represent all the information needed to describe the requirements, functional and non-functional, behavioural and structural, of a software system. For example, Figure 25.1 illustrates part of a Rose model developed for a real-world system built by JayDee Technology. This Rose model has links to Word documents (such as Overview), screen designs (such as APSFrameView), design notes (APS-MVC-Design), classes (APSFrameController, APSFrameModel, APSFrameView) and sequence diagrams (View SQM Questions), as well as class diagrams, collaboration diagrams, Visio diagrams (in pseudo-UML as well as screen layout designs indicating panels, layouts and components), Activity diagrams etc. Thus the models are (an important) part of the documentation of a system, but only a part.

2. *Modelling implies a heavyweight software process*
Again this is not true. The fact that you are using some form of modelling to describe your system does not mean that you must be using a formal software development process. It may well be that placing the modelling task within the context of a development methodology will help, but modelling does not equate to a software process.

3. *You must "freeze" the requirements*
The point here is that many people believe that you must be able to freeze the requirements before you start to model. In theory this would be great. If you had all the requirements presented to you before you started modelling then all the questions about what the system should do would be answered at the start and it would make deciding on what should be in the model easier. How-

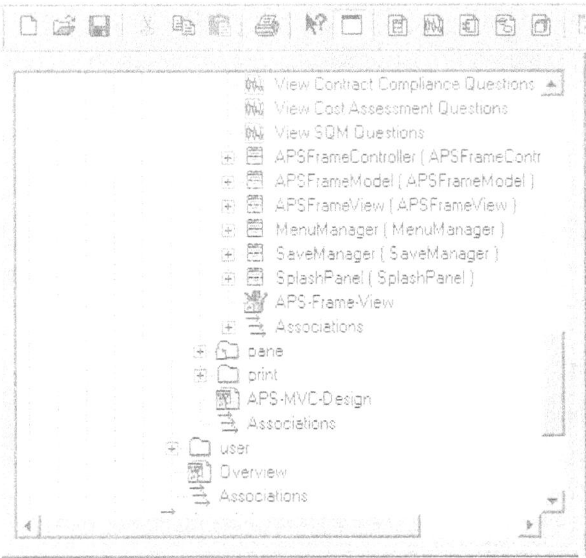

Figure 25.1 Part of a Rose model.

ever, that is theoretical; in reality requirements change (even in the smallest projects). This can be for a variety of reasons. For example, those who wrote the requirements missed out some details (which may only come to light when the development is progressing), the users may find their needs change during the lifetime of the project, or the project is a Greenfield software system in which the requirements are difficult to ascertain up front (or any combination of these). Thus, although for contractual reasons you may need to formally freeze the requirements, the reality is that these requirements will change, and thus the design and implementation of the system may need to be "agile" enough to keep pace with these changes (either during development or in subsequent iterations).

4. *Your design is carved in stone*
This is a leftover from the more traditional waterfall-based approaches to software development. In an ideal world you would like to remove as many unknowns and variable elements from software development as possible. Therefore to have the design "fixed" and never changing would be great. Again this does not work in reality. This is for a variety of reasons, including changing requirements, but also because designs are an abstraction of the implementation. This means that as an implementation is progressing, some elements of the design will be found to be unimplementable, inefficient or fatally flawed. Thus during the implementation some changes may be required to the design to ensure a working system etc. In addition, there may be some situations in which it is difficult to define more than a highly abstract model, as not enough is known at that point about how the system should work. Thus the model will need refinement at a later date when some missing information or understanding becomes available. I know that you may be thinking that you should not move on from the modelling phase until you have this information, but in the real world there are times when you don't have a choice.

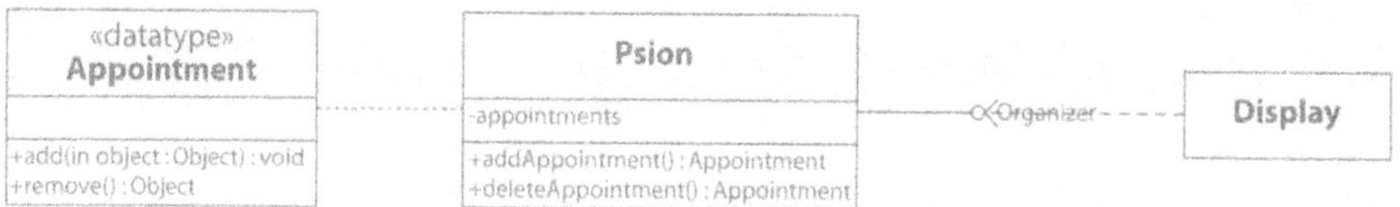

Figure 25.2 Classes diagram produced in Visio.

5. *You must use a CASE tool*

By this I mean that if you are going to do some modelling you must use some sort of Computer-Aided Software Engineering tool, such as TogetherSoft's Together Control Centre or Rational's Rose. Of course, these tools may well make things easier, but they are not mandatory. Indeed, in the past I used the UML modelling features of the Microsoft tool Visio to generate all the models presented. As a comparison, Figure 25.2 is a diagram in Visio while Figure 25.3 is from Rose and Figure 25.4 is from Together. As an extreme, I once worked for a software company, writing Smalltalk software for the financial industry, where they wanted me to use Microsoft Paint to draw class diagrams. Note that all of these (as well as hand-drawn diagrams) represent models.

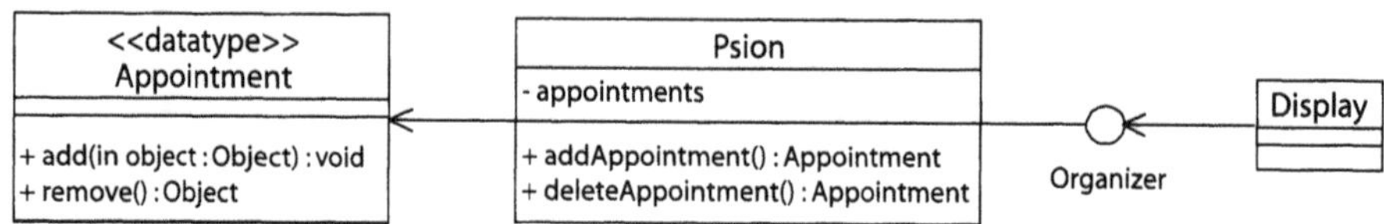

Figure 25.3 Class diagram produced in Rational Rose.

6. *All developers know how to model*

Generating appropriate, correct, well-formed, understandable models is not trivial. It takes time to get familiar with whatever tools, notation and approaches are being used. Just as with programming itself, the more modelling you do, the better you get. In addition, the more you study the models generated by yourself or your colleagues, the more you will learn. Thus just taking some developers and asking them to start creating a sound robust model of sufficient clarity and abstraction is generally a flawed approach.

7. *You can think of everything from the start*

One problem with UML-style models is that they are static – that is, you cannot execute them. Thus it is hard to determine whether they cover "enough" or whether you have missed some critical areas out. Therefore believing that you can think of everything and cover all eventualities at the start is wrong for all but the simplest systems.

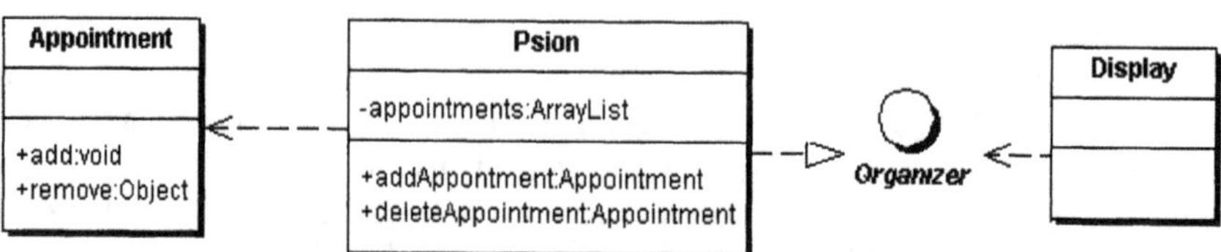

Figure 25.4 Class diagram produced in Together.

8. *Modelling is a waste of time*
This myth represents the extreme opposite of that promoted by the waterfall approach's proponents – that is, designing models has no benefit, so just get on with the coding; that's what you are delivering after all. You can, of course, see where these people are coming from. The model is not what gets delivered to the user and is not what will meet their eventual needs. However, let me ask you this: "Which would you prefer to live in: a tower block in which the architect first draws up plans, scale models and prototypes to confirm any outstanding issues, or one where the builders just got on and did it?". Personally I would be happier in the one where some models were generated, and to some extent software is the same. On a personal level I have found that working on software that can be placed within the framework of a model and in which the model provides the starting point, the basic structure and the context is extremely useful, and I believe that it helps to produce more robust systems. For example, on a recent project the products of four software developers were integrated for the first time within an hour. I believe that this was achieved because we had generated appropriate designs and that at the core of these designs were the models!

9. *The world revolves around the data model*
That is, the data model describing, for example, the information in the database is the centre of the universe and the object-oriented model is based on this. This is a view that is prevalent in organizations with a very strong database culture or in those that have migrated from a more data-oriented language. However, while there is certainly a mapping between the object and relational worlds, it is not the case that the data model dictates the object model. The two may be very closely aligned or they may be quite distinct – it depends on the application. It is also important to remember that the relational world of a database and the object world of, say, Java have very different requirements when it comes to performance, maintainability and reusability, and that these elements will affect the design of their models. It is also not true that either is less important than the other. Almost every commercial system I have ever worked on has had a database at its heart. Therefore the data model used with the database is very important. However, the database was only one part of these systems and the other parts were just as important. For example, a gearbox is very important within a car, but there are many other parts that go to make up the car, and designing a care solely around its gearbox would be a mistake!

So what about the issue being discussed in this chapter – modelling in a dynamic, iterative and incremental process? Well, issues 3, 4, 7 and 9 are the most important myths or misconceptions to refute. This is because these issues are in general wrong, and thus we need to adopt a different approach to modelling (an agile approach).

25.3 The Manifesto for Agile Modeling

There is a growing movement that promotes the use of an agile development philosophy. This movement (see references at the end of this chapter) came together in February 2001 to form the Agile Software Development Alliance (often referred to as the Agile Alliance). They produced a manifesto that they hoped embraced the philosophies that they commonly supported and which they believed helped to produce better software. From this manifesto they defined a set of principles for Agile Software Development. The manifesto proposed the following values, summarized (very briefly) below:

1. *Individuals and interactions over processes and tools*
This refers to the fact that it is the people involved and how they communicate that typically have the largest bearing on the success (or failure) of a software project. Yes, software development processes, methodologies, tools etc. can help, but they are still not the overriding influence. Thus you should encourage the best people and group interactions.

2. *Working software over comprehensive documentation*
There are times when (and I am sure I am not alone in this) it can feel that all you seem to be doing is producing reams and reams of documentation. Sometimes this is aided (even determined) by the CASE tool, and sometimes it is merely the process being followed. However, ultimately it is the software produced by a development project that will be used by a user, not the documentation. Therefore documentation should not be a major goal in and of itself. Instead it should be a supporting medium for the actual product – the software.

3. *Customer collaboration over contract negotiation*
Remember that these are values – thus time should be spent on working with customers and in getting them involved in the software development rather than on detailed contract negotiations. Of course, in the real world this can be difficult, as although your direct clients may buy into this philosophy, their legal and financial departments may not. For example, we have worked with a number of clients where the legal (and or financial) departments have imposed a contract and associated negotiations because they want something to hit us with if things were to go wrong.

4. *Responding to change over following a plan*
Finally, agile software development embraces change rather than saying "It's not in the requirements or the plan so we can't do it". That is, it is agile!

Based on these value statements a set of twelve principles have been identified. The aim of these principles is twofold. Firstly, they are intended to help people gain a better understanding of what agile software development is all about. Secondly, they can be used to help to determine whether you as a developer are following an agile methodology or not. Note that these principles do not specify a method, but rather define a set of guiding statements that approaches under the banner "Agile" should conform to. Thus agile methodologies should conform to these principles:

1. Highest priority is to satisfy the customer.
2. Welcome change.
3. Deliver working software frequently.
4. Business people and developers must work together daily.
5. Build projects around motivated individuals.
6. Face-to-face communication is best.
7. Working software is the primary measure of progress.
8. Promote sustainable development.
9. Continuous attention to technical excellence and good design enhances agility.
10. Simplicity – the art of maximizing the amount of work not done – is essential.

11. The best architectures, requirements and design emerge from self-organizing teams.
12. Introspection – teams should regularly review themselves and their processes to try to improve.

Some of the above may seem obvious and others may appear more contentious. In general they appear quite vague ("Welcome change"). However, they have been defined to help guide agile methodologies rather than to actually be a methodology. For example, an agile methodology should promote the frequent delivery of working systems rather than a single "Big Bang" delivery. One way that this can be interpreted is that an iterative and incremental approach is better than the more traditional waterfall approach to software production.

25.4 Agile Modeling

So what is Agile Modeling? Firstly, it is not a complete methodology in the sense that you can do Agile Modeling and that is sufficient. Rather, it is an approach to the modelling aspects of a software development method; that is, it is an add-on to an approach such as the Unified Process (or indeed XP). Remember that the Unified Process is actually a framework. It has often been described as being heavyweight. This is true if you adopt the whole of the Unified Process. However, that was never the intention except for very large, very long-lived projects. Instead, you should adopt the aspects of the Unified Process that meet your requirements and integrate additional methods or techniques as appropriate (as was suggested with CRC in Chapter 22). Figure 25.5 was presented earlier in this book to illustrate this idea.

The use of Agile Modeling is just another technique that can be used to augment the Unified Process. Thus adding Agile Modeling to the Unified Process is completely in keeping with the original aims of the Unified Process. This is illustrated in Figure 25.6.

So Agile Modeling is an approach to modelling and not a complete methodology. What is that approach? If it is possible to summarize the concept of Agile Modeling in one sentence then it is an approach that "aims to model just enough and no more"! Allied to this is the aim to use the simplest, appropriate tools for this modelling. Another way to put this is that the right tool should be used for the job. We shall come back to this issue of tools again later.

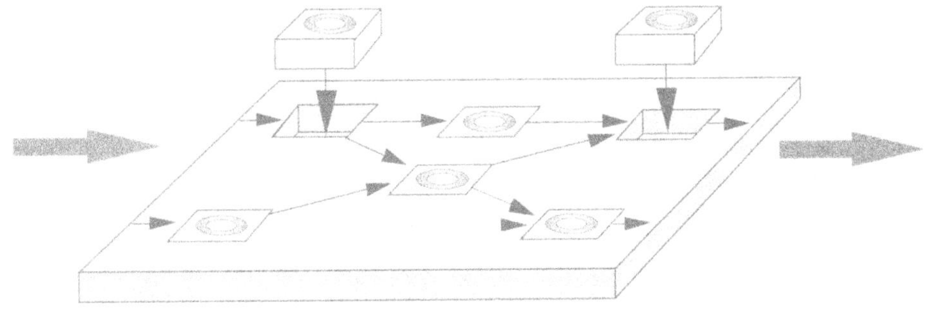

Figure 25.5 The Unified Process as a framework.

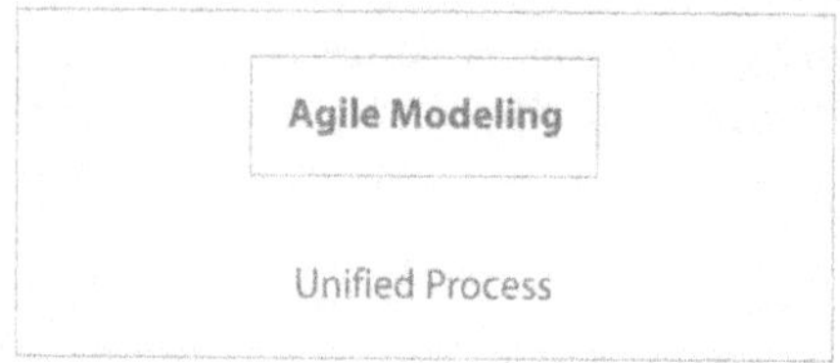

Figure 25.6 Augmenting the Unified Process with Agile Modeling.

So Agile Modeling "aims to model just enough and no more", but what does this mean? What is "just enough" and how do you know when you have done just enough? We will try and clarify some of this below.

First, Agile modelling assumes that modelling is a means to an end and not the final goal in itself (remember that one of the principles of the Agile movement is that working software is the aim). Thus you do not need to model every aspect of a software system if some of those aspects are either obvious, straightforward or may not be needed. Instead, model what is actually required to understand what the software should do, how it will fit together and how it will operate. To put it another way, a model is an abstraction of the software to be produced, so by its very nature it should not be as detailed as that software, nor should it be as complete (otherwise you are writing the software just in a different language – which is generally a waste of time and effort).

An associated idea is that you should model with a purpose – and not just model. This aims to help you to determine what should be modelled and at what level. For example, when creating a model you should ask yourself "Why am I creating the model – how will it be used?". If the answer is "I don't know" then you need to either find out or not create the model. If the answer is "to explain to John how this part of the system is structured" then you have both the purpose and the level of detail. For example, in Figures 25.7 and 25.8 we have the same class diagram.

In Figure 25.7 we show a great deal more detail than in Figure 25.8. However, which diagram do you think is better at showing the structure of the EventManager framework? Personally, Figure 25.8 shows me all the detail I need to know to get the basics of the framework. And certainly early on in the design process, this may be as much as anyone needs to know, other than the methods and properties that define the public interface of this framework; that is, the contract interface between the EventManager and the rest of the application. At a later date, if we need to, we can fill in the details of the classes (possibly by reverse engineering the code).

This leads us to another important concept within Agile Modeling: that of promoting incremental change. That is, we should model in small increments (where small is relative to the size of the system). These small increments should then be validated (for example by implementing them) before moving on to the next piece of modelling work. This means that you are always modelling relevant and pertinent aspects of the system (i.e. they are about to be implemented) and are not modelling potential features that may never be implemented. It also means that any corrections to the model identified during implementation can be fed directly back to the model if appropriate.

Taking the concepts of modelling with a purpose and incremental modelling, we can now draw a flow diagram illustrating the overall Agile Modeling process. This is presented in Figure 25.9.

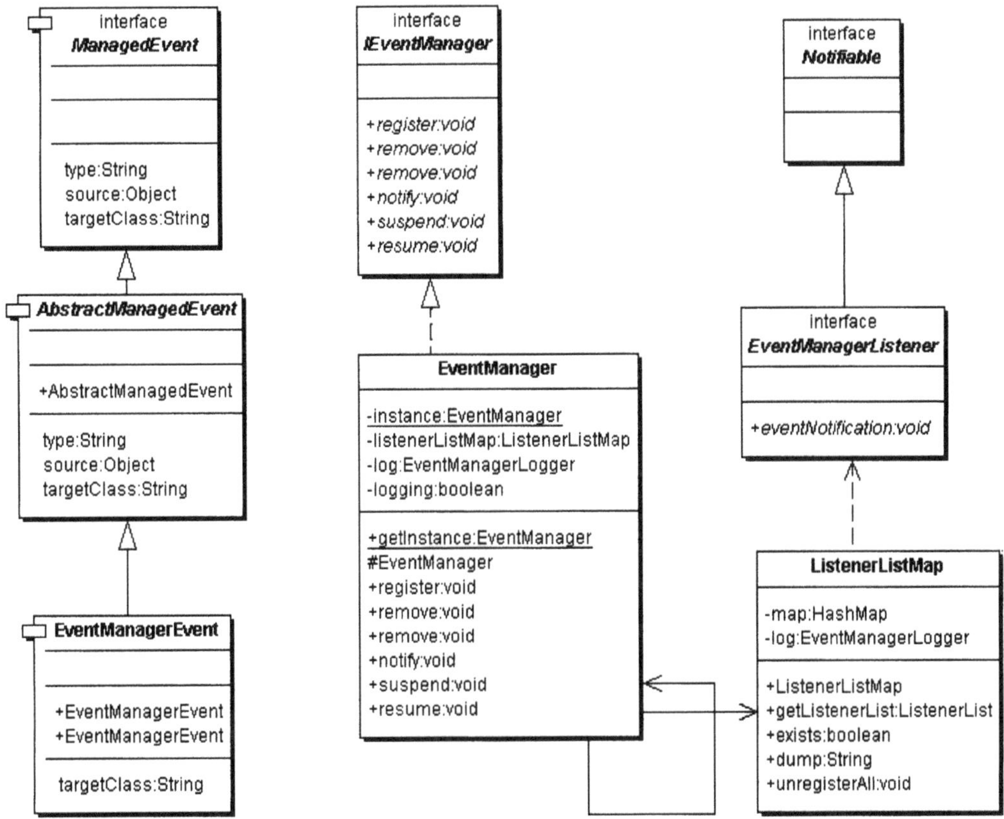

Figure 25.7 Detailed UML class diagram.

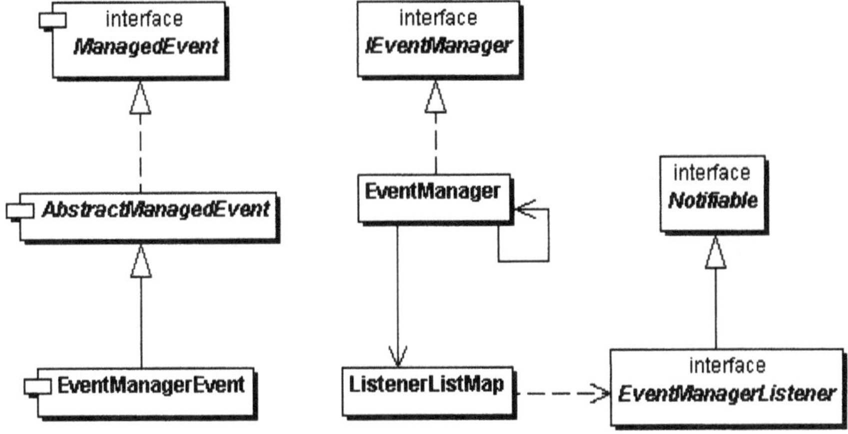

Figure 25.8 UML class diagram with much of the detail hidden.

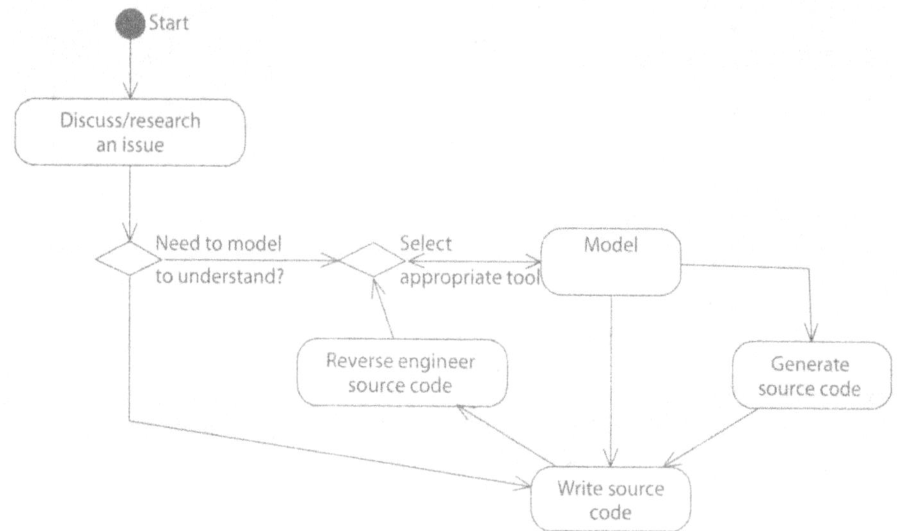

Figure 25.9 Agile Modeling flow diagram.

Figure 25.9 illustrates the basic Agile Modeling process. First identify the issue (or features) to be analyzed. This may involve client discussions, group analysis or some form of research. Once this is done the first thing you need to ask is "Do I need to carry out any modelling to understand this in more detail?". If not, then you can immediately start to write the code. For example, if what you are doing is writing a single class that loads images from a file and writes images back to files, then you probably don't need to model it.

If, however, you need to carry out some modelling to help in the understanding of your task (or how it integrates with other elements of the system etc.) then you need to select the most appropriate modelling tool and do some modelling. Notice that this is a two-way process. I might start off by modelling on paper or a whiteboard. I might use this as a medium for discussion and peer review. Once I am happy with the model (and decide that the model is worthy of preservation – see later) I can then select a different modelling tool (such as a CASE tool) to represent the final version of the model. Once I have completed my modelling task I can write the code for the model. This might be done completely by hand or may involve some automated code generation. For example, one of the very nice features of TogetherSoft's Together system is that it generates classes as you create the models. Thus when you come to "implement" the model, the basic structure is already there. Once this is completed you can reverse engineer the final result back into your modelling system (this happens automatically in Together) so that the model remains up to date.

Another important aspect of Agile Modeling is that the models need only be sufficiently accurate and consistent. That is, you do not need to worry about crossing very "t" and dotting every "i". Allied to this idea is that the model (or models) should be comprehensible for their intended audience (but by implication not necessarily comprehensible to everyone, or at least sufficient for everyone) and sufficiently detailed for that audience. Finally, the models should be as simple as possible without losing their message. That is, unnecessary details need not be included.

For example, if I am using a street map to try to get from one location to another and I find that the map and the real world differ slightly (because of changes since the map was printed) I do not necessarily throw the map away. I may instead annotate the map at that point, or use the map to find another route. Equally, my map probably does not show every house on my street; rather, it gives an impression of a number of houses. That is enough for me to know that this is a built-up area and that if I go to this street I will find houses on it. In many cases that is sufficient for my needs.

However, such a map would probably not be sufficient, accurate enough or detailed enough for a utility company wishing to provide fibre optic cable to all the houses in my street. The company would need a different type of map. Indeed, such a map may well not only provide a great deal more detail of the actual houses and street, but may also show details that I do not wish to know (such as what exactly is underneath the road outside my house).

Another key idea in Agile Modeling is that content is more important than presentation. For example, the hand-drawn diagram in Figure 25.10 may not be the prettiest UML diagram you have seen – the lines are not straight, the classes not complete etc. However, it is the message it conveys that is important. If this diagram is sufficient and effective in conveying that message, then that is enough!

Agile Modeling is also an incremental and iterative modeling technique. It promotes incremental change (and suggests attempting to model in small increments) with rapid feedback in the form of peer review comment, proof by implementation or from discussion groups. Part of this emphasis on small increments and rapid feedback is that if you find you need to throw away the modelling you have just done (perhaps because it has been shown to be unimplementable), then you are not throwing away a great deal.

One more point to note about Agile Modeling is that you should use whatever diagram or diagrams best suit the information you need to present, discuss or understand. This does not mean that you must produce many different models, merely that if what you need to describe is best presented as a class diagram then use it. However, if it is better to use a

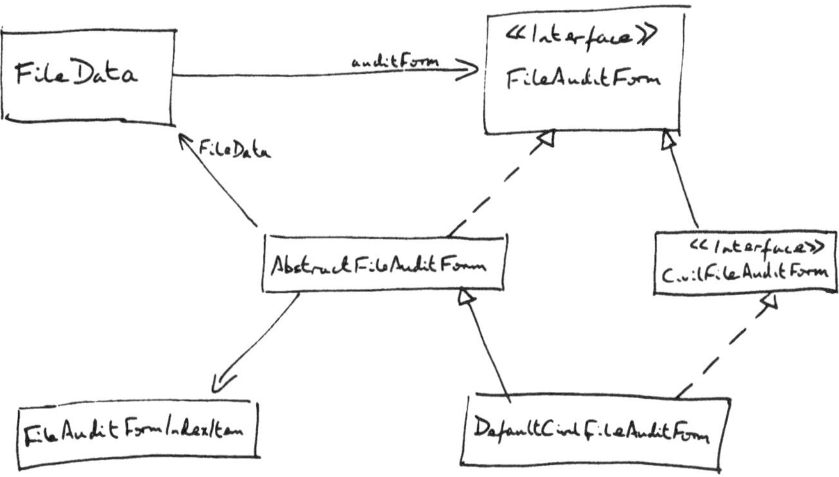

Figure 25.10 A hand-drawn UML diagram.

sequence diagram, use that. In addition, if something is proving difficult to understand or work through in one type of diagram, move to another – it may be that this will help. Also, do not feel afraid of mixing diagrams. Placing some data modelling on a class diagram may well help describe your problem. The key here is to use whatever tools and techniques are available to you to win the modelling battle. In general it is likely that you will need to use multiple modelling techniques to understand a problem. Personally, I rarely find that a class diagram is suitable in isolation. In general I will create a class diagram in parallel with at least one other behaviour-describing diagram (be it a sequence diagram, collaboration diagram, activity diagram or statechart, or simple flow chart etc.).

Finally, we come to the question of when you should update the models you have created. The general gist of when this should be is "when it hurts"; that is, when you actually need to. What does this mean? Take, for example, the case on a recent project we carried out. On that project we created models of what we would implement, which helped us to understand what was required and the structure that would be used. However, for various memory and performance reasons it was found that the implementations had to change to try to reuse as many Java Swing components as possible. This necessitated quite a few changes to the behavioural aspects of the system and some changes to the structure of the system. However, at that point we did not go back and rework the models, as they had served their purpose – they had helped us to understand the requirements and how the system should be structured (in addition, they still gave a flavour of the system). If those models were never needed again, reworking them would have been a waste. Some six months later this aspect of the system was to be updated. It was at this point that the models were updated by a software engineer, reverse engineering the classes. He also worked through the code to update the behavioural aspects of the model. This had two effects: firstly the models were updated in a timely fashion and secondly the software engineer involved gained a detailed understanding of this part of the system before he commenced further design.

In addition, some models may never be required again and can be thrown away. For example, the hand-drawn models used to allow myself and a colleague to understand how two areas of the system will interact do not necessarily need to be saved for posterity. These existing models may more than suffice. Therefore the hand-drawn model (created to help our understanding) can be thrown away. This means that it does not need to be maintained, fully documented, recorded, reviewed etc. This can be taken further for more formal models created using tools such as Rose. However, I tend towards caution and feel that if the model was established enough to have been created in a CASE tool then it should at least be stored in a version control tool (such as CVS or SCCS) so that it can be retrieved if necessary at a later date (otherwise the effort used to create the model may be lost altogether!).

25.5 Agile Modeling and the Unified Process

Unfortunately (or maybe fortunately) the Unified Process does not describe a modeling methodology as such. Thus you are free to employ your own approach to modeling.

Let us first review a few important points about the Unified Process. Firstly, it is a framework that encourages you to adapt it to your own needs. In particular, you should not slavishly produce the deliverables from all disciplines unless they are actually useful.

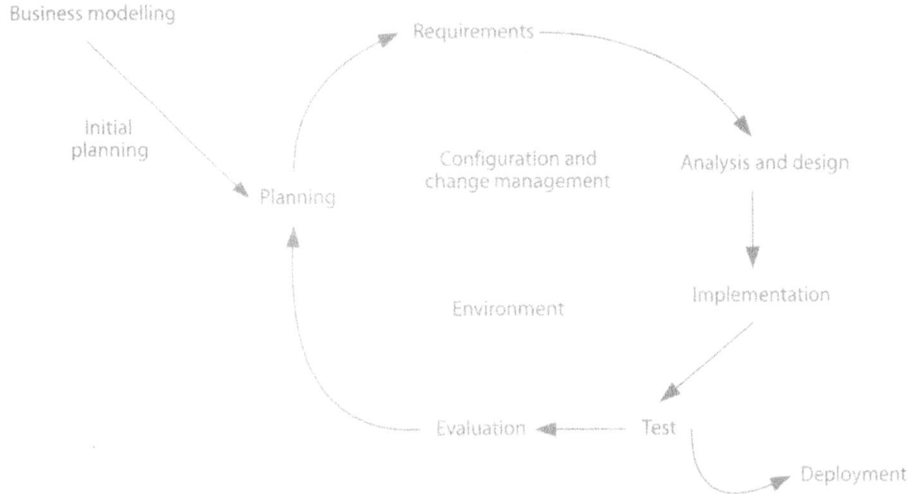

Figure 25.11 The Unified Process: iterative and incremental.

Secondly, the Unified Process actively encourages an iterative and incremental approach to software development (as illustrated in Figure 25.11). Indeed, it is one of the Unified Process's key elements. However, this can be lost in the detail when organizations implement the Unified Process themselves. In particular, it is easy to end up with an approach that promotes each discipline as part of a waterfall-based methodology (partly this is because such an approach is more familiar to those trying to move to the Unified Process and thus an easier fit with what they already know). However, as illustrated in earlier chapters of this book, the incremental and iterative aspects can easily be emphasized instead.

Thirdly, there is nothing in the Unified Process that assumes that *all* the modelling must be done up front. Indeed, if you adopt an incremental and iterative style, then each iteration will generate its own set of models. Some of these models may replace existing ones, others may augment them and some may be completely new.

This brings us nicely to the role of Agile Modeling within the Unified Process. There is very little in the Unified Process that actually describes how you should model. In this book we have examined how to identify the elements of a model, how to refine those elements and what the elements are (for each type of model). However, we have not, until now, discussed how you go about building up a large model for a complex software system. Such a model may encompass years of person time, client and server architectures and technologies, multiple editions of the software etc.

The Unified Process contains nothing that explicitly or implicitly prohibits the use of Agile Modeling (and remember that Agile Modeling is more a philosophy than an actual method). Indeed, there is much in the Unified Process that actively promotes a style of development that naturally encourages an Agile Modeling approach.

However, it is too simplistic to suggest that all you need to do is to plug Agile Modeling into the Unified Process. The following lists some of the adaptations you should consider to the Unified Process to promote the integration of Agile Modeling.

- You may need to lower the emphasis on "use case-driven": although the style is still model-centric and still iterative, it is harder to determine all use cases up front, and agile model is less use case-focused.
- Use cases should be used to help identify the core of the architecture and potentially the elements of the first iteration. The use cases form the basis of your starting point (but are a subset of all the potential use cases that could have been identified).
- Subsequent iterations need to identify their own use cases (or requirements), which will help to focus and drive that iteration.
- Treat the architecture as the key to enabling the integration of the results of Agile Modeling, but be careful not to try to design in all eventualities and "What ifs?" – you may never need them and the architecture may have evolved by the time you do, so that they are obsolete.
- The architecture is still the key to the infrastructure, but now Agile Modeling works within the spaces left by the architecture.
- Don't go over the top with the architecture. In particular, select appropriate models and views as necessary for your project's requirements.
- Don't go over the top with design patterns! They can be very useful, but you need to know where and when to apply them, and they can make software more complicated.
- The architecture is more interested in the contacts between areas than with a fixed skeleton of code (this skeleton itself may be subject to incremental and iterative modeling and implementation).
- The architecture itself can be modeling in an agile manner. That is, the architecture is not fixed: it may well change and evolve, but this change will be controlled and will be effected in an agile manner (only those areas that need to change should change). Other aspects of the "architecture" may not be fleshed out (or even designed) until they are actually needed.
- The iterations and increments are more than likely to be smaller rather than larger. That is, each increment may represent a sub-release of a software system (say from 1.4.1 to 1.4.2) rather than a full release of a software system (from say 1.4 to 1.5).

The key philosophy underlying the above is to try to do only what you need to do in terms of modelling for each iteration in the Unified Process, and that Agile Modeling can help you to do that. Of course, this is where experience is so important. That is, knowing what must be done up front and what can be left until later is not a hard and fast science. For example, security in a Web application is a very good case. Trying to factor this into an existing system may require major redesign of the whole system, so although security may not be an important criterion for initial builds it might be good to design it into the initial architecture.

25.6 Agile Modelling and Documentation

It is important to realize that adopting an agile modelling approach to your modelling task does not mean that you do not need to produce documentation. Rather, documentation encompasses the models you create just as it would have done before. The issue is that you only create just enough models (and by implication documentation) to support the tasks required. For example, in general the documentation you need while creating a software system is different from the documentation you need once that system is built and you need to support it. On a recent project, for example, we were taking a system we had built previously for a client and adding a set of new features and a new class of information to be managed. One of the documents written early on described how the existing architecture and classes would need to be revised and refactored for the new requirements. This document was of great use during development, but was obsolete at the end of the project. What was needed now was documentation to support future maintenance of the system – not a document describing how to migrate from a previous (and now historical) version of the system.

To conclude this section, agile models and their associated documentation are "lean and mean" and fulfil a specific purpose. They are intended to be good enough for those who should be expected to read them.

25.7 Tool Misconceptions

At this point it is worthwhile considering some misconceptions and myths relating to the use of tools, modelling and UML.

1. *UML requires CASE tools*
This is certainly not true – I can draw a UML diagram freehand on paper, using a simple program such as Paint or with a tool such as Together. It may well be true that to strictly adhere to the UML notation it is easier to use something which knows about UML(and Visio might be such a tool). It may also be true that, if you want to generate code from the UML diagrams, using a CASE tool such as Rose or Together makes life easier. But it is not a prerequisite.

2. *Modelling requires the use of CASE tools*
An extension of the last point is that if you are going to create models as part of your design you need a CASE tool that can manage, manipulate, cross-reference etc. your models. While these features may well be useful, they are not necessary. I can (and indeed have) used simpler tools such as Visio to perform all the modelling necessary for the design of a system. Obviously the larger the system and the larger the amount of modelling performed, the better a CASE tool may be.

3. *Agile modellers don't use CASE tools*
This is a common misconception by those starting with Agile Modeling. This is partly due to the emphasis of Agile Modeling on using the simplest appropriate tool, and if that tool is a whiteboard or a piece of paper then use it. The key word here is *appropriate*. If I need to work something through with one of my colleagues we might well use a whiteboard or a piece of paper and not worry too much about the accuracy of the UML notation being used. If, however, I am trying to describe a complex structure that will need to be referenced by a variety of developers, possibly in multiple locations, then a CASE tool might well be the most appropriate.

4. *UML is all you need!*
Some take the view that UML is all you need in terms of notation – if you can't do it in UML (or the design tool you are using) then it is either not relevant to an object-oriented system or not important enough to document. This is not true. There are many aspects of a software project that you

wish to document but that do not fit within the remit of a UML diagram; for example GUI storyboarding or data modelling.

5. *The CASE tool is master*
This is more a perception than a misconception. It is a perception because users often feel that they are battling with the CASE tool and that they have to work in the way prescribed by the CASE tool. Certainly I know that some of my colleagues have an almost irrational hatred of one well-known CASE tool because of the way it forces them to work. Some of this can be overcome with training and some by choosing a suitable tool. The important thing is that the CASE tool should *not* be the master but the servant. It should help you with your work and not hinder it. Thus finding an appropriate tool (or tools) is important. For example, in our case Together has proved to be particularly well suited to our way of working and to the developers' experience and background.

25.8 Summary

Agile Modeling is an approach to model generation that takes account of the inherent uncertainty in most (if not all) software development. It provides a style of modelling which fits particularly well with an iterative and incremental software development methodology. As the Unified Process is itself inherently iterative and incremental, Agile Modeling can provide the framework within which the model creation aspects of the Unified Process can be accomplished. This is of course not the only approach that could be taken, but it is at least a feasible one.

25.9 References

Ambler, S. W. (2002). *Agile Modeling: Effective Practices for Extreme Programming and the Unified Process*. John Wiley & Son, New York.
Cockburn, A. (2002). *Agile Software Development*. Addison-Wesley, Reading, MA.
Boehm, B. (2002). Get ready for agile methods, with care. *Computer*, January, pp. 64–69.

25.10 Online References

Agile Software Development Alliance: `http://www.agilealliance.org/`
Agile Modeling mailing list: `http://www.agilemodeling.com/`

UML Notation

A.1 The UML Notation

The UML notation can be broken down into the various parts which comprise it. This can be very useful in helping to think about the different diagrams and the various notations used on those diagrams. Figure A.1 presents one possible organization of the elements which comprise the UML.

In the remainder of this appendix, a visual glossary of the UML components presented in this book is provided. Note that the UML is undergoing continual refinement. As such, the notation presented in this appendix is based on the UML 1.3 specification. A number of UML elements have been omitted (such as swim lines). However, these are conceptually very simple.

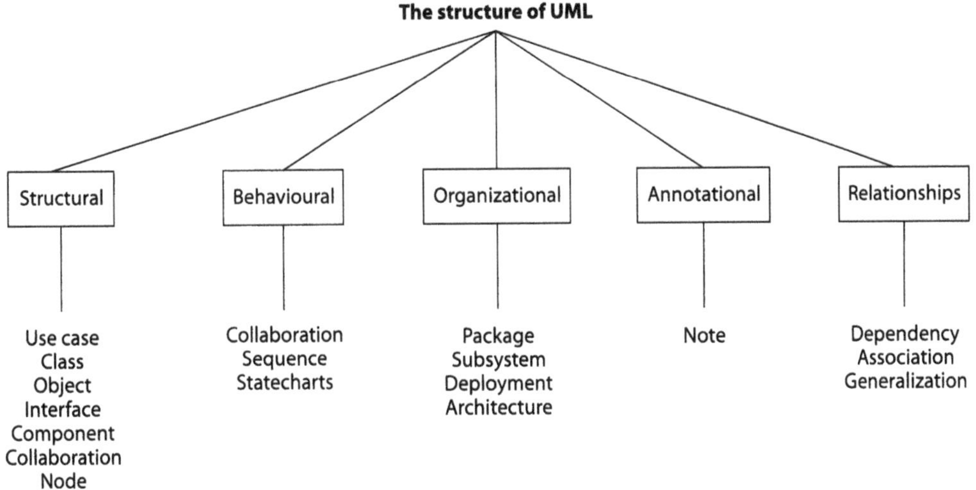

Figure A.1 Providing a structure for the UML components.

A.2 Use Case Diagrams

Use case diagrams are often the starting point for many people in the world of the UML (the other typical starting point is the class diagram). Use case diagrams are made up of actors, use cases (and their relationships) and the boundary of the system being considered. The elements which comprise a use case diagram are presented in Figure A.2.

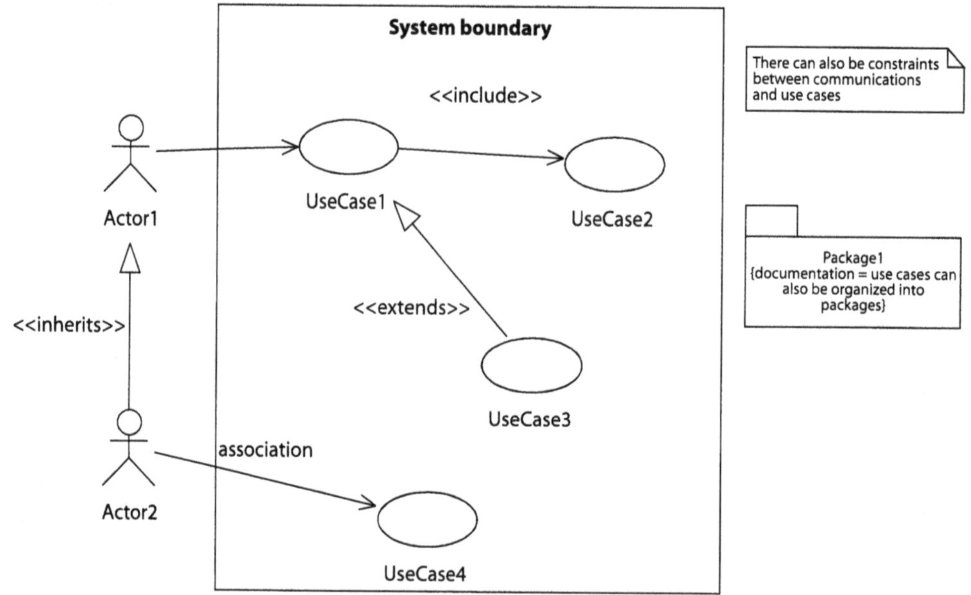

Figure A.2 The components of a use case diagram.

A.3 Collaboration Diagrams

Collaboration diagrams are one way in which the UML allows the interactions between various elements in a system to be described. The other way is through sequence diagrams. The Unified Process makes a great deal of sequence diagrams and places much less emphasis on collaboration diagrams. However, as tools such as Rational Rose allow you to generate one from the other, you can pick whichever diagram best suites your needs. Figure A.3 illustrates the elements in a collaboration diagram using analysis stereotypes and Figure A.4 illustrates a collaboration diagram using standard object notation.

A.4 Class Diagrams

The UML class diagram acts as the core element for the whole of a design. It represents the static structure of the system being designed. As such, it contains the classes, interfaces, relationships

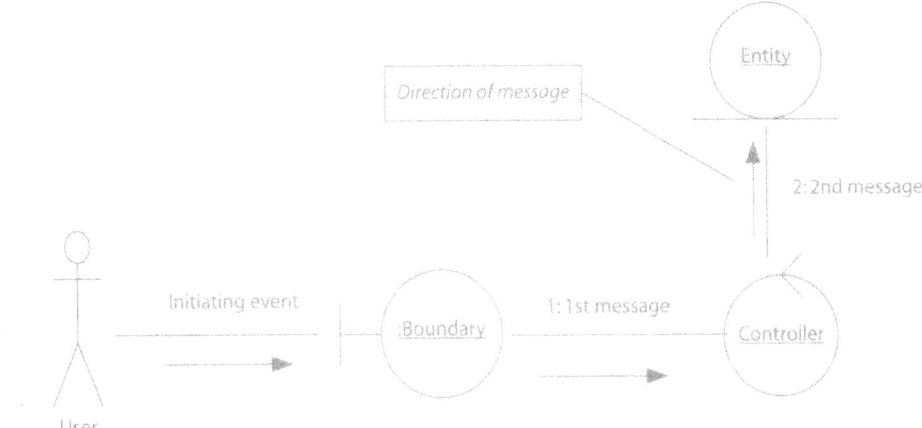

Figure A.3 The elements in an analysis collaboration diagram.

etc. present in the system. Figure A.5 illustrates some of the elements of the analysis workflow class diagram components.

Much of what is used in the analysis workflow is also used in the design workflow. The major difference is that the boundary, controller and entity stereotypes are not used. Figures A.6 and A.7 illustrate the components which comprise the UML elements used in a design workflow class diagram.

Figure A.6 includes many of the structural elements in a class diagram, such as classes, interfaces and stereotypes. Figure A.7 presents the majority of associations that can occur between the various elements present in a class diagram.

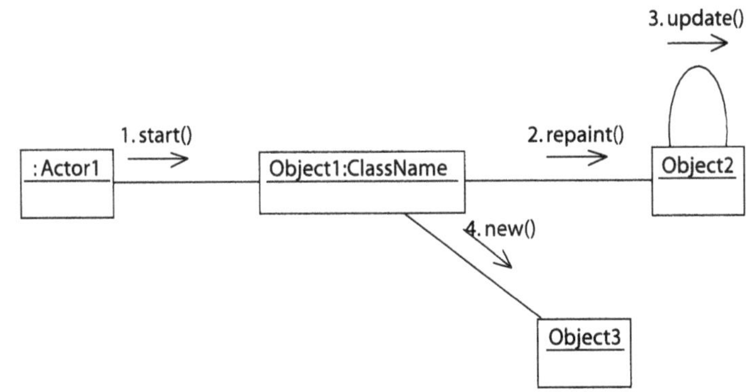

Figure A.4 Design collaboration diagram elements.

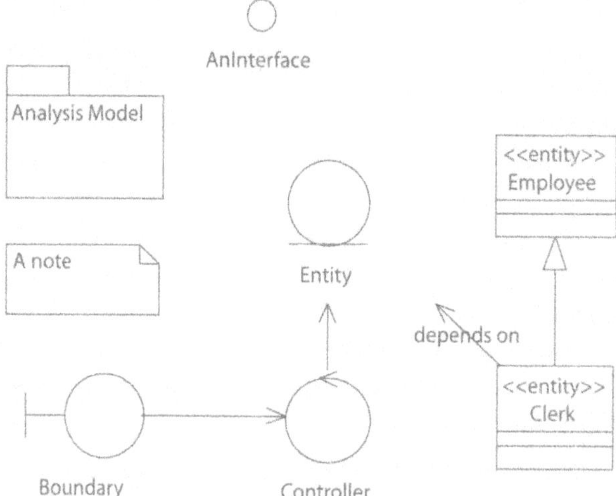

Figure A.5 The analysis workflow class diagram components.

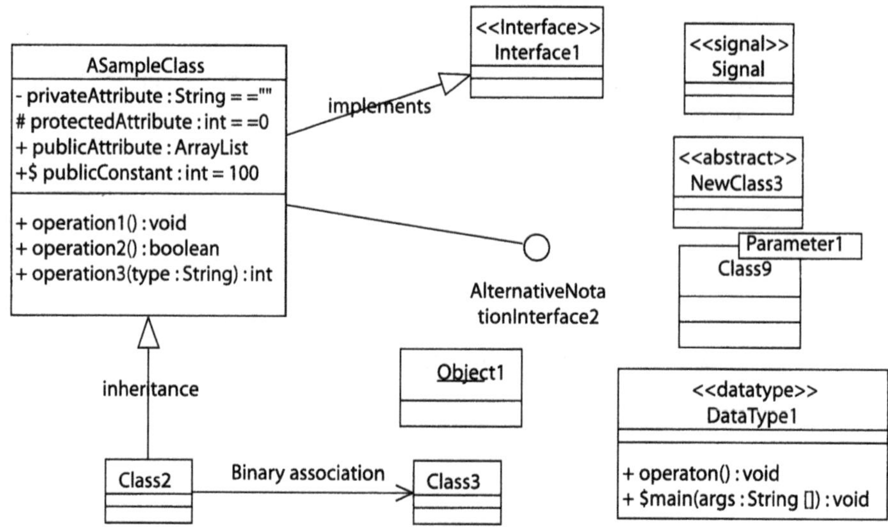

Figure A.6 UML elements used in a class diagram.

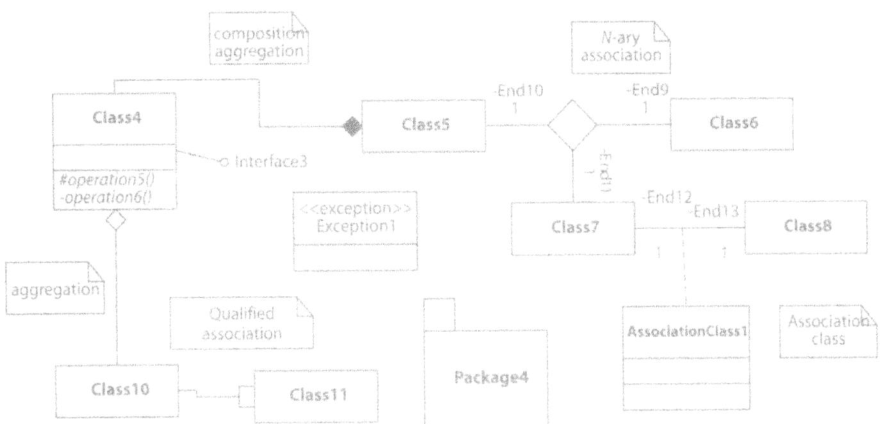

Figure A.7 Further UML elements used in a class diagram.

A.5 Activity Diagrams

An activity diagram can be used to express how a particular operation is performed. It is similar in purpose to pseudocode in other design methods (which can also be used as an alternative to an activity diagram if preferred). Figure A.8 presents the UML elements used in an activity diagram.

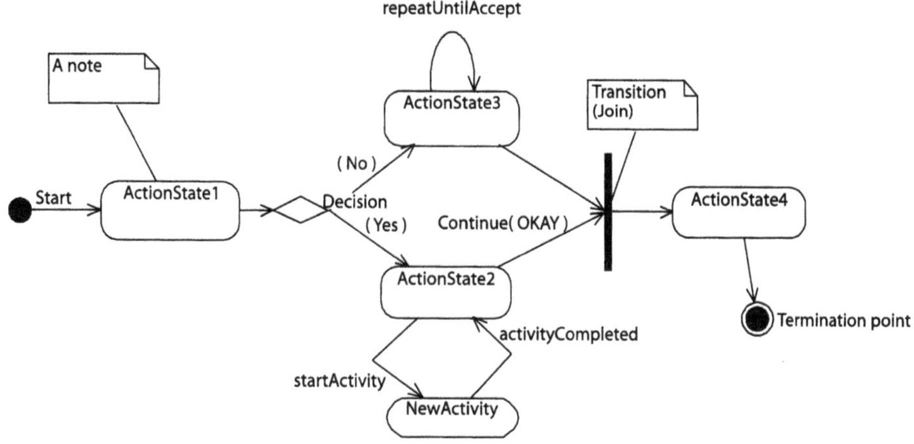

Figure A.8 The elements in an activity diagram.

A.6 Sequence Diagrams

As mentioned earlier, sequence diagrams are a form of interaction diagram, along with collaboration diagrams. The primary elements in a sequence diagram are presented in Figure A.9.

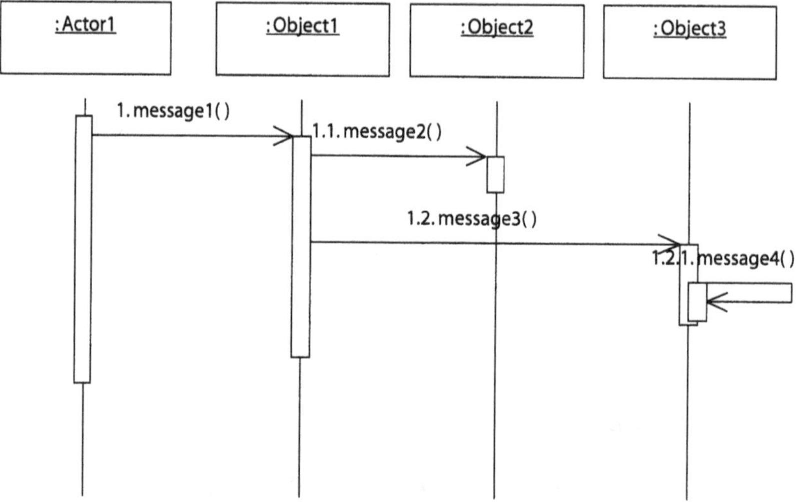

Figure A.9 The elements in a sequence diagram.

A.7 Statechart Diagrams

Statecharts are a very useful formalism for describing the dynamic behaviour of an object-oriented system (they are particularly useful for real-time systems). Figure A.10 illustrates the elements that make up a statechart diagram.

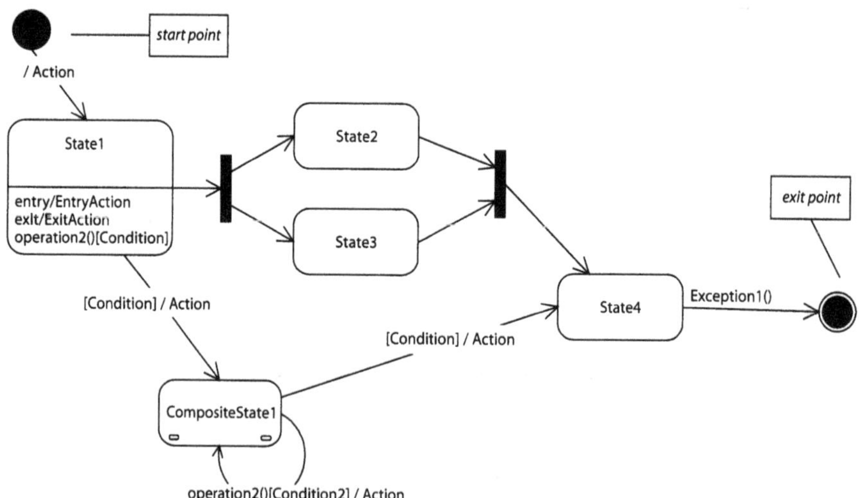

Figure A.10 The elements in a statechart.

A.8 Component and Deployment Diagrams

The final figures (Figures A.11 and A.12) in this appendix illustrate the notation used for both components and nodes with UML.

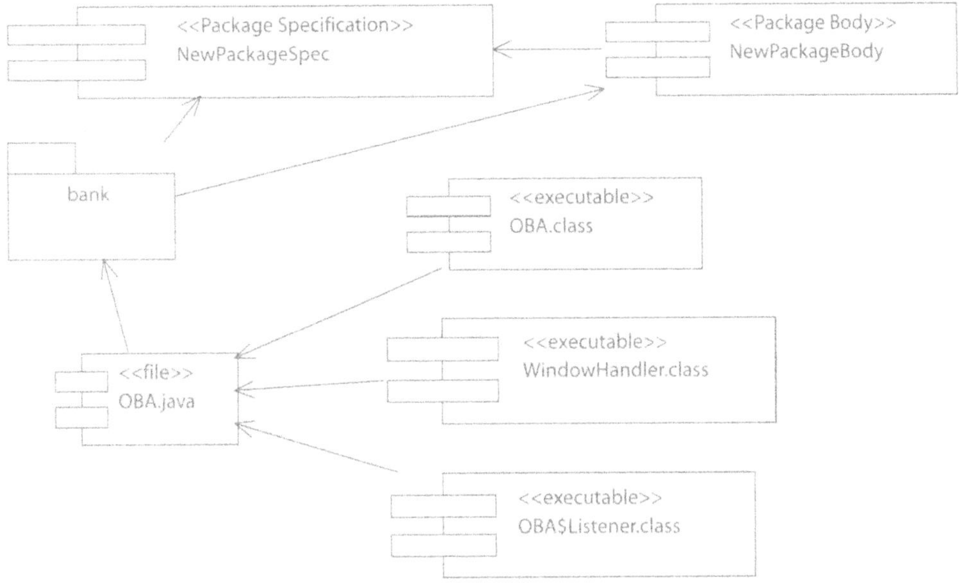

Figure A.11 Components diagram elements.

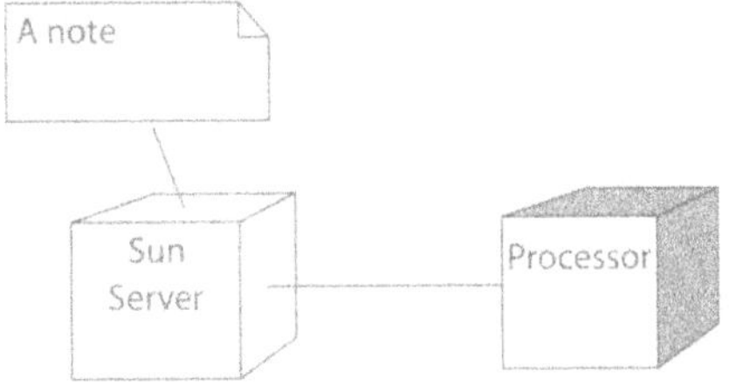

Figure A.12 Deployment view elements.

A.9 Reference

Fowler, M. and Scott, K. (1999). *UML Distilled*, 2nd edn. Addison Wesley, Reading, MA.

GPSR Compliance
The European Union's (EU) General Product Safety Regulation (GPSR) is a set
of rules that requires consumer products to be safe and our obligations to
ensure this.

If you have any concerns about our products, you can contact us on

ProductSafety@springernature.com

In case Publisher is established outside the EU, the EU authorized
representative is:

Springer Nature Customer Service Center GmbH
Europaplatz 3
69115 Heidelberg, Germany